Chinese Face/Off

POPULAR CULTURE AND POLITICS
IN ASIA PACIFIC

Series Editor
Poshek Fu

*A list of books in the series
appears at the end of this book.*

Chinese Face/Off

THE TRANSNATIONAL
POPULAR CULTURE
OF HONG KONG

KWAI-CHEUNG LO

UNIVERSITY OF ILLINOIS PRESS

Urbana and Chicago

First published in 2005, this title is available from the University of
Illinois Press except in Asia, Australia, and New Zealand, where it is
available from Hong Kong University Press.

The University of Illinois Press	Hong Kong University Press
1325 South Oak Street	14/F Hing Wai Centre
Champaign, IL 61820-6903	7 Tin Wan Praya Road
www.press.uillinois.edu	Aberdeen, Hong Kong
ISBN 0-252-02978-x (cloth)	www.hkupress.org
0-252-07228-6 (paper)	ISBN 962-209-753-7

Library of Congress Cataloging-in-Publication Data
Lo, Kwai-Cheung
Chinese face/off : the transnational popular culture of Hong Kong /
Kwai-Cheung Lo.
p.   cm. — (Popular culture and politics in Asia Pacific)
Includes bibliographical references.
ISBN 0-252-02978-x (cloth : alk. paper) — ISBN 0-252-07228-6 (pbk. :
alk. paper)
1. Popular culture—China—Hong Kong. 2. Hong Kong (China)—
Civilization—21st century. 3. Hong Kong (China)—Civilization—
Foreign influences. I. Title. II. Series.
DS796.H75L557   2005
306'.095125—dc22   2004018122

Contents

Acknowledgments

IN THE PROCESS of writing this book, I have met new friends, received encouragement, and incurred personal and professional debts to more people than I can name here. I owe the successful publication of this book primarily to Poshek Fu, who has given me enormous support; Joan Catapano, Carol Betts, and others at the University of Illinois Press, who offered indispensable assistance throughout the production process; and three anonymous reviewers of the manuscript, who provided generous comments and useful suggestions.

At different stages many people have had an impact on my intellectual life and helped me formulate my ideas even though those individuals were not directly involved in the production of the book. My thanks go to Gisela Bruche-Schulz, Peter Canning, Christopher L. Connery, Arif Dirlik, John Nguyet Erni, Lawrence Grossberg, Lynne Joyrich, Ping-kwan Leung, Dean MacCannell, Juliet Flower MacCannell, Gina Marchetti, Meaghan Morris, Shu-mei Shih, and Esther C. M. Yau. I feel very fortunate to have the generous support and friendship of Rey Chow and Austin Meredith, who have helped me through many difficulties.

Finally, I would like to express my greatest gratitude to my wife, Laikwan Pang, whose intellectual and emotional support gives me nourishment, and to our baby boy, Haven, who gives us tremendous joy. This book is for them, with all my affection.

Note on Transliteration

SINCE MOST READERS know more of standard pinyin romanization than Cantonese transliteration, all Chinese names and terms throughout the book are romanized in pinyin, the system of romanization for Chinese written language based on the pronunciation of the northern dialect of Mandarin Chinese. In some cases, however, Cantonese romanization will be used, but only when the Chinese words are originally meant to be read in Cantonese or when the recognized English names or transliteration of persons and things are available.

Chinese Face/Off

Introduction:
The Chineseness of Hong Kong's
Transnational Culture in Today's World

"HONG KONG SHOULD BECOME the Switzerland of Asia," said Wang Zhan, director of the Shanghai Municipal Government Development Research Center, an influential government think tank, when a Hong Kong journalist asked him to comment on the future of postcolonial Hong Kong (Lu and Lu 2002, 49). Could the Special Administrative Region (SAR) of Hong Kong, returned to the People's Republic of China (PRC) after 150 years of British colonial rule, manage to transform itself into an entity as internationalized as Switzerland? There is no lack of advice as to what post-1997 Hong Kong should do to redefine and rejuvenate itself. Some believe that the best future for the city involves improved integration with China; that is to say, further sinicization would be the path to tread.[1] Others insist that the very strength and uniqueness of Hong Kong depend on its autonomy and rule of law, which keep China at a safe distance. People from many different fields hope to see Hong Kong transform itself into a regional center, dominating the areas of high technology, logistics, tourism, and academic research and maintaining its key position as a bridge between China and the West. Advice from Shanghai, Hong Kong's greatest potential competitor in the twenty-first century, could have a questionable motivation. "If Hong Kong becomes increasingly sinicized, it will only face more competition from other mainland cities and may even become another Shanghai," Wang Zhan elaborated in the interview (50). Wang may have strong reasons to encourage Hong Kong not to imitate and compete with Shanghai but to shape its postcolonial future as the Switzerland of Asia.

Switzerland is a small nation-state sandwiched among its powerful neighbors. But when the great European countries do business, Switzerland is able to serve as an intermediary for their dialogue. As an Asian economic tiger, Hong Kong has striven to be a leading international financial hub and a commercial center for Asia and the Pacific Rim. The prolonged economic downturn triggered in 1997 by Asian financial turmoil was a terrible blow to the people of Hong Kong. The postcolonial city has been struggling with a domestic crisis of confidence. The capability and leadership of the SAR government to guide Hong Kong into the twenty-first century have been questioned. Under these circumstances, it is not surprising that the Hong Kong media trumpeted Wang's words. Nowadays an insecure Hong Kong is receptive to advice as to how it should readjust its own position. It may be too early to tell whether Hong Kong can become the Switzerland of Asia. Perhaps it is simply wrong to urge Hong Kong to do so, since the city has been playing such a role for quite some time. Does it make sense to say one should become what one already is? In any case, the mention of the Swiss experience by a mainland Chinese scholar may reveal, or even underscore, Hong Kong's relationship to its neighboring powers, not only economically but also culturally.

Swiss culture is renowned for its international flavor and its simultaneous assimilation of the adjacent German, French, and Italian cultures and distinction from them. Like Switzerland, which is in Europe but not the European Union, Hong Kong is both inside and outside of China. Its porous borders (to capital, information, and travelers) and special status (once a British colonial outpost and now a Chinese SAR) historically have enabled Hong Kong to achieve a mission impossible elsewhere. Exposed to many foreign influences, Hong Kong also promotes the flourishing of a modern Chinese popular culture that has been in virtual hibernation in mainland China. For decades, this colonial city, once second only to the United States in film export, has been a prolific production center of Chinese diaspora culture and one of the most important platforms for Chinese-Western cultural mediation. Precisely because Hong Kong has played a major role in the representation of modern popular Chinese culture throughout the world, I would argue that the contemporary meanings of being Chinese are revealed by studying the city's culture, which would provide a new understanding of Chineseness and its interplay with today's world.

A Transgression Inherent in the Meaning of Chineseness

My study, unlike many previous scholarly works,[2] does not intend to assert the uniqueness of Hong Kong culture, which is actually an untenable position. I am far more interested in the ways in which that culture could be used to actualize its potential Chineseness within the symbolic structure. Presumably, it is the culture, rather than simply ethnicity, that figures prominently in defining Chineseness. Such a unified culture, in terms of beliefs, rituals, behaviors, worldviews, written script, socioeconomic institutions, and practices, shared by the Han Chinese with a common ancestry, is said to have successfully assimilated the small proportion of non-Han racial groups within the homogeneous nation. The myth goes so far that the tremendous modernization of social and economic life in various Chinese societies, ranging from the mainland to diasporic communities all over the world, would even enhance rather than weaken such unique cultural characteristics.

To many foreign visitors, Hong Kong already appears to be a very "Chinese" city.[3] It was used to exhibit Chineseness when the "real" China could not be accessed. In fact, the returned Hong Kong may serve as an exemplar of Chineseness not because the colonial city disassociated from Chinese culture in order to produce a Hong Kong identity, but because it has been producing and reshaping Chineseness since the early colonial era. For decades, Hong Kong's popular culture has succeeded in creating and perpetuating an abstract kind of Chinese nationalism and identity for a global audience.[4] The Chinese nationalism expressed through Hong Kong kung fu films exported to the Chinese diaspora, however, carries no political substance. At various times, Hong Kong popular culture has even gone so far as to disavow and negate its Chineseness in order to make itself less parochial and more modern—that is to say, westernized. But, in other historical moments, film and other carriers of culture produced in the colonial city have manifested strong patriotic feelings and nostalgic sentiments for China.

Hong Kong's position toward Chineseness has often shifted. Sometimes Hong Kong provides a safe haven for sinicist ideology; many exiles and émigrés from the mainland expressed in their Hong Kong works nationalistic and melancholic imaginations, especially prior to the 1970s (Tan 2001). At other times Hong Kong appropriates Chineseness as a means to realize its own identity formation. For example, in the 1940s some Hong Kong filmmakers used Chinese nationalism to conjure a hybrid local identity (Fu 2000a). Sometimes the sinicist ideology enables the Chinese culture to realize its full potential. And very often Hong Kong ruthlessly exploits Chineseness for commercial purposes. These shifts comprise an all-encompassing space in which sociopolitical tensions between different Chinese societies might be obliterated and in which members of various communities might somehow relate and recognize themselves as Chinese. In this sense, Hong Kong's Chineseness offers the broadest representativeness, not because it typifies the majority of the Chinese population, nor because it occupies a premier place in the Chinese cultural hierarchy, but because it has no proper place within that hierarchy and thus constitutes a site of conflicting determinations of the contemporary meaning of Chineseness.

Elizabeth Sinn, a Hong Kong historian, has claimed, "Hong Kong is a window to the world for China, as well as one for the world to look into China. In Hong Kong, the Chinese, the foreign, the new, the old, the orthodox, and the unorthodox are mixed in a melting pot, with various contradictions acting as a catalyst, out of which arises a pluralistic, fluid, exuberant cultural uniqueness" (Sinn 1995, iv). Hong Kong's Chineseness is a site of performative contradictions. It is like a crack in the edifice of Chineseness. Its existence is simply a living and contingent contradiction, in the sense that the city's culture both exaggerates and negates Chineseness in the vicissitudes of its sociopolitical milieux. However, this contradiction actually embodies the fundamental imbalance and inconsistency of the cultural totality of contemporary China. Hong Kong culture may appear to be an obstacle to the full actualization of the Chinese subject. What should not be overlooked is that the contradiction or "defect" constitutive of Hong Kong's Chineseness is effectively the Chinese subject itself in the contemporary world.

This may be why I do not argue for the existence of "Hong Kong-ness," although works that attempt to affirm the uniqueness of Hong Kong continue to appear. If there is such a thing, it operates according to the logic of a fantasy that affirms the ideological power of what it means to be Chinese, rather than any determinate local position.[5] The subject of Hong Kong emerges only at the moment that it fails to be "subjectivized" (in both senses—that is, to be its own agent as well as to be a member of the Chinese state) within the traditional Chinese symbolic order. Perhaps Hong Kong should willingly assume its own "nonexistence." It would no longer be so easy to declare its so-called uniqueness to be in opposition to the Chineseness of (mainland) China. My study of Hong Kong is not exactly a search for a unique Hong Kong subjectivity. Instead, I consider how Hong Kong culture operates as an articulation of "transitional Chineseness." Rather than consciously aiming at a construction of a particular local identity, the popular culture in and of Hong Kong moves toward or away from Chineseness at different historical moments in order to accommodate the changing needs of different ideological groups. The Chineseness of Hong Kong culture itself is by no means fixed. It is instead a process of becoming, generated by various national forces and interests rather than by a single origin. It is especially true that after being colonized by the British, Hong Kong would never relate to Chinese sovereignty as simply another version of the colonial narrative. The new horizon confronted by the postcolonial city is instead the possibility of redefining its own position in relation to nationalism. The complex connection between Hong Kong's historical development with that of China in a way denies the facile kind of postmodern arguments that designate the city a site of timelessness and placelessness. The process of becoming, on the other hand, entails a mutual transformation of the two parties involved: Hong Kong and Chineseness. Hong Kong cannot become Chinese without the Chinese changing into something else. The post-1997 subjectivization of the Hong Kong people as Chinese nationals demonstrates that a different notion of Chineseness can always gratify new demands and that the return of the colony to its motherland might present a challenging perspective from which to examine the supposedly incontestable status of national identity.

However, the Chineseness with which Hong Kong has been grappling does not necessarily coincide with the multiple and hybrid kinds of Chineseness described and promoted by critics who defy the notion of a monolithic Chinese identity. Tu Wei-ming, a neo-Confucian scholar, argues, in his overarching tripartite division of "cultural China," that, while Chinese culture is disintegrating at the center, which consists of mainland China and other societies populated predominantly by ethnic Chinese, it will be the periphery, composed of diasporic Chinese communities throughout the world and individuals who try to understand China intellectually, that will set the economic and cultural agendas in the twenty-first century (Tu 1994). But Rey Chow has already pointedly questioned the validity of such promotion of the pluralization of Chinese identity: "[S]hould we from now on simply speak of Chineseness in the plural—as so many kinds of Chineseness-es, so many Chinese identities? Should Chineseness from now on be understood no longer as a traceable origin but in terms of an ongoing history of dispersal, its reality always already displaced from what are imaginary, fantastic roots? As is evident in other intellectual movements, the course of progressivist antiessentialism comprises many surprising twists and turns, and the problem of Chineseness is, one suspects, not likely to be resolved simply by way of the act of pluralizing" (Chow 2000, 18).[6] In my view, it is not exactly pluralization that allows Chineseness to become an open signifier, able to anchor all kinds of meaning. In fact, a multi- or trans-Chinese vision generated from such multiplicity may only help to make the cultural and national ideology of Chineseness more powerful, oppressive, and dominating. Precisely by emphasizing that "it is living and changeable" and that it is a "product of a shared experience whose record has continually influenced its growth," as Wang Gungwu did in "The Chineseness of China," Chineseness always "would be distinctively and recognizably Chinese and that may be all that matters" (Wang Gungwu 1991b, 31, 34).

In this sense, a postmodern politics of plural or multiple identities or subjectivities, or a reversal of center-periphery hierarchy will never be political enough since it collaborates with more than subverts the domination mechanism. There have been—and likely will continue to be—many attempts by local and foreign scholars to describe the specificity of Hong Kong in terms of the development of its culture, identity, and local consciousness. These scholars agree that the specificity of Hong Kong culture is complex and difficult to describe in any coherent and unitary form. So for some cultural and literary critics, the amorphous, elusive, hybrid, slippery, and inconsistent nature of Hong Kong culture becomes its only consistent, identifiable characteristic. The very elusiveness and ambiguity of Hong Kong's specificity might not contribute to the formation of its own unique identity. Instead, it paradoxically smoothens the process of Hong Kong's reintegration with China and facilitates its convergence with the global economy in such a way that its cultural specificity as an indefinably multiple entity would easily give way to any kind of larger system.

My understanding of Hong Kong's Chineseness tells a different story about the openness of Chineseness. Chineseness, as examined through Hong Kong culture, is the master signifier of the Chinese nation—nothing but an empty sign standing for an impossible fullness of meaning, insofar as there is no way for its content to be positivized. The pluralism or multiplicity of Chinese identities only presents more choices for a general idea of "Chineseness," which, instead of providing anything precise, simply conceals the fact that "Chineseness" is an empty term.

I argue that rather than appearing as a plurality or as one among many species, Hong Kong represents an "inherent transgression" of Chineseness itself.[7] That which has been publicly disavowed is actually the ultimate support of the existing order. From the orthodox perspective of earlier Chinese Communist officials, the colonial enclave had indulged moneymaking, class exploitation, drugs, gambling, prostitution, gangs, and unrestrained freedoms that not only offended socialist principles but also violated traditional Chinese moral values. But far from being subversive to the social and cultural order of China, the disavowed "dirty" freedoms enjoyed by the Hong Kong Chinese community actually helped define what it means to be Chinese in today's world. It is this "obscene" side of Chineseness found in Hong Kong that sustains a positive notion of Chinese cultural identity. Hong Kong culture is "good" for Chinese identity insofar as it is "bad" and belongs primarily to the realm of "low" culture; as China said repeatedly before the handover, in support of Hong Kong's autonomy and its lifestyle, *wu zhao tiao, ma zhao pao* (literally, "keep on dancing, keep on horse racing"). In the eyes of the Chinese Communist Party, legalized gambling and prostitution epitomize the corrupt lifestyle of the capitalist colony.

Having been designated the bad, contaminating element, Hong Kong culture generates a certain degree of distancing or disidentification from the symbolic structure of China, thereby implicitly supporting the power of the great, proper Chinese tradition. After 1949 the colonial rule of Hong Kong obviously would not have been possible without the consent of Communist China.[8] The Chinese tolerance of such a capitalist enclave under British rule cannot be explained merely by economic and strategic factors. In a public address, Li Ruihuan, a member of the Politburo Standing Committee, once described Hong Kong as a hundred-year-old teapot from Yixing, the value of which lies solely in the residual sediments inside of it. Tea drinkers know that the real value of the teapot is in the residue of tea leaves lining its interior. Should a well-intentioned person come along and scrub the stains from the vessel, the cleaning would destroy the teapot's worth to its owner. Li Ruihuan implies that Chinese authorities are well aware of the fact that Hong Kong's value to China resides chiefly in its lingering taint. It is perhaps not an exaggeration to take this idea one step further and to say that the authoritative power itself relies on its bad and obscene side in order to legitimize and maintain itself. The transgression is actually inherent in the edifice, although it is always dismissed or kept hidden. Hong Kong serves precisely this function for China at a time when the nation desperately needs a culturally cohesive force to maintain its power.

The inherent transgression of a Hong Kong that lends its obscene support to Chinese cultural coherence no longer goes unnoticed. Indeed, China today is far more "obscene" than Hong Kong in terms of its relentless capitalization, cruel exploitation of its working class, unlawful business transactions, fraud and false accounting, government corruption, drugs, gambling, prostitution, gangs, and other "capitalist" crimes. This capitalization is the emblematic showcase of the violent return of the repressed in Communist China that has to take place in order for the existing power structure to justify itself. China's increasing integration with global capitalism severely undermines the homogenization and essentialization of its national and cultural identity. The only way that the given reality of contemporary China can achieve its unity is through the agency of an exceptional signifier—a signifier that is not part of its reality but that can provide a point of reference for the unity and identity of a certain national and cultural ideological experience. Historical circumstances have always enabled Hong Kong to enjoy exceptional rights, to transcend national boundaries and engage in things that many Chinese can only fantasize about. A typical example would be the return of Dr. Li Shaomin to Hong Kong in 2001. Li, a U.S. citizen teaching at the City University of Hong Kong, had been convicted of spying for Taiwan and deported to the United States. Soon after his deportation, however, Li was allowed to return to his home and his teaching job in Hong Kong. The scholar's return demonstrates Hong Kong's autonomy under the "one country, two systems" arrangement. In addition, Hong Kong is still the only piece of Chinese soil on which the anniversary of the Tiananmen Square massacre can be publicly commemorated. Insofar as the appearance of integrity, unity, and order of Chineseness has not been encroached, Hong Kong is permitted an "obscene underside." As an exception, Hong Kong is structurally necessary to the domain of Chineseness. It is always the singular exception that enables one to formulate the totality as such.

Hong Kong's Chineseness is not one of the particular Chineseness-es to struggle with the origin by displacing it in its own specific ways. By no means is my study an empirical search for and attempted generalization or representation of "real" Chineseness. I argue instead that only what is exceptional and singular, such as Hong Kong's Chineseness, will help establish the cultural norm. The Chineseness of Hong Kong emerges as a correlative to some traumatic remainder or to some excess that cannot easily be integrated into Chinese symbolic space. Its very negativity signals the presence and actuality of a positive, definitive meaning of Chineseness. Precisely because Hong Kong culture does not present distinct national characteristics (because of its transnational character and its lack of immediate political threat), it can refer to an abstract wholeness that is implied by a singular element that is structurally displaced and out of joint. Within a given cultural totality, it is precisely that exceptional element that stands for that culture's all-encompassing dimension.

The Changing Gaze of China in a Global World

Dismissed for decades as a "cultural desert" and a place insensitive to "high" culture as well as indifferent to political ideologies, Hong Kong today is increasingly sought by its critics and by sinologists to mediate the relations between China and the world. Compared to China, Hong Kong seems too small to produce any enduring cultural effects. But because of its smallness, this most westernized of Chinese cities could project images of grandiose national fantasies. The widely acclaimed Shanghai writer Yu Qiuyu has argued that, contrary to popular opinion, Hong Kong has never been a cultural desert. At a seminar organized by the Hong Kong SAR government a few years after the historic handover, Yu claimed that "Shanghai has never been able to compete [with] Hong Kong's culture, [which] is so diverse and sensitive to both Chinese and Western cultures, and it serves as a bridge between the two" (A. Leung 2001).[9] Since the people of Hong Kong have felt increasingly threatened by the revival of Shanghai's cultural and economic status, Yu's remarks might have brought relief to the city. However, the description of Hong Kong as a bridge between Chinese and Western cultures is of course clichéd; Hong Kong locals have heard it for years and repeated it to themselves over and over like a mantra. But a cliché, paradoxically, can say something "original," if it has reached the point at which its concept reflects back only on itself. Perhaps what is novel about this description is not what it says about Hong Kong's role with regard to China and the West, but rather how it attests to a recognition of that role on the part of mainland Chinese intellectuals. Before that, mainland intellectuals had rarely used this "bridge" idea to describe the colonial city. Even while the impact that the handover has had on Hong Kong is being examined, China itself is undergoing fundamental cultural changes in the process of modernization.[10]

Reflecting on the conditions of contemporary Chinese culture, Wang Shuo, a popular mainland writer and pioneer of Chinese "hoodlum literature" (*pizi wenxue*),[11] frankly and sardonically acknowledges the major vicissitudes in China's reception of Hong Kong culture over the last two decades of the twentieth century:

> Twenty years ago we said that Hong Kong was a "cultural desert" whenever the place came up in conversation. Saying this helped us to maintain some sort of psychological balance in the face of the city's prosperous economy and enviable standard of living. At that time, the image of the Hong Konger in my eyes was someone who was loud, loquacious and vulgar. . . . The commercial activities that today are called our lifestyle or our mode of consumption first arrived with a remarkable Hong Kong chop. In those days I had no idea that these things could be culture: live performances in restaurants developing into karaoke and live bands; pop music broadcast over cabbie radio exclusively for car owners; popular magazines, pirated discs and pirated computer software sold at the clothing market; prostitutes directly creating the prosperity of night

clubs, saunas, and beauty salons; and more importantly, the gossip topics provided by tabloids and fashion magazines. . . . Hong Kong's and Taiwan's cultures are openly integrated parts of Chinese culture. They are the successors of Chinese entertainment culture, its *legitimate inheritors,* or in fact *its authentic roots.* After 1949, the revolutionary culture overwhelmed us here. The leisure and the "Mandarin Ducks and Butterflies" of old China went over there. Over the years, they ceaselessly continued to merge traditional Chinese, Japanese and the Japanese-mediated Western cultures into a culture that was institutionalized, industrialized and serialized. Now they return to give us make-up classes. Shouldn't we be happy? . . . At least we are fortunate enough to see the old culture—I shouldn't use this term because it sounds so derogatory—at least we can witness *the traditional Chinese culture . . . that has been entirely restored in China these days.* (Wang Shuo 2000, 2–3, 42; my emphases)

Ah Cheng, another mainland writer of the school of root-searching literature (*xungen wenxue*), also sees Hong Kong as an oasis of the Chinese secular and people-oriented culture that is repressed on the mainland. Without Wang's sarcasm, he comments on this in a rather embarrassingly eulogistic way:

My first visit to Hong Kong was in 1985. I immediately liked the place because I liked its unrestrained secular culture and its bustling energy. . . . The colors of Hong Kong restaurants are sharp reds, greens, golds and silvers. The restaurants are very noisy. Northern Chinese find it too rude and tasteless. But if you have read Tang poetry, you could recognize this secular culture, which is extravagant but lively. Hong Kongers enjoy good food and colorful clothing. They don't care whether it is Chinese or Western. Neither do they boast about their Chinese culture. Such attitudes reproduce the vigor and openness of the Tang dynasty. . . . Mainlanders always say Hong Kong is a cultural desert. I don't agree. Hong Kong has everything. It just depends on what kind of thing you want. . . . There were large numbers of mainlanders living in Hong Kong after 1949. They preserved their lifestyle in spite of migrating there. The secular high culture that disappeared on the mainland was able to survive in Hong Kong, and in a lively form. (Ah Cheng 1994, 83, 85–86)

The Tang dynasty occupies a significant place in the Chinese psyche. It was a time when China achieved greatness in its civilization and was remarkably open to foreign culture and trade. While the great China was in hibernation, the tiny Hong Kong, westernized through colonialism, occupied a retrospective space in the Chinese imagination. Hong Kong is imagined by some mainland intellectuals to be a Xanadu-like place safeguarding traditional Chinese culture otherwise damaged by political turmoil on the mainland. Once a re-minder of the humiliating history of the colonial experience and comprador-capitalism, Hong Kong grew to be one of the driving forces of China's mod-ernization and nationalization. The city evolved from disseminator of low culture to preserver of the essence of Chinese identity, transforming itself dra-matically under the gaze of a changing China.

Ironically, the colonial city has become a stand-in for the Chinese identi-ty lost to the motherland. It is not unlike the fantasy created by the Nation-alist government that fled to Taiwan in 1949: the mainland was turned into the so-called "Communist areas," and Taiwan, the temporary home of "Free China," upheld itself as the legitimate place of "real Chineseness" in response to the threats of the Communist mainland and of the Taiwanese indepen-dence movement. Precisely because Taiwan has made a claim for the agency of "genuine Chineseness" before, the island has been progressively develop-ing its separate identity. Hong Kong movies could be given the privileges and favors by the Taiwan government to be categorized as the "national cinema" (*guopian*), which helped the industry to dominate the Taiwanese market until the 1990s, since Taiwan had a strict quota on foreign films. But, while Tai-wan's role as a repository of traditional Chinese culture diminished by the end of the twentieth century, how could Hong Kong, this colonial enclave, suddenly have become a protector of Chinese civilization or Chineseness in general? How did this port city help to restore cultural order and virtue to a motherland that has suffered years of political chaos and social decay? At a time when Communism no longer has a powerful ideological grip on main-land China and nationalism has risen to fill the moral vacuum, Hong Kong, as an international Chinese city, may have become an illuminating model for compatriots seeking to understand what it means to be "Chinese" in a glo-bal age. China has been obsessed with its glorious past, which could conceiv-ably affect its future rise to global prominence. Recent Chinese media cov-erage of the discovery of a community of Chinese with blond hair and big noses, thought to be the descendants of Romans (Liu 2001, 10); the excava-tion of Caucasian mummies in the Taklimakan desert of northwest China (Halbertsma 2001); and the controversy over the construction in Beijing's Tiananmen Square of a futuristic opera house designed by a French archi-tect all demonstrate contemporary China's enthusiasm for globalization and its longing to reclaim its position in the international community.[12] The Chineseness preserved and reconstituted in Hong Kong is a light at the end of the tunnel for China, demonstrating how global and internationalized the

Chinese people can be, seemingly without losing any of their national and cultural essence.

As a transnationalized metropolis that is efficiently incorporated into global capitalism, Hong Kong is generally understood to be a portent of the future of many other Chinese cities. In Hong Kong, China's influence is more pervasive than the West's; strong Chinese characteristics linger throughout its cosmopolitan culture. Some critics believe that, as China's most affluent and diverse city, Hong Kong has created new traditions for all Chinese people. But this Chinese aspect of Hong Kong is conditioned by a certain kind of marginality. The postcolonial scholar Gayatri Spivak writes, "The center wants an identifiable margin[;] claims for marginality assure validation from the center" (Spivak 1990, 221). Many scholarly studies emphasize the positive contribution to the center made by this identifiable margin. Helen Siu, an anthropologist from Hong Kong, has asserted that "Hong Kong's cosmopolitan city-life and associated Western civic values are posed against a reified 'Chineseness.' . . . What Hong Kong has offered in this unique position has fueled China's reentry into the world community" (Siu 1999, 108, 110). One critic even states that Hong Kong's hybrid culture is an imaginative new source of Chinese culture: "Every old civilization needs a 'savage' to rejuvenate itself. It is what Africa means for modern European arts, what the West means for American spirit . . . what Hong Kong means for China, and what 'bantang-fan' [half-Chinese and half-Western] means for Hong Kong" (Chan Koon-Chung 1997).[13] However, what I am trying to argue in this book is not simply that the eclecticism or bricolage of Hong Kong culture provides China with an example of how to face the challenges of modernity. Rather, I point to the fact that the totem of Chineseness—this totem is more a token—created in Hong Kong is a fake or approximation, concealing the structural inconsistency of Chineseness itself. With the advent of globalization, the conventional senses of Chineseness have been severely undermined even in China. Hong Kong is both a remedy for and an obstacle inherent in the Chinese symbolic order of cultural and national identification, making such identification possible even as it blocks its actualization from within.

Western Representations of the Free-Floating City

Hong Kong's strategic role in the construction of Chineseness in the contemporary world, however, does not stop at the nation's borders. The dialectical role of Hong Kong's Chineseness may contribute to a more sophisticated understanding of the function of racial differentiation and national identity in a global society in which conventional borders no longer hold; that is to say, Hong Kong's Chineseness obscures its problematic nature, or its presence conceals its absence. The Chineseness of Hong Kong culture has been perceived by non-Chinese as an object of fantasy or a semblance of being that demarcates the world. In the eyes of the West, the significance of Hong Kong lies precisely in the challenge it poses to China;[14] at the same time, the city is living proof of the aggressive expansion of the Chinese cultural zone—the "clash of civilizations," in the words of Samuel Huntington. Huntington points out that even before 1997, Hong Kong, as one of the "few small imperial remnants" of the West, was becoming increasingly oriented toward, involved in, and dependent on mainland China—a potential threat to the Western domination. "A Chinese cultural nationalism," says Huntington, "is thus emerging, epitomized in the words of one Hong Kong leader in 1994: 'We Chinese feel nationalist which we never felt before. We are Chinese and feel proud in that.' . . . There developed a 'popular desire to return to what is authentically Chinese, which often is patriarchal, nativistic, and authoritarian. Democracy, in this historical reemergence, is discredited, as is Leninism, as just another foreign imposition'" (Huntington 1996, 106).

The signifier "Hong Kong" indicates far more than the place itself. China's assumption of sovereignty over Hong Kong after 1997 has never been regarded simply as a "Chinese national event." Rather, it has been seen as a critical test for China as well as a criterion by which to measure how the rising China might challenge the hegemony of the West. As Michael Yahuda summarizes it, "a display of tolerance for an autonomous Hong Kong would consolidate its new relations with the Chinese communities outside China, strengthen Beijing's stance regarding Taiwan, reduce anxieties in Southeast Asia, ease China's relations with the USA and Japan, enhance the process of China's integration with the Asia-Pacific region, and improve China's international standing generally" (Yahuda 1996, 1). The Hong Kong issue, when put in the context of international politics, is never confined to a local or national problem but is conceived in terms of a "global design" for the remaking of the power hierarchy in the world.

Long before the 1997 handover, when I was still living in the United States, the American media seemed to have a strong interest in the news in Hong Kong. Just one year after the June 4, 1989, incident in Tiananmen Square and Hong Kong's million-citizen demonstration in response to it, Western correspondents presented Hong Kong as distinct from China. The American audience was shown news coverage of numerous issues, including the correlation of Hong Kong's Hang Seng stock index to the political fluctuations of mainland China, and especially to the health of then-premier Deng Xiaoping; Chris Patten, Hong Kong's last colonial governor and a self-proclaimed champion of democracy, in heated disputes with the Chinese officials over the democratization of the colony; the question of whether the candle-light commemoration of June 4, held annually in Victoria Park since 1989, could continue after the transfer of sovereignty; a fatal stampede on New Year's Eve 1992 in Lang Kwai Fong, an entertainment district frequented by Westerners and expatriates; a donation of one hundred million U.S. dollars to Princeton University by Gordon Wu, a Hong Kong businessman; and the brain drain from the Hong Kong film industry to Hollywood. But the various stories about Hong Kong always boiled down to a single event: the 1997 handover. "The Hand-over: they called it the Chinese Take-away and it was now the old refrain," writes Paul Theroux in his novel *Kowloon Tong,* which itself does not avoid the old refrain: "It was the only news in Hong Kong—and news related to it, the economy, land reclamation, sales of commercial property, the price of petrol, the new airport, the noisy fears of anxious politicians, all of it was tied to the Hand-over" (Theroux 1997, 6).

When Hong Kong does make itself heard in the West, it is monotonously univocal. If the chance arises for Hong Kong to speak, its voice is allowed to resonate only with the tone set by dominant groups. So my point is not that Hong Kong as subject has been silenced, neglected, erased, or constructed as absent in various discourses; rather, within the dominant conceptualization of the East-West binarism, its voice remains muffled and unexpressed. Thus, its inclusion only underscores the violence of its effacement. Apparently, Hong Kong became an interesting—and at the same time flat and hackneyed—object for the Western media at the time of the city's historic transition from a colonial port under British rule to a Special Administrative Region under Communist China. The passage was considered bizarre because this advanced capitalist free port was handed over by a Western democratic country—albeit one that had practiced imperialism in the past—to an Asian Communist regime that came to power through repressive force rather than by direct election. The world has continued to watch this unprecedented transition, not to observe how the laboratory idea of "one country, two systems" could work in practice, but to see how it might fail. This kind of watching is not uncommon in our international community. The fall of Communism in Eastern Europe once attracted the eager attention of Western media. According to Slavoj Žižek, what initially fascinated the West about that disintegration was the reinvention of Western democracy: "[It was] as if democracy, which in the West shows more and more signs of decay and crisis and is lost in bureaucratic routine and publicity-style election campaigns, [was] being rediscovered in Eastern Europe in all its freshness and novelty" (Žižek 1993, 200). However, after witnessing the necessary evils—such as high unemployment and crime rates, financial turmoil, and moral chaos—brought about by the liberalization of the political and economic systems, and after observing the growth of ultranationalism within the Eastern European states, the West gradually gave up its enthusiastic anticipation of the re-idealization and recreation of its own image there.

In comparison to the conversion of the ex-Communist countries to liberal-capitalist nations modeled on Western democratic systems, Hong Kong's story is one of transition as well as of transnationalism. The significance of Hong Kong for the West lies in its challenging or subverting of an emerging China and also in its mirroring of a superior Western cultural identity and values. The former British colony is a potential trump card, allowing the West some control over China's domestic affairs in terms of preventing human rights violations in Hong Kong or protecting the city's autonomy, which was promised by the Sino-British Joint Declaration of December 1984. Hong Kong has also been upheld as a symbol of Western strength that is supposed to prevail along with a system of Western values, institutions, civil liberties, and democracy. On the one hand, the example of Hong Kong runs counter to the "Asian values" promoted by many authoritative Asian leaders. Hong Kong's success is a slap in the face to those who reject Western ideals and insist on Asian cultural advantage. On the other hand, the growing visibility of Chineseness in Hong Kong as perceived by the West could be manipulated to support the notion of "essential cultural differences": collectivism versus individualism; the values of authority and hierarchy versus liberty, equality, and democracy; and the supremacy of the state versus the propensity to distrust government and oppose authority. The idea of Hong Kong perpetuates the East-West binarism in today's world, although such a culturally essentialist structure should have been seriously questioned long ago.

The Collaboration of Nationalization and Globalization

To call attention to the Western "globalization" of the Hong Kong issue is definitely not to suggest that the question of Hong Kong should be grasped beyond the framework of the dichotomy between China and the West; hence the "correct" notion of the city lies in its cultural and sociopolitical particularities (neither does the conventional differentiation between East and West offer any help). My insistence not on Hong Kong–ness but on Hong Kong's role in constructing Chineseness in the global age could be understood as a way to lay bare not only the ideological mechanism of cultural and national identification but also the void of subjectivity that such an ideological force attempts to conceal.

In this book I describe the popular culture in or of Hong Kong that is spread as transnational culture throughout Chinese and other ethnic communities. Hong Kong's transnational culture refers to the cultural impacts of the movement of the Chinese population and capital not only within mainland China but also to other countries. The Chinese diaspora has not necessarily created a mutant culture of dislocations and discontinuities. On the contrary, the encounters of the diasporic Chinese with their adopted countries constantly remind them of the differences of their locations and of the boundaries separating them from those countries.[15] These differences end up producing a strong desire on the part of Chinese emigrants to hold on to their ethnic culture and to derive from it a sense of certainty and security. It is not at all surprising that the Hong Kong emigrants who left the city a decade or more ago still largely depend on Hong Kong's popular cultural products for their daily entertainment and spiritual consolation. Popular culture is a kind of empowering force for the diasporic Hong Kong Chinese in foreign environments.[16]

The Chineseness of Hong Kong's transnational culture not only serves a purpose for China and the Chinese diaspora; it also plays a supporting role in the multiple processes of globalization, and not simply because its mechanism of constructing a hybrid and fluid identity operates beyond the nation-state and is not bound by any geographical region. Insofar as it effectively reterritorializes the ongoing process of deterritorialization, the flexible and reproducible Chineseness of Hong Kong's transnational culture acts as a seal that fills the void of nationality and cultural unity resulting from a global economy and the self-initiating circulation of capital. Because global capitalism is only an inconsistent amalgam of diverse elements, national and cultural direction will continue to be sought as part of an attempt to secure identities and political positions on what has become slippery ground. The Chineseness is a veil to cover up the loss of substantial national particularity in a world operating with the logic of global capitalism. As Žižek argues, "[the] very reference to a particular cultural [background] is a screen for the universal anonymity of Capital. The true horror lies not in the particular content hidden beneath the universality of global Capital but, rather, in the fact that Capital is effectively an anonymous global machine blindly running its course; that there is in fact no particular Secret Agent animating it. The horror is not the (particular living) ghost in the (dead universal) machine, but the (dead universal) machine in the very heart of each (particular living) ghost" (Žižek 1999, 218).

In a world where homogeneity is becoming the norm, the global circulation and consumption of Hong Kong popular culture could serve as a comforting sign to make believe that cultural difference is still safely in place. As a culture of obsolescence, a throwaway culture especially designed not to endure, Hong Kong's transnational culture, with its fluid and malleable nature, is well suited to contribute significantly to the creation of a global culture that poses no threat to any states. Furthermore, the Chineseness established by the worldwide popularity of Hong Kong culture may present a distinguished point of identification for the East's constitution of its national positions and for the West's reestablishment of a racial other. Even though Hong Kong popular culture is not exactly "indigenous" to other Asian countries—and many of them are generally hostile to Chineseness—it can still articulate the Asian experience of adapting to a westernized modernity in common terms. Compared to white American celebrities, Hong Kong stars are definitely more stimulating to Asian viewers, because these viewers can more "closely" identify with them. Although Hollywood's assimilation of Hong Kong Chinese filmmakers and movie stars—such as John Woo, Jackie Chan, Jet Li, Chow Yun Fat, and Michelle Yeoh—might demonstrate the adaptability of the global entertainment syndicate to alien cultures, more essentially (through the popular cinematic representations of their Chineseness with possible racialist, if not racist, undertones), a significant ethnic difference could be reintroduced to designate how "foreign" the Asian minority groups are in order to delineate a sharper identity in the eyes of the mainstream white American. The Hollywood film *Kiss of the Dragon* (2001) presents Jet Li as a superhero who can destroy an entire police station with his bare hands, just as Schwarzenegger did in *The Terminator* (1984). This kind of trendy, "Hongkongified" movie glorifying a small Chinese martial artist actually contributes to a legitimization of the white supremacy and racism being acted out not on screen but on the streets; now white people could have their liberal conscience firmly supported in this type of hyperbolic action film, which is seemingly good enough to offer glamorous but mythologized representations of the ethnic minority without really changing the existing racist fantasy.

Since the mechanism of global capitalism provides human beings with no directions and no goals (or, too many directions and goals, giving rise to unwanted confusions and chaos), racial and cultural distinctions appear to be a means for preventing the horrible collapse of the symbolic order of a world that is still categorized by racial, cultural, and national identities. The production of Hong Kong–styled Chineseness in transnational popular culture, along with the surge of other nationalisms and ethnic identities, can be viewed as an attempt to reestablish some kind of order in a universe governed by the logic of global capitalism, and to find a frame of reference that would lend the world a cognitive mapping in the face of its possible total breakdown. Perhaps, in this sense, Hong Kong's Chineseness serves as the appearance as appearance—it is nothing but its own surface, pretending that there must be some reality behind it. It is still the appearance, not any substantial content, that helps establish the distinction between the self and the other. Such a Chineseness is an illusory feature that accounts for the essential difference of the identity.

However, I would like to emphasize that the Chineseness produced by Hong Kong's transnational culture underscores the fact that the external difference (the so-called clash of civilizations) is actually an internal one; there are always more clashes within a culture than among cultures. Self-contained cultural unity is basically impossible, as differences can always be found within. The external limitation of cultural unity is indeed reflected from within and is manifested by a culture's inherent inability to become fully itself. The manifest Chineseness of the looming Chinese century is in fact the expression of its exact opposite—a total release of an ideological and political grip that would govern people's minds. In this sense, Hong Kong culture acts like the child in Andersen's "The Emperor's New Clothes," openly announcing the illusory nature of Chineseness, or any kinds of national and cultural identity, while others only whisper about it in secret.

Structure

This book is divided into three parts. Part 1 focuses on language—the ways in which written and spoken Chinese languages have been reshaped in Hong Kong popular culture. Part 2 deals with images—the production of cinematic images in relation to the (re)construction and identification of Chineseness. Part 3 concerns objects—the real and imaginary objects found in the post-colonial city's theme parks.

Chapter 1 looks at local Chinese print culture, focusing on local newspaper columns in order to examine how the "Hong Kong way of life"—which

China politically and emphatically promised would continue after the hand-over—has been shaped, policed, and protected by the columns. The local newspapers' perpetuation of a so-called Hong Kong lifestyle is in fact an illusion that conceals the city's very lack of a political identity. The column writing found in the Hong Kong dailies has the potential to subvert the cultural and national totality. To a certain extent, column writing follows the model posited in Chinese book culture, but it also transgresses that model by moving away from its breeding ground of subject formation and into an economy of prodigal self-dispersion.

Chapter 2 examines subtitles in Hong Kong cinema and television and explores the relationship between globalization and cultural particularism, on the one hand, and the construction of cultural identity within a trans-Chinese context, on the other. I consider the Chinese subtitling in Chinese films and TV programs to be a visual articulation of a split in the national forms of speech, both spoken and written, that defies any easy identification. I present three interrelated instances of Hong Kong subtitling that illustrate how the assimilation of the particular into something much larger—say, the national or global—always yields some leftover that eventually nullifies the assimilating system. These are the English subtitles in Hong Kong cinema prepared for Western audiences; the standard, written Chinese subtitles in television programs prepared for the Hong Kong viewership; and the Cantonese subtitles of films and TV broadcasts prepared for the local audience. I argue that the clumsy English subtitles that attempt to represent a certain cultural specificity or designate certain ethnic characteristics are a hindrance that—paradoxically—facilitates globalization. The renaturalization of capitalism through the very reference to Chinese nationalization is borne out by a close look at the Western reception of subtitled Hong Kong cinema. I attempt to document the politics of the subtitles by pointing to the subtle form of power manipulation that occurs when the radical ambiguity of the voice is eliminated in its translation into a "comprehensible" and "readable" written text. My reading suggests that, if hearing oneself speak implies an experience of immediate, transparent self-presence, the local audience hears and sees itself speaking, although what it hears and sees is never fully itself but an alien body at its very heart.

Chapter 3 addresses the muscular body as seen in Hong Kong popular cultural forms such as the action movie and kung fu comics. I concentrate on how the failure of representation, which is essentially inscribed in Hong Kong subject formation, simultaneously contributes to and subverts the heroic and nationalist Chinese masculine body. By its very insufficiency, the logic of the sublime embodies the negativity of the idea of Chineseness that prevails in the world of global capitalism and according to which a deep nihilistic void is always present in our being. Chapter 4 examines the way in which the recent "Asianization" of Hong Kong cinema is simply a strategy of "global localization" or "glocalization." It looks back at the films of the 1990s in order to emphasize that although Hong Kong appears to address its differences from others, the city is actually struggling with itself, with its place in the world, and with its own invented sense of Chineseness. The depiction of localism in Hong Kong films proves to be a circular journey in which the more globalized localism becomes, the more it is nationalized—or relocalized. However, it never returns to its starting point because the so-called national or ethnic point of origin is continually differentiated.

Chapters 5 and 6 explore new possibilities of representing Chineseness by discussing the "Hongkongification" of Hollywood films, especially those of Jackie Chan, John Woo, and Jet Li. I argue that the transnational dissemination of Hollywood by members of the Hong Kong film industry provides a justification for continued domination and exploitation by the Western (global) entertainment industry; but I assert that it also initiates a negation of the symbolic realm of Chineseness. The transnational intersection of Hong Kong cinema with Hollywood may produce something that could generate a new and useful reading of cultural globalization, yet it also could reveal the absurdity of identity formation at large. The Chineseness in Hollywood films is stereotyped in order to assert its dominant (American) self. Hong Kong audiences may be offended by such portrayals of Chineseness, but they forget that their so-called authentic identity is no less artificial. If the Chineseness constructed in local Hong Kong film is an empty notion without a specific ethnic object, then Hollywood–Hong Kong film is the ethnic object without a proper notion of Chinese national identity. Losing one's memory, mixing with or even becoming part of another ethnic group, and selectively deploying Chineseness in order to advance one's own interests are the characteristics of some of the heroes of these Hollywood–Hong Kong films. All of them suggest that a transnational Chinese hero should rejuvenate himself by symbolically cutting himself off from his past and repositioning himself as a subject with a fluid identity within a global economy. The issue of racial passing comes up in these films, which construct the fantasy of transgressing a stable Chinese racial authority and which rewrite racial identity so that it can easily move between Chineseness and any other kind of ethnicity. The Chinese person who "passes" can always find a way to return, paralleling the movement of capital in the Pacific Rim. These "Hong Kong films" of the new Hollywood help to reinforce visible ethnic distinctions at the same time that they further affirm whiteness as natural, de-localized, and universal.

Chapter 7 is dedicated to Ang Lee's *Crouching Tiger, Hidden Dragon* (2000) and takes up the issue of appearance in a discussion of what I call transitional Chineseness. This film, the highest-grossing Chinese-language film in the West, is a strong indication of a Chinese cultural diaspora and represents the extremely fluid spatiality of Chineseness, although Chinese critics in particular have complained that the film's content is too westernized. Drawing on the conceits of film noir, I argue that the opposition of false appearance and hidden truth is itself deceptive, and that the film's ethnic appearance, beyond being sheer illusion, is, in accordance with the logic of global capitalism, devoid of substance. The so-called mystery behind the appearance is itself a phantasmic deceit. The theme of the discovery of an inner truth in Lee's blockbuster is probably a reflection of its exact opposite, namely, the growing loss of a hidden dimension of an authentic cultural or national self. The appearance of Chineseness throughout the film signifies something beyond superficial phenomena and conceals the fact that there may be nothing inside.

The final chapter looks at how postcolonial Hong Kong is turning itself not only into a fantasy of its own, but also into a fantasy of the mainland's, as evidenced by the construction of theme parks and the importation of both real and phantasmic animals such as Ocean Park's giant panda and Disneyland's Mickey Mouse. By attempting to fill the void created by its new subjectivity and erase the antagonism of its past experience of modernity with the magical effects of new fantasy objects, Hong Kong unwittingly exposes the internal contradictions in the modernity of the Chinese nation-state. In its circularity, the fantasy of post-1997 Hong Kong fills the gap it opens up by bearing witness to what it is supposed to cover. The advent of "Disneyfication," heralded by Hong Kong's Disney theme park, is viewed by the mainland Chinese government as a way of sorting out the internal problems of modernity and of helping to integrate its economy into the global system through a neutralization of the political dimensions of social life. By becoming the theme-park city of China, Hong Kong serves to shield the naked truth that virtual reality has already permeated a country with both a Communist name and pervasive commodification. Thus, the theme parks of Hong Kong are designed to allow China to (re)locate its Chineseness and its position within the new global picture. Probably the ultimate mission of the small Hong Kong is to provide this transitional Chineseness for its great motherland.

PART 1

From Voice to Words and Back in Chinese Identification

1

Much Ado about the Ordinary
in Newspaper-Column and
Book Culture

IN STARK CONTRAST to the colonial language policy in place else-where, 150 years of British colonial rule did not produce an influential English print culture in Hong Kong. There are only two major local English newspapers published in the former colony, and their popularity cannot be compared with that of the Chinese-language dailies. In 2001 there were fifty-three newspapers available to the six million people of Hong Kong, and twenty-five of these papers are published in Chinese. The city's vibrant Chinese newspapers may reveal how Chineseness survives in its urban culture. Hong Kong Chinese readers subscribe to English-language newspapers mainly for utilitarian purposes, such as looking for high-level jobs, polishing their English skills, or simply showing off their Western educational background and middle- or upper-class status. Hong Kong's local print culture is predominantly Chinese in the sense that it has employed primarily Chinese language and has identified with Chinese race and culture, even under British colonial rule. The British government did not enforce a radical colonial language policy in Hong Kong because, critics argue, the Chinese identify strongly with their traditional culture and language. A wholesale Anglicization would have met with fierce local resistance. Historically, Hong Kong was seen as a British outpost in mainland China. The colonial regime initially desired little involvement with this island. The establishment of the People's Republic of China and the tie of kinship between mainland and Hong Kong Chinese also convinced Britain that the implementation of a colonial language policy would be ineffective (Tay 1994; 1998, 5–6).

The transformation to English did not take place in the print industry or in everyday language practice, although the colonial government officially recognized the legitimate status of the Chinese language only in the 1970s.[1] English is the language choice in the business world and in schools, where Chinese learning has been marginalized and even categorized as lesser learning.[2] The cultural tolerance and minimal engagement of the colonial government in print culture seem to have allowed the local Chinese to gradually develop a linguistic form of cultural and ethnic representation. But this local consciousness still must rely on the prevailing Chinese writing system based on standard Chinese (*bai hua,* which is a written form of Chinese based on the vernacular Mandarin), since Cantonese—the everyday dialect of Hong Kong people—is primarily a spoken language, though it sometimes infiltrates the local written texts. This form of Hong Kong cultural identification is, first and foremost, nationalized by the use of Chinese script. It is widely believed that Hong Kong is essentially a monoethnic, monolingual Cantonese-speaking community. But recent studies have challenged this myth. Scholars find that Hakka, Hoklo, Chiu Chau, Fukien, Sze Yap, and Shanghainese together with Mandarin/Putonghua are the minority Chinese dialects spoken in many Hong Kong families. But these "home dialects" appear to have decreased rapidly in the thirty years between 1961 and 1991, because of the increased educational opportunities giving every child the chance of schooling through Cantonese, growing pressure toward conformity in Hong Kong Chinese society, and the emergence of a sense of Hong Kong identity (Bacon-Shone and Bolton 1998).

A Phenomenal Cultural Practice

More than a dozen Chinese-language newspapers are on sale daily at newsstands, and almost all of them offer supplements (*fukan*) that carry serial columns (*zhuanlan*). The serial newspaper column is a uniquely local phenomenon that defines the experience of everyday modern metropolitan life. Some assert that one would be hard put to find the same variety of daily newspaper columns anywhere else in the world. A leading Chinese-language daily that covers local and overseas general news puts out no fewer than thirty columns on various topics in its daily supplements. It has been estimated that there are about a thousand columnists who regularly contribute to Hong Kong newspapers. The daily columns cover a vast array of topics and styles. The columns range from writings intended to edify (commentary on world

politics, critiques of local and Chinese affairs, advice on international investment, and cultural criticism) to those meant purely to entertain (recipes;
restaurant, film, and music reviews; celebrity gossip; travel guides; health tips;
gardening and pet care information; horoscopes; horse-racing previews;
nightclub listings; literary essays; and serialized fiction). Critics find that the
supplement pages look more and more like magazines and they compare the
variety of offerings to those of a supermarket (He Liangmao 1997, 53–57).

In the December 20, 2002, *Mingpao Daily News,* there are thirty-two columns in the seven pages of the supplement. Apart from three comics, a poem,
and special pages devoted to cuisine, travel, health, parenting, and shopping
tips, the rest of the columns defy categorization. They are predominantly
individual commentaries on a number of current-affairs topics, including
Article 23 legislation (a bill required by the Basic Law to introduce national
security laws on treason, sedition, and official secrets to postcolonial Hong
Kong). Because the city has actively debated the Hong Kong government's
proposal to introduce the highly controversial Basic Law Article 23—which
may limit the freedom of people in the name of national security—there are
an unusual number of columns addressing the issue. However, columns are
associated with the ordinary and prosaic as much as with vibrant and dynamic elements of social reality. These columns average about five hundred
words in length, and the writers usually adopt a relatively soft approach and
accessible language so as not to alienate their readers, rendering most column writing indistinctive and mediocre.[3] Despite its nondescript character,
column writing indoctrinates its readers, influencing the ways they feel and
live, what and whom they believe, and what and where they eat and shop.
These columns present information on everyday living that may be free from
the constraints of social abstraction but never from the logic of commodification.

The production and consumption of newspaper columns are phenomenal. Perusing them has become a daily habit for many newspaper readers
in Hong Kong. Because of their diversity of subject matter and widespread
appeal to different classes, columns play a significant role in cultivating and
shaping Hong Kong's way of life. This phenomenon serves as a momentary reminder of how the everyday is rooted in the lived urban experience.
Many believe that the reason a small place like Hong Kong can support so
many newspapers is not the quality of the reporting but the popularity of
the supplements—where most of the columns are published ("Women
meitian de jingshen shiliang" [Our Daily Spiritual Food] 1989, 7). As a forum in which different concerns are raised and different histories are lived,

columns may sometimes manage to orchestrate the coexistence of different narratives and temporalities. However, homogeneity is the norm in column writing, whose standardization is not limited to issues of length. In November 2002 most local column writers, along with many movie stars, condemned the tabloid magazine *Eastweek* for publishing a photograph of a local actress showing her topless and taken when she was kidnapped many years ago. An old Chinese proverb, "tian di bu rong" (intolerable both by heaven and earth), has been used to describe this sort of sensational tabloid journalism. The event ignited a fiery debate among columnists about media ethics. Despite their role in the commercialization of the local press (whose major concern is circulation and profit), in this instance column writers collectively resorted to traditional Chinese moral values to criticize capitalist operation and to ensure that Chinese society remains Chinese.

Supplement pages are by no means uncommon in the newspapers worldwide, but Hong Kong supplement sections carry an exceptional number of columns.[4] The supplement section, derisively nicknamed the "tail" or the "butt" of the newspaper (*baoweiba* or *baopigu*), is considered by Chinese critics to be characteristic of printed media in Chinese communities (Feng Bing 2001; Xiang 1995). Chinese-language newspapers started carrying supplement sections in the late nineteenth century, when they featured mainly poems, literary essays, and fiction. Aided by the growing circulation of newspapers, fiction attained an unprecedented popularity in the late Qing dynasty (Lee and Nathan 1985). Hong Kong newspapers have further developed the entertainment function offered by the supplement. Besides adopting the conventional practice of publishing fiction and literary articles, Hong Kong newspaper supplements since the 1970s have become more commercially oriented in order to cater to the diversified interests and tastes of their readers. The new offset-printing technology that replaced traditional block printing intensified the competition among local dailies, motivating editorial boards to redesign their supplements and introduce new columnists to maintain readership and attract additional readers (Yip 2000). It was also during that time that columns published in the supplement section were given fixed numbers of words and preset layouts, which facilitated the systematic editing and organized production of the commercial dailies. The 1990s witnessed drastic changes, supported by computerization in newspaper supplement production and the trend of "supplementization"—or "tabloidization"—of other pages, led by the successful newcomer *Apple Daily.*

Founded in 1995, *Apple Daily* is a pioneering local press that competes for readership by making innovative use of style and entertainment supplements.

Word-based articles have given way to image-based features, indicating a visual transformation in Hong Kong print culture. Colorful design and graphic layout have prevailed over the written language. Visual appeal and graphic attraction are now in the spotlight, to the detriment of the printed word. Print media has transformed itself in imitation of television and has become more fragmented and incoherent, emphasizing sensation and feeling over reason. Indeed, the full-scale market-orientation strategy is not restricted to the supplement sections. Having become the number-two bestseller in a very short time, *Apple Daily* is well known for its brazen, sensational news coverage. By imitating supermarket tabloids and slick gossip magazines, *Apple Daily* apparently panders to the tastes of a mass audience with its provocative content, and it succeeds in arousing the active participation of the readers by forcing them to make sense of its fragmented and discontinuous narratives. Legitimate political and social topics have been supplanted by sex, sensational crimes, the rise and fall of celebrities, scandalous paparazzi investigations, rumors, and even sham news.[5] One of the most outrageous examples was the exclusive coverage of a Hong Kong man who patronized prostitutes in mainland China shortly after his wife threw their two young children out of their high-rise apartment and jumped to her death after them. It was later disclosed that *Apple Daily* reporters paid the man to philander in China.

Although the backlash against the story was severe and the press later printed an apology, the success of *Apple Daily*'s strategy has proven to be a model for its competitors. Nowadays local popular dailies print colorful and eye-catching photos and graphics in preference to traditional, written-word reporting. Coverage of a bank robbery is typically accompanied by colorful cartoons or illustrations that dramatically recreate the action. It is tempting to argue that this "process of supplementization" that many popular Hong Kong local newspapers have undergone is a byproduct of globalization, since by relying heavily on the graphic, the pictorial, and the sensational, the Chinese-language dailies now have greater potential of overcoming the barriers of language and regional culture. Despite these "global" tendencies in Hong Kong newspapers, the locally targeted Chinese-language column remains popular, even though it is gradually losing ground to the more visually appealing features in the commercial papers. Column culture may signify that no matter how globalized Hong Kong's economy has become, Chinese language and culture still lend structure to the city's everyday life.

Examining the issue from a different angle, we find that the power of globalization is apparent only with the awareness that Hong Kong is not fully globalized, and that there is still something culturally unique that cannot be assimilated by a world economy. The preservation of local cultural specificity is probably the ideological basis of globalism. Rather than holding antagonistic positions, the global and local would then have a symbiotic relationship. Stuart Hall points out that "what we usually call the global, far from being something which, in a systematic fashion, rolls over everything, creating similarity, in fact works through particularity, negotiates particular spaces, particular ethnicities, works through mobilizing particular identities and so on. So there is always a dialectic, a continuous dialectic, between the local and the global" (Hall 1997, 62). Globalization can be understood as a process of creating a world in which differences and particularities are celebrated as well as overcome. Today's globalism is far more powerful and terrifying than one that conceives the world as universal, transcending and denying the particular interests of individual localities. Now we tend to think of globalization not as a movement toward a singular, unitary cultural form, but as one of decentering, and of living with and adapting to differentiated particularities and local conditions. The success of this new form of globalism depends on a "multilocal" or "translocal" mode of operation, which means that it can prevail only by establishing partnerships with the local. This new globalism is so pervasive that there is no particular interest it cannot articulate, no local identity it cannot recognize, and no marginal position it cannot incorporate.[6]

The popularity of the newspaper column in Hong Kong could be explained by its accessibility, diverse content, and responsiveness to the changing world, all of which perfectly match the pace of life in an advanced capitalist city. Besides serving as a receiver of information from all over the world, the columns in the supplements domesticate the foreign elements and cater almost exclusively to local interests. After the terrorist attack in New York on September 11, 2001, many Hong Kong columnists related the incident (albeit in a farfetched manner) to local concerns to appease the city's appetite for gossip. On the day after the attack, Tsao Chip, a popular columnist, ironically predicted that Hong Kong tabloid newspapers, infected with what he called "bubbling headline syndrome" (*biaoti paomozheng*), would use the largest fonts for headlines relating to the attacks, since the scandal rags did so even for matters so trivial as movie stars going sixty hours without peeing (Tsao 2001). Another popular column writer, Lee Pik Wah (Lillian Lee), remarked that Osama bin Laden looked like a local TV star, Lawrence Ng Kai Wah; she suggested that fortune tellers should examine bin Laden's face, palms, date of birth, and other personal information in order to have a better understanding of this terrorist (Lee Pik Wah 2001). The columnists succeed at creating gossip topics for the community that are incomprehensible to foreign visitors and non-Chinese-speaking residents. With its fragmentary form of expression, column writing is capable of quickly transmitting bits of information and snatches of ideas to the public, thus promoting the spreading of rumors and idle conversation throughout the community. In 1992, there was a widespread rumor concerning a Kowloon-Canton Rail Corporation television commercial. The thirty-second commercial featured a group of little children playing "train" by lining up with hands on each other's shoulders. A caller to a phone-in radio program claimed that in that line of children was a ghost who bled from the mouth and hovered above the ground. Many columnists dismissed the rumor as nonsense, interpreting the motives behind it (local media always help perpetuate rumors in order to boost ratings or sales), yet all the while they generated more talk and fanned the flames of an already hot issue.[7]

Intended for casual and leisurely reception, the ephemeral columns are more like elusive voices in the wind than permanent cultural artifacts. As Walter Benjamin observed of the print culture in the 1920s, "locust swarms of print, which already eclipse the sun of what is taken for intellect for city dwellers, will grow thicker with each succeeding year" (Benjamin 1985, 62). More than three-quarters of a century later, the swarms of column writing in Hong Kong have become almost unimaginably thick. The number of columns featured in Hong Kong newspapers over the last several decades defies any simple summarization or empirical measurement.[8] However, column culture does chronicle and register the transient, the fleeting, and the contingent in the locality, typifying modernity and revealing community concerns and conflicts.

The intellectual attitude toward column culture is generally critical and negative. Column writing is discredited for its shallowness and superficiality. To respond to events in a rapid and timely manner, a column has to be produced in a very short time. A professional columnist sometimes contributes several articles a day to various newspapers and hardly has time to engage in serious contemplation of a subject. A famous example is the 1960s columnist Gao Xiong. Dubbed the "columnist king," Gao wrote for local and overseas Chinese-language newspapers under a number of pen names; on a daily basis he wrote over ten thousand words in a variety of genres, including satire, literary fiction, detective stories, and porn. Lam Chiu Wing, one of the most versatile popular writers of the 1990s, contributes daily columns to two newspapers, writes short stories for *Mingpao Daily* three times a week, hosts weekly radio talk shows and television programs, and writes occasional film scripts. Because of the special layout of Hong Kong newspapers, the length of columns is usually restricted to between three hundred and one thousand Chinese characters. This further limits the possibility of coherent arguments or profound and substantial thinking. The newspaper column is like fast food for the mind. Columnists seek only to entertain the reading public rather than strive for any new vision. The writing is criticized for being ephemeral, fragmented in form, and schizophrenic in content. Columnists are often derided for being sloppy and inconsistent in their arguments.

At the same time, column writing is highly commercialized. A column can be nothing more than a thinly veiled commercial with a stylistic or personal touch (columnists are sometimes commissioned to promote certain products, such as Hollywood movies or computer software). Columnists themselves are commodities; newspapers promote those "stars" that achieve celebrity status in order to boost newspaper circulation. To borrow Adorno's critique of the culture industry, the star system—appropriated from the romantic notion of individualistic art—serves only to reinforce the dominant ideology of the existing reality by strengthening blind obedience to authority and impeding the development of the autonomous individual (Adorno 1991). Many newspaper columnists are multimedia people who host radio talk shows and even television programs to increase their public exposure. For example, the Jackie Collins–style columnist Lin Yanni has been very active in upper-class social circles and since the 1980s has been a celebrity in her own right. Tsao Chip, who writes for the *Oriental Daily* and the *Mingpao Daily,* also cohosts a weekly radio talk show and television program. Hence, there are worries that the public forum offered by the columns is being dominated by a small circle of writers who have achieved the most media exposure.[9] After all, Hong Kong column culture is a distinctive experience of everyday modernity that is mediated—if not dominated—by commercialization and consumption.

It is not difficult to see that this critique of Hong Kong column culture comes from a standpoint of elitist taste and high modernist criteria. When the value of the columns is affirmed, it is due primarily to their reflection of local lifestyles, which serves the interests of historicism and sociology. From a sociological perspective, newspaper columns are like social documents that bear witness to the historical development of the city, even though what the columns reflect is the sheer reality of cultural commodification.[10] One critical approach aims at excavating column writings with intrinsic literary merit (such as creativity, individual style, or sense of social responsibility) from the mass of cultural data and instating them in the "canon" of Hong Kong literature.[11] Without a doubt, newspaper columns have played an important role in the development of Hong Kong literature written in Chinese. Well-established Hong Kong Chinese writers of different generations, such as Liu Yichang, Xi Xi, Ye Si (pseudonym of Leung Ping-kwan), Ng Hui Bun, Wong Bik Wan, and Dung Kai Cheung, wrote regular newspaper columns, and many of their major novels were first serialized in dailies.[12] While acknowledging the necessity of differentiating "literary works" from columns to the study of Hong Kong literature, I would point out the exclusivity and elitism inherent in such an undertaking.

Both reflectionist and restorative approaches may fail to capture the cultural implications of column writings as much as the negative dismissal of them does. There are those who have come to consider column writing to be a major constitutive element in the formation of a public sphere (Leo Lee 1995; Leung Ping-kwan 1996b, 76–79), in which a variety of opinions may be voiced and through which a common cultural identity is fabricated. In their view, column writing provides a form of expression for differentiated groups, since the multifarious backgrounds of the columnists represent different social strata, and with its emphasis on local interest, column writing offers a kind of meeting place that is supposedly open to all. Hence, column culture can unite, for a time, a populace that is learning how to find its own voice and mode of living.

My approach to column writing is neither to rediscover its inherent literariness nor to integrate these popular texts into the continuum of the local historical narrative structure. The task of examining Hong Kong newspaper columns may not necessarily coincide with the agenda in contemporary cultural studies of empowering marginalized and oppressed cultural products. It is debatable whether Hong Kong column writing secures the democratization of the cultural sphere or supports a mass manipulation and reification. To a large extent, the cultural function of column writing can be compared to Lacan's understanding of the role of the chorus in Greek tragedy. Lacan asks:

> And what is a Chorus? You will be told that it's you yourselves. Or perhaps it isn't you. But that's the point. Means are involved here, emotional means. In my view, the Chorus is people who are moved. . . . When you go to the theatre in the evening, you are preoccupied by the affairs of the day, by the pen that you lost, by the check that you will have to sign the next day. You shouldn't give yourselves too much credit. Your emotions are taken charge of by the healthy order displayed on the stage. The Chorus takes care of them. The emotional commentary is done for you. . . . It is sufficiently silly; it is also not without firmness; it is more or less human.
>
> Therefore, you don't have to worry; even if you don't feel anything, the Chorus will feel in your stead. Why after all can one not imagine that the ef-

fect on you may be achieved, at least a small dose of it, even if you didn't tremble that much? (Lacan 1992, 252)

In a similar vein, if you don't feel anything in the alienated and reified world, the newspaper column will feel for you. When you are bored and numbed by the banality of the daily world, the columns create an invisible, artificial, enthusiastic public that feels and reacts for you. This public assures us that we are inscribed in the social and cultural order of the community. Like Benjamin's "voluntary memory," columns offer a shield for the reader's self, protecting it from the shock evinced by the experience of modernity. Events may be mediated by the intervention of column writing to satisfy partially the demand for telling the changing conditions of everyday existence. Column culture represents an everyday practice that Heidegger would label a "site of inauthenticity," wherein personal discourse is dominated by public talk and the self is integrated into the standardized realm of the majority (Heidegger 1962, 223). Easy access to local affairs, foreign cultures, and global information, by means of the supplement writing in the dailies, facilitates the merging of the personal into a syncretic world. Through the mapping of the details of everyday life by the daily columns and supplements, "we" are able to comment on any event, be it nearby or far away, as if "we" know all.

The media coverage of the outbreak of atypical pneumonia, better known as SARS (severe acute respiratory syndrome), in April 2003 was an outstanding example of such "chorus-like" mediation. Throughout the entire month, all the headline news and columns in Hong Kong were overwhelmingly preoccupied with everything about SARS, creating an impression that almost no crimes or other social events ever happened in the city. The media made SARS sound like the great influenza outbreak after the First World War that killed more than twenty million people worldwide. The city was in a panic under the endless bombardment of the media coverage. Although the SARS outbreak was far from being of historic plague proportions (the virus has stricken less than two thousand of Hong Kong's seven million people, with a death rate among affected patients of about 15 percent), people were clearing the shelves of pharmacies in the hope of protecting themselves against the disease, and facemasks, latex gloves, and sterilizing solutions had been sold out for weeks. Everybody wore facemask day and night. Indeed the fear of SARS spread much faster than the illness itself. Hong Kong people almost forgot that they had more chance of dying from other diseases or from being hit by a car than they did from SARS. Anxiety and fear were mounting in the city as authorities daily announced more cases, and the media trumpeted the effects. A citywide hysteria was surely induced by the saturated media coverage. Schools and universities stopped classes. Social activities were cancelled. Many people stopped going out and there was a huge drop in customers at many popular shopping malls and restaurants. In early April, a fourteen-year-old schoolboy created a further panic by downloading a page from the Web site of the *Mingpao* newspaper and filling it with a bogus story that Hong Kong was about to be declared an "infected city" with all businesses ordered to shut down. Without using their own judgment, people moved fast to stock up on rice and other supplies by stripping supermarket shelves before authorities put out convincing denials and arrested the hoaxer. Notwithstanding the SARS panic was due to the media's penchant for exaggerating and alarmist reporting, Hong Kong people showed pride in the performance of the city's media, which was in stark contrast to that of the mainland press, on which the Chinese central government had a firm grip in the early stage of the outbreak. People believed that the choruslike media had made the government more transparent and kept the citizens more informed.

This illusion of omniscience always conceals the incompleteness of the media in general and column writing in particular. The dissemination of information and ideas can make one feel like one belongs to the world of public opinion and even that one is genuinely enlightened. In addition, current hot topics—those of "self-examination," "getting in touch with your true feelings," "keeping a healthy balance," or "understanding yourself in a sexual relationship or marriage"—are hooks by which newspapers engage the reader not only in public life but also in his or her own unique self. Like the world constituted by the discourse of column writing, this self is, of course, an illusory image readily accepted by isolated and self-absorbed individuals in a media-saturated and monotonized world. Perhaps the reified daily life defined by column writing is that of the same and the repeatable, which constitute the homogenized content of a highly commercialized culture. This site of inauthenticity constructed by the discourses of writings in supplements and columns always acts as an agent of arbitration, sustaining the symbolic efficiency of the public world and effecting a seemingly total transparency in our everyday experience by interpellating—requiring us to occupy an assigned place within the sociocultural order.

Column writing is definitely a medium that imposes a narrative structure on the events of our lives and connects our personal life-stories to the larger drama of our community and even to the international world. It is in terms of the narrative mode made accessible in comments, gossip, anecdotes, remarks, and stories circulating in the public discourse of supplement and column culture that we come to see what is at stake in our situations. In this sense, supplement and column writing in Hong Kong functions as a symbolic support for the individual, inasmuch as it gives him or her a sense of consistency in which to identify his or her preordained place in society. But such symbolic seizure of the individual operates not only at the local and everyday level. Political and ethnic subjectivizations also exercise their authority in local everydayness, by directing individuals via their ideological mechanisms in a transnational context.

Policing Lifestyle in a Transnational Context

The everydayness manifested in Hong Kong newspaper columns is not only constrained by the logic of commodification but also has been historically marked by ideological conflicts between political forces. Hong Kong newspapers certainly have long been used as loci for the ideological and political struggles between the mainland Chinese Communist regime and the Taiwanese Nationalist Party. Both camps founded their own papers and used the columns, along with news coverage and editorials, to propagate political ideas. The British colonial government intervened in the struggles between the two Chinese political parties only by expelling the leftist and the rightist writers from the colony (including the anti-Communist novelist Zhao Zhifan, who was deported to Taiwan in the 1950s) and by banning a pro-Communist newspaper, *Ta Kung Pao*, for eleven days in 1952, when the regime felt threatened by its radical speech. Otherwise there has been almost no overt political censorship of the print culture. The pro-Communist and pro-Nationalist papers continue to disseminate political propaganda, although their markets remain limited in comparison to those of politically neutral dailies. The idea of what it is to be Chinese in Hong Kong is perhaps more evident in print culture than it is in other popular cultural products, such as films or pop songs. This is not simply because of political solicitation and nationalist indoctrination by the Communist and Nationalist parties. The identity presented in print culture is manifested through Chinese language, a written economy that has not been greatly affected by political domination (i.e., British colonialism) or phonological mutation (since Cantonese, not Mandarin or Putonghua, is the language of Hong Kong). But there is always something left over, something that continues to escape the scriptural precision or code, no matter how hard the two Chinese political parties attempt to nationalize the local to suit their own interests.

On the one hand, the local as embodied in the Hong Kong newspaper column is receptive to global culture and information, while, on the other hand, it evokes a relatively keen sense of national consciousness that is attached more to a culture and a language than it is to any political regime. However, it would be too facile to assert that these characteristics of Hong Kong print culture, especially column culture, contribute to the formation of a unified cultural and national identity, that is, to a sense of identification based not on a place or ethnicity but on a language or a cultural consciousness. It may be true that the creation of solidarity among various interest groups via the column or supplement is especially important in the overseas Chinese communities. For several decades, Hong Kong has been the center of capital, talent, and information for overseas Chinese-language newspapers and media in Southeast Asia, North America, and Europe. Since most of these overseas Chinese media were operated at very low cost with small staffs, they had to rely heavily on clippings from Hong Kong dailies, despite a time lag of one to two days. It was thus a very common practice to reprint many Hong Kong columns and supplement pages in overseas Chinese-language newspapers (Wang Shigu 1998, 92–93). "There emerges an interesting phenomenon," a critic observes. "Although overseas Chinese-language newspapers are founded all over the world, their layout and coverage (especially of mass culture) look very consistent and similar[;] from Jin Yong [a Hong Kong best-selling martial arts fiction writer] to Qiong Yao [a popular Taiwanese romance novelist], from Teresa Teng [a pop singer] to Andy Lau [a movie star], they all become familiar topics to overseas Chinese readers" (M. Cheng 2001, 249). In the 1970s, many Hong Kong newspapers began to publish overseas editions. The *Sing Tao Daily* was the first to open offices in New York, San Francisco, Toronto, Vancouver, Melbourne, and London. As these overseas editions of Hong Kong newspapers became better financed and carried more attractive supplements, they became more competitive than locally run Chinese-language dailies. But in the 1990s, the overseas Chinese populations began to change, owing to the increasing number of emigrants from mainland China. Hong Kong–style newspapers and media gradually gave way to mainland-style journalism in overseas Chinese communities: the printed characters changed from traditional (*fanti*) to simplified (*jianti*), the orientation of lines of print changed from vertical to horizontal, and the writing style also was adapted.

In the 1990s, mainland Chinese emigrants started setting up news Web sites that focused on current events in the PRC. Although these Chinese news sites seem to form what is tantamount to a virtual community or a diasporic public sphere for Chinese expatriates, they still underscore the articulation of a collective, national identity and rely heavily on a nationalist discourse inherent in the concept of a nation-state (Sun 2000). Thus the global dimension of cyberspace has not been fully embraced by the Chinese Internet. At the same time, Hong Kong newspapers created Web sites to cater to the needs of Hong Kong emigrants in North America, Britain, and Australia. However, the Internet versions of Hong Kong daily newspapers seem to be aimed at accommodating the changing habits of the Chinese readers rather than at reaching a worldwide audience. Even in the "cyber age," North American Chinatowns and suburbs are full of shops in which daily newspapers and tabloid magazines from Hong Kong are readily available. Column culture is well suited to emigrants who do not immediately adjust to their new environments and still cling to Hong Kong customs of dressing, eating, behavior, and treatment of others. For instance, in the suburbs of Toronto, such as Scarborough, the Hong Kong lifestyle is evident in numerous Hong Kong–style shopping malls, in which overseas editions of many Hong Kong newspapers and magazines are sold daily.

It is undeniable that column culture pertains to a certain lifestyle. If this lifestyle constitutes an identity that manages to reach and affect Hong Kong emigrants worldwide, how does this identity differ from the one promulgated by the propagandist writings of (pro-PRC and pro-Taiwan) political newspapers? Beginning in the mid-1980s, when the Sino-British Joint Declaration was signed and the handover of Hong Kong became a certainty, the increasing influence of the mainland became evident in the folding and retreat of pro-Taiwan rightist papers such as the *Hong Kong Times Daily*. Some of the politically neutral dailies quickly were transformed into pro–Hong Kong papers that aligned with the pro-China camp by embracing a local specificity that did not necessarily oppose China. At the same time, there emerged a rigorous effort to define, through the study of its popular culture and social structure, a Hong Kong identity distinct from that imposed by Chinese nationalism. In other words, there is commonly believed to be a unique and authentic subjectivity evident in the everydayness of the Hong Kong lifestyle.

In an article on Hong Kong political cartoons, Rey Chow (1997, 42) argues that the word "lifestyle" is an ambivalent term appropriated by both Britain and China to obliterate Hong Kong's claim to a political identity as such.[13] In discussing Larry Feign's political caricature of Hong Kong daily banality, she observes that

> the physical impurity of the everyday as such is underscored by another kind
> of impurity—the indistinguishability of the everyday from a ubiquitously dom-

inant type of discourse in whose interest that everydayness must remain a mere nonpolitical "lifestyle." In other words, precisely because of the concerted efforts by both Britain and China to deny it a political identity, Hong Kong's "lifestyle," even in its most carefree and leisurely "everyday" moments, is all the more indivisible from the cruelty and treachery that are spilled over from the twin legacies of colonialism and totalitarianism. (Rey Chow 1997, 42–44)

If the word "lifestyle" is generally understood to be the everyday decisions made from among a plurality of possible options and to be intimately connected to the (re)making of self-identity (Giddens 1991), the Hong Kong lifestyle, according to Chow, is not so much "chosen" as "handed down" by colonial history and the possibility of future totalitarian rule. In other words, the creation of lifestyle in Hong Kong, given its specific political circumstances, is less interwoven with the process of individualization than integrated into an illusion that belies the very lack of an identity. In this sense, although it does not avoid open criticism of China, the *Apple Daily*, with innovative supplement pages and tabloid reporting that promotes an idea of local lifestyle, only invalidates its political stance and pushes everyday life further into the realm of global capitalism: lifestyle, especially a highly commercialized one, is nothing but a substitute for politics. The everyday routines presented by newspaper columns with the aim of "policing" consumption, diet, dress, living, and investment contribute to a cultural identification that is not merely ideological; it is illusory. This may explain why an experienced scholar of Hong Kong culture like Ng Chun-hung complains that "after all these years we were still basically at the stage of *asserting* the presence or otherwise of a Hong Kong way of life" (Ng Chun-hung 1996a, 123).

A number of studies have been devoted simply to proving the existence of a Hong Kong lifestyle. Appropriating the Marxist critique of capitalism and ideology, sociologists such as Tai-lok Lui, Ng Chun-hung, and others, who are Hong Kong born, have focused their attention on mass media culture from the perspectives of class relations and power structures. They understand Hong Kong culture in the context of its colonial history and seek a particular local identity or consciousness stemming from larger social forces. What they discover is that local consciousness is grounded mainly in popular cultural representations, which are fragmented in nature and thus give an inconsistent and non-unitary image of Hong Kong. Their accounts of the colony's local history confirm the common belief that the emergence of such a consciousness or identity has nothing to do with the influences and interference of British colonialism and Chinese traditional values (Lui 1983, 1997; Ng Chun-hung 1998). In other words, the local consciousness fundamentally develops from the so-called autochthonous culture, which is explicitly distinguished from and, to a certain extent, opposed to the hegemony of the colonial ruling class as well as the prevailing ideology of Chinese cultural tradition. However, local consciousness or lifestyle is not a complete entity in itself. If the so-called Hong Kong lifestyle is only an illusory or sham identity, how can that lifestyle be sustained without the simultaneous establishment of an authentic identity, especially when lifestyle is precisely that which concerns the very core of identity formation? A possible answer is that the identity created by the Hong Kong lifestyle must be one that poses no threat to China. It is an imaginary identity deprived of any oppositional dimension or political edge. But an identity without political meaning can be only a false one—an illusion that hides its own impossibility.

Suffice it to say that the cultural identification of the Hong Kong lifestyle portrayed in newspaper columns designates an ideological interpellation that is addressed by the other in order to constitute its addressee as a subject. This subject, however, is deprived of political substance and national tradition at the hands of the Sino-British agreement allowing life in Hong Kong to remain unchanged for fifty years. In a sense, it is against this background of closure and confinement that a production of a Hong Kong subject can occur; but this involves a subject without subjectivity. A post-1997 Hong Kong identity is denied not by censorship or military repression, but by popularizing it and trivializing it as a "lifestyle," which as a mass phenomenon displays characteristics that can be dictated and ultimately emptied of any political content. How, then, can we say that an authentic self is constituted in the Hong Kong lifestyle, if this daily life is not able (or not allowed) to produce a political identity? What if the "true nature" of this authentic self is rendered possible only by external impositions and political restrictions? The paradox is that a "true Hong Kong self" emerges only in the absence of a political identity, as a stand-in for an authentic existence.

Internal Mutations in the Book-Concept of Chineseness

The Hong Kong newspaper column seems to provide a favorable environment for the smooth process of reintegration with China, since its language and target audience are Chinese. Unlike Hong Kong films that can always arouse the interest of a universal or global audience, column writing addresses only Chinese readers and, to a large extent, addresses essentially Chinese issues. This emphasis on Chinese interests in particular has great appeal to overseas Chinese communities and exerts a powerful transnational Chinese influence. Many popular Hong Kong columns are reprinted in the Chinese-language newspapers of Southeast Asia, North America, and Europe, even though the intended audience is not Chinese emigrants but Hong Kong locals. For decades, Hong Kong was the only Chinese society to enjoy considerable freedom of speech. Perhaps for this reason, the comments expressed and the information circulated in Hong Kong newspapers attracted the interest of the diasporic Chinese. In this sense, Hong Kong column writing, with its emphasis on nonpolitical Chineseness, is capable of reaching a huge transnational Chinese audience. Ironically, the transnational Chinese network and sense of cultural identification for Chinese emigrants are themselves bereft of a true identity. The formative element for a Chinese identity as such is without any positive and definitive (i.e., political) substance. Does this not imply that Chinese identity as such may also have no objective, substantial content but is a subjective stance assumable by many individuals and represented by arbitrary features?

Owing to the standardization of the written Chinese language, column writing seems to have a unifying power with respect to Chinese emigrants and their cultural cohesion. However, the nature of column writing also undermines the unity of the Chinese written economy. It is a form of writing that challenges the traditional concept of the book, if the book represents the structure of unification and totalization. Historically speaking, with the advent of block printing, the Han government of the Song dynasty (960–1279) supplied every school with a set of officially approved versions of the Confucian classics for the students to study and memorize. This demonstrates the book's usefulness to political and ideological unification. The book established the foundation for a culture unified by a written language and written signifiers. The book stands for the everlasting value of the cultural tradition. It not only enables the preservation of cultural knowledge over generations but also enforces the hegemony and continuity of a print-language over the diffusion of numerous dialects. Hence, voices are de-privileged by the totalizing tendency of written signifiers. Even though linguistic unification is unimaginable in Chinese culture, the book lends a fixity and stability to language and helps to build an image of antiquity and commonality, which is crucial to the idea of a nation-state. The book as written record ensures the permanence of national affairs and removes them from unreliable and intractable utterance and memory. Knowledge reproduced in book form becomes the common property of the nation, attaining a standard that may, like that of law, be applicable to all. Not only does knowledge take on a new consistency by means of the book, it also becomes the "truth" that lays the ground-work for exchange and written communication. Gilles Deleuze and Félix Guattari have inventively analogized the book to the tree: "A first type of book is the root-book. The tree is already the image of the world, or the root the image of the world-tree. This is the classical book, as noble, signifying, and subjective organic interiority. . . . The radicle-system, or fascicular root, is the second figure of the book, to which our modernity pays willing allegiance . . . but the root's unity subsists, as past or yet to come, as possible" (Deleuze and Guattari 1988, 5).[14]

The book is used to organize and unify conceptual structures in print form. However, column writing in the Hong Kong dailies may subvert the idea of the book's inherent totality.[15] The fragmentation and transitoriness of column writing is in direct opposition to the homogeneous and steady root-form of the book. Although many popular columns have been reprinted in book form, they simultaneously promote and transgress "bookness." The publication of column writing in book form is a merchandising ploy to promote the colum-nist's reputation and sustain readers' interest in following the daily columns, besides maximizing profits in the print market. Many popular columnists have anthologized their daily columns. Tsao Chip has published in six years twenty-four books collecting his columns. The conventional concept of the book as a totality is undercut by the "columnized" book that defies the book's typi-cal orderly progression of ideas. It simulates the old book form as well as deviates from it. A columnized book may still be organized into chapters, but the reprinting of the daily articles conveys a strong sense of disparateness that subverts any notion of central unity. The "chapters" of the columnized book are intended for casual and disjointed consumption and not to imply the centrality of an overarching meaning. The columnized book disrupts the cir-cuit of intentions of the usual form of the book through its excess and heter-ogeneity. One can open the columnized book at any point. As opposed to the linear unity of the typical book, the collection of columns always has multi-ple entryways and exits. The linear constraint of the book is, in a way, under-mined by the relatively itinerancy of column discourse. But, as mentioned earlier, column discourse cannot separate itself entirely from the culture of the book. The two exist in a certain balance.

The hierarchy that values the permanence of the book over the imperma-nence of column writing does not apply to columns published in book form. The columnized book can easily be categorized as a frivolous byproduct of ephemeral daily writing. Unlike the root-book, column writing can connect any point with any other point, without forming a unified structure. However, it does not necessarily contrast with the durability and timelessness of the serious book. There is no such thing as randomness in writing. The so-called nonlinearity is in fact a flexible but limited multilinearity. Traces of continuity and regularity are preserved in column discourse. All that column writing evokes still remains within the domain of the book.

Perhaps the ephemeral character of the columnized book exemplifies the rapid transmission (and transition) of knowledge in our capitalist society. Anthologized columns, in a sense, erase the difference between the steady presence of the book and the momentary characteristic of column writing. The book is thus transformed by column writing into a different entity, which may be comparable to the content available on the Internet. Nevertheless, column writing does not simply negate the book. The book, as a totalized and unified presence, is effaced at the same time that it remains distinct. Column writing practically extends and renews this concept of the book by manufacturing a new form of printed work. Hong Kong column culture has always promoted the subjectivity of the columnist through his or her writing; that is to say, the columnist writes what he or she thinks, feels, eats, drinks, loves, and hates in everyday life. The major selling points of column writing are its cordiality, spontaneity, and intimacy. The columnist writes as if talking casually and freely to close friends. In his column at the *Hong Kong Economic Journal,* Dai Tian usually told his readers about the people with whom he had dined, how he enjoyed these social activities, and what sorts of books he received from friends or admirers every week. Not dependent on sophisticated rhetorical or literary techniques, column writing is meant to be a direct and naked expression of the self. It is a writing that expresses the inner voice, reinvesting language with the presence of the author. This proximity of voice and the meaning of being produce the self-presence of the subject, according to the Western idea of phonocentrism.

However, we have to bear in mind that the self-presence produced by column writing is temporary and elusive. The moment the subject is produced is also the moment of its obliteration. Column writing is a technique of "erasing its own trace" and is an act of forgetting. This is not simply a problem of the gap between representation and the speed of current events—things in everyday life go so fast and become so intangible that the available forms of representation are unable to keep up with them. If the book has a strong tendency to fixate its reader through the use of a unified written language, and thus to form the embryo of national identification, column writing follows the concept of the book up to a point but transgresses it by moving from a breeding ground of subject-formation to one of prodigal self-dispersion. The book is built around the concept of the individual, rational human monad, incorporated into the social body by free will and a distinct voice. However, column writing evokes this voice of the subject at the same time that it allows it to subside. It may fetishize the voice, but it also breaks open a gap within it. It is well known that, insofar as a columnist is a celebrity, he or she does not have to be a good writer. Movie stars, pop idols, and other well-known people, merely because of their fame, are always invited to write columns for newspapers. The aura of authorship is no longer built on the writing itself. But instead of shaking the foundations of the book, column discourse is a "mutant" that basically inhabits the order and value of book culture at the same time that it engages in an unmistakable structural critique of that order.

As a mutated mode of writing and communication, the newspaper column is still endowed with the old fantasy of authorial authenticity. The romantic idea of the creative, original genius upheld by the book carries on in the realm of column writing. Quite a number of columnists are packaged as "gifted writers" (*caizi*) or "talented women" (*cainu*). Such a concept of authorship, however, mingles anachronistically with the mechanization of writing in late capitalist society. The popularity of the column depends principally on its mechanical reproduction. But in the age of mechanical reproduction, as Benjamin suggests, the traditional privileges enjoyed by writers are stripped away because "at any moment the reader is ready to turn into a writer" (Benjamin 1973, 234). On the one hand, column writing invokes the dated myth of the authenticity and uniqueness of authorship; on the other hand, the rapid development of the means of reproduction and the increasing number of readers-turned-writers confirms the death of the author as Godlike creator. In other words, column writing insinuates a certain "hollowness" at the very heart of the traditional concept of authorship. The absence of a distinct individual human monad or creative genius is posited as an empty presence. What is harbored in column writing is merely a simulacrum bereft of the ultimate referent. Hence, the concept of authorship is reintroduced or reiterated in the column only by effacing or eradicating it. A column may still be attributed to a subject, but it no longer is a permanent referent, since it is easily and ceaselessly replaced by other referents. What column writing reveals is that there is no definite link between an individual person and the position of authorship. The embodiment of the voice that hears itself speaking (*s'entendre-parler*) in column writing does not entail a favorable condition for the emergence of a unique subject.

What, then, is this "voice" of column writing if it is not the voice of self-presence ascribed to a particular subject? How do we understand the lack of a political Hong Kong identity through the problematization of this voice? I argued earlier that the functions of column writing are to promote lifestyle, consumption, and products and to constitute identities. But I also argued that unlike the root-book that unifies multiple voices and provides forms of identities and practices as a bulwark against disruption of its unity, column writing has a specific nature similar to what Deleuze and Guattari call the "rhizome" that constitutes networks and connects one already differentiated realm to another. If Hong Kong column writing stands for the formation of the local, it is a local that is already permeated by the logic of globalization. It connects different localities in such a way that the local mode of life is incessantly reshaped by ideas and events occurring at a distance, and it is controlled and determined by capital drives that are much more powerful than it. If column discourse represents a dimension of Hong Kong culture, all its mutated and transgressive tendencies still operate within the Chinese logocentric order. It is therefore unable to offer a real alternative to the established national discourse. Owing to the political conditions of postcolonial Hong Kong, the local is not allowed to be a force of resistance. All it can do is to smuggle "shit" or "trash" into printed discourse and shock the old order with its vulgar use of the Chinese language. Under British colonial rule, newspaper columns were free to appropriate the local to promote a national consciousness. Hong Kong as conceptualized by Britain and China is destined to be globalized—a world center of capitalist development. In Hong Kong newspaper supplements and column culture, we find a paradoxical combination of nationalist identification, heterogeneous local lifestyle, and corporate capitalist reproductive logic that precludes any politicization of local identity. It may be true that under Chinese rule, Hong Kong seems to have become more pluralistic, multicultural, globalized, and even "promiscuous," in the sense of mixing indiscriminate realities. The outcome of globalization is not necessarily the overgeneralization of local cultural forms or the ranking of one locality over another. On the contrary, it may even encourage a new understanding of translocal connection, as evinced in Hong Kong column culture, and undermine the simplistic notion of a single local condition or national identity. However, this kind of cultural globalization points toward a proliferation of the locals or multiples that also neutralizes their political dimension. In this age of globalization, we hear many different voices. But all of these voices, like the various newspaper columns, are secure in their proper places as determined by the new global order.

2

Leftovers of Film and Television Subtitles in a Transnational Context

THE INTENSE RELATIONSHIP between world-market globalization and cultural particularism that characterizes the agenda of contemporary cultural studies should be reexamined when it comes to the question of subtitling in Hong Kong cinema and television. Subtitles tell us about the dialectical interactions of words and images taking place in the transborder film viewing process under the heightened speed of globalization. As a specific form of making sense of things in cross-cultural and cross-linguistic encounters, subtitling reveals realities of cultural domination and subordination and serves as a site of ideological dissemination and its subversion. A relatively marginalized topic underdeveloped in film and cultural studies, the problem of subtitling is appropriated here not only to open up the discussion about the power relations between different cultures in the process of film spectatorship, but also to rethink the subject formation under the myth of one language in Chinese culture. In the transnational context of Hong Kong film and television reception, subtitling is never confined to a translation of one language to another. It also involves the tensions between voice and script and between dialect and standard language.

In addition to helping local cultural products merge more smoothly into the global economy, the subtitles of Hong Kong films and television programs tie into the construction of transnational Chinese ethnic identity. Although postsynchronization, or dubbing, is normally seen as a strategy for injecting the film into consumer cultural contexts worldwide, subtitling is still a much cheaper and more common route the Hong Kong film industry takes to export its productions to different national audiences. Indeed the overseas market has always been one of the most—if not the most—important target for the distribution of Hong Kong films. Unlike other film industries such as those in the United States and India that possess a huge domestic market, Hong Kong cinema has to rely on overseas markets to survive. Local box-office generally occupies only one-fifth or one-third of total revenue. Therefore, "the great majority of Hong Kong pictures are made with an eye to the overseas market, with the local market being a secondary consideration" (Leung and Chan 1997, 149). From the mid-1980s to the early 1990s, the industry's production output and total exports sprang to their peak. But the industry gradually declined after the mid-1990s, and Hollywood products have increasingly usurped Hong Kong film's market share in Asia.

Dubbing and subtitling films definitely create different effects in terms of meaning and reception.[1] Historically, Hong Kong cinema has appropriated the two different strategies for its overseas marketing. Although Cantonese is the major language spoken by the city's population, Hong Kong cinema has not been confined to this single dialect. The industry had produced different Chinese dialect movies to cater to various overseas Chinese communities in the past. Beginning in the 1960s, Taiwan became the major market of Hong Kong films and remained as such up till the nineties. Many Hong Kong productions are either made or dubbed in Mandarin. In the fifties and sixties, the diasporic Chinese communities in Singapore, Thailand, Malaysia, Taiwan, and the Philippines were the chief markets for Hong Kong Chaozhou-dialect and Amoy-dialect films.[2] By 1970s and 1980s, Hong Kong pictures were exported to Japan, Korea, America, Europe, and elsewhere around the world.

Dubbing and subtitling are juggled for different markets' needs. For instance, in Japan, all Hong Kong films are released with Japanese subtitles since Japanese audiences love foreign things and believe the original audio recording can preserve their exotic genuineness (Yeung 2000, 152–53). But during the "kung fu craze" of the early seventies in the States, Hong Kong films were mostly dubbed in English, though their postsynchronous sounds were far from ideal. The hurried dubbing and release of many more Hong Kong kung fu films by fly-by-night companies only attempted to "capitalize on a craze that wouldn't, couldn't, last much longer" (Desser 2000, 20). After the craze, viewers continued to see Hong Kong films but in subtitled versions in Chinatown theaters or on video, until Jackie Chan's dubbed *Rumble in the Bronx* made its way to the top of the American box-office list in 1996.

All Hong Kong films, even those released locally, have been subtitled in both Chinese and English since the mid-1960s. It was said that this was because English subtitles were mandatory under British colonial law and the standard Chinese subtitles are necessary to those Chinese who do not speak Cantonese. However, there has never been any colonial rule to enforce the English subtitling. Actually it was the more cosmopolitan, outward-looking Mandarin cinema under the Shaw Brothers Studio that began the bilingual subtitling practice since the Shaw productions mainly relied on the overseas markets to make their money.[3] It is worthwhile to note that, after World War II, Hong Kong cinema was mainly produced in two dialects, Mandarin and Cantonese, despite the fact that most Hong Kong residents are Cantonese speakers. The Mandarin films were the work of left-wing artists who left for China after 1949 and of Shanghai capitalists fleeing the 1949 Communist regime. Mandarin cinematic output increased steadily in the 1950s and 1960s and almost extinguished Cantonese cinema in the early 1970s. But by 1979, Mandarin cinema in Hong Kong was entirely wiped out by the reemergence of Cantonese movies.[4] Most of these Mandarin and Cantonese films in the early period, however, were rarely subtitled in standard Chinese since their audiences did not intersect. Only some of them had been subtitled in foreign languages to cater to the needs of overseas viewers. As noted earlier, it was not until the mid-1960s that the Shaw Brothers Studio and the like started regularly subtitling their products in both Chinese and English to attract wider attention. Such bilingual subtitling soon became the norm of Hong Kong cinema, and now the overseas-market-oriented industry usually does not even bother to release an unsubtitled copy for Hong Kong local viewers.

In a study about the politics of cultural difference in the global context and the particularity within Chinese culture, subtitled Hong Kong films and television programs, rather than the dubbed versions, are an appropriate object for representation and evaluation; the words onscreen always consciously remind viewers of the other's existence. Like all translation, the practice of subtitling involves the "filtration of meaning through ideological and cultural grids" (Shohat and Stam 1985, 46), although this process is seldom addressed in film criticism or cultural theory. The process of subtitling often draws attention to itself, if only because of its tendency toward incompetence.[5] The "failure" of subtitling may reveal how film translation usually "smoothes over its textual violence and domesticates all otherness while it pretends to bring the audience to an experience of the foreign" (Nornes 1999, 18). The collaborative and mediative functions of subtitles are open to criticism when the process of converting speech into written text is involved in a cross-cultural exchange that ultimately serves the dominant powers. As Trinh T. Minh-ha argues, "If in most translated films, the subtitles usually stay on as long as they technically can—often much longer than the time needed even for a slow reader—it's because translation is conceived here as part of the operation of suture that defines the classical cinematic apparatus and the technological effort it deploys to naturalize a dominant, hierarchically unified worldview" (Trinh 1992, 207).

In order to resist the suppression of cultural specificity and the naturalization of a unified worldview that are inherent in the practice of subtitling, one critic even calls for "abusive subtitling" as a "gesture of respect" for other cultures. That is to say, rather than smoothing out otherness and turning the source culture into something easily comprehensible or pleasurably consumable for the target audience, the "abusive translator" would locate the subtitles in the place of the other by confronting foreignness without erasing it (Nornes 1999). The most frequently cited example of an abusive strategy—or "kidnapping"—of subtitling is a Hong Kong kung fu movie, *The Crush*, which a French leftist group has renamed *La dialectique peut-elle casser des briques?* (Can the Dialectic Break Bricks?), in which a dialogic exchange during a sequence of karate combat is accompanied by subtitles such as "Down with the bourgeoisie!" or a flirtatious scene between a fighter and a young woman is changed to a discussion of commodity fetishism.[6] Whether abusive subtitling actually brings otherness to the foreground or simply leads to its further containment invites further analysis. Since film is generally seen as a transcultural product that efficiently facilitates the circulation of global capital, subtitles that remind the audience of a film's cultural origin can sometimes become an undesired obstacle to the film's international success and prevent it from "ceasing to be a 'foreign' film in order to become just a film" (Ascheid 1997, 40). In the case of the subtitling of Hong Kong films and television programs, however, foreignness or cultural difference is never the only issue to be considered, since the subtitling is bridging not different cultures but different Chinese communities sharing a national language.

As mentioned earlier, Hong Kong Cantonese movies, since their reemergence in the seventies, have been released with both English and Chinese captions. The majority of Hong Kong Cantonese-speaking viewers (who do not need the Chinese subtitles) accept the practice and seldom complain about the visual distraction the subtitles present. The subtitles are for the most part ignored or filtered by mental or psychological processes. They are visible but also invisible—material that cannot be integrated into the experience of the film. Just as stains on the screen affect the visual experience, subtitles undermine the primacy and immediacy of the voice and alienate the aural from the visual. Local viewers are used to blocking the subtitles from their vision simply because they are not relevant. I am always oblivious to the onscreen captions in a Hong Kong Cantonese movie even though they are definitely there. That Hong Kong cinema has been so action-oriented for many years has probably allowed local viewers to not care about the words at the bottom of the screen.

I am also aware of the fact that, paradoxically, even Hong Kong viewers cannot avoid reading the subtitles onscreen. Most Hong Kong movies are shot postsynch in order to save time and money. The soundtrack is added to the film only after the entire film is shot.[7] Therefore the visual is never intimately tied to the aural. Usually, sound and image have incongruent speeds, and the difference can create an interesting complement of rhythms.[8] To make things worse, some Hong Kong stars have voice doubles. In the heyday of Hong Kong cinema, stars made several films at once and did not have enough time to dub their own voices. The first time I heard Jackie Chan's voice, it was not in one of his local action flicks but in a Hong Kong-produced American movie, *The Big Brawl* (1980), in which Chan played an English-speaking immigrant. Instead of using a voice double, Chan delivered his lines himself—perhaps to demonstrate the effort he had put into learning English.

The subtitles, then, only widen the gap between sound and image in Hong Kong films. If a local viewer feels compelled to read the subtitles while watching a Hong Kong film, his experience of being immersed in the already-not-immediate living world of speech is exacerbated by the spoken word's being overwhelmed by the written. Such an experience may be summed up by the Chinese expression *ting de jian* (literally, "listen and see," which means "perceive by listening"). The subtitles become a kind of verbal "stain" that partially obscures the field of vision. It is like living in a world of comics, where one would continuously see one's own speech and the speech of others.

Since the early 1990s, Hong Kong television stations have subtitled many of their own productions in standard Chinese to benefit the hearing-impaired and new immigrants from mainland China. Eighty percent of prime-time Cantonese-dialect shows already carry Chinese subtitles.[9] On the small screen, viewers who don't need subtitles might find it particularly difficult to ignore them. If they are not bothered by the visual distraction, perhaps local audiences regard the captions as some kind of additional entertainment or simply as a supplement in case they do not catch something that was said. As subtitling has been made obligatory by the Broadcasting Authority, and television is free entertainment, there is little grumbling on the part of local viewers.[10] The habit of reading subtitles is probably involuntary, or a result of the karaoke boom. Song lyrics always appear at the bottom of the karaoke screen in order to guide the singer. Subtitles can give words additional weight by compelling the spectators to read them. As one critic puts it, subtitles "also have the effect of 'doubling' the spoken words˙. . . [thus] mak[ing] the words more pithy and prophetic . . . [and causing the audience to] become both word-dependent and word-oriented, so that if a scene appears in which there are no subtitles, [audiences] feel at a loss" (MacDougall 1998, 174).

Because the concept of Chineseness is significantly grounded in a written language that serves as a symbolic system for the integrity of the national culture, Chinese subtitling in Chinese films and TV programs paradoxically creates a doubleness within the original text—not by juxtaposing two mutually incomprehensible national languages, as other subtitled films do, but by reinforcing the split between the spoken and written languages, thereby destroying the possibility of any easy identification.

Hong Kong subtitling, although it invites a reconception of the articulation of a national subject position, is not confined to the realm of Chinese cultural consumption. The most popular Chinese cultural product ever produced for the global market, subtitled Hong Kong cinema has carved a special niche for itself in an industry otherwise dominated by English-language and Hollywood films—not by its perfect integration into the lingua franca of the English-speaking world but rather for the "bad" English subtitles with which Anglophone viewers associate them. To a presumptuous Western audience, the poor English subtitles make Hong Kong films more "Chinese" by underscoring the linguistic difference. Such a designation of "Chineseness" in Hong Kong films circulated in the West may produce an "outside" perspective from which to look at the so-called inherent ethnic subject position. I will examine three separate but interrelated aspects of Hong Kong subtitling: English subtitles in Hong Kong cinema as received by Anglophone viewers in the West; standard Chinese subtitles in television programs as seen by Hong Kong viewers; and Cantonese subtitles in local films and TV broadcasts as viewed by the local audience. These illustrate how the assimilation of the particular into something much larger—say, the national or global—always leaves certain unabsorbable excess that eventually nullifies the assimilating system.

Excessive Pleasure and the Lure of Cultural Difference

As I mentioned earlier, English subtitles in Hong Kong cinema may stand for the integration of the city's self-positioning and self-representation in world-market globalization. Since Hong Kong film depends largely on overseas revenue, the desire for an ever-expanding market motivates the industry to develop an aggressive attitude toward establishing connections with regional markets in Asia and worldwide. Hong Kong movies are subtitled in both Chinese and English upon release. Subtitles are available on videotape, laser disc, video compact disc (VCD), and digital video disc (DVD) releases.[11] This practice is believed to promote the international circulation of these films. In recent decades, Hong Kong cinema was able to hold the dominant share of Asian markets and draw attention from the West because of its extraordinarily outlandish character. The Hong Kong kung fu movie craze in the United States began in the early 1970s, but white audiences lost interest in the genre quite quickly (Desser 2000). Hong Kong action flicks remain popular among Asian, African American, and Hispanic minority groups in the States. For various reasons, there was renewed interest in Hong Kong cinema among white audiences in the 1990s, and even Hollywood took notice of the genre (Bordwell 2000b, 82–97). For many North American audiences and film critics, Hong Kong cinema is appealing because it evokes Hollywood's long-lost energy and the sheer visual pleasure of the silent film. Jackie Chan has been repeatedly compared to Buster Keaton. The outrageous delights offered by popular Hong Kong films remind Americans of early Hollywood, before the great divide between entertainment and art had opened.

What attracts international eyes is first and foremost the explosive action of the kung fu genre—a genre that prioritizes muscle and hustle over the meaning of words. In the 1970s, Bruce Lee's heroic pictures introduced to the world a unique martial arts tradition that demonstrated the fascinating maneuverability of the human body. The deliberate use of the body immediately developed into a language that anyone watching Hong Kong kung fu or action movies believed he or she could easily grasp. In the 1980s and early 1990s, Jackie Chan, John Woo, Tsui Hark, and their compatriot filmmakers pushed this body language to a sophisticated level with more spectacular stunts and high-speed editing. Although kung fu and the well-choreographed action of Hong Kong cinema could be interpreted as a manifestation of Chineseness (stemming from the traditions of Chinese martial arts and Peking opera), they are a kind of cultural and ethnic particularity that is not opaque or incomprehensible to foreigners. As Hong Kong films are so eagerly consumed worldwide—and by viewers who know nothing of Chinese or Cantonese—a discussion of English subtitles might not seem superfluous or irrelevant. We can see the importance of the English subtitles in Hong Kong cinema and the Western reception of them and consider their implications both for the culture of globalization and for the construction of ethnic identity.[12]

The participation—since the mid-1990s—of Hong Kong film talents in the making of several Hollywood films may represent a trend of cultural globalization that would eliminate the barriers imposed by local ethnic traditions. Some Hong Kong filmmakers and stars are able to leave their cultural ghetto and achieve international renown. However, no matter how far some of its talent has gone internationally, Hong Kong cinema is still tainted by its self-imposed English subtitles, which are by nature "excessive" and which impede integration into the global economy. Hong Kong cinema is said to be too idiosyncratic and extravagant (its subtitles are only one of its wild elements) for mainstream Western viewers. English subtitles in Hong Kong film often appear excessive and intrusive to the Western viewer. Unlike film industries that put a great deal of care into subtitles, Hong Kong cinema is famous for its slipshod English subtitling. The subtitlers of Hong Kong films, who are typically not well educated, are paid poorly and must translate an entire film in two or three days.[13] Perhaps the dubbed versions of Hong Kong films could better meet the industry's goal of conquering regional and world markets. I would rather focus on the problem of subtitling because it provides an important framework within which to examine the role of local particularity in the politics of market globalization, as well as how the globalization of the Hong Kong local interferes with Chinese subject reconstruction.

An apparent contradiction is not difficult to see: although the Hong Kong film industry is eager to sell its products overseas, it pays very little attention to issues of translation and seems to make the English subtitles as useless as possible to non-Chinese viewers. Cultural theorists, depending on their political and ideological stances, might arrive at different interpretations of the English subtitling in Hong Kong cinema. Some might say, "Look! This is a typical example of unscrupulous Hong Kong modernity—take the easy money and run!" The combination of fast output and cunning entrepreneurship typifies exploitative capitalism in cross-cultural transmission. All that Hong Kong film investors and producers are interested in is the bottom line—not the quality of their films or the messages conveyed by them. Other critics, however, may take the opposite tack and romanticize slipshod English subtitling in order to characterize the "lumpen modernity" of the postcolonial city, and they may assert that the clumsy subtitles constitute a symbolic (if unintentional) form of resistance that hinders the unstoppable flow of global capital.

Despite the validity and insight of these observations, the bungled and unrefined subtitles are probably one kind of cultural particularity that does not contradict but rather facilitates world-market globalization. I am not saying that if Hong Kong films were all dubbed into English or if the English subtitles were improved, the films would merge more smoothly with the process of globalization.[14] On the contrary, globalization is facilitated by the "hindrance" or the "symbolic resistance" inherent in the clumsy English subtitles—which represent a certain cultural specificity or designate certain ethnic characteristics of the port city (for example, the bad, impure English used by the ex-colonized, or the Hong Kong pidgin referred to as "Chinglish"). It has been well documented in Western fan guides and critical studies of Hong Kong films that the English subtitles are not viewed simply as troublesome but also as great fun for Western viewers. In the West, Hong Kong cinema enjoys great popularity among nonconformist subcultures—festival circuits, college film clubs, Internet fanzines, and fan groups—in which cult followers and lovers of camp celebrate the exploitation and peculiarities on display (Bordwell 2000b, 82–97; Hammond and Wilkins 1996); its wild and weird subtitles further elevate the cinema's fetishistic status and exotic flavor. The tainted object that obscures part of the screen and confuses the signification has been sublimated into a cult element by hardcore fans who look for off-center culture and down-market amusements.

In an examination of the English translations of song lyrics in Hong Kong action film, Julian Stringer attempts to describe his disorientation in the following way: "While watching the Chinese-version of [John Woo's] *A Better Tomorrow*, first distributed in North America by the video company Tai Seng, the pleasure I take from this text is inadvertently enlarged by the less than perfect subtitles. Confronted with my favorite one-liners ('Singing jollity like the sunbeam,' 'Learning. That's what you've to learn!' 'Don't trust those cunny!') I am left lost and linguistically floundering, adrift on an alien sea of undecipherable phonic substance" (Stringer 1997, 37 n. 20). The fractured English subtitles may puzzle the viewers who need them, and yet they also give rise to a peculiar kind of pleasure. The articulation of the loss of proper meaning offers a pleasure of its own to those who treasure alternative aesthetics and practice a radical connoisseurship that views mass culture's vulgarity as the equal of avant-garde high art.

What is suggestive about Stringer's remarks is that pleasure is described in terms of being adrift. Drifting pleasure occurs when definite meaning can no longer be grasped. Bad English subtitles may kindle a kind of pleasure that was never meant to be there. It is only when words collapse or fail to communicate properly that the viewers—especially those hardcore fans—can experience this strange pleasure. As native speakers of English, the hegemonic language of the film world, American fans are privy to the "jokes" in inept English subtitles and are able to distinguish between what is properly expressed in English and what is not. The crudity of the English subtitles could easily be viewed as a peculiar mode of expression characteristic of nonwhite ethnic cultures. What fascinates American fans about the subtitles is their unpretentiousness—a rough but honest expression from another culture—which mainstream American movies or subtitled European art films could never have. This view of the subtitled Hong Kong films in the West is of course narcissistic and inevitably orientalist. Aspects of Hong Kong film that are taken seriously by Chinese audiences may be seen as sheer comedy by Western viewers. To mock and laugh at the absurdities and unintentional offenses of an Asian movie is a posture of self-congratulating supremacy. Gordon Chan's *Beast Cops* (1998), a thriller that won an award for best film in Hong Kong, has been called a "super funny movie" and a "crazy-ass martial arts dynamo ass-kicking midnight film that rocks the party" by one American reviewer, for whom the most laughable element was the subtitles: "The dialogue is in Cantonese with English subtitles, but the two don't always match, sometimes by a wide margin. Most of the [American] audience laughed uproariously whenever Michael [Fitzgerald Wong, who is not a native Cantonese speaker] flubbed his Cantonese lines. . . . [S]ometimes he would even just say his lines in English, with a different English subtitle displayed onscreen. When he yells out: 'What the Fuck!!', on screen it read 'You bastard!'" (mat x 2002).

Another not-so-sympathetic American reviewer makes similar ironic comments on the same issue: "Hong Kong cinema is in clear disarray with the transfer to China, a star system in virtual collapse, talent dispersing throughout the world, and a general who-gives-a-damn attitude. At least the translators are still employed, and the fractured subtitles continue to thrill" (G. Morris 2002).

A reviewer may be impatient with the lousy low-budget films made in Hong Kong, but for him the films are redeemed by the wacky English subtitles: "The pacing is slow, the mood trashy-sentimental with flashes of lowbrow humor. Bizarre subtitles abound, but two demand quotation: 'I must declare: she's goldfish!' and 'I refuse to fever in the lousy ballroom of Mongkok!'" (G. Morris 2002). But there are also some real admirers who cherish the unpredictable energy of the subtitles. The way one Western fan describes the English subtitles of Hong Kong cinema makes manifest their uncanny effects on the Western viewer:

This splintering of the Queen's English adds additional—if unintended—entertainment value for those of us who have no idea of what to make of the rapid-fire Cantoflow. We've collected our favorite "hex errors," divided them into categories, and sprinkled them throughout the rest of the book. If you are like us, some of these epithets will stick in your head, springing from long-term memory at the oddest times. Drop a cup of coffee, and out pops "Damn you, stink man" (*Caged Beauties*); when someone cuts you off in traffic, you spit "You bastard, try this melon" (*Gunmen*); and for no good reason, you'll find yourself whispering "Suck the coffin mushroom now" (*The Ultimate Vampire*). (Hammond and Wilkins 1996, 68)

This description of English captions in Hong Kong films is somewhat similar to the description of the uncanny: the "additional entertainment value" provided by Hong Kong subtitles is readily absorbed but then repressed; the subtitles can suddenly return at unexpected moments to haunt the subject. A subtitled Hong Kong film received in the West produces a residual irrationality that fascinates its hardcore fans. Apparently, a dubbed Hong Kong film would not offer the same sort of additional fun. The distorted meaning of the English subtitles is not to be overlooked. On the contrary, the distortion is written into the very essence of Hong Kong films and is one of the major appeals for Western fans.[15] It is an unexpected boon that increases the viewer's already considerable enjoyment.

Although clumsy English subtitles would seem to be excruciating to viewers already frustrated by the disunity between subjectivity and cinematic image created by subtitling, some Western fans see the subtitles of Hong Kong films as an extra pleasure and a magical experience whose effects linger long after the viewing. It has been said that "the subtitled version contains a number of reflexive elements which hold a much larger potential to break cinematic identification, the suspension of disbelief and a continuous experience of unruptured pleasure . . . and makes room for intellectual evaluation and analysis. At the same time, it destroys the usual unity between the spectator and the cinematic world she or he experiences. This results in the perception of 'difference' rather than the confirmation of 'sameness' and identity, which potentially leads to a considerable loss of pleasure during the experience" (Ascheid 1997, 33–34). In the case of subtitled Hong Kong films, these arguments are no longer valid. The disruption of cinematic identification and the perception of difference might generate extra enjoyment but never a "loss of pleasure." Rupture does not necessarily give rise to "intellectual evaluation and analysis";[16] rather, it lends to a film's fetishistic appeal.

In regard to these Western reactions to the subtitles of Hong Kong films, I would boldly speculate that, in the postmodern global market, which supposedly threatens the continuity of local ethnic traditions, ethnic excessiveness manifested through cultural differences has been essentialized and fetishized but not made to disappear. Global mass culture does not long for homogenization or domestication of all differences. Instead, it embraces differences, celebrates their crowd-pleasing creativity, and fully incorporates them into established consumption and reception patterns. What originally might have been a disgusting stain on the screen instead provides additional enjoyment for the viewer. The mysterious veil that conceals the ethnic other, protects its integrity, and even defies the gaze of the Western viewer is now transformed into a kind of added value, destined for thorough exploitation. If Hong Kong cinema has really "thrilled global audiences," "attained cult status in the West," "become one of the success stories of film history," and "influenced international film culture and the development of film as a medium,"[17] credit is due not only to the industry of this postcolonial city. As a matter of fact, the high praise given to Hong Kong cinema in the West is fundamentally related to the articulation of a new form of global mass culture.

The traditional cross-cultural encounter between East and West is now characterized by a desire to recognize and absorb those differences and excesses within a larger framework of perception. The possible conflicts of cultural particularities in transnational exchange are thereby depoliticized—reduced to mere forms of entertainment, or even fetishized as cult objects that can provide tremendous and mysterious fun. The excessive enjoyment Western viewers derive from English subtitles in Hong Kong cinema may signify a unique situation in today's globalized cultural economy. The very materiality of the broken English in subtitles and its excess of meaning (or nonmeaning) are rapidly rearticulated and "spiritualized" into a spectral fetish that can be enjoyed in the world market. The formidable aspect of the global cultural economy is its ability to incorporate transgressive urges arising from cultural differences that threaten the economy's normal operation. The acknowledgement of the added value of the subtitled Hong Kong film can by no means be understood as a conventional recognition of the radical otherness of a different culture. It is a different kind of recognition of otherness. Hong Kong cinema is basically perceived as a "good other" to the American viewer insofar as it is analogous to the old Hollywood. Although Hong Kong cinema is culturally different and its subtitles carry a "grain of voice" that is not immediately transparent to the Western subject,[18] it is never inexplicable or hostile to the West. Indeed, the subtitles as good and pleasing otherness are actually founded on the exclusion of the political dimension usually immanent in the encounter of the cultural other.

By eliminating the political content of cultural difference, global mass culture generates another ghostly specter. The "bad" English subtitles that are happily consumed in the global economy, which is good at negotiating and incorporating differences, contribute to the formation—in Western eyes—of a more unified Chinese subject in Hong Kong culture. Since cultural identity is established through the mediation of the other's gaze, and English subtitling in Hong Kong film is generally considered to be a peculiar mode of ethnic expression, an "authentic" though hyperbolic sense of Chineseness—Hong Kong's being-for-the-other—is thus constituted. Hong Kong cinema, placed in the context of the global cultural market, represents a distinct Chineseness and clings to a particular ethnic heritage.[19]

When different cultural products enter the global market, their differences are not suppressed but highlighted—and promoted as a stand-in for their ethnic communities. This multiculturalist ideology of global capitalism is of course an inverted form of racism. It seemingly respects the other's identity and culture as something "authentic" but actually conceives the other from a privileged position. Undoubtedly, this privileged position is occupied by those Western viewers who see the off-kilter subtitles in foreign films as extra fun and who can cross linguistic boundaries without actually knowing any foreign languages.[20] Western viewers could self-congratulate their open receptiveness to other culture and their superior idiosyncratic taste of turning the bad movies from Hong Kong to a subversive subculture against the Hollywood mainstream. As Bordwell writes, Hong Kong could offer downmarket pleasures to the young American fans. "[F]rom the first years, the florid acting and outrageous plot twist [with the laughable subtitles] made Hong Kong products into 'bad movies we love.' 'It is entirely possible,' wrote the *Times* reviewer of *King Boxer* (1972), 'to take the film as a joke.' Run Run Shaw recognized that whereas [Hong Kong] local audiences took kung fu seriously, 'Americans see it as comedy.' Run Run proved prophetic. In Europe and North America young people come to screenings of [John Woo's] *The Killer* (1989) determined to ridicule its excesses" (Bordwell 2000b, 92). A certain otherness, even if it is too much sometimes, is always required as a license for the ethnic subject to participate in the world economy that can tolerate, consume, and assimilate all differences.

Faint Voices in the National Resubjectivization

Hong Kong film subtitles tell us about the mechanism of globalization that celebrates and essentializes rather than eliminates cultural and ethnic differences. Yet they also reveal how cultural and linguistic nationalization aggressively engulfs and encompasses the internal otherness. Without a doubt, the 1997 return of Hong Kong will be given a prominent place in modern Chinese history. Historians may celebrate the movement of Chinese people toward national unity in the third millennium. But this problematic transition, whereby Hong Kong people supposedly have become part of a "reunified" Chinese subject, cannot be easily described by an overarching explanation of the long-term rationality of history. So-called rational historical development is only a history of how the predominant ideological system manages to accommodate subversive elements that threaten it. Hong Kong people are solicited or "interpellated," as Louis Althusser puts it, by a new system of representations in which they must see their specifically designated place in a peculiar and historically changing cultural and sociopolitical formation as inevitable, natural, and real in order to meet current conditions for existence. However, the transition to a new representational framework, or a newly designed Chineseness, may not be as smooth as one would assume. After all, the transition means more than substituting the British colonial flag with the Communist Chinese one. Subtitling, I will argue, provides a means of examining how Hong Kong people are making the transition to a new form of social reality and subjectivity, as well as how they consciously and unconsciously resist ideological solicitation.

Many cultural critics have indicated that the so-called Hong Kong cultural identity is derived from the former colony's idiosyncratic use of the Chinese language. Cantonese, the mother tongue of the majority of Hong Kong people, is primarily a spoken language and must be "transcribed" into a standard form of written Chinese. Many believe that the vitality of Hong Kong's language lies precisely in its intractability and refusal to be "tamed" by standard Chinese. Hong Kong provides a perfect example of how language constitutes a contested terrain in which a local identity strives to assert itself. The language of Hong Kong has been considered by many scholars to be a "unique" phenomenon, for its form of orality is a schizophrenic contextual combination of vernacular Cantonese, written Chinese, and oral, written, and "broken" English. Cultural critics of Hong Kong are proud of this hybrid language, and they see in this linguistic predicament and language incompetence a positive opportunity both for constructing a critical discourse of resistance to the "pure" Chinese national tradition and for problematizing the classic East-West binarism (Q. Lee 1994). In the last two decades, as a result of the increasing influence exerted by Hong Kong mass culture, Cantonese has become a dominant language in many popular cultural products like commercial films and pop songs widely circulated in diasporic Chinese communities. Many Chinese who are not speakers of Cantonese as their first language can still enjoy Cantonese humor and listen to Canto-pop.[21] However, Cantonese writing certainly creates difficulties for Chinese readers elsewhere (I will elaborate on this issue later). Generally speaking, Cantonese does not necessarily separate Hong Kong from the mainland or anywhere else. The view of Hong Kong's linguistic hybridity that can resist against the Chinese language hegemony represented by mainland China could be merely a romantic fallacy.

The relation between Hong Kong Cantonese and standard Chinese operates in a subtler manner. Modern concepts of the sign may help us to better understand the cultural politics of Hong Kong in the transitional period.[22] Meaning is generated by signifiers not just in relation to their signifieds but also according to their differential relation to other signifiers. It is the signifier—and not the signified—that has the capacity to combine with other signifiers to form meaning. The return of Hong Kong to mainland China does not necessarily mean an elimination of the differences between the two places. On the contrary, it is precisely this integration that might lead to a cultural transgression of Chineseness as a presumably stable signified, because the secure realm of the signified is now facing the threat of penetration by a material but elusive signifier.

I would like to make it clear that in discussing the linguistic implications of Hong Kong's cultural politics in terms of its relation to China, I am not proposing that China and Hong Kong are two opposing parties that defy reconciliation.[23] Rather, I propose that difference is constitutive of origin, and that the basis of Chinese cultural studies has to be grounded in the disjunction and fragmented historical configurations of various Chinese communities. What should be problematized, then, is Chineseness as a presumed referential unity within the cultural studies of various Chinese communities. I would argue that in the process of the resubjectivization—or "becoming Chinese"—of the Hong Kong people, some revealing moments may occur and could illuminate studies of national culture and related issues.

Subtitling in Hong Kong TV programs offers an opportunity to investigate resubjectivization during the transitional period. It is a relatively new (1990s) phenomenon, and it represents a specific point of rupture in the transition process launched by the nationalist linguistic project (although subtitling is not unfamiliar to consumers of Hong Kong mass culture). Perhaps, subtitling makes a strong case for the failure of national resubjectivization, in spite of the people's willingness to embrace their new Chinese identity.[24] Whether or not Hong Kong people are willing to accept a new national identity and political context, the unpredictable contradiction and subversion inherent in the process of resubjectivization may motivate Chinese cultural scholars to rethink the question of cultural totality and national unity. Interestingly, local television channels began subtitling their programs in the early nineties, which tells another story about cultural changes in the transitional city.

That the Chinese language employs a single written form has become a myth. The Chinese themselves generally believe that although Chinese of different regions speak many different dialects, when they write, they write in a unified fashion: the multiple (if not actually conflicting) voices are governed by a single script, which separates itself from the barbaric world of voices. Writing is not merely an act that traditionally distinguishes the educated from the illiterate; it also serves as an ideological apparatus that helps create cultural nationalism. Written language, accompanied by print capitalism, constitutes the basis of national consciousness by unifying the media of exchange and communication and by hierarchizing one dialect over the others.[25] This scriptural economy could be compared to the economy of perspectivism, which conquers exteriority from a dominating, geometrical point of view. The field of language becomes a place of production to be mastered by the writing subject. Writing enables the subject to occupy a position from which to control his space—a space that is distinct from others and in which he or she can carry out his or her own will. Jacques Derrida may not be completely correct when he says that writing is the forgetting of the self and that voice is closest to the signified (Derrida 1976). In many cases, writing inscribes the mastering subject in his space of articulation, whereas voice is driven outside the scriptural empire to collide with a slippery chain of signifiers.

An example of this is a television documentary on Hong Kong history, entitled *Hong Kong: One Hundred Years* (Xianggang cangsang),[26] aired by China's central station in early 1997. It represents a scriptural enterprise that seeks to provide itself with a new space with respect to the past, to write itself anew, and to produce a consistent and unified national history. Since the documentary was first nationally broadcast in the mainland and only later on the Hong Kong cable network, apparently the primary political aim of the program was to reeducate the mainland Chinese audience about the colonial history of Hong Kong in order to celebrate and propagandize the return of the former colony to the Chinese homeland. Using the conventions of documentary, *Hong Kong: One Hundred Years* is built around a series of interviews, with a combination of voice-over narration and montage of historical footage. However, like many Chinese government propaganda films, its voice-over narration is authoritative and does not hesitate to make comments and judgments about political and historical events, despite its attempt to interview people with different points of view. There is a segment in which mainland Chinese reporters interview the passersby on a Hong Kong street. They ask them why a street in Hong Kong Island is named "Station Street" (its Chinese name is "Shuikengkou" [literally, "puddle's mouth"]). It was, of course, a leading question asked simply to demonstrate Hong Kong people's ignorance about their colonial history. The street is named after the nineteenth-century installment of the first British army garrison on the island.

An interview is a record of voices. Every enunciation of the interviewee is defined and measured according to a system of language established by scriptural production. Even though the program is full of individual voices (of the interviewees and of the narration itself), these voices are used in a collective fabrication of national unity. In theory, there is no need for the diversification of these voices in the process of writing or rewriting the nation. The documentary characterizes the early colonial history of Hong Kong as one of national struggle against the British imperialists, in which the Chinese side was always a unified front. Nevertheless, there are some revealing moments when the scriptural system attempts to write those voices and to find a proper place for them in the documentary "text."

Orality has to be written in the national discourse as much as the "voice of the people" has to be written in the official historiography. The aural must be transformed into visual texts for consumption by a hungry viewership. The documentary subtitles the words of its interviewees, although most of them spoke Mandarin. It may be said that in some cases, since a few Hong Kong Cantonese interviewees do not speak "proper" Mandarin (by mainland Chinese standards), subtitles become necessary. But the act of subtitling the interviews of the mainland Chinese becomes an implicit acknowledgment of the political chaos caused by the voice, a chaos that disrupts the tidiness and self-transparency of the logo of the nation. To a certain extent, the documentary does prove that there is relative freedom of speech in China nowadays, since people feel comfortable voicing their opinions on camera. The national and political discourse at least seems to concur that there is something significant expressed by these voices, but it also assumes that these forms of utterance do not fully comprehend the importance of individual voices. Thus, the scriptural system has the responsibility of clarifying and eradicating the "hiddenness" of these voices by transcribing them into written text.

In the politics of subtitles, therefore, we are witnessing a subtle form of power manipulation. In the cultural politics of mainland China and Hong Kong, there is no longer any simple suppression of different voices. Instead, there now exists a mechanism that seeks to eliminate the radical ambiguity of the voice by translating it into a "comprehensible" as well as a "readable" scriptural message; this is precisely the function of subtitles. The transcription of the oral into the written becomes a legitimate operation because the production of "meaning" depends on the textualization of all hidden or indistinguishable voices. In short, through these subtitles, the self-transparency of the nation as a logo and as a legitimate representative of Chineseness is no longer hindered or obscured by disruptive, senseless voices. Voice is now brought under control by the rational articulation of the written, so that it will not threaten the established order fixed by writing.

In the early 1990s, rather than introducing new Mandarin programs, Hong Kong television stations began captioning preexisting Cantonese programs, including broadcast news programs and soap operas, in standard written Chinese. These subtitled programs are meant, it is claimed, to cater to the needs of the hearing-impaired and immigrants from mainland China. However, it is commonly joked that the captions are provided for the sake of non-Cantonese-speaking Communist Party officials in Hong Kong, lest they assume that the soap operas disseminate anti-Party propaganda (at one time, vilifying images of mainland Chinese were common in Hong Kong cinema and television). The captioning of Hong Kong television programs does not necessarily mean that Hong Kong's voices are subordinated to the authority of the scriptural text or that the hybridity of these voices is vanishing into an integrated national form of speech. It is a longstanding film industry practice to subtitle their productions in standard Chinese and English; are we overestimating the significance of subtitling in Hong Kong television? After all, isn't this just another marketing strategy of the cunning Hong Kong people to cater to the taste of mainland Chinese? I believe that the act of subtitling TV programs has a special significance.

Derrida's critique of phonocentrism is that the voice produces the illusion of hearing oneself speak, and that it provides the speaking subject with the sense of an immediate transparency of self-presence. Now the majority of the Hong Kong audience, who are Cantonese, watch television programs in their own language and at the same time hear themselves speak; however, whatever illusion of self-identity they might derive from the voice alone is regularly punctured and edited by the written words on the screen. When interviewees on news programs stutter or say something redundant, the subtitles immediately tidy up their words in order to clarify their speech. So the excessiveness of spoken words and the inaccuracy of verbal expression are steadily being eliminated in the written form. The "cleaning" performed by the subtitles also points to the fracture and the insurmountable difference between the voice and the text. The text endeavors to cite and alter the voice, but it is not able to erase the specificities of speech within the parameters of scriptural reconstruction except by simply ignoring them. What this means is that a Hong Kong audience can hear itself speak but cannot hear itself think or rationalize, for its voice fails to coincide with the distinct logic of meaning and thinking offered by the written Chinese text. To use Derrida's argument, writing (or subtitling, in this case) does, in one sense, supplement the voice. But writing has also become a usurper, and the production of the meaning is now, from an official standpoint, confined to the written text alone. Voice, meanwhile, has not disappeared. Instead, it has turned into an opaque object that continues to render the self-presence of the written subject impossible. In other words, it is voice, not writing, that now occupies the place of what Derrida calls the "dangerous supplement."

What, then, is the political implication of this dissolution of self-identity in the cultural relationship between Hong Kong and China? The return of Hong Kong to China is overdetermined by a narrative that emphasizes ethnic reunification and a national totality. In the (post)transitional period, Hong Kong people are already undergoing a process of resubjectivization as "Chinese" citizens under the polity of one nation. Insofar as a Hong Kong individual is a captive of the signifier of the other, he is, we might say, inevitably inscribed in the universe of the other's (China's) desire (he desires what China desires). Television captioning, then, can be read as a Lacanian *capitonnage* (quilting) of the national resubjectivization project, which attempts to anchor Hong Kong people to a unified identity. What results, however, is something else entirely: even though the individual is captioned or quilted by the other's signifier, he is not in reality inscribed squarely in the other's desire and cannot become a subject that desires exactly what the other desires. His path toward subjectivity is undermined by an excess—the voice that eludes the scriptural conquest. The hindrances embodied by this obscure voice undercut the self-presence of the national subject and ensure that the identity imposed by writing will be forced from its trajectory by nontranscribed or nontranscribable differences. If resubjectivization is based on a smooth transition from one signifier to another, we may say with regard to subtitling that a piece of invocatory material will inevitably fall out of the signifying chain and will not be successfully reintegrated into a clear-cut identity with self-transparency. The trend toward reconstituting a new Chinese identity is unstoppable, but the process of subjectivization can never remain pure or unruffled. The excessive voice defying any attempt at rational subtitling and other kinds of rupture-points signified by Hong Kong mark a fundamental failure in China's linguistic nationalist project.

The Estranged Other in One's Voice

The case of television subtitling indicates that voice is always coerced to submit to the imposition of scriptural or writing order, conveying the tensions between the local and the national, between Hong Kong and China in the process of unification. However, the full identification of words with voice in the Hong Kong cultural and linguistic sphere does not necessarily suggest the self-presence of a local subjectivity in place. That a Hong Kong subject writes what he speaks does not guarantee him a full identity. On the contrary, the complete agreement of voice and text, as in the following case of Cantonese subtitling, may alienate the narcissistic self from within, suggesting the impossibility and untenable position of Hong Kong subjectivity.

Voice, in many theoretical discourses, is considered a significant factor in the process of subjectivization. Althusser describes a typical example, in which an individual walking along the street hears the voice of an officer behind him: "Hey, you there!" The individual turns around, believing that the call is for him. As Althusser puts it, "by this mere 180–degree physical conversion, he becomes a *subject*" (Althusser 1971, 174). The call of the voice solicits an individual to become a subject and confers on him an identity. However, this sort of subjectivization not only designates the becoming of the subject but also denotes the reality of subjection. In short, a subject is produced by its readiness to submit to the voice of law, and this submission is redeemed by the assurance of one's own existence.[27] According to the deconstructive critique, the self-presence and self-transparence of the subject is derived from the primordial experience of hearing-oneself-speaking (*s'entendre-parler*). However, a different and even conflicting understanding is also invoked to rehabilitate the complexity of voice. Voice is far more ambiguous and intractable than is its safeguard of self-presence. Rather, it is treated as something threatening to the law and order of the scriptural empire and, for this reason, is subordinated to the rational articulation of written word. Instead of disclosing the totality of being and meaning, voice is perceived as the locus of the negative (Dolar 1996; Agamben 1991). Further elaborating the Derridian interpretation, Žižek states that "the founding illusion of the metaphysics of presence is not simply that of 'hearing oneself speaking,' but rather a kind of short circuit between 'hearing oneself speaking' and 'seeing oneself looking': a 'seeing oneself looking' *in the mode of 'hearing oneself speaking*,' a gaze that regains the immediacy of the vocal self-affection" (Žižek 1996, 95). The accord between seeing and hearing—the effect that modern media attempt to achieve—constitutes the fundamental illusion of the immediacy of self-presence and self-transparency.

Nowadays, an increasing number of Hong Kong and foreign films shown in Hong Kong are captioned not in standard written Chinese but in Cantonese dialect—the "living voice" of Hong Kong. This phenomenon of subtitling in Cantonese is also often found in local television programs. Would Cantonese subtitles provide a better accord between seeing and hearing and create a stronger illusion of the immediacy of self-presence for the Hong Kong subject? Standard Chinese subtitling on television was, as noted earlier, initially meant for the hearing-impaired and new immigrants from mainland China. Hence the message of national unity (Hong Kong and other parts of China are one nation under the universal script) is highlighted by the practice of television captioning. Nonetheless, this argument may no longer apply to the peculiar phenomenon of Cantonese subtitling. What the Hong Kong local viewers see at the bottom of the screen is not standard written Chinese but the Cantonese they use every day. Since Cantonese is only one among hundreds of Chinese dialects, the so-called common Chinese language is fundamentally determined by the written text. In this sense, Cantonese subtitles not only transmit the "living voice" of the Cantonese-speaking Hong Kong audience, but they also challenge the hegemony of the standard Chinese text. However, the well-known columnist and film critic Sek Kei disapproves the practice of Cantonese subtitling in film:

> [Someone] has complained that the Chinese subtitles of some foreign films shown in Hong Kong are translated into Cantonese dialect that Chinese audiences from other provinces will not understand.

I don't like this practice either. I feel uncomfortable when I see the Cantonese subtitles. In the past, subtitles were usually translated into standard Chinese. Even nowadays, there are some excellent translations. But since the last ten years, there has been an increase in the incidence of Cantonese subtitling. It is probably because more and more Hong Kong people cannot read and write standard Chinese. They use Hong Kong–style Cantonese and change it into "Hong Kong language." Not only the Chinese from other provinces, but also the Cantonese reader from Canton may be unable to understand some popular Hong Kong idioms.

Being of Cantonese origin, I support Cantonese culture but I don't support the Cantonese subtitling of foreign films. I believe the popularity of "Hong Kong language" would further limit Hong Kong's development. People in Hong Kong are not good at Mandarin. They are already lagging behind. If we convert even standard Chinese into "Hong Kong language," what kind of future will be left for us? (Sek Kei 2002)

Many people may share Sek Kei's idea that a unique Hong Kong linguistic identity only impedes the city's integration with the motherland. To subtitle Cantonese dialogue into a vernacular script seems to be self-defeating because it serves no purpose to help non-Cantonese speakers understand the content. However, it would be facile to conclude that Cantonese subtitling, which has been becoming popular since the 1990s, represents a counterstrategy on the part of the locals of resisting the scriptural imposition of a unified Chinese national identity. It might be misleading to say such an act would constitute an attempt to reactivate the lost transparency, plenitude, and authenticity of Cantonese speech in the face of the dominant standard Chinese script. The Cantonese subtitles apparently do not target new Chinese immigrants; if they did, they would then interpellate the Chinese individuals into a Hong Kong subject rather than upholding a united Chinese identity built upon a common written text. The language of Canton, or Guangzhou, used to be considered the most authentic, but due to the overwhelming influence of Hong Kong's media and popular culture, Hong Kong Cantonese has become the spoken standard. From a chauvinist Hong Kong perspective, the message is loud and clear to new immigrants: if you live in Hong Kong, you have to speak like a Hong Konger. It is the voice—or living speech—that distinguishes a local subjectivity.

There is anti-immigrant sentiment in post-1997 Hong Kong though the local population is mainly composed of first- or second-generation immigrants and their children. But the accents of new immigrants from other parts of China are ridiculed by the locals. Since physical appearance may not indicate the difference between a Hong Konger and a new immigrant from the mainland, voice becomes the criterion of authenticity of cultural identity. The notion of voice taking precedence over writing is reiterated in the cultural politics of China–Hong Kong relationships. In this sense, Cantonese subtitles are presumptuously categorized as an ideological tool delineating the boundaries of the locality. A strong sense of community and loyalty to the place is evoked by dialect. The retention of local accent or voice, through a bizarre transcription of the patois into a literary script, may show the unwillingness of the Hong Kong people to cede their subjectivity to an all-encompassing Chinese identity. It fosters a myth of belonging and togetherness that reinforces the "naturalness" or historical factuality at the heart of Hong Kong's cultural position.

However, such an interpretation may overstress Hong Kong's cultural separatism from China and misread the dialectical relations between voice and writing. The transitional period foretells the mutual destinies of Hong Kong and its neighboring Chinese cities. On the one hand, Hong Kong is a model of modernity and advanced capitalist metropolis for other Chinese cities; on the other hand, the postcolonial city is also producing more and more Chineseness in order to adjust to its changing milieu. Not necessarily something inherited, the Chineseness of Hong Kong is as much a product of self-invention as it is the consequence of conforming to a dominant structure. Traditionally, Hong Kong film and music industries have created a pan-Chineseness to promote their products to the lucrative overseas Chinese markets. In this sense, Cantonese is by no means perceived by Hong Kong people as the "other" language vis-à-vis standard Chinese.

Nevertheless, "written Cantonese" for Hong Kong locals is more like an estranged other than a familiar text. Although Cantonese is the major language spoken in Hong Kong, when Hong Kong people write, they write in the standard Chinese linguistically based on classical language as well as Mandarin. This so-called "common speech" (*Putonghua*) is standardized modern Chinese, in which Beijing speech serves as its phonetic basis, and modern classic works written in the vernacular form its grammatical basis. Cantonese is regarded only as a spoken dialect that defines a provincial culture rather than a unitary national literate culture. In fact, it is difficult to write every word spoken in Cantonese because many Cantonese words are slang and cannot be written without being recreated from standard Chinese characters. Local Hong Kong students are generally discouraged (or even forbidden) by their Chinese language teachers from using Cantonese in their essays (written Cantonese is quite popular in the youngsters' cyber-communications), though the medium of instruction in many Chinese schools is Cantonese. So, ironically, Cantonese is being used for teaching standard Chinese language in school; however, as a language, it is not taught (Bruche-Schulz 1997).

The ideological concept of a China unified by a universal script existed even during Hong Kong's colonial era. There is a distinct divergence between the Chinese literacy as representative of national culture and the localized aspects of everyday orality. Cantonese as a written language is definitely repressed in formal and official channels. The silenced dialect is certainly alienated from its users textually, but by affirming its silence in writing, Cantonese becomes more expressive. Throughout the city's history, the realm of the written Chinese has occasionally been penetrated by the Cantonese patois. Many popular forms of writing—such as newspaper columns, comics, commercials and Canto-pop lyrics—have incorporated the spoken dialect into their textual production in order to highlight realism, vitality, humor, and common ground with the audience. Vulgarity is central to Cantonese's expressiveness. In a way, its devalued status enables the local language to continually reinvent itself.

The rise of written Cantonese in published media is closely tied with the growth of local Hong Kong culture and its sense of identity. For centuries, Cantonese words and vocabulary have appeared in low-prestige popular texts written primarily in classical Chinese or standard Chinese that generates a hybrid style coined as *saam kap dai*.[28] But since the 1960s, growing numbers of texts published in Hong Kong have been written entirely, not merely partially, in Cantonese. More and more newspaper articles, magazines, advertisements, and pocket books use Cantonese as their written language. Texts in Cantonese are marketable products and some of them are very successful commercially. The increasing popularity of written Cantonese in Hong Kong daily life reveals the escalating focus of the residents on the city's local life and the corresponding decline in identification with and interest in greater Chinese culture. As Donald Snow pointedly says in his comprehensive research on the history of written Cantonese in Hong Kong, "It can no longer be said that Cantonese appears only in cheap publications dealing with 'low-class' content matter for a poor or uneducated audiences. Instead, the use of Cantonese is becoming more closely associated with entertainment based on local themes, and with publications intended for local audiences rather than Chinese-speaking audiences outside Hong Kong. Of particular importance is the fact that Cantonese is used widely in leisure reading popular among young people, especially students, the same group in which identification with Hong Kong is the strongest" (Snow 1991, 4–5). However, almost all the uses of written Cantonese in Hong Kong are still found in entertaining materials that are associated with oral culture.

Oralization of the written text is usually viewed as a contamination or debasement of "high" literary culture. The practice is confined primarily to popular culture. The tradition of Chinese literary or textual culture enjoyed a privileged position even during the British colonial era. It is precisely in the face of the commanding grip of the classical Chinese antiquity that Cantonese subtitling can carve a niche for itself in the forms of communication and subjectivity that are closely associated with the development of technology. The polarized concepts of orality and literacy constructed by Walter Ong apparently cannot facilitate an exploration of the multiple modes of thought and cultural expression created by new technologies and media (W. Ong 1993). It may be valid to insist that the emergence of electronic media generates an awareness of the contrast between writing and voice and poses a challenge to the dominion of the printed word. But the assertion that the electronic age represents a comeback by oral culture is simply not true. It is the combination of sound effects, speech, written words, and visual images—and the manipulation of them—that mold the production of films or television programs. Modern media productions cannot be characterized in terms of a unitary sensory experience. Therefore, the voice of the Hong Konger that is "seen" in the motion picture has to be understood within the context of the multiplicity of expressive means that constitute today's media.

I want to emphasize that when Hong Kongers watch a local movie or television program and simultaneously see their dialect in print, it does not necessarily mean that the life of their immediate speech and the totality granted by the self-sufficient voice have been restored, since the life breath of this voice is always already mediated by the act of looking or reading. The usual organization of space and time in film is constrained by the spatial medium of written text. The voice in print cannot be simply equated with self-presence or hearing oneself speaking, which is the very basis of experiencing oneself as a living being. This "written voice" in Hong Kong popular media does not necessarily promise the instantaneity of vocal being. I would say that the immediate written transcription of the living voice, although different from translating the oral and vocal into the literary, is not an act of sovereign being. Rather, the viewer hears and sees himself speaking, yet what he hears and sees is never fully himself but is an alien body at heart. There is from the outset something about the voice that prevents the subject from embracing its immediate presence and fullness. The familiar and intimate dialect embodied in the written voice suddenly becomes an estranged other. The perfect coincidence of the vocal and the textual brings the viewer to a point at which his narcissism is no longer bearable. I would say this is the point at which the self is confronted with its "double."

This "double" is the very projection—or echo—of the living voice of the Hong Kong subject, materialized in Cantonese subtitles. It is by virtue of the double that one can become endowed with an ego and can establish oneself as a subject. However, when the viewing subject watches the subtitles, the subtitles are also looking back at it; the object of vision returns its gaze to the subject and makes the subject aware of itself in the picture. The "double" that looks back is the manifestation of otherness in the field of vision. It is the otherness that cannot be denied in the subject's constituting self-image. However, this "double" is not simply an image double or a vocal double that the subject can reduce to its objective counterpoint. The "written voice" of Cantonese subtitles is not a typical reflection in which one can recognize oneself on screen. Although it contains strong vocal elements, the "written voice" remains a printed sign. The line between self and other, subject and object, and seeing and hearing remains ambiguous. It subverts the standard opposition of subjectivity and objectivity. By definition, the objectivity of Cantonese subtitling is that it exists independently on screen, and it becomes subjective when it is consciously perceived and experienced by the viewing subject. However, the real function of Cantonese subtitling is evident only when it (bizarrely) becomes "subjectively objective" to the local viewer—things seem subjective only to him even though they actually are that way. The Cantonese subtitles are there although they are experienced as if they were not. So when the subject actually encounters the "double," he would still say to himself that he could never consciously have that experience.

The popular Hong Kong movie *Her Fatal Ways IV,* one in a series of blockbusters satirizing mainland Chinese bureaucrats, caricatures a mainland policewoman (played by a Hong Kong actress, Dodo Cheng Yu Ling) who has decided to settle in Hong Kong and become an authentic Hong Konger.[29] It is common in Hong Kong cinema for mainland Chinese characters to be played by Hong Kong actors. This is not due entirely to the star effect (not many stars from mainland China are well known to Hong Kong audiences); rather, Hong Kong stars playing mainland characters can create a "subjectively objective" effect, allowing the audience to ridicule the characters from a critical distance and to identify with them. The ugliness of Chinese culture—from which the Hong Kong Chinese community is not exempt—thus lies somewhere between fiction and reality. Hence, the most intimate "subjective" (in the sense of being part of the subject's conscious intuition) experience that Hong Kong people can share with mainland Chinese may be "inaccessible" or partially closed to them. The inaccessibility may render the subject empty. However, a distinct Hong Kong subject position can emerge in this Chinese community precisely because of the repression of cultural closeness. The female protagonist's dream of becoming an "authentic Hong Konger" is a projected one through which the narcissistic reflection of Hong Kong is mediated by the other. In this way, local media affirm Hong Kong's cultural superiority, but only tentatively.

In the eyes of the female cop in *Her Fatal Ways IV,* Hong Kong Chinese are westernized, and all are proficient in the English language (ironically, this proficiency is not evident in the English subtitles of Hong Kong film). She has difficulty learning English and the comedy makes fun of her lack of sophistication as well as her poor English. Since she sees English as the key to becoming a Hong Konger, she predictably falls for a Westerner—the Scottish officer who lives upstairs from her. To her surprise, the Scot does not conform to her expectations. Instead, he has embraced Hong Kong culture: he loves egg tarts (a Hong Kong–style pastry that the female protagonist hates), sings Cantonese songs, and speaks the dialect like a native. In a funny but romantic rooftop scene, the subtitling produces an unexpectedly alienating effect. Like all Hong Kong movies, the film's subtitles are in English and Chinese (in this case, Cantonese). Since the characters speak English and Cantonese in mixed modes, the English and Cantonese subtitles are sometimes redundant. At this point in the film, our protagonist believes she has found her ideal love in the handsome Scot, but she has not yet discovered that he can speak Cantonese. The pretentiously romantic Scot sings to the protagonist. His song is an English rendition of a traditional Cantonese ballad, "Sim Yuen Chung Sing" (The Temple Bell Tolls). The English lyrics are stupid and intended to inspire laughter. The protagonist joins in and sings the same song with different English lyrics. Encouraged by the female protagonist, the Scot expresses his love more directly, by singing a song he wrote for her. The subtitles change from Cantonese to formal written Chinese. Finally, the Scot proves to be able to speak Cantonese as competently as the protagonist. She is embarrassed because she has opened her heart to him in Cantonese—believing that he couldn't understand a word of it. The subtitles return to Cantonese (see the text in note 30).[30]

What are the implications of these changes in the subtitles? The initial juxtaposition of Cantonese and English subtitles, accompanying the mixing of English lyrics and a Cantonese tune, makes perfect sense to the local audience. A large number of Canto-pop songs are cover versions of Japanese, Taiwanese, and English songs. Canto-pop has always been regarded as cosmopolitan because of its stylistic blending and it is a representative cultural form of which Hong Kongers are proud; but the music is also criticized for its lack of creativity and for being a mere manifestation of the conformist and short-sighted attitudes of the general population. The English version of the Cantonese melody in the film, however, presents an eagerly accepted illusion that this is a creative form that embodies the people's half-Chinese and half-Western cultural hybridity. The message, apparently, is that no matter what your origin, Hong Kong culture, like the song sung by the *gweilo*—(literally "demon"— a Cantonese label for Caucasians) and the *biuje*—(literally "cousin-sister"— a derogatory Hong Kong Cantonese term for mainland Chinese women), can envelop you in its imaginary sameness. In a number of foreign films released in Hong Kong, such as *Trainspotting* (U.K., 1995), *Run Lola Run* (Germany, 1998), or *The Iron Ladies* (Thailand, 2000), the Chinese subtitles are in idiomatic Cantonese.[31] The translators may believe that stressing the equivalence of social and cultural contexts takes precedence over the cultural differences. But what is uncanny about *Her Fatal Ways IV,* that is, in the familiar suddenly turning into the alienated, is that the voices of the "not quite foreign" characters—the Cantonese-speaking Scot and mainland Chinese woman cop—are reproduced verbatim in the Cantonese subtitles. The pretension to universality and coincidence, which is definitely one of the phantasms consigned to logocentrism, inaugurates a difference, however minute, that points toward the otherness constitutive of voice-as-presence itself. As shown in this movie, the speaking subject of auto-affection could be *another* as well as constituted by *the other.*

A deliberate shift in the subtitles from the oral to the literary happens in the second stage. The English folksong sung by the Scot integrates the earlier stupid and senseless words into a meaningful signifier of love. His confession of love makes it difficult for the female protagonist to resist. Almost mechanically, she falls in love with him. Here love is like an autonomous mechanism that automatically changes the inscrutable mixture of dialects into the proper written text. It is no longer a funny matter when the other addresses you formally to express his love. The subtitles cannot afford to play around with a flippant amalgam of Cantonese and English. However, this is not necessarily a resumption of the scriptural order. The written text could be a dangerous implement that brings about a breakdown in language. The uncanny is at work here again, orchestrating the shuffling between the oral and the literary. Writing is freely employed to challenge the complacency of a self-presence based on vocal immediacy. There is always an estranged other popping up in the closed world of the self-affecting speaking subject. Love, as a desire for oneness, is a missed encounter in the sense that lovers may express too much or too little passion for each other, and either too early or too late, but never coherently and together. One may not find one's ideal image in the eyes of one's beloved, just as appropriate language may not be found in the subtitles.

The restoration of Cantonese to the subtitles in the third stage bears witness to an uncanny force by which inscription and erasure of the local voice constitute a gap within the Hong Kong subjectivity. The fundamental division in the subject perhaps typifies the struggle of the Hong Kong people in their insistence on a unique local subjectivity in the face of being resubjectivized in the postcolonial period. The theory of the mirror stage in psychoanalytic theory suggests that the recognition of oneself in the reflection has already produced an inevitable split. It is only when one sees oneself as the reflected other that one can identify oneself as "I." The mirror double that helps to construct one's ego identity also, paradoxically, stands for the dimension of eternal loss and division. Thus, doubling entails the loss of uniqueness. The lost uniqueness of Hong Kong could easily be interpreted as the byproduct of political transition, in which the city's historical and cultural specificity is expected to vanish.

However, in Cantonese subtitling, the written voice as double appears to grant the Hong Kong subject access to its imagined primordial being, the immediate self-being supposedly lost in the objective reality of the handover. Of course, the loss of self-being is false from the very beginning, because the subjectivity of Hong Kong was already marked by division and emptiness. Hong Kong is undergoing a process of healing, dealing with the "loss" of this imaginary self-being by resubjectivizing itself within the unified Chinese national identity. But the part that is lost approaches the subject through the reincarnation of the "written voice." The once familiar now changes into the other that disrupts reality and haunts one from the inside. It sticks out and destroys the harmony of united Chineseness. This recovery of something that is lost does not reassert Hong Kong's identity. Rather, it disrupts Hong Kong's process of integration. The locals are effectively stuck; they are no longer Hong Kong subjects but not yet Chinese. We must bear in mind that the Hong Kong subject and Chinese identity are not diametrically opposed entities. The Hong Kong subject that sees itself speaking is not a subject beyond the purview of Chinese identity. It merely stands for the inherent inconsistency of the Chinese national identity itself. The self-seeing or self-reading subject is not a principle that would lend coherence to a national subjectivity organized by a universal written language.

Cantonese subtitling in Hong Kong films and television programs designates a constitutive other within the totality of Chinese identity. Subtitling, normally used to translate a foreign language, is like the resounding Echo (in the myth of Narcissus), who may have a voice but can no longer use it. Its existence cannot be ignored, and yet it is not a creative, autonomous force of its own. English subtitling in Hong Kong film is an Echo that sings out of tune; it deviates and produces something excessive even while it tries hard to resonate with the original tune. At the same time, Cantonese subtitling appears narcissistic. Perhaps it is historical context that makes Hong Kong people fall in love with an inchoate image and mistake it for substance. Cantonese captions describe the formation of a local subject via a process of visual as well as spoken identification. It is too late for the local Narcissus to recognize himself in the reflection and resonance. There is already an internal division at work: Narcissus cannot recognize himself and at the same time be one with that image. The encounter with its double only discloses the disunity of the subject and questions the promise of future wholeness that sustains the subject. However, a subject position that has been subverted locally could be transformed, in a larger context, to one with a veneer of consistency and a place in global society.

PART 2

Image Is Everything

3

Hong Kong Muscles and Sublime Chinese Subjectivity

LESS THAN A YEAR before the colony's return to China, a locally trained female windsurfer, Lee Lai-shan, won Hong Kong's first Olympic gold medal in the international world of sports. The victory had special meaning for the postcolonial city. On the one hand, Hong Kong people associate windsurfing with the image of the Chinese sailing boat—a red junk—that the Hong Kong Tourist Association (now called the Hong Kong Tourism Board) has used for decades as an official cultural icon for the city. On the other hand, a Chinese athlete had never won a gold medal in the Olympic windsurfing race until Hong Kong did it on the brink of the political handover. Symbolically, Hong Kong was able to flex its muscles and assert its own identity through the body of its female Olympic gold medalist, showing the new sovereign of mainland China that the decolonized city deserved some respect even in regard to its long-considered weak spot.[1]

In the hundred years of its colonial history, Hong Kong athletes were hardly able to excel in the international arena. The colonial government had not been very interested in any long-term programs for nurturing and training professional local athletes to compete on an international level. Hong Kong people were able to find their moments of glory in sports only when the People's Republic of China returned to international competition in the early 1980s.[2] The triumphs of China's team or individual sports in transnational games always aroused the Hong Kong people's Chinese national identification and pride. However, many locals are also well aware of the transitory nature of their Chinese-nationalist sports enthusiasm, to which they ironically refer by saying something like "it's probably the only moment that I feel closest to China and am proud to be Chinese." Perhaps what is even more ironic is that the resurgence of male-chauvinistic nationalism in the male-dominated sports world surrounded mostly by fervent male fans is instigated and supported by Chinese female athletes. The international achievements of the Chinese women's volleyball team in the 1980s and the Chinese women's soccer team in the 1990s, and the overall greater international successes of Chinese female athletes in comparison to those of their male counterparts, have captured the national imagination of not only Hong Kong Chinese people but also numerous diasporic Chinese.

With the international success of Chinese sportswomen, it is not surprising to see that their female "musculinity"—a term coined by Yvonne Tasker—has become a nationalized body of signifying elements appropriated by the nation-state as well as the male-dominated sports market. By and large, the nature and structure of Chinese nationalism in sports fundamentally eliminate any feminist voice even in women's games (Brownell 1999). The defeminized bodies of Chinese sportswomen have been delicately intertwined with the generally feminized Chinese male bodies in the Western media. When Chinese men fail to exert the power of their bodies in global competitions, Chinese women have no choice but to fill in the void left by the male body, in order to construct a national identity for their compatriots. To a certain extent, Hong Kong also occupies a somewhat symbolic "female" position for the construction of masculine Chinese identity. What I mean by a "female" stance here is a functional role made out of the very thing missing in the Chinese male-dominated national identity. Not necessarily characterized by the conventionally designated "female" qualities of passivity and subordination, Hong Kong's position in the making of the masculinized Chinese identity could have both constructive and subversive potentials. As if defined as a woman within the patriarchal society, Hong Kong always relates itself to China as its outside or marginal other. But Hong Kong is never China's real other (since that is always the West). Rather, Hong Kong is only the very becoming of China's other. If China is traditionally defined as the national being and as the self-evident ground of a national identity or subject, Hong Kong thus functions as a way of "becoming-woman," not as a complementary being, but as an element of instability that surrounds and re- or disorganizes the Chinese being.

Though Hong Kong has rarely been able to find a distinct place for itself in the transnational sports arena, the bodies exported from the former British colony ironically do enjoy a wide popularity throughout the world and play a significant role in the (re)definition of Chineseness and nationalist sentiments. Kung fu and action films made in Hong Kong have been conducive to the emergence of a transnational Chinese nationalism and identity of the abstract and symbolic kind. It is commonplace to associate action movie stars and superhero figures with the (dis)play of their body. Hong Kong popular culture has become famous for its export of muscular Chinese bodies—from Bruce Lee, through the kung fu comics, to Jackie Chan—to Chinese communities and other Asian countries. The importance of hypermasculine action bodies produced by and exported from Hong Kong, however, does not necessarily contradict its relatively marginal position "feminized" by the mainland political discourse. After all, these hyperbolic bodies are considered by such presumptuous attitudes as something belonging only to the trashy popular culture realm (Wang Shuo 2000), but they have nothing to do with the really serious national affairs.

John Woo's tightly choreographed gunfight sequences are a sheer deployment of virile bodies. In the movies of Tsui Hark and Wong Kar-wai, the action bodies go beyond their physical dimensions and constitute a new kind of signification. These bodies are identified as the unique contribution that Hong Kong has made to cultural production in the world, as well as the reconstitution of a muscular Chinese identity. They play an important role not only in the self-invention of Hong Kong but also in the remasculinization of the Chinese body. Under the orientalizing perception, China is recognized in the West as feminine and passive. Many Chinese men on the streets indeed appear to confirm the Western stereotypes of Chinese male sexuality. Although China definitely has its own aggressive, militant, macho, and tough-guy tradition, as exemplified by the multiple images of one particular military god, Guan Yu (Hodge and Louie 1998; Louie 2002), it is Hong Kong's cultural production that has enhanced and developed such a tradition into an affective and compelling global representation.

However, while the male Chinese bodies from Hong Kong appear solidly material on screen or page, they are of a peculiar make and significance. When global circulation of films and comics makes these bodies conspicuous as Hong Kong cultural products, they remain at some levels inscrutable. Despite their importance as components of the self-invention of Hong Kong and revirilization of Chinese culture, they allude to no positive, descriptive cultural features from which Chinese identity can easily be drawn. As such, their import evades its own articulation and, by the same move, escapes representation in familiar critical discourse. Instead, the Hong Kong Chinese male body serves as a "sublime body" that paradoxically presents what is "unrepresentable" in the making of Chinese national identity. That is not to say that Chinese identity is some transcendent and unattainable entity that no proper representation could match. Rather, what the sublime Chinese body made by Hong Kong popular culture can provide is precisely a failed and negative representation of this subject position, one that paradoxically reveals its true, positive nature. This logic of the sublime body, by its very insufficiency, lends a body to the negativity of the idea of Chineseness within the world of global capitalism, according to which a deep nihilistic void is always found in our being.

What "sublime" generally refers to is something measureless, incommensurable, unimaginable, and formless.[3] It is often described as a feeling one has in the face of raw nature—though, I will explain, there is no "raw nature" when it comes to bodies, and specifically, in this case, "the Chinese body made in Hong Kong." Nonetheless, the word usually designates the inadequacy of form to content. I would like to use this concept of the "sublime" to understand the complex cultural formation of Chinese identity through the Hong Kong muscular body. As a sublime entity, this body is paradoxically a material signifier of that which is unsignifiable. This itself is a product of material conditions. Because of its historical specificity, Hong Kong culture is situated in between Chinese tradition and Western influence, but problematically, a commitment to Hong Kong cannot simply mean reclaiming native culture or identifying with British colonial traits, either of which will only eliminate the possibility of cultural agency. Hong Kong's cultural self-awareness is said to be an awareness of its "in-betweenness," its impurity, its difference at the origin, or its changing indeterminacy. This impossible representation of Hong Kong cultural identity has been discussed perspicaciously and rigorously by a number of critics.[4] In this chapter I concentrate, through a reading of how the muscular body is portrayed in popular cultural forms, on how the failed representation is inscribed as an essential part of Hong Kong subject formation, which simultaneously contributes to and subverts from within the heroic and nationalistic Chinese body.

The pumped-up bodies of the Hong Kong kung fu movie stars and the heroic figures of the comic books have a fantastic quality that cannot be fully articulated by historical interpretation. Although these bodies are the products of the history of Hong Kong, they cannot be approached directly as so many positive ontological entities that endorse a definite historical meaning of national or cultural identity. However, their peculiar quality does not refer to a timeless world or a place beyond history. On the contrary, these sublime bodies occupy an empty space without a positive content or intrinsic meaning, and their void can only subsequently be filled through the specificity of their particular historical milieus. What they indicate is only the impossibility of fixed definition. The sublimity of the muscular body thus creates an initially empty place for the emergence of a particular transnational Chinese subject made in Hong Kong, which is correlatively embedded in this "hole" of identification. The body may fail to offer a completely coherent representation corresponding to Hong Kong Chinese subject formation, but its inadequate presentation constitutes the real dimension of this subjectivity. This is the reason why neither a total denial of any symbolic meaning nor a conventional historical explanation of the Chinese bodies represented in Hong Kong kung fu culture could ever grasp the complicated mechanism of subject construction.

In a historical study on the construction of Hong Kong identity from the 1960s on, Matthew Turner argues that, after the political separation from China, the image of the Hong Kong body was designed to fit the modern Western mode of health, posture, and physique. He points out two particular types of Hong Kong male bodies popular at the time: those associated with Fei Jai and Mr. Hong Kong. Fei Jai was a rebellious teddy boy who gelled his long hair, wore sunglasses, and led a "corrupted" Western lifestyle, whereas Mr. Hong Kong was a muscle-building competitor associated with the image of Western wrestling shows on television. Both types converge into the seventies' image of the popular movie star Bruce Lee and the comic-book figures of Wong Yuk Long's *Siu Lau Man* (Little Rascals), later renamed *Lung Fu Moon* (Dragon and Tiger Kids). Turner explains, "Icons of the Hong Kong male were transformed from the weaklings of earlier Cantonese comedies and given new identities as stylish playboys or muscular heroes. A unique combination of Western body building and Chinese Kung Fu (with an admixture of James Bond karate and Mainland flying action) were brought together in the figure of Bruce Lee and the characters of Wong Yuk Long's early comics" (Turner 1995, 38).

For Turner, the representation of the Hong Kong body functions almost like an ideological state apparatus (although Althusser's name is never mentioned in his text). As a chronicler of the social control of Hong Kong identity construction, Turner focuses on the ways in which the formation of identity is monitored to meet the political, economic, and cultural demands of the times, or how the individual in Hong Kong is interpellated as a Hong Kong subject rather than just a Chinese one. In this sense, Hong Kong identity is a mere reproduction of the existing power structure; the bodies are basically created and trained by the rules of the dominant colonial system. A visiting British scholar in Hong Kong, Turner launched the project studying the general designs of local architecture, fashion, exhibitions, advertisement, school textbooks, and other popular icons beginning from the sixties. According to his research, the rhetoric of local community and sense of belonging was first manipulated by the colonial government on a large scale as anti-Communist counterpropaganda after the 1967 riots instigated by the proletariat Cultural Revolution in mainland China. The identification with China was gradually displaced by an ambiguous but inclusive discourse of local and communal cultural identity. For him, Hong Kong identity is a discursive object intentionally made by the colonial regime in order to alienate the local people from attaching culturally and politically to mainland China. The popular representations of Hong Kong were basically inseparable from the perceptions of the colonial authorities. However, the colonial government's official support of the separateness of local cultural identity began to fade with the impending return of Hong Kong's sovereignty to the mainland. This change, as Turner observes, had less to do with acceding to China's disapproval than with justifying the British decision to invalidate the right of abode of the three million Hong Kong British passport holders. Turner comments that such a designed identity "that can be possessed can also be taken away, just as the Hong Kong people have been 'divided,' constituted as a 'community,' only to be dissolved, reconstituted and dissolved again with the ebb and flow of politics" (Turner 1995, 31).

However admirable his empirical studies of Hong Kong history, Turner's perception of the relationship between history, identity, and the body is based on a simple model of causality. The design, dissolution, and rearticulation of identity are for him always the result of a political cause. Determined by a political break, the subjectivization of individuals into "Hong Kong people" occurred, according to Turner, in the sixties, a period that demarcates a "before" and an "after": "Before the sixties, Hong Kong exhibited an ambivalent identity, like many displaced *huaqiao* (Chinese expatriate) communities and overseas Chinese. . . . A decade later it was evident that local life-style was displacing traditional cultural attachments as the basis of identity, to the point where, in the mid-eighties, the great majority of the population identified themselves as 'Hong Kong people,' not 'Chinese people'" (Turner 1995, 23–24).

Yet the clear historical cut in this analysis trims off the radical heterogeneity of the effect by tying it up neatly with the cause. Such an approach of mechanical determinism fails to acknowledge that the surface phenomenon itself could be more than the appearance of an underlying content. The body as a representation of Hong Kong identity is precisely not a transparent medium for straightforward historical explanations. The body should be thought of in its specific autonomy in relation to subject formation. The Chineseness of the new formation of the Hong Kong body under the design of the colonial power could never be totally contained or neatly separated. The ideological interpellation of "Hong Kong people" through the machine of colonial ideology has never fully succeeded. On the contrary, there is always a remainder or a leftover of traumatic, nonintegrated Chineseness sticking to its distinct subject position. Far from preventing the submission of the subject to the ideological command, the remainder of Chineseness found in Hong Kong culture provides the very condition of the subjectivization.

Nevertheless, if Turner's approach is too direct, missing that dimension of Hong Kong's Chinese subjectivity that resists historicization, I also do not concur with those film critics who read Hong Kong kung fu culture as pure visual and aural spectacle and bliss. Typical examples of this response are often found in nonacademic, popular writings like the following: "[I]n describing Hong Kong cinema . . . film-school polemics fail. There is no pointy-headed, white-wine-and-baked-brie philosophizing that adequately describes its 'scalding propulsion,' the force that blasts you out of your seat and rearranges your popcorn, because over-intellectualizing the film denies the primary purpose of moviegoing: entertainment. And Hong Kong movies are, simply, some of the most entertaining films on the planet" (Hammond and Wilkins 1996, 11). The popular reception of Hong Kong movies—especially of John Woo's films—in the West always celebrates their notorious staging of violence. Many Western critics writing for popular magazines eulogize the excessive violence in Hong Kong cinema as ballet choreography or as the orchestration of pulverized bodies. The question of how the violence relates to the semantic function, the narrative articulation, and the historical, cultural, and ethnic background is seldom raised.[5] For these critics, the spectacle of kung fu has no historical or ideological association. Rather, it performs the function of undoing all narrative and representational fixities in its simple excitement, vitality, and electricity.[6] In this view, the *jouissance* of bodily spectacle defies all meaning and designates the limit of historicization and ideological interpretation. The antihistorical understanding of Hong Kong muscles may succeed in substantializing the body as a new object of study, but it ignores the body's intimate connection with the political reality of the postcolonial city.[7]

In distinction from both of these approaches, I propose to understand the relationship between the cultural identity of Hong Kong and its male body image in relation to the construction of Chineseness, by focusing on the unrepresentable, corporeal aspect of subject formation—that is to say, the body part that eludes a direct ideological critique and that cannot easily be symbolized in any objective historical sense. On the one hand, this bodily aspect is not a simple reflection of the meaning of history; it is always already a part of the historical transformation of Hong Kong Chinese self-(re)construction. But, on the other hand, the unrepresentable corporeality can only be made sense of in its inherent connection with the historical changes of Hong Kong society. It is like a remainder of history that can be neither directly symbolized nor fixed by historical explanation; yet an ahistorical approach would entirely fail to grasp its existence.

The cultural identity of Hong Kong may not be readily articulated or presented in any positive terms, such as distinct values, customs, or lifestyle. On the contrary, that identity is something that might be determined by a series of negativities and contradictory properties. To put it differently, Hong Kong Chinese identity may be accessible to the local inhabitants only in a way that both Chinese nationalist discourse and a Western global perspective fail to grasp or fully understand. But, at the same time, that identity is so fragile and unstable that it is constantly altered, dissolved, endangered, and threatened by the mere presence of other subjects, including new immigrants, British colonial bureaucrats, and Chinese Communist officials. In what follows, I examine Hong Kong's body culture (focusing primarily on kung fu cinema and comics) in relation to its Chinese subject formation, and I argue that the subject posited is not always a definite, substantial entity but is rather a site of indeterminacy or an ambivalent space to be filled out with different historical contents.

The Hole Punched Out by Bruce Lee's Body

Without any doubt, Bruce Lee was the most popular kung fu star in the West, and he has become a token of Hong Kong action cinema. If the image of Bruce Lee facilitates and promotes the construction of Hong Kong identity, the role of agency it plays is far more complicated than that of being an ideal ego for identification. When Lee came back from the United States to Hong Kong to make his first kung fu movie, *The Big Boss* (1971), the Hong Kong Cantonese film industry was in a severe decline because of the competition from Mandarin films.[8] Lee's films were all originally dubbed and released in Mandarin.[9] He never spoke the common dialect (Cantonese) of the majority of Hong Kong people in any first release of his kung fu movies.[10] The characters Lee played were also more generically "Chinese" than distinguishably "Hong Konger." He was generally viewed as a Chinese hero who used the power and philosophy of kung fu to defeat the Westerner and the Japanese, arousing a Chinese nationalistic fantasy within the Hong Kong audience more strongly than any particular local identification.[11] If Lee's onscreen figure primarily advocated an encompassing Chinese national spirit, how then can we account for his contribution to the invention of a Hong Kong subjectivity?

It is possible to clarify Lee's unlikely role in the formation of Hong Kong subjectivity only by deviating from the traditional inquiry into the meanings of his filmic image.[12] What is at stake in understanding the connection between Bruce Lee and Hong Kong is neither a stable signifying link nor any positive causality, but rather the inherent inconsistency of Lee's signification, implying the inconsistency of Hong Kong subjectivity in the making of Chinese identity. What prevents Lee's image from falling entirely into the category of a "Chinese hero" is paradoxically the kind of Chineseness invoked in his films. The China portrayed in Lee's films is a remote space emptied of social and political reality, an imaginary and void China with which Hong Kong inhabitants and many other diasporic Chinese can associate. The nationalistic feeling stimulated by Lee's kung fu exercised its influence through this alienation and distance. As such, Hong Kong identity or the cultural identity of overseas Chinese could be said to have derived from an ambivalent emotional attachment to a fictional China. The ambiguity cloaking a fantasy object of identification—the fictive China—is further complicated by Lee's own background. His mother is Eurasian, and he was born in San Francisco; he married an American and was himself an American citizen. Before making the Mandarin films, he was already known to the people in Hong Kong through his appearance on the U.S. television series *The Green Hornet* (1966–67).[13]

Herein lies the impossibility of the linear determinism of Hong Kong identity through Lee's body. Consistency of identification derives from an inconsistency of the signification. If being the first Hong Kong movie star to become widely famous across the world qualifies Bruce Lee for a role in the constitution of transnational Chinese subjectivity, there is nonetheless little trace of Hong Kong local culture in his movies. His fame is as a foreign body, an inconsistency in the field of symbolic signification. But it is precisely because of this lack of localism that a Chinese as well as Hong Kong identification with Lee is possible. His alien body ("alien" both as a deficiently localized figure and as a superhuman screen image) gives new symbolic meaning to the community even though—or because—he is not an integral part of it. The icon that his body image provides for identification is not immanent but comes from afar; it does not belong to that symbolic order which it is made to uphold, and it even pierces a "hole" in the conventional signification of that identity. Suffice it to say that Lee's body is unable to offer a solid ground for locating a specific entity, be it "Hong Kong" or any particular Chinese community. However, this hole becomes the new symbolic center for identity construction. The invention of Hong Kong and Chinese subjectivity is structured around this hollow space punched out by Lee's muscular body. It is the exceptional or the alien part that helps constitute the whole.

To illustrate further this problem of causality, I want to focus on the famous gimmick used in Lee's movies: the shrieks and wails he emits to disturb his opponents in combat. The tactic of shrieking or sneering at the opponent has been interpreted as bespeaking a profound bliss in the self, a reinforcement of Lee's own subject position (Rayns 1980, 112). But as far as I can see, although Lee's mouth moves, the shrieks do not come from a particular source or subject.[14] The animal-like voice is all-pervasive and free-floating, unfixed to any definite visual object on the screen; it is not a noise caused or uttered by any individual subject. Disembodied, this animal voice, this sound from nowhere, seems to have a life of its own, even as it is, conversely, looking for a body to fill out. The chain of cause and effect is thus somewhat reversed here. The ecstatic and intoxicating sound associated with Lee as star suggests more of a loss of control than mastery by any speaking subject. This mythic voice is an object that cannot be mastered by the subject but is rather constitutive of that subject, acting precisely like an empty placeholder in the causal chain.

The Two Surfaces of Wong Yuk Long's Kung Fu Comics

Though different from Bruce Lee's impact on Hong Kong and transnational Chinese culture in the seventies, the connection between Wong Yuk Long's popular, violent comics[15]—(another form of image making through the sheer exhibition of bodies)—and Hong Kong local subjectivization in the same period is equally telling. While Bruce Lee's image presented a fantasy element for identification, his body was real. The bodies of Wong's heroic figures, created in the bloody, violent world of his comic books, are on the other hand entirely imaginary. In the early period of Wong's Little Rascals (1971), characters like Wong Siu Fu (Little Tiger Wong) and Shek Hark Lung (Black Dragon Shek) resemble the figures in Japanese cartoons who have disproportionately big eyes and long legs. Their opponents are always depicted like Westerners with crooked long noses and colored, fluffy hair. Every character, good or evil, has an exaggeratedly delineated muscular body (which undoubtedly can be cross-referenced to Bruce Lee's body) and is dressed up in then-fashionable seventies styles (like the image of Fei Jai). Defenders of law and order as well as aggressors scrambling for new turf, the little heroes of Wong's comics represent emerging local ideals. The spirit advocated is a collective one, marking a difference between Wong's comic violence and Lee's ultra-individual heroism. Wong's characters are gang members engaged in group fights, a depiction that was closer to the reality of his grassroots readers, who lived mostly in Hong Kong government housing estates.

But despite this bit of "realism," other local features are missing from the comic books. It is, interestingly, only the villains in Wong's work that give the readers a feel of localism. For example, their nicknames refer to different areas in Hong Kong: "The Fifteen Wolves of Wan Chai" or "Four Bulls from Ngau Tau Kwok." Wong's villains also interact more with the community than his heroes do, although the interactions are typically criminal, involving extortion and the like. But local places appear only as names in the comics; undefined in any detail, they are mere combat stages. With the chaotic appropriations of various cultures in the comics, the climax is typically a confrontation between the "good" Japanese-like heroes from nowhere and the "evil" Westerners or colonizers of the local areas. Furthermore, regional flavor disappears entirely when the setting moves to Japan in a later development of the story. (By this time, the comic book had been renamed *Dragon and Tiger Kids*.) Indeed, this erasure of local traces from Wong's work points to a transformation occurring within Hong Kong identity itself. If the identity evoked by Bruce Lee was built on an elusive nationalist feeling, such an antagonistic attitude toward foreigners is no longer a basis for subjectivity in Wong's comics.[16]

Thus, the significance of Wong's comics for Hong Kong "Chinese" cultural identity is not the same as that of Bruce Lee. This time the subjectivization is even more elusive because the locus of identification is no longer confined to the body found within the fictional world. Here, identification crosses the borderline separating the inside from the outside of the comics; that is to say, the attraction lies not merely in the body image of the comic-book heroes but also in the world of comic-book production, which is no less intriguing and violent than the cartoon story itself. Like his own comic creations, Wong Yuk Long is a legend in his own right, a legend he has constructed and overseen directly. For years, as a supplement to his weekly comics, Wong has published a column in which he answers his fan mail, narrativizes his publishing experience, and generally enlarges his ego. It is the story of Wong himself, as told by Wong. He has also described his comic books as autobiographical, even though he knows no kung fu, his body is not muscular, and he denies being a gang member. But the artist still asserts that, visually and thematically, his protagonist, Little Tiger Wong, is modeled on himself. As Chan Koon-Chung, who has interviewed Wong in the 1970s, says, "I have discovered in this interview that the appearance of this long experienced comic-book artist who is only twenty-seven years old rather looks like his character, Wong Siu Fu, in *Little Rascal*. They both have round faces, big heads and rough eyebrows. Wong Yuk Long himself explained, 'Also my hands are chubby, so are Wong Siu Fu's.' Then I understand that while there are so many people working in the comic field there are only two or three artists who can really excel—Wong's comic-book heroes are his alter-ego. He imagines himself to be his characters" (Chan Koon-Chung 2001, 186). A closer look at the development of Wong's comics may help us to better understand this relationship.

The story line of the *Little Rascals* period tells how the gang of Little Tiger Wong assists the innocent people of Hong Kong in their fight against evil gangs and crime organizations. Every fight they win expands their turf and sphere of protection. But in the period of *Dragon and Tiger Kids,* the moral principles of helping the poor and protecting the weak are rarely mentioned. The goal instead is to destroy the enemy with violent and spectacular kung fu. The world of the comics is thus reconstituted as an arena for the fighters whose sole aim is to destroy the opponent. The major opponent of Little Tiger Wong's gang is a powerful Japanese cult group that is organized like a huge multinational corporation. With the enlargement of the comic book and the introduction of more sophisticated techniques in printing and drawing, including the addition of color pages, glossy covers, and the integration of filming techniques,[17] the fight scenes in the later series became highly aestheticized. Simultaneously, and as previously mentioned, the plot was virtually eviscerated of any local social elements, the very concept of the local having been shifted from a ghettoized Hong Kong to the multinational arena. The enemy also underwent a major change; no longer local thugs, Wong's villainous gang, although Japanese (the traditional Chinese enemy) in name, resembles a global organization.

Unlike many kung fu films and comics of the time that used the Japanese as an opponent to assert their own pan-Chineseness, Wong's comics make use of anti-Japanese rhetoric as part of a globalization of the local. In a way,

Wong appropriates the empty body of Bruce Lee (namely, the form of a national hero fighting against Western and Japanese imperialists) and infuses it with a new idea of the local. This new local has a strong tendency to redefine itself as multinational rather than as ethnically and regionally bound. The development of the comic books' story has an interesting parallel with Wong Yuk Long's own ambitious project of empire building, a story he has chronicled in his personal column. Thanks to adventurous investing and management, Wong's company, Jademan Corporation (named for the English translation of "Yuk Long"), has dominated Hong Kong comics since the 1980s. Wong was the first comic-book artist who placed advertisements for his products on television and radio (in the early 1970s, a comic book sold for twenty cents while TV advertising cost several thousands of Hong Kong dollars). And when comics were attacked by moral leaders for their violent content and threatened with government bans, Wong toned down and appeased the detractors. Meanwhile, he hired the biggest talents to work for him, including those who once competed with him for market share. His empire developed new genres of comics, extended the scale of production, bought up publishing houses, undertook several short-lived daily newspaper ventures, adapted the comics into movies and television programs, and explored overseas markets. Under his empire, the comic industry began to promote its artists' drawing skills, elevating their products to the status of art rather than presenting them as senseless entertainment for teenagers and grassroots readers.[18]

The Jademan Corporation expanded quickly, attracting investment money and changing the public image of comics production, a profession that had previously been considered socially unrespectable. Through Wong's company, comic-book production underwent a drastic transformation, changing from a small-scale, family-like, low-tech business with slim profit margins to a major corporate enterprise under modern management. Thus, a parallel can be drawn between the story in Wong's comics and the story of Wong's comics. The dragon characters in Wong's comics are like the "Four Little Dragons" of Asia; they succeed and grow miraculously from modest and simple modes of production. Of course, the success story of Wong is not very different from that of many Hong Kong tycoons, such as Li Ka-shing. But Wong is a muscular Li Ka-shing, even though his body is of a sublime, phantasmic nature. Furthermore, the story of Wong's comics empire is not exactly a direct allegory of Hong Kong's economic success; Hong Kong is not necessarily the source of meaning within Wong's story. On the contrary, it is Wong's double story that (re)invents a Hong Kong identity. It tells a Hong

Kong story in a double key. The protagonist of this narrative makes his living by making body images as well as making his own body into an image.

In fact, the way that Wong's personal struggle is intermingled with the jungle world of his comics gives a sense of reality to the fictional construction of a local identity: his running of his empire is reputed to be no less vigorous than his comic-book heroes' use of their fists and kicks. For example, in the late 1980s, Jademan was in dispute over a new contract with its brightest star, Ma Wing Shing (whose comic book *Chinese Hero* topped the sales charts for years).[19] During the long negotiations, Ma was assaulted twice by unidentified armed men. The attacks finally convinced Ma to leave Jademan to establish his own company. Around the same time, Wong was indicted for false accounting and was later convicted and sentenced to prison for four years. The trading of Jademan shares was suspended, and the company suffered a big financial setback. Since his stint in jail, Wong has returned to his comics empire. His company, Jade Dynasty Publication Ltd., retains a major share in the comics market and remains one of the most established corporations in the industry (the sales of model weapons from his kung fu comic books always draw a long line of his fans and attract the most media attention at the annual Hong Kong book fair), despite the humble origins of the company and of Wong himself.[20] In the new millennium of information technology, Wong wants to reinforce his muscles in cyberspace. He established the Web site www.Kingcomics.com to promote locally created comics to every corner of the world over the Internet. Within half a year after the launching of his site, more than a hundred thousand comic lovers from Hong Kong, Macau, Taiwan, Malaysia, Singapore, England, and North America have registered as members. Since the Hong Kong comics industry has already taken up a major share in many Asian countries, the aim of the online comic is to challenge and crack open the strongest comics empire of Japan. In a way, the plot of Wong's comics thereby crosses over to the world of his kingdom expansion. It thus is no surprise that like the fascinating scenes in his comics, his own spectacular ups and downs exert a strong pull on the gaze of Hong Kong people and present a legendary story of a transnational Chinese capitalist.

The interpellating function of Wong's story is based on a synchronization or a coincidence of the interior and exterior of his comics world. Any approach that attends simply to one side can only be reductive, for the Hong Kong subject is constructed in the oscillation and curved movement of the two (in this case, the "imaginary" site of kung fu violence and the "real" site of Wong's empire building). Any direct allusion to either side will fail to do justice to the complexity of this identity construction. The muscular bodies of Wong's comic-book heroes are not simply the manifestation of the underlying essence of Wong Yuk Long's history. Nor are the two sides two opposite surfaces. More accurately, they form a model of twisted space, like a Moebius strip. Proceeding from one side and entering the violent comics world, suddenly we may discover that we are already on the other side, on the surface of the flesh-and-blood story of a transnational Hong Kong entrepreneur.

Wong's body projected onto the kung fu story does not form a clear mirror image. Rather, it distorts the familiar representation, confuses the idea of the local, and unfolds an ambivalent space for the new self in Hong Kong culture. The subject brought about in such a twisted topological structure is not a subject of unity or one with definitive meaning. It is a subject that is torn between the local and the multinational, between the imaginary world of violence and the violent business world. Wong's double story thus suggests the futility of the quest for a unified notion of Hong Kong identity; there is always something that will slip away from the grip of totalization and perturb the balance of identity structure. The twofold surfaces of Wong's empire-building trajectories displace the opposition between the depth of Chinese being or value prevailing across borders and the shallow façade of its sensible copies. He is never merely a "flexible" Hong Kong entrepreneur who makes personal gain and profit by appropriating Chineseness for his own good, such as selling skin-deep Chinese kung fu to overseas Chinese communities. His depth is always the surface of the comics world he has created. The interplay of Wong's two surfaces, which constitutes his Hong Kong position, is a heterogeneous effect of the Chinese symbolic order, but an effect that is irreducible to its cause.

As the examples of Bruce Lee and Wong Yuk Long's comics have shown, a direct historical interpretation fails to comprehend the complexity of subjectivization in Hong Kong because identity formation is never a simple transition from an individual to a subject, or a linear movement from a cause to an effect. Thus a search for a stable historical meaning to explain subject formation will always miss the point. The genesis of the subject is only a retroactive reconstruction. It is only when we have the outcome that we can understand the historical genesis and gain access to the historical conditions of the emergence of the subject. There is always a fantasy element in subjectivization, in how a person falls into (or identifies with) a certain subject position. It is never enough to denounce the subjectivization as false or nonhistorical. Rather, we have to grasp the senselessness or the irrationality of this subject formation in order to see its multidimensional "truth."

The Outtakes of Jackie Chan

Bruce Lee's body reveals the hollowness of transnational Chinese identity whereas the body image of Wong Yuk Long's comics, inside and out, points to the impossibility of a unified subject. What does the image of Jackie Chan, that well-known muscle man, tell us about the mechanism of Hong Kong's Chinese identity construction? Over the last two decades, Hong Kong has changed from a local community to an international metropolis. Although Hong Kong culture may not accurately be described as a national culture, its colonial history and its need for a specific identity in the face of the 1997 handover to China do not allow Hong Kong to let go of its particular local elements. The muscular image of Jackie Chan developed over the years by Golden Harvest, a Hong Kong–based multinational film production company, also reveals the ambiguity of being both local and international at once. As a result of this position, Chan is never like a conventional kung fu movie star since he occupies both a local and a transnational space simultaneously. Also, he is more like a comic-book hero become real, occupying the roles of hero and comedian simultaneously. Generally seen as the successor of Bruce Lee, Chan tells an American reporter in an interview: "'How can I get rid of the Bruce Lee shadow and be Jackie Chan? Then I look at Bruce Lee all the film. O.K. When Bruce Lee kick high, I kick low. When Bruce Lee punch, he is the superhero; when I punch, ahh!'—he shakes his hand. 'It *hurts*'" (Dannen 1995, 33). This is how the reporter tries to capture Chan's funny tone as well as the flaws in his English. Chan does not mind exposing his weakness to the public, which he does with good humor.[21]

Several years ago, watching David Letterman's *Late Show* on CBS, I was surprised to find that Jackie Chan was the show's second guest, there to push his new release, *Rumble in the Bronx* (1995). Asian faces, especially those directly from Asia, are rarely shown on U.S. television. And at the time, Jackie Chan had not yet achieved widespread popularity in the United States. I happened to be teaching a course on Hong Kong popular culture at an American university, and my students were excited about Jackie Chan's action movies. I can't remember exactly how I felt when I saw Chan on Letterman's show, but I might have been a little bit nervous. I did not really want to admit that I was concerned about Jackie Chan, or about his popularity in the United States, or about what he said on the show, partly because we come from the same place, but also because, in addition to the news footage of Hong Kong's 1997 handover to China, Chan was the only popular Hong Kong subject consistently covered by the American media—(Chan also appeared on Jay Leno's *The Tonight Show, Entertainment Tonight, The MTV Movie Awards,* and *The Academy Awards* around that time). But I was eager to have my image "correctly" represented by a Hong Kong action hero, especially since I was living in the States at the time. I would prefer to believe that I was concerned because I wanted to see my teaching materials transcend the restricted boundaries of academic area studies and become a part of everyday life. Perhaps I fantasized that Chan's celebrity would elevate Hong Kong from its location in a particular field to a universal realm, moving from the ghetto of Chinatown to the blockbuster chart of the first-run theater in Hollywood (such dreams did come true for Jackie Chan and a number of Hong Kong filmmakers and stars).

What fascinated the audience of the *Late Show* that night were the clips of acrobatic action scenes and the incredible physical stunts from Chan's movies. Chan showed off his athleticism live by somersaulting to his chair and kicking bottles from a table. He teasingly told Letterman that his American fans had asked him to come to kick the host's butt. Letterman responded by exchanging his jacket with Chan's and trying it on to demonstrate that he was bigger than the Asian star. For a while, the show was full of jokes about bodies. I felt embarrassed afterwards.

In front of the American audience, Chan played the role of silent film comedian or cartoon character. I worried about his representativeness for Hong Kong people. Would the American audience see the Hong Kong subject as a muscular, though slight, man who only knows how to use his body to amaze them and make them laugh? My worry was not ungrounded. The transnational media considers Chan more as a representative of the Chinese in general than simply a particular Hong Kong subject. The issue of Chan's being the Chinese national representative was brought up by the Chinese media in response to the comic pairing of the "short" Jackie Chan and the tall ex-NBA player Kareem Abdul Jabbar, who had been invited to present the Oscar for the short film at the 1996 Academy Awards ceremony. To infuriate the Chinese audience further, Abdul Jabbar raised the announcement letter high up in the air to force Chan to leap to catch it. What was treated as "good humor" for the American audience was perceived by Chinese spectators as a humiliating act of "dwarfing the Chinese" (qtd. in Shih 2000, 99).

But Chinese audiences are not aware that it is actually Chan who is in the driver's seat to appropriate black culture in his Hollywood career, such as in the films *Rush Hour* (1998) and *Rush Hour 2* (2001). Gina Marchetti has nicely elaborated how the elements of Africa, the African diaspora, and African

American culture are already in use in Chan's Hong Kong films such as *Rumble in the Bronx* (1995), *Mr. Nice Guy* (1997), and *Who Am I?* (1998). She points out that "the use of 'blackness' as a signifier in each of these vehicles enhances their marketability across various audiences, including white, middle-class, suburbanites who can place Chan within the defined parameters of 'multicultural' spectacle found in the Hollywood action genre" (Marchetti 2001, 157). This link between the Chinese and the black communities through Hong Kong kung fu movies could of course be traced back to Bruce Lee, who became one of the first martial arts masters to train non-Asians and blacks. In fact, Kareem Abdul Jabbar was Lee's student and appeared with him in *Game of Death* (1978). For quite some time Bruce Lee has been considered as a cultural symbol to give oppressed black people a sense of personal worth for collective social and political struggle, notwithstanding that a yellow-and-black alliance has been converted into an "opportunistic combination of ethnic niche markets" (Prashad 2003, 78; 2001, 146). The pairing of Abdul Jabbar and Chan might convey multiple meanings though Chinese viewers saw it only as a sign of humiliation. Chan's five-foot-nine height and his muscular body would by no means be seen as small within the Chinese community. The body of the Hong Kong Chinese star apparently serves as a cultural and ideological terrain of negotiation for different values and interests seeking to shape their own senses of identity.

Beyond his own body, Jackie Chan seems to possess a sublime body that incarnates the so-called pan-Chinese soul to cover up the lack in the Chinese symbolic order. The movies Chan makes are more like action-packed comedies than traditional kung fu films. It is Buster Keaton, not Bruce Lee, who is Chan's role model. In every new movie Chan made in Hong Kong, his ambition was to outdo the most daring stunts of the previous one. In Bruce Lee's films, especially in *The Way of the Dragon* (1972), combat is a serious, intense duel between two equally powerful kung fu masters who have to perform a series of rituals before and during the fight: taking off their outer clothes, flashing their muscles to warm up, pausing when an opponent falls down, and so on. By comparison, Chan's combat is a street fight. There are no rules, and it can happen in any place at any time. He does not even have the time to take off his street clothes and warm up. And though he is the star, the action sequences of Chan's films are not just solo performances; they heavily depend on collective work and coordination. Chan's movies are thus multiple loops of actions and stunts. The narratives are weak and the messages ambivalent: spectacular performance, not heroism, occupies the center stage. Indeed, a signature feature of Chan's films is the homage they pay, tongue in cheek, to stunt-driven action.

Chan's movies began a tradition of showing the closing credits against outtakes of stunt mishaps.[22] No Jackie Chan fan will leave during the closing credits of his films. Significantly, it is precisely the outtakes of the flubbed stunts that create the myth of Jackie Chan. Portrayed as a comedian, a common man in the films, Chan becomes a superhero in his outtakes. The clips do not really debunk the illusionism of the movies. Instead, they reveal to the audience how hard Chan works. Real flesh-and-bone is imperiled before your eyes; these are not the workings of blue screens and computer technologies. Chan may be only an ordinary human being who makes mistakes and gets injured, but precisely because he does not have an invincible body the stunts produce a fantasy effect. As with other films, viewer identification is with superhuman accomplishment. Yet revealing the failed stunts explicitly acknowledges the existence of a subject willing to believe. The credibility of the film is solidified by this imaginary subject. Because of the presence of this believing subject, the outlandish stunts are given a reality status, even though they are just made for a movie. Through this combination of "real" and "imaginary" elements, the films confirm the "truth" of the spectacular stunts, and the audience is posited to identify with the "subject supposed to believe," that is, someone who believes for us, even as its limits are exposed.

At first, there may seem to be no point in watching Chan fall fifty feet from a clock tower and hit the ground with his head (*Project A*), or jump off a railing in a department store and crash through several glass ceilings (*Police Story*), or hang dangling from a flying helicopter over the city of Kuala Lumpur and bump into a billboard on a skyscraper (*Super Cop*), or skip across a snowy mountain with only a sweatshirt to keep himself warm (*First Strike*). Clearly, his stunts are imbued with masochistic intensity for comic effects. However, these spectacular abuses of the human body perform another function as well. In the revelation of the outtakes, they become part of the structure of the entire "reality." In other words, it is the fantasy element (the subject supposed to believe) that gives consistency to the "reality" of Chan's body image. The international stardom of Chan emanates from the support of this fantasy identification with "unreal realism": the outtakes' revelation of the enactment of the impossible.

In *Armour of God* (1986), directed by Chan himself, he plays an Indiana Jones type of character named Asian Hawk. He is a world-famous adventurer who is good at stealing ancient treasures. Some satanic monks abduct his ex-girlfriend in order to force Asian Hawk to give them the "Armour of God" (an antique five-piece set). The Armour of God acts as the "MacGuffin" of the movie.[23] The MacGuffin is an essential but ultimately irrelevant object, around which all of the action turns. The object sets off the story and the chase, but it has no significance in itself at all. Unlike the treasures of the Indiana Jones movies, the Armour of God has no magical power or special contents. It is not even mentioned at the end of the film. It is just a pure medium or empty form that instigates action and incites relationships among the characters. In many ways, the mission of Asian Hawk is itself like a MacGuffin. It has no purpose but to affirm the unconditional desire for action. The hero is portrayed simply to satisfy Asian audiences' fantasies about the ideal image of the Asian hero before the Western gaze of highly developed societies: he is well respected by Westerners and drives a high-tech sports car manufactured by Mitsubishi (which is also the film's sponsor), chasing other cars off-road in a European city. From the African tribal group from whom he steals the Armour of God to the evil European monks whom he battles, Asian Hawk denounces and sneers at all beliefs and rituals. He presents himself as a pure action hero supported by unlimited resources but not motivated by any inner conviction. The image of Asian Hawk offers no ideological cause with which an audience might identify. As an icon and sublime figure, he is neither global nor particularly local—or perhaps this is what Hong Kong's transnational Chineseness means: an eye-catching face and spectacular action with no inner substance. However, the pure action itself is the very thing that calls for identification; it does not signify but only indicates a space that gives a sense of reality to the impossible, nonexistent "Chinese" subjectivity of Hong Kong.

The Virtualization of Chinese Bodies

In the transition from the 1980s to the 1990s, the representation of Hong Kong kung fu culture began to lose its physical dimension. For instance, as Ackbar Abbas argues, the real heroes in Tsui Hark's martial arts movies are not the kung fu stars but the special effects (Abbas 1996, 298). The bodies stand as an alibi for a "culture of disappearance."[24] Abbas further explains that the problem new Hong Kong cinema faces is how to represent a subject that is always on the verge of disappearing. He goes so far as to suggest that the local, not only in Hong Kong cinema but also in other cultural forms, is "already a translation" (Abbas 1997, 12) that is always dislocated from a specific place or a particular race. The local is experienced as a field of instability, discontinuity, and elusiveness that transforms any available models of culture. Abbas's comments about the local give rise to a kind of theoretical playfulness that deconstructs the nationalized grounding of the local as something exclusive, essentialized, and closed. This elusive, translated local can come to presence, paradoxically, only when it is going to become extinct with the possible disappearance of its former lifestyle after the 1997 handover. This may explain why Abbas believes that the history of the Hong Kong people seeking a local identity is relatively short. It began only in the early 1980s when the Sino-British Joint Declaration announced the return of Hong Kong to China, causing anxiety about the possibility of such a social and cultural space's disappearing. That worry has led people to look at Hong Kong "in all its complexity and contradiction for the first time, an instance, as Benjamin would have said, of love at last sight" (Abbas 1997, 23).

My notion of disappearance, however, has a different focus. As I have explained above, the sublimation or the disappearing of the material bodies is a necessary condition for understanding the history of Chinese identity constitution in Hong Kong. I would also suggest that Hong Kong's Chinese identity is constructed historically at the expense of female bodies. Even though the positive status of masculine bodies in popular cultural forms has become weakened, it does not follow that women can therefore take on a more progressive role in representation. It is true that the muscle men in Tsui Hark's films—(such as Yuen Biao and Sammo Hung in *Zu: Warriors from the Magic Mountain* [1982], or Jet Li, who is originally from mainland China and was made a star by Hong Kong cinema, in *Once Upon a Time in China* [1991], or all the characters in *Legend of Zu* [2001])—are probably pretexts for intense special effects, though Tsui has to rely on the skills of these martial arts masters to do his postproduction works. Interest in kung fu technique and human athletic ability do not survive his obsession with creating a political allegory for modern Chinese and Hong Kong history. Not bodies but excessive technical prowess, over-rapid editing, breakneck-speed narration, and video-game-like cinematography are what convey the impossible representation of Hong Kong culture in its chaotic transitional moment. Even though the phobia of losing one's virility and literally becoming a woman, as is evident in *Swordsman II* (1992), produced by Tsui, might suggest a materiality of bodies,[25] in Tsui's films the Hong Kong body is actually no longer confined to any individual or sex. It encompasses a larger social body characterized by restlessness, high-speed movement, the force of dislocation, and instantaneous comings and goings. The only stabilizing force acting on the Chinese body made in Tsui's films is the constant play of flux or incessant motion.[26]

A different and subversive manipulation of the figure of the kung fu master is seen in Wong Kar-wai's two action films, *Ashes of Time* (1994) and *Fallen Angels* (1995). Wong's ultrastylistic productions not only redefine the kung fu and action genres (*Ashes of Time* is a historical martial arts genre freely adapted from the popular swordsman fiction by Louis Cha [Jin Yong], and *Fallen Angels* is a hit-man story with John Woo–inspired violence), but they also reshape the heroes' bodies by filling them with a desire for love. The heroes and the heroines in both movies fall in love with the ones they cannot have; like their opponents, all their love objects are elusive and unattainable. In *Ashes of Time,* the hero, Ouyang Feng, is deeply in love with a woman, but because of his pride he does not express his love to her. The woman, who has the same affection for Ouyang, is angered by his pride and marries his brother. Ouyang exiles himself to the desert to hurt the woman, who still cares for him, and each year she sends someone to spy on him there. In *Fallen Angels,* the female assistant of the hit man falls desperately for the hero, even though circumstances forbid their rapprochement. As these descriptions suggest, the sexual drive in these two movies corresponds with the drive for combat, but love does not lead to physical intimacy or consummation. Precisely because of the elusiveness and impossibility of the objects of love, desire can never be extinguished and action is futile. While the traditional action genre stresses the hero's masculinity and physical invulnerability, Wong's movies empty out the bodies and fill them with excessive emotional drives.

The bodies are haunted and persecuted by the pure desire for the impossible; the desire that dominates them presents itself as an unconditional imperative. Desire in its pure form has no object, yet it is only via this empty form that desire constructs and affects the subject. The spectacular imagery of the wild desert and the wide-angle shots of the Wan Chai streets supply somber ambiance for the futile maneuvers of these subjects and objects. But since pure desire has no goal outside of itself, movement will bring about nothing but the failure of action. Kung fu, violence, or love, as Wong Kar-wai's films show, cannot achieve anything; they only affirm action's invalidity and impotency. In both films, the action heroes have lost whatever it was that might have defined their beings. Their angst bespeaks the social atmosphere of Hong Kong near the end of time and its ambivalence to Chineseness. A history of the Chinese body manufactured in Hong Kong popular culture is a history of its gradual virtualization. No matter how show-offish the Hong Kong muscles are, they are only a fetish marking a sublime absence and giving positive existence to a modern Chinese subjectivity. Tsui Hark actually is not a pioneer in using special effects in Hong Kong film production. The early martial arts movies of the 1950s had already appropriated some relatively primitive special effects to highlight the supernatural power and kung fu skills of their protagonists. After Bruce Lee's real kung fu combats and Jackie Chan's death-defying stunts, Hong Kong muscles are becoming more dependent on computer effects than on their natural given. The new popular action-movie stars, such as Andy Lau, Aaron Kwok, and Ekin Cheng, are no martial arts masters. They are like every other Hollywood star who desperately depends on stuntmen when shooting dangerous action sequences. The myth of powerful Chinese kung fu skills perpetuated by Bruce Lee, Jackie Chan, Sammo Hung, and the like has basically vanished in the new generation of Hong Kong action stars. Jackie Chan can no longer proudly say that even Steven Spielberg and George Lucas cannot make the action films that he does.[27] The edge of the Hong Kong action film disappears with the dwindling of its traditional markets and the Hollywood absorption of many of its martial arts talents. The return of Hong Kong cinema to the essence of Chinese martial arts now passes through the process of digitization.

The most successfully digitized kung fu movie made in Hong Kong to date is *The Stormriders* (1998), which is adapted from Ma Wing Shing's martial arts comics.[28] Having imitated the Hollywood film (with what he described as the Chinese version of *Star Wars*) and mimicked Hollywood marketing strategies, the director, Andrew Lau, still insisted that *The Stormriders* has a strong Chinese flavor. It is a high-budget, homegrown endeavor to combine "Hollywoodization" and traditional Chinese national characterization in a post-1997 production. But the Chineseness it offers is "the Versace look with some of the costume" (Ho 1999, 44), since the style of the comics itself is already hybrid, mixing Japanese popular *manga* (comic book or graphic novel) and extravagant Chinese *wu xia* (martial arts) fiction. The "masculine" subject constructed by the computer-generated effects of the film is a pure fictional void from which all substantial content of Chinese kung fu is taken away. Like Andrew Lau's other popular film series, *Young and Dangerous,* which is also based on local comics, *The Stormriders* is often injected with animated and hand-drawn comic scenes to highlight its fantasy nature. Real kung fu combat has been displaced by the supernatural videogame-like battle.

Though *The Stormriders* comic series has been running for a decade and the movie adaptation was a post-1997 production, it shares its theme of being orphaned and its implication of ambivalent attitudes toward different father figures with many local, allegorical films and reminds its audience of the Hong Kong identity issue triggered by the 1997 handover. The two young heroes are each orphaned as children and then adopted by the merciless and ambitious Lord Conquer (played by the veteran Japanese action star Sonny Chiba, who may symbolize the tribute Hong Kong comics pay to their Japanese origin). It is in fact Conquer who has killed the boys' fathers, and he wants to raise the youths as his own sons because, according to the words of a prophet, Conquer's success at dominating the world and even his own destruction hinges on the two young men. Not surprisingly, the movie ends with the collaboration of the two young heroes, who seek to eliminate the evil Conquer in a death duel laden with special effects.

What is revealing about this post-1997 production is its orientation toward Chineseness in its digitized reconstruction of masculinity. The film could be considered both as a return to tradition and as a new step forward for the local film industry. It returns to the costume swordplay epic and thereby may allude to the classic period of Cantonese cinema and to a genre that was temporarily revived by Tsui Hark and Ching Siu-tung but quickly ran out of steam by the mid-1990s. On the other hand, it also explores the production style of Hollywood, by borrowing heavily from the Hollywood-dominated area of computer-generated imageries and by executing strategic marketing, from preproduction promotion, to computer games, to all sorts of merchandise tie-ins. However, the intense reliance on Spielberg-like special effects has almost completely dislodged the glittery tradition of Chinese acrobatics and Beijing opera skills that Hong Kong action cinema has derived, refined, and further developed into a flashy performance spectacle. Hence, while the film still holds on to Chinese martial arts, it empties out all the "substance" of its Chineseness. Perhaps it is a paradoxical kind of Chineseness that has to annihilate its own being in order to make it appear and come to light again.

Such a move seen in this post-1997 film actually parallels the tactics used by the Hong Kong Special Administrative Region government, which has claimed a patriotic stance toward Chineseness (as defined by the central government of the mainland) by means of its growing conservative political policy, and which has simultaneously (re-)privileged English language and all kinds of internationalizing trends in order to cater to the economic exigencies of the local and the global. Thus, though the Chinese image appears to stand strong in postcolonial Hong Kong, its phantom status or virtual existence is also unprecedented. If Hong Kong cinema has been exporting Chineseness through the male body of its action cinema and manufacturing a public space and a visible point of identification for the Chinese diaspora, ironically, it is now the comic book's heroic figures, largely generated by computer technology, that embody the macho stereotype for transnational Chinese representation. This tradition is almost monopolized by men, whereas the female body remains at the margins of this scene or merely functions as a national symbol. Undeniably, there is never any lack of action heroines in Hong Kong cinema. The pervasive presence of fighting women such as Michelle Yeoh, Cynthia Khan, Brigitte Lin, Maggie Cheung, and others, in Hong Kong kung fu movies does destabilize the sexual hierarchy in cinematic representation. Though these women warriors might have exerted an infectious influence in Western popular culture, most female action figures in Hong Kong cinema are still confined to playing masculine or masculinized roles, raising very little feminist awareness.[29]

While the cyber subject in *The Stormriders* paradoxically embodies the new void of Chineseness in Hong Kong film, its virtual and nonsubstantial existence is also intentionally created to broaden its appeal for the world market. If Hong Kong cultural products have been good at faking and fabricating Chineseness, and ultimately evacuating its substance almost to the breaking point, they could go further and play with different racial masks. In the new century of cyber technology, when films such as *Final Fantasy: The Spirits Within* (2001) can be created entirely by computer and when dramas no longer need real actors, Chineseness could be definitely embodied by non-Chinese vehicles. By such vehicles, I do not refer to the creation of virtual performers, computer-generated humans, or any resurrected "synthespian" replicas of deceased celebrities through the digital manipulation of stock footage (Rickitt 2000).

I would like to call readers' attention to the phenomenon of three Hong Kong directors, John Woo, Ringo Lam, and Tsui Hark, having marked their Hollywood debuts with action films starring the "muscle from Brussels," Jean-Claude Van Damme, in *Hard Target* (1993), *Maximum Risk* (1996), and *Double Team* (1997). As Tsui has ironically observed, "It's become a sort of ritual for [Hong Kong] people to work with Van Damme to get into Hollywood" (Major 1997). The ritual may even turn into a convention, since Tsui and Lam's second Hollywood movies, *Knock-off* (1998) and *The Replicant* (2001), respectively, continue to use Van Damme as the leading man. Instead of using and advertising their ethnicity as a key to success in the West, they make use of white masks to cover up their minority faces. On the other hand, that Hollywood hires Asian talent in front of and behind the camera in order to penetrate the Asian market is paralleled by other American corporations' hiring of Chinese talent to expand their market in China. For example, in 2002, the seven-foot six-inch Yao Ming from Shanghai signed a contract with the Houston Rockets as the number-one pick in the premier National Basketball Association (NBA) draft. He established himself in the NBA quickly and soon became a source of national pride for millions of Chinese. The NBA also took the chance to double the number of its games broadcast in China. Yao is not China's first player in the NBA. Back in 2001, the seven-foot Chinese basketball player Wang Zhizhi, nicknamed the "Great Wall of China," joined the NBA by signing a deal with the Dallas Mavericks. Similar nationalist sentiments about Wang's move to the NBA were played up on both sides. The Chinese authorities attempted to use Wang as a bit of basketball diplomacy in order to land the 2008 Summer Olympics for Beijing. For the NBA, drafting a Chinese player to the league might obviously help expand its market in Asia, since it already has signed a television deal in China to broadcast NBA action to over 150 million people. The Mavericks' assistant coach Donnie Nelson also boosted the nationalist ideology: "This is more than just a basketball player going to the U.S. Wang Zhizhi is synonymous with and represents the spirit of China" (Herskovitz 2001).

Yet, in the case of Hong Kong talent in Hollywood, this is not necessarily a global strategy that goes beyond any particular identity politics, a subversive act of a minority who performs in whiteface, or a "reactionary co-optation into a dreamworld of postethnicity" (Ma Sheng-mei 2000, 148).[30] I would argue instead that the use of a white male body as a vehicle for Hong Kong directors to launch into Hollywood probably designates the point of breakdown for the Chinese male body, or its self-referential negativity. Although many Chinese critics love to look for traces of Chineseness in these Hollywood films of Hong Kong directors, the imagination is here strained to its utmost and, I would say, the failure of the search appears at its purest. Hollywood films with an entirely white cast but made by Chinese directors from Hong Kong are just like any other Hollywood films. Perhaps the white body in these Hollywood–Hong Kong films appears as a sublime object that, in the field of representation, offers a negative view of the dimension of what is unrepresentable about Chineseness. The films' very inability to represent Chineseness adequately is inscribed in the films themselves. Paradoxically, this is a "successful" representation by means of failure. The positive body of Chinese identity created by Hong Kong is nothing but an embodiment of its pure negativity. The radical otherness of the white male muscular body in these Hollywood–Hong Kong films may reveal a significant point about the logic of the representation of transnational Chinese muscles through the agency of Hong Kong popular culture.

Hong Kong is always charged with playing double agency for China and the West. An ethnic Chinese double agent from Hong Kong could of course assume a white face to please the white audiences if he has been good at appropriating national characteristics to entice his Chinese patrons. Hillel Schwartz in *The Culture of the Copy* discusses those who take on the role of double agency, writing of "blacks passing as whites, Jews as Christians, gays as straights, women as men, colonial subjects as their colonial ruler." He states further that "with these impersonations, people take on malign second bodies in order to escape hurtful demands upon the native body" (Schwartz 1996, 77–78). As I have said earlier in this chapter, the native body of Hong Kong is problematic. It starts from a second body or an empty carcass with which to incarnate changing contents in various contexts, generating copies of copies with a hint of faking the origin.

4

Transnationalization of the Local in a Circular Structure

THE CONCEPT OF transnationality offers a new way of studying the social and cultural conditions of Hong Kong cinema in the 1990s and poses a daunting challenge for rethinking the concept of the local. Hong Kong, once the second-largest source of film exports in the world (Leung and Chan 1997, 143), has been undergoing an unprecedented process of decolonization and at the same time is forming a newly unified national identity under the regime of Communist China in the name of "one country, two systems." Although it would be expected that films produced in Hong Kong would be harnessed with a more distinctive national image after 1997, this has not turned out to be the case. It is true that, since the early 1980s, Hong Kong cinema has been infiltrating the mainland by coproducing with Chinese studios and by importing films (and also through video piracy).[1] Although this kind of cooperation and interaction does not necessarily lead to a stronger sense of unity within the cultural and cinematic productions of the two Chinese communities, it does reveal a freer flow and more pervasive penetration of transnational capital in the mainland market. Hong Kong films made during the transitional period and even the post-1997 productions are actually becoming more transnationalized than nationalized, offering a provocative reconception of what we usually mean by "local" and inadvertently subverting the concept of the nation.

In the past, the Hong Kong film industry had much closer ties with Taiwan than with the mainland, not only in terms of capital investment and market distribution, but also in the areas of exchange of talent, story materials, and even legal status.[2] Many Hong Kong productions have been directly financed by Taiwanese capital ever since Hong Kong commercial films began to dominate Taiwan's film market in the early 1980s and Taiwanese businessmen found it more profitable to invest in Hong Kong films. In the eighties, Hong Kong also served as a middleman for Taiwanese investment in the mainland film industry because the Nationalist government in Taiwan strictly regulated the screening of films shot in China. In the 1990s some Taiwanese companies even began moving their main offices to Hong Kong in order to facilitate their transnational investments both in Hong Kong and on the mainland.[3] Some Chinese films made by the fifth-generation directors of the mainland, such as Zhang Yimou's *Raise the Red Lantern* (1990) and *To Live* (1995) and Chen Kaige's *Farewell My Concubine* (1995) and *Temptress Moon* (1996), were financed by Taiwanese companies registered in Hong Kong.

The direct financing of Hong Kong movies enables Taiwanese investors to dictate casting and genre and to make other production decisions. Taiwanese investors had a strong voice in the logistics of Hong Kong productions for a while, but it is arguable whether Taiwanese capital is really capable of steering the development of the Hong Kong film industry. Meanwhile, Hollywood has been importing a number of Hong Kong directors and stars to shoot action films and comedies. Japan also occasionally has hired Hong Kong directors, such as Lee Chi-Ngai for *Sleepless Town* (1998), and cast some Hong Kong stars in their movies and TV productions, such as Andy Hui in Shunji Iwai's *Swallowtail Butterfly* (1996), Michelle Reis in Takashi Miike's *The City of Lost Souls* (2000), Kelly Chan in Isamu Nakae's *Between Calm and Passion* (2001), Karen Sun in *Ichi the Killer* (2002), and Kelly Chan and Faye Wong in some Japanese TV dramas. Wong Kar-wai has signed a contract with a leading Korean television station to produce a 100-episode drama series.

At the same time, Hong Kong film distributors have increasingly introduced other Asian films to the local audience. The popular ones include the Thai films *The Iron Ladies* and *Ong Bak;* South Korea's *My Sassy Girl, Christmas in August,* and *Shiri;* and many sequels or imitations of the Japanese horror film *The Ring.* Hong Kong production companies have also collaborated often with other Asian countries like Japan, South Korea, Singapore, and Thailand. Casting Japanese actors or actresses has even become chic in many local films; examples include the casting of Sonny Chiba in *The Stormriders,* Toru Nakamura in Jingle Ma's *Tokyo Raiders* (2000), Norika Fujiwara in Stanley Tong's *China Strike Force* (2000), Tokako Tokiwa in Daniel Lee Yan-Gong's *Moonlight Express* (1999) and *A Fighter's Blues* (2000), Takao Osawa and Kaori Momoin in Stanley Kwan's *The Island Tales* (2000), Junna Risa in Jacob Cheung Chi-leung's *Midnight Fly* (2001), Takashi Sorimachi in Johnnie

To Kei-Fung's *Fulltime Killer* (2001), and Takuya Kimaru in Wong Kar-wai's *2046*. Biracial actors such as the half-Chinese half-American Michael Wong and the half-Chinese half-Japanese Takeshi Kaneshiro, and those Chinese "new species" (*xin renlei*) who have been brought up in North America and speak English much better than Chinese, such as Edison Chen, Maggie Q, Daniel Wu, and Christy Chung, are getting more popular on the local screen. Because of the diversified cultural elements added to the productions, the dialogues of these local films are no longer delivered simply in Cantonese, Mandarin, or any other Chinese dialect but also in English, Japanese, Thai, and other foreign languages. Yet, the cross-cultural breeding of Hong Kong cinema comes at a time when the local industry is suffering a severe decline. Even though some Hong Kong filmmakers become successful in Hollywood and the film industry is oriented to a kind of trans-Asianization, Hong Kong cinema is actually losing its competitive edge to Hollywood productions in its Asian markets. It is precisely this crisis that opens up new opportunities for the transnationalization of local film production.

The Local Constituted in the Transnational

Peter Chan, who has already made his first American feature, *The Love Letter* (1999), for Steven Spielberg's company, believes that Hong Kong "could take the lead in Asia to organize other industries such as Japan, Taiwan, Korea, etc., to produce an 'Asian cinema.' The trend is towards non-local development, just like in Europe. We could produce a unique Asian system. At present, it is difficult to distinguish a European picture and make out whether it is French or Italian. A European feature can utilize French actors, Italian directors, Polish cinematographers. Why can't we do the same?" (S. Cheung 2000, 137).[4] Chan founded Applause Pictures in 2000 in order to produce pan-Asian films, as he believes Hong Kong could serve as a bridge for the Asian mentality versus the Western one. The company has already released some Hong Kong–Thai collaborations, such as Nonzee Nimibutr's *Jan Dara* (2001), the Pang brothers' *The Eye* (2002), and a Hong Kong–Thai–Korean product, *Three* (2002). However, the reason why Hong Kong cinema may not exactly follow the European model is that no matter how many Asian crew and cast members are used, the film remains a Hong Kong one rather than an Asian one. What happens is more of an appropriation or assimilation according to the logic of flexible accumulation rather than a real cooperation between equals.[5] Indeed, the concept of a single "Asia" is nothing but a creation of the colonial West. Reappropriation of such a concept in Hong Kong cinema could not be immune to its inherent ideological content.

The word "Asian" is generally used in Hong Kong to refer only to East Asians, those from China, Japan, and South Korea. People from elsewhere in Asia, such as the brown people from the Indian Subcontinent and Southeast Asia, are often ignored or excluded when the media identify an "Asian" organization. Some of these "Asian" individuals even turn out to be exclusively Chinese. Critics point out that a hierarchy of Asians, divided according to the degree of lightness in skin complexion and according to economic strength, can easily be seen in some Hong Kong movies. For instance, in the self-acclaimed "Asian movie" *Fulltime Killer,* the two protagonists are "white Asians" of Chinese and Japanese ethnicities, while their victims are all "black Asians" from Malaysia, Thailand, or Pakistan. It is not surprising that when the SAR government proclaims Hong Kong to be "Asia's world city," it uses the very traditional Chinese cultural symbol of a flying dragon as its official logo. Hence, the irony is that the further the postcolonial city wants to be Asianized and transnationalized, the more it appears nationalized.

The call for Asianization in Hong Kong cinema is apparently more economically oriented than culturally oriented.[6] The transnational circulation of Hong Kong films has already been influential among Asian countries. Bhaskar Sarkar, an Indian film scholar, writes that Hong Kong, through the wide dissemination of its cinema, has become the "emergent transnational imaginary" for Asia. He says, "For many Asians, upward mobility is coterminous with a one-way ticket to Hong Kong. Deepa Mehta's film *Fire* (1997), an Indo-Canadian coproduction, dramatizes this tendency in the figure of a video-store owner from Delhi who loves martial arts films, has a Chinese girlfriend, and dreams of migrating to Hong Kong" (Sarkar 2001, 159). In Japan, the interest in Hong Kong films and stars is not motivated merely by hunting for novelty and for trendy cosmopolitan things, but also by a nostalgic yearning for a different Asian modernity. As Koichi Iwabuchi observes of this Japanese fandom of Hong Kong popular culture, "A sense of coevalness perceived by Japanese fans toward Hong Kong finds its expression in the critical reflection on Japanese cultural modernity but even more urgently accompanied efforts of self-transformation. . . . An accompanied self-reflexive praxis thus marks out their appreciation of the different cultural modernity of Hong Kong" (Iwabuchi 2002, 194). However, from a different viewpoint, Hong Kong films, besides Japanese popular culture, have been considered the agency of a new type of cultural imperialism by some of the city's neighboring areas (Lii 1998).

Perhaps, "Asianization" for Hong Kong cinema is only a strategy of "global localization" along the line of Sony's policy to become sensitive to local needs and incorporate the perspectives of the dominated in order to sell the standardized commodities throughout the world (Robertson 1995). Although there have been repeated attempts by Hong Kong–based film companies such as the Shaw Brothers Studio in the 1960s and 1970s (Fu 2000b) and the Golden Harvest Films from the 1970s to 1990s (Fore 1994) to break into the mainstream markets of the West, especially the United States, they could hardly achieve their goals, and the major arena for Hong Kong movie industry remains in the Asian regional marketplace. Hence, the trend of Hong Kong filmmaking is never simply toward a nonlocal development but rather toward a local transnationalized. That is to say, all external differences of Asia are reappropriated and reinscribed into the inside of this expansionist and even imperialist localism of Hong Kong. The external differences of other Asian cultures are incorporated into the conditions of possibility for the development of Hong Kong localism. The local does not use the external differences as the frame of reference for its development. Rather, it directly rewrites itself by using those differences to fill in its gaps. Appearing to deal with and appropriate the external differences, Hong Kong localism is actually struggling with itself and with its own invented sense of Chineseness.

China has politically guaranteed that the Hong Kong local way of life would not be changed for fifty years after the handover. The unifying national ideology has been asked to respect Hong Kong local forms of life. The Hong Kong people themselves have desperately searched for a unique local identity that they could hold on to during the transitional period and have attempted to convert the longing to belong into the insistence that members conform to that way of life and identity. Despite all this, the local in fact has been undergoing fundamental changes. The issue of the local as seen in Hong Kong cinema is not just a choice between integration into the Chinese national or imperial culture and the celebration of multiculturalism or cosmopolitanism. Hong Kong culture has a long history of juggling, syncretizing, and simulating Chineseness. "Re-sinicization" (E. Ma, 1999) is actually not a new thing in Hong Kong, though exigencies of allegiance to nationality in the political world have loomed larger and larger after 1997. On the other hand, Hong Kong culture never really promotes any consciousness of cultural diversity or pluralism. Knowing about other cultures through local films or popular culture does not necessarily increase tolerance or undermine bigotry.[7]

The so-called particular identity and way of life in Hong Kong is indeed an object for the other's gaze. Hong Kong localism is a chip for China to use in negotiating with the West and also an excuse for the West to intervene into Chinese affairs. There has never been a strong sense of community and loyalty to the place that could be passed on by descent. Any cultivation of intense feelings toward the locality is only temporary, or it is strategic for warding off the large-scale domination of the nation-state. I would call this kind of local attachment a "perverse structure." What is absent in this local structure is the deficiency of nationality. That is to say, the rule of colonialism is believed not to affect the unique features of Chineseness in the city. But, on the other hand, the perverse structure is also a defense against the threat and imposition of a too powerful national culture. No matter whether confronted with Englishness during the British colonial era or Chineseness throughout the entire history of the port city, Hong Kong could always seize its local way of life as a symbolic substitute for the absent national identity. The world created by this local perverse structure is a world of comedy, in which whatever the crisis and danger and no matter how bad the predicament is, the weak or the little guy will surely survive, escape all the obstacles, and find his way out. The comic dimension of this structure is that, at one point, the local even believes it is able to shape and change the national. Such a perverse structure of the local is also a way in which Hong Kong situates itself as an instrument of the other's *jouissance,* by means of which China can happily improve its international image by fulfilling the promise of preserving Hong Kong's way of life and the West can congratulate itself for successfully monitoring the smooth transition (of the local adaptation to the national). Insofar as what has been disavowed will return in different forms, Hong Kong films bear witness to this formation of the local, which I call transnationalization.

Hong Kong cinema enters a transnational space in which tensions and ambivalence resulting from encroaching national representation and borderless capitalization have generated a new kind of complexity in its filmic production.[8] What will happen to Hong Kong cinema when it becomes more transnational in these changing times? On the other hand, how do local filmmakers react to the increasing influence of the national from mainland China and to the economic pressures of other foreign investors? This chapter is concerned with how some Hong Kong films, in this transnational situation, attempt to constitute a "local" site in the field of relationships shaped by those contradictory pressures and tendencies. What the local implies in this context is no longer a realm of resistance to global capital; nor is it a form of desire to return to one's cultural origin or to a lost past. Rather, the local constructed in the Hong Kong cinema of the 1990s is an area of negotiation within which dominant, subordinate, and oppositional cultural, economic, and ideological elements are mixed in various permutations.

In terms of the antagonistic relationship between the local and the global, the former is always designated as the primary source of national identity against the penetrating forces of multinational capitalism and cultural imperialism. It is also considered a site of resistance to the coercive linear and teleological development of Western modernization. But the local constructed in Hong Kong cultural and filmic production may not necessarily meet this definition. On the contrary, the local site, rather than being an enclosed place for delineating a well-established homogeneous identity, is relatively fluid and porous to the infiltration of alien elements. I would argue that the meaning of the Hong Kong local is always already overdetermined by the framework of the transnational that structures our perception of its reality. In the case of Hong Kong, the local is the transnational itself in its becoming. It emerges in between the national discourse and global structuralization and remains fluctuating and unsettled rather than being fully articulated and self-present. The local is a moment not of closure but of openness or undecidability that can even disrupt and call into question some fundamental structures and preconceptions of self-identity. This may explain why the local in Hong Kong filmic production is never asserted as a nationalistic entity against the universalistic drive for modernization. Instead, the Hong Kong local is always accompanied by a tinge of modernity in the sense that the capitalist narrative and the claim of westernization are not easily repudiated by it.

In other words, there is a correlation or codependence between the transnational and the local that, however, is not merely an objective correlative to the force of globalism. It is the transnational itself in its changing and pliable existence that serves as a kind of stand-in for the local, which cannot be recuperated in a simple positive form. Thus the conception of the local always goes hand in hand with transnational development and resists a separate comprehension. For Hong Kong, it is never an absolute either-or issue. As Arif Dirlik observes, "Hong Kong is indeed a global city, where it may be difficult to conceive of places as an alternative to globality. . . . What is remarkable, however, is the emergence of an articulated place consciousness in Hong Kong in response to the political pressures of the last decade. . . . Hong Kong is still a global city, but the globality now finds a counterpoint in the claims to a particular Hong Kong culture, a particular Hong Kong identity, and Hong Kong as a place of memory that distinguish the people of Hong Kong from other locations on the globe, as well as within the new political space of the People's Republic of China in which Hong Kong has been relocated" (Dirlik 1999, 55).

A trend of transnationalization of the local was evident in kung fu movies early in the 1970s. The martial arts films or swordplay films made in Hong Kong, inheriting the Chinese opera tradition, emphasized the tactical skills of the kung fu–master actors and closely captured minute changes in the actors' posture, stance, and appearance. As David Bordwell points out, this aesthetic of highlighting the concreteness and clarity of each gesture in kung fu cinema must come from the traditions of martial arts and Peking opera (Bordwell 1997, 81–89). However, the action director Zhang Che, one of the pioneers of the Hong Kong new-style martial arts pictures in the 1960s, has said that the kung fu skills displayed on screen are never authentically nationally inherited: "Hong Kong cinema at the time used the southern school of kung fu and though the pictures freely mentioned the names of Shaolin and Wudang, the actors did not express the movements of these two schools. . . . The main pillar of martial arts in Cantonese opera was the Longhu (Dragon and Tiger) masters of martial arts which was derived from Peking opera. However, this was not a genuine strand of martial arts acting from Peking opera since it came from the serialized libretto play of the 'Shanghai stream' of Peking opera" (Zhang Che 1999, 19). It is precisely this "localism" that differentiates Hong Kong action cinema from its national origins as well as from its Hollywood counterpart and intrigues many audiences.

Esther Yau comments that action directors like Zhang Che in the 1970s urged Hong Kong filmmakers to work on a new kind of localism, combining native legends, "yanggang" masculinity, and modern cinematic mise-en-scène in order to compete internationally (Yau 1997). The "local" boosted in Hong Kong kung fu cinema is not really intended to empower native awareness. Rather, it is a strategy of overseas marketing undertaken to serve commercial purposes. Although Bordwell convincingly argues that the concrete and powerful action sequence in Hong Kong kung fu cinema is mostly manifested by a pause-burst-pause pattern in which the actor's continuous movements are separated by intelligible breaks of stasis (Bordwell 1997, 84), the main rhythm of this action genre is still predominantly characterized by unimaginable speed—a speed that, as Tsui Hark's films abundantly demonstrate, can no longer be performed by human bodies but has to be supported by special effects and advanced technology. It is also a speed that can easily merge into the superhighway of the global flow of capital, becoming synonymous with transnational circulation, progress, and change.

Hong Kong films of the late 1980s and early 1990s offer more reflections on the concept of the local. For New Wave directors and filmmakers like Allen Fong, Ann Hui, Stanley Kwan, Mabel Cheung, and Clara Law,[9] localism no longer pertains to the culture and customs of a particular place. It is thought of in relation to other cultures and other localities, rather than simply being a thing that stresses its self-same identity. The construction of the local relies on what differentiates. In short, the local consists of a sequence of representations that are all by definition differentiated. In Allen Fong's *Just like Weather* (1986), Ann Hui's *Song of the Exile* (1989), Stanley Kwan's *Full Moon in New York* (1987), Mabel Cheung's *An Autumn's Tale* (1987), and Clara Law's *Farewell China* (1990), the local is scrutinized in terms of its being displaced in different spaces and different times. These films were mostly shot in foreign locations and deal with the problem of local subjectivity through the relationship of the local to the other. Though they could be considered transnational in their inclinations, these works still see the foreign other as a differentiating entity from which a distinct Hong Kong or Chinese identity is constituted. However, in other productions of the 1990s that I will discuss shortly, the local culture or identity depicted shares a very blurred boundary with the foreign. The other is always incorporated as an essential part of the local. The local is never a single, unified given; rather, it is a multiplication of various cultures and different times. What is revealing about these productions is that the so-called Hong Kong localism has become even more ambivalent in the further transnationalized context of the last few years of the twentieth century and the first few years of the twenty-first.

Creating Trans-subjectivity

Hong Kong cinema went through a slump in the 1990s. The uncertainty attending Hong Kong's return to China in 1997 exacerbated the loss of talent and the take-the-money-and-run attitude in filmmaking that were helping to create a flood of slapdash productions, resulting in a serious drop in ticket sales. But the most critical factor contributing to the industry crisis was the rapid shrinking of its overseas market shares, which traditionally had made up 30 to 80 percent of the total income of each production. The increasing loss of overseas markets was caused by the decreasing standards of many Hong Kong productions and keen competition from Hollywood cinema (Leung and Chan 1997). The crisis in the film industry, however, created opportunities for new talents and new companies to renovate conventional genres and explore innovative ideas. Spending large amounts of money on stunts and explosions for action thrillers became far less common in the local cinema of the 1990s. Hong Kong filmmakers, knowing that their movies had fallen out of favor among foreign film buyers, have been attempting to give priority once more to the local audience. They believe, with a certain arrogance and pride in spite of adverse circumstances, that what is popular in Hong Kong will be widely appreciated by other Chinese audiences in different places.

As Peter Chan puts it, "The Chinese communities in Southeast Asia always see Hong Kong as their role model. They accept almost everything that is popular in Hong Kong. This means that the taste of the people of Hong Kong would be warmly received by other Chinese communities. It is only a matter of time" (He Wenlong 1994, 50). In the new marketing strategies of the Hong Kong film industry, the local stands for the transnational Chinese. This notion of Chinese transnationality is, however, different from that of the Chinese diaspora. Whereas the concept of the Chinese diaspora is still built upon the "Middle Kingdom complex," in which the hierarchical relationship between the Chinese cultural core and the peripheral status of the dispersed Chinese communities dominates,[10] transnationality depends more on economic and informational-cultural deterritorializing drives than on the centripetal force of Chineseness. Thus, the transnational character in the Hong Kong cinema of the 1990s was not exactly a manifestation of the cultural identification of the Chinese diaspora. It was less a symbol of ethnic unity than a form of desire for capital growth. For instance, a diasporic Chinese may be eager to find another space to relocate the ethnic community, but a transnationalized local would attempt to remake or dislocate a given space in order to loosen it up for more fluid economic and cultural flows.

The current Hong Kong filmmakers have refocused on the concerns of the local market, but their works are not confined to narrow, parochial interests. They endeavor to simulate the quality of Hollywood productions on much lower budgets and, consciously or unconsciously, imitate the characteristics of the globalist American cinema, with its emphasis on movement and an ease of crossing frontiers, a concern with communication and service, a relative downplaying of subtle emotions in human interaction, and a focus on violent action or sexual activity.[11] The popularity of their movies may tell us about the changing cultural conditions of the local community. It also tells us why Hong Kong films attract many Asian audiences, insofar as they demonstrate how American or Western cultural forms can be negotiated, appropriated, and domesticated for achieving local purposes. The producers and directors Peter Chan and Lee Chi-Ngai and the production company United Filmmakers Organization (UFO), which was founded in 1992, were outstanding examples of this new trend in Hong Kong cinema. Meanwhile, some other less prominent companies founded in the 1990s produced films in which the interplay of transnationalization and localism can be tracked. These companies' films have in common low budgets, contemporary settings (for the most part), commercial orientation (though good art direction as well), and close ties to the current issues of Hong Kong daily life—for instance, the problems of cultural identity and migration. Nevertheless, UFO relied more on the star system, which might explain why the company has done better in terms of box-office receipts and attracted more media attention.

Back to Roots (1994),[12] directed by Ray Leung, is a film that touches on nationhood, but anachronistically: a Hong Kong gangster fleeing a murder charge ends up in a primitive Shanbei village on the loess plateau of northern China. The film's images of the yellow rural landscape, the hardships of peasant life, and women's subordination to the patriarchal system, all accompanied by a soundtrack of folk songs, repeatedly remind the viewer of another film, Chen Kaige's *Yellow Earth* (1985), which was set in 1939. For the contemporary citizen of Hong Kong, what signifies China—an estranged homeland to which Hong Kong Chinese have to return—is still the lofty natural landscape, poverty, and primitive living conditions, as well as a harmony and intimacy in human relationships. The typical "Chinese features" presented in imagistic terms in *Back to Roots* do not necessarily generate the same effects of cultural identification as those in the works of the fifth-generation directors from mainland China did among audiences in the West. Perhaps it is not simply that a Hong Kong film is incapable of correctly representing authentic and pure "Chineseness." Precisely because of its powerful technology, which can recreate a rural China as visually impressive as the real thing on the mainland, Hong Kong film transforms Chinese local culture into a simulacrum for the tourist's gaze and renders its authenticity suspicious.

The message of *Back to Roots* is "politically correct": the Hong Kong exile and prodigal son recognizes his identity in the Chinese homeland and is determined to go back there after serving out his sentence in a Hong Kong prison. But that identity is never place-bound and has no communal loyalty to any particular locale; instead, it is constituted by simulated images from contemporary Chinese cinema. It is a Hong Kong transnational fantasy of Chinese localism, created by privileging its isolated ethnic signifiers while depoliticizing the cultural and native experiences. Invoking as a political message not only the dichotomy between the evil city and the saintly countryside, the film also points to the opposition between the Communists and the Nationalists (the Hong Kong gangster is the grandson of a deceased Nationalist soldier who had been exiled to Hong Kong, while the father figure he meets in Shanbei village is a retired Communist soldier participating in the Long March). Yet, this opposition can be overcome by the myth of a shared Chineseness and by male bonding (the Hong Kong gangster sees in the retired Communist his own Nationalist grandfather and regains from him lost fatherly love and meaning in his life). This fantasy is often upheld in Hong Kong cinematic productions, such as Alfred Cheung's *Her Fatal Ways* (1990) and its sequels. In a way, this film reconstructs an exotic but hospitable China in terms of surface imagery and simulated concepts. But the last shot is ambiguous: the protagonist, who wears decent modern clothing and carries an Adidas bag, walks away from the camera in the direction of the village. Is he abandoning corrupt Hong Kong society for the new horizon of an idyllic China? Or is he bringing with him the global force of the late-capitalist city to penetrate the nature of the supposedly precapitalist enclave?

At first glance, Gordon Chan's *First Option* (1996) appears to be an attempt to reassert the integrity of the local in the face of threatening internationalism: international terrorists (mainly former U.S. Marines) traffic in drugs and challenge the local police force.[13] Instead of remasculinizing the loner hero, a Special Unit cop who is suffering after being ditched by his girlfriend, the film emphasizes the spirit of teamwork and collective discipline. The film differs from the Hollywood terrorist genre in that the hero of *First Option* is not rewarded with a woman—that is to say, he does not return to being the "real man" he once was—after winning the battle with the terrorists. Localism is not delegated by any individual masculine hero. On the contrary, the local world is represented by various members of the law-enforcement group, especially the female customs officer, who knows she is no match for the terrorists in terms of military training and weaponry but still insists on doing her duty. However, even though the unified local triumphs over the internationalist threat, the film exemplifies certain globalist attitudes. First of all, the male lead, played by Michael Wong, suggests the hybrid and multicultural nature of the local subject. The local is never in a truly antagonistic position with respect to the global culture. The hero himself is an American-trained specialist who transfers his foreign knowledge to the local officers in order to combat the terrorists. The film stresses the performativity rather than the origins of ideas, things, and people. Second, the terrorists are portrayed as rapacious thieves who have no commitment to any global cause. Even though these global professionals have done the evil deeds, there is no direct linkage to the transnational system itself. The film is by no means about the antagonism between localism and globalism. Rather, it is about which system could be more effective at managing crisis—which, of course, allegorizes the utilitarian attitude of the Hong Kong locals.

Interest in the creation of transnationalism is better demonstrated in Peter Chan's popular comedy *He's a Woman, She's a Man* (1994), UFO's greatest hit, which plays on the gimmick of (mistaken) sexual identity and projects a fantasy of the transnational power of Hong Kong's music industry. The film begins with an ordinary local teenage music fan, Wing, who idolizes the glamorous female vocalist, Rose, and her composer boyfriend, Sam. Sam's record company organizes an open audition to look for a new male talent. Seeing it as an opportunity to get close to her idols, Wing poses as a man to go to the audition. "He" wins the contest and, in this disguised identity, becomes a popular teen idol; "he" even gets involved romantically with Sam. Apparently, the film's humor is based mainly on false identity gags and gender confusion. It could be read as subversive since it provides an anti-essentialist understanding of sexuality by revealing gender identity to be an artifice or a performance. The director makes a concrete claim, through Wing's male pose, that gender identity is more a costume than a given, more a social construction than a biological essence. But another myth is built upon the film's deconstruction of the gender myth. As a local nobody, Wing is reconfigured by the transnational capitalist power into a new, de-corporealized "trans-subject." Her unbound sexual identity is, in fact, more compatible with the fantasy of the global flow of capital than with criticism of traditional concepts of gender. The film also calls the audience's attention to the fact that the logic of commodification dominates the local popular culture: the individual style and talent of the artist simply comprise a package produced by the music industry, while the fans are not too innocent to take advantage of their idols by selling their photos of them and accessories they have used. The local culture is therefore depicted as totally capitalized and commercially exploited. The only uncontaminated place left is exotic "Africa," to which Sam is always longing to go. He identifies with Paul Simon, who uses African music as a new source for his creativity. He falls for Wing because she is Africa for him. In this respect, *He's a Woman, She's a Man* is in line with many Hollywood movies that join in the privileged and globalist appropriation of peripheral, localist cultures for mainstream reimagining.

Although the film looks forward to a new trans-subject whose identity can blur into another's and who is no longer constrained by any frontiers, it dresses itself in a nostalgic ambiance. Its Chinese title, *Jinzhi yuye* (Golden Branch and Jade Leaf), is the Chinese translation of the title of the 1953 American film *Roman Holiday,* starring Audrey Hepburn. The sweet Mandarin melodies of the 1950s and the Beatles songs incorporated in the soundtrack of *He's a Woman* induce an emotional yearning for Hong Kong's past and at the same time remind the viewer of a local identity that is always already multicultural.

Recognition of the Transnational as Home

Another Peter Chan blockbuster, *Comrades, Almost a Love Story* (1996), also makes good use of old music. The old song here is presented not only for nostalgia and narrative comprehension but also for the contemplation of identity. The Chinese title of the film, *Tianmimi* (Sweetness), is a popular song by the female Taiwanese vocalist Teresa Teng (Deng Lijun in pinyin). Teng's songs swept through Taiwan and Hong Kong during the 1970s, but their influence subsided in the 1980s. However, thanks to mainland China's version of a market economy, outmoded popular cultural goods from the two capitalist Chinese communities, namely Hong Kong and Taiwan, can always get a new lease on life in the People's Republic. Different versions of Chineseness, in a way, keep recycling over various times and spaces to generate new meanings and new identities.[14]

Teng's oldies became huge hits among the mainlanders in the early 1980s. Her popularity was even comparable to that of another Deng: the engineer of the modernization campaign and the political leader at that time, Deng Xiaoping. Because of this time lag in the reception of the same cultural products among the Chinese, their choices and tastes easily reveal their different local identities. Chan's film cleverly appropriates this delicate difference in pop-song tastes in order to rethink the question of Chinese cultural identity. *Comrades, Almost a Love Story* is a romance of two mainlanders who first meet in Hong Kong and, ten years later, reunite in New York. Like many formulaic movies, the plot depends greatly on chance and coincidence. The film begins on March 1, 1986, in the Kowloon train station where the two protagonists, Li Xiaojun and Li Qiao, both arrive at the same time, at this point still strangers to each other. The closing scene of the film reruns the opening scene by showing that they actually fall asleep back to back on the same train, reiterating the myth of fate in the romantic relationship. It is rather a commonplace in popular romances that the other person contingently encountered always, predictably, turns out to be the love object prescribed by providence. But the "magic element" that thematically and structurally ties the couple together across all boundaries is Teng's songs, which are heard both diegetically and nondiegetically.

The film makes apparent the audience's cognition of Teresa Teng as well as her songs' narrative functions. Unlike films that affirm their music's self-effacement and unobtrusiveness, *Comrades* foregrounds the sweet voice of Teng to help the audience notice structural unity and narrative coherence. Teng's song first appears nondiegetically when Xiaojun is giving a bike ride to Li Qiao on the busy streets of Hong Kong. Xiaojun, who has a mainland-er's skill in maneuvering the bicycle, inscribes a transnational space into the congested traffic of the colonial city and turns the urban area into a pastoral field, with Teng's music playing in the background while the noise of the city street totally disappears. Li Qiao, sitting behind him on the bike, enjoys the ride so much that she is humming Teng's song, unconscious of the fact that she is thereby revealing that she herself is a mainlander, a fact she wants to conceal from Xiaojun.

This inscription of a different space in the local site of Hong Kong could be interpreted as the desire of homeless Chinese to construct their own sense of locality. It destabilizes the binarism between city and country, homeland and hostland, self and other. The spatial reconfiguration of the bicycle ride in the urban city is imbued with eruptions of memory and nostalgia for a cultural identity the protagonists miss. Thus, the newly inscribed space is not only trans-nationalized but also nationalized. As new immigrants suffering from culture shock, poverty, and discrimination, the protagonists have achieved a transcendent unity and a community of one not by any traditional, folk-cultural forms but, ironically, through an "alien" commercial Taiwanese song.

There is another bicycle-ride scene, roughly near the end of the film, which considers the transnational spatial reconfiguration. By this time Xiaojun and Li Qiao have already gone their separate ways, but, coincidentally, both are in New York City. When Li Qiao is deported by U.S. immigration officers and is on the way to the airport—she is on the run with a Hong Kong mob boss (played by Eric Tsang who is, however, killed in a random street crime)—she catches a glimpse of Xiaojun. He is working as a bicycle deliveryman for a Chinese restaurant in the busy streets of New York. She unhesitatingly jumps out of the car, chasing Xiaojun's bike as well as running away from the immigration officers. She cannot catch Xiaojun, nor can the officers catch her. The bicycle ride indirectly saves her from being deported from the lo-cale of her lover. On the other hand, it also keeps her from reuniting with him, since she is not fast enough to catch up with the bike. Unlike the first bicycle scene, which conveys a (temporary) sense of harmony and suggests a growing intimacy and emotional bond between the protagonists, the bike scene in New York produces feelings of alienation, loss, and anxiety owing to separation and the tensions of acculturation. However, even in a Western metropolis, the trajectory of the Chinese-food delivery bike ridden by Xiaojun becomes a lifeline, rescuing Li Qiao from the hands of foreigners. The rootless Chinese are not totally lost in an adopted country since there is always a nationalized or ethnicized route for them to follow whereby they may find temporary asylum and, eventually, a home.

Asked if he originally intended to make a film about Hong Kong–born residents who have emigrated, Peter Chan said he was really talking about "the rootlessness of the Chinese as a people, and of their continuing search for a new home." "Subsequently," he elaborated, "I realized that the story is also a reflection on the lives of Hong Kong natives of my generation, people like me who are trying to cope with a deadline called 1997" (Tsui 1997, 26). The story of "Hong Kong natives" is told as the story of mainlanders within a transnational context, and the specific issue of 1997 is universalized into a problem of exile and the loss of home. In this way, the local question is reconsidered by the filmmaker in the light of an intertextual, cross-cultural and translational vision. Peter Chan has used the term "Hong Kong natives" because, though he was born in the city, he migrated to Thailand with his family when he was twelve, then was educated in the West and came back to Hong Kong to start his movie career. He explains his cultural identity by saying that "we all share an identity crisis because we are going round in circles. . . . I did not feel that I was Thai. I consider myself a Hong Kong person, but that does not mean I consider myself Chinese. I am Chinese by ethnicity but not by nationality. So I eventually came back to Hong Kong. I thought I was coming home, but ironically, I came back the same year . . . when China and Britain sealed the fate of Hong Kong. . . . To me, it is the circular structure that counts" (Tsui 1997, 26–27).

As mentioned earlier, Teresa Teng's song, besides ensuring continuity, creating atmosphere, and providing background music, performs a narrative function in the film. Its primary function is to narrate and reinvent a fluid and multiple trans-Chinese identity of social migration and transcultural production. Repeatedly, it is Teng's songs that diegetically bring the protagonists together romantically. It first happens when Li Qiao sells Teng's cassette tapes in the Chinese New Year's Eve market. Being a big fan of Teng, Li Qiao forgets that Teng's songs are no longer popular in Hong Kong and that new immigrants from the mainland would avoid buying Teng's tapes in public in order not to reveal their not-so-respectable backgrounds. Her business flops but she gains a deeper understanding of Xiaojun, and they begin their relationship and sleep together that night. When the second diegetic cue of Teng's song appears, it is several years later, Xiaojun has married his fiancée, and Li Qiao has become the mob boss's mistress. Obviously they still have strong feelings for each other. On the way home with Li Qiao, Xiaojun turns on the car radio and Teng's song is playing. As if to remind the viewer even more of the importance of Teng's music in the film, the protagonists run into Teresa Teng on the road. Xiaojun gets out of the car to ask her to autograph the back of his jacket. The appearance of Teng and her melodies triggers Xiaojun and Li Qiao's repressed passions, and they start their love affair again.

The last noticeable instance of Teng and her music in the film is the announcement of her sudden death. The news plunges the protagonists into deep reminiscence and they wander the streets of New York in this reverie. Each stops in front of a shop window to watch a television program reviewing Teng's life, and right there they have their final reunion. Teng's songs have a crucial representational and expressive function in the film, intensifying the protagonists' love affair. The style and cultural connotations of Teng's love songs allow the viewer to easily attribute a particular emotional cast to the musical accompaniment of various scenes in the film. But what is telling about the film's score is that the identification of the musical expression involves transnational cultural codes and differences under a seemingly unified national representation. The romantic desire for unity is overdetermined and structured by a transnationalized musical mode rather than by any indigenous folk songs.

The filmmaker never really uses the national image and the ethnic tradition to construct cultural identity. In fact, the local represented in the film always enacts the reconfigured space of national deterritorialization and reinvention. Xiaojun's aunt, Rosie, a prostitute who runs a brothel, is constantly indulging in her memory of the happiest day in her life—one she spent with William Holden while he was shooting *Love Is a Many Splendored Thing* in Hong Kong. And the brothel is a multiracial place where Thai girls work and which Westerners frequent. The mob boss has on his back a Mickey Mouse tattoo that implies not only the pervasive presence of American culture but also his transnational runaway life and the ultimate reunion of the protagonists in the United States. In addition, the protagonists have their first rendezvous at McDonald's, the multinational fast-food restaurant. In a way, the film paints a utopian picture to show that different races can get along well (which, however, is slightly disrupted by the killing of the mob boss by a multiethnic youth gang in New York) and dreams can cross cultural and national boundaries. This transnational and transcultural fantasy is indeed very common in Hong Kong cinema of the 1990s. It is not merely a conscious strategy of transnational marketing but also part of a hybridized production process. As Yau succinctly puts it, Hong Kong filmmakers "have refashioned a cinema that is eclectic in cultural imagination: modern, local and Americanized, but also premodern, Westernized, Japanese and Chinese. A complex hybridization has been taking place for the last two decades that is more conducive to a theory of chaos . . . than the lateral model of cross-fertilization between East and West, or the critical model of colonial hegemony and subjugation" (Yau 1997, 111).

The reimagining of the local realm into a hybrid wonderland is evident in other works produced by UFO—for example, the collective neighborhood modeled on those of the Cantonese classics in *He Ain't Heavy, He's My Father!* (1993), the Japanese-comic-inspired local street in *Dr. Mack* (1995), and the fin-de-siècle city waiting for a savior in *Heaven Can't Wait* (1995). These imagined spaces cannot be understood simply as the anachronistic or atemporal worlds of fairytales. Indeed, they are like a loop (it is the circular structure that counts): by moving toward the past or toward an alien culture, they come back to where they already are. Far from being the kind of fantasy spaces that offer the audience the illusion of escape from immediate reality, these dreamlands provide a defamiliarized perspective from which to view the present. If localism is understood as a desire to return home, the films discussed above designate a home that is ultimately always a fantasy. It is a home imagistically built, through the mediations of transnational capital, more on deterritorialized cultures than on national ones, on reinvented memories than on inherited ones, on forms of creolization than on a unified and integrated ethnic content. The sense of the local, in Hong Kong films of the 1990s, is sustained through the syncretization of images and information the origins of which are external to the existing forms of cultural life. What is discovered at the kernel of the local is always a self-estrangement. Thus there always remains, in the process of constructing the local, a nonlocal that can provide a viewpoint from which the local can identify itself as something other than itself. These estranged, transnational elements are the local's otherness, which, however, is closer to the local than anything it can set against itself.

In Lee Chi-Ngai's *Lost and Found* (1996), another UFO production, the local sceneries of a relatively old, shabby, and nostalgic Hong Kong are presented against a striking Celtic folk tune, Leonard Cohen's "Dance Me to the End of Love," creating a surprisingly compatible feeling of melancholy and restraint. Though every scene takes place in the Hong Kong of the nineties, the opening shot of the film establishes a nostalgic tone in black and white as the hand-held camera pans from the glamorous skyscrapers and gorgeous harbor view to the dirty narrow streets and the expressionless faces of the poor inhabitants and lower-class manual laborers to convey a sense of dinginess and banality in contrast to the splendid modern life of the globalized Hong Kong. The film attempts to portray a typical local that has been ignored, oppressed, or even exploited by the global development of the metropolis. And it seems to suggest that a search for identity and for meanings of life has to be rooted in the reassertion and recognition of the local. However, the suggestive Celtic music introduces an external gaze or fundamental otherness to examine the Hong Kong local. The opening sequence of *Lost and Found* may not be so different from that of the classic Hollywood production *The World of Suzie Wong* (1960), in which the American tourist played by William Holden walks to Wanchai, a poor Chinese neighborhood, to "discover" all the exotic food and local ways of life. In Lee's film, the female protagonist may share a similar exotic perspective from which to view the local, since she comes from a wealthy family and has been educated in the West. She becomes interested in the local only when she finds out she has leukemia, starts searching for the meaning of her life, and "discovers" the sufferings and miseries of other people.

At first glance, *Lost and Found* is just another Hong Kong movie obsessed with the 1997 motif. The plot sounds very melodramatic, invoking many elements of the "illness melodrama" told from the perspective of the female protagonist, Lam: a beautiful young women with a terminal illness looks for a reason to live in the time she has left and for someone to fall in love with before she dies. A daughter of a shipping-business mogul, Lam meets a sailor named Ted who comes from a barren island in the North Sea off the coast of Scotland, which the natives call "the Edge of the World" (*tianya haijiao,* the Chinese title of the film). It is a place which everyone leaves, returning there only to be buried. Lam associates the place with her own fate, and she develops romantic feelings for Ted. Suddenly Ted disappears (he has to leave for his grandfather's funeral and to inherit his inn on the island). Lam then encounters a Mongolian-Chinese with the funny name of That Worm (a Cantonese expression that is opposite to "Dragon," the Chinese symbol), who runs a "Lost and Found" company. Predictably, Lam hires him to look for Ted, whom she calls her "hope." In their journey to search for "hope" and help others find what they have lost, Lam finds true love in the upbeat and energetic Worm. But she decides to leave him so that he will not be hurt by her impending death. Near the end of the film, all three of them end up on the coastline of Scotland, "the Edge of the World," reaching the resolution to find the world as their "home." Lam and Worm get married and have a baby girl. Lam later dies. The film ends with family and friends grieving after Lam's funeral at a gathering in her father's house. Lam's spirit appears and stands between her two men, Worm and Ted, to take up her final position in the family picture. In the closing credits, the hand-held-camera shots of the Hong Kong local scenery shown at the beginning of the film are rerun, but this time in color, suggesting that human suffering can be meaningful.

Some critics dislike the film for the heavy-handed metaphorical language it uses to symbolize the 1997 issue. Others are moved by this skillfully crafted and beautifully shot weepie. The Hong Kong Film Critics Society calls it "probably the most controversial Hong Kong film of 1996" (Hong Kong Film Critics Society). Though sentimental in its story, the film has a lively and witty tone. Like many other local films, especially those produced by the UFO, that synthesize melodrama with other genres, Lost and Found is a mélange of melodrama and romantic comedy. Exoticizing, hybridizing, and transnationalizing the local community or traveling far away to a really foreign, exotic locale called "the Edge of the World" turns out to be a circular trip back home, which is paralleled by the return to the traditional genre of melodrama. The allegorical meaning of Lost and Found is not simply about handling a deadline named 1997 through the fatal illness of the female protagonist in a melodramatic setting, but about accepting the limitations of one's origin and identity. Though melodrama is all about excessive talk, emotional openness, and overexplicit speech about the meaning of life and love, the stake of the genre actually hinges on the unsaid, on what cannot be spoken of (Kozloff 2000, 242). What Lost and Found struggles to express is that no matter how far Hong Kong cinema manages to Asianize or transnationalize itself, it cannot really leave its Chineseness behind. While the message of the film is to treat the world as one's home, it has recourse at the same time to an old Chinese saying (*sihai weijia*, "making one's home wherever one is") to legitimize its stance of transnationalization. Between the not-really British, half-Scot and half-Chinese sailor (played by the half-American, half-Chinese Michael Wong), and the not-really Han Chinese, Mongolian-Chinese (played by the half-Japanese, half-Taiwanese Takeshi Kaneshiro), the female protagonist (who symbolizes Hong Kong ravaged by the 1997 deadline) can only relocate her spectral body in the Chinese family hierarchy, as revealed in the last scene of the film.

The notion of the local in Hong Kong cinema exists in the form of a desire to become what it is not, in the hope of losing as well as simultaneously reconstituting itself in the process of globalization, which marks a new possibility of self-representation. The full power of the idea of the local is reached in the sense of aggregates and conglomerations of various cultural particulars—national or global—intertwined on the same field. Hong Kong cinema of the 1990s does not necessarily demonstrate that, under the dynamic changes brought by the forces of globalization, all cultures become more creolized and more pluralistic in relation to their origins. But the more the Hong Kong filmmakers invest in constructing a site of the local in the field of relationships, the more they find the local to be inseparable from the transnational modes of living and imagining. This portrayal of the local in the Hong Kong film industry of today as constant mutability in the terrain of continuous cultural and political intervention and reformulation may have nothing to do with the homogeneous synthesis of late capitalism. Instead, it may lie much deeper, in the nature of the passing experience of constructing the local itself.

5

Charlie Chan Reborn as Jackie Chan in Hollywood–Hong Kong Representations

RIDLEY SCOTT'S MOVIE *Blade Runner* (1982) depicts a futuristic world in which a number of "replicants," who look like human beings and are implanted with artificial childhood memories, misperceive themselves as human beings. What is most traumatic for the replicants is that their self-perception as human is never secured. Just like human beings, they are plagued by doubts about the truthfulness of their memories and their human subjectivity. Perhaps it is too quick and easy to conclude that their uncertainty about being human paradoxically makes the replicants "human."[1] Nevertheless, the example of the replicants' dilemma can help to shed light on the influx of Hong Kong film stars and filmmakers into Hollywood.

As John Woo, the most successful Hong Kong director working in Hollywood today, once exclaimed, "It is ironic that Hollywood began to imitate Hong Kong movies in the late 1980s and 1990s because Hong Kong films (to a certain degree) are imitations of Hollywood films, so Hollywood is imitating Hollywood!" (qtd. in Stokes and Hoover 1999b, 309).[2] Does this comment suggest that, with respect to the significance of their presence in filmmaking, the Hong Kong film talents working in Hollywood are nothing but its replicants? In spite of participating in some of the blockbusters produced by Hollywood's global entertainment syndicate, these members of the Hong Kong film industry still maintain a suspicious subject position within the construction of a cross-cultural media network.[3]

This is not to say that Hollywood is simply a vampire-like creature sucking the fresh blood of Hong Kong film talents. Nor am I suggesting that even if they become successfully integrated into the world of Hollywood, these film people from the postcolonial port city are no longer themselves and have therefore lost their original "humanity." Rather, the problem is located elsewhere. If the replicants in Scott's movie are created by humans as an alibi for a loss of humanity, the transnational migration of Hong Kong film people to Hollywood perhaps also provides an alibi for the continued domination and exploitation of the Western globalizing entertainment industry. Perhaps we need to see the limited "Asianization" of Hollywood as a displacement of the old hegemony, in which the West displaces itself into new representations of itself and the world. In the scenario of the Western fabrication of its global self through cinematic representation, is Hong Kong identity "doubly negated" since, in these Hollywood productions, (1) the Hong Konger's place of origin always remains underrepresented to the American audience, and (2) Chinese ethnicity is always emphasized over Hong Kong cultural specificity? Does the "lure of Hollywood" catch Hong Kong red-handed in its "forgery" of both Chineseness and Hollywood film style? Can Hong Kong migrants, or any other postcolonial people, negotiate and renegotiate their own cultural identity within such a transnational context?

To begin with, the success of Hong Kong film talents in Hollywood is not always considered to be identical with the success of Hong Kong cinema. On the contrary, the drain of stars and filmmakers out of Hong Kong and into Hollywood indicates the rapid decline of a dominant local entertainment industry in Hong Kong that was once a significant exporter of films in the world. The golden age of this extravagantly outlandish cinema is perhaps over. What comes as a surprise to most people is that the passing of its glorious movie era was not caused by the city's reunion with mainland China and the implied increase in political censorship, but rather was brought on by multiple, not so obviously political reasons including video piracy problems, a lack of high-quality productions, and the loss of many traditional overseas markets. People in the Hong Kong film industry are therefore being presented with the opportunity to compete in Hollywood at the same time that they are losing the battle of being able to compete with Hollywood in their Asian markets. The appearance of Hong Kong film talent in Hollywood therefore alludes to a vanishing Hong Kong movie empire. But this does not mean that Hong Kong cinema is engaged in an antagonistic relation with Hollywood, like many other national cinemas fighting for their survival in the face of encroaching American media imperialism. Hong Kong cinema has never been opposed to Hollywood. It has always wanted to be it, like a replicant wanting to be human. The ambition of Hong Kong film talent to achieve Hollywood success never wanes. But just as in the case of the replicants, the desire of Hong Kong cinema to break into globalized Hollywood's circuit of sameness produces an irresolvable difference within that circuit.

This chapter examines how the historical mutation of Hong Kong cinema in the 1990s was accompanied by tangible changes in the postcolonial city's cultural identity, which had been extensively grounded in and largely represented by its local cinema and which came to display a stronger awareness of the deeply ambiguous, contingent, and precarious character of its existence. To what extent can we discuss the complex mechanism through which Hong Kong's Chinese identity is reconstituted in those Hollywood productions involving Hong Kong filmmakers and movie stars? This question should also cause us to wonder if the so-called locality of Hong Kong in the 1990s does not necessarily refer to any entity belonging to a particular locality and culture, but rather is determined by a framework of transnationalism that structures our perception of its local social reality. The so-called reconstruction of Hong Kong Chinese cultural identity in Hollywood films can also be understood in terms of a double negation, both insofar as (1) two negations happen simultaneously there and (2) a negation of a negation happens there.

As I already mentioned, Hollywood movies involving Hong Kong film people diegetically negate the cultural identity of Hong Kongers by characterizing them as mainland Chinese at the expense of Hong Kong's particularity. And yet in the American mainstream press, in television profiles and Web sites, their Hong Kong identity is highly exposed. In the media hype of the 1997 Hong Kong, their personal stories intensely converged with and were engulfed by the narratives of political transition and commercialism related to the postcolonial city. The fact that this distance separates the stars from their characters in Hollywood films suggests that the subject called "Hong Kong" by the Western media is reserved primarily for real, external portrayals at the same time that it is virtually excluded from the fictional, diegetic world. The Hong Kong identity formed in Hollywood is therefore never simply a given but rather a negation of itself, as something other than what is given.

On the other hand, in Hong Kong cinema the formation of local identity is connected to a certain negation of Chineseness,[4] although this negation is still very much confined to the Chinese cultural symbolic realm. At the same time, Hong Kong's transnational crossover to Hollywood initiates another negation that negates the symbolic realm common to Chineseness. My focus therefore will be on the way in which the Hong Kong film talents working in the different symbolic realm of Hollywood reappropriate their agency through the production of a transnational narrative of their cultural identity that takes place in light of this double negation.

When I refer to the negation of negation within the process of Hong Kong identity reformation, I am not referring to a loss and its consequent recuperation; it is not that the negation of a negation results in an affirmation. There is no dialectical logic in supposing that the negative result has a positive outcome; hence, because the particularity of the Hong Kong subject has been evacuated in the postcolonial era, this vacuity therefore provides the best opportunity for regaining the unique self. In fact, double negation changes almost nothing in itself but only self-referentially repeats what already was, revealing its own self-contradictoriness. By negation, the symbolic Hong Kong subject portrays itself as something beyond Chinese national identity and then holds on to this negative position. However, reunification with China makes the Hong Kong subject aware that such a position is no longer tenable. Hollywood, on the other hand, offers a chance for the subject to return magically to its particular identity; this move is the double negation that acts as an imaginary "way out" that paradoxically only leads right back to the starting point. But it is never simply a return to the original, un-negated state. Rather, it involves a circular return of something negative inherent in itself. Double negation is a movement toward its own "other" (Buck-Morss 1977). I propose that it is only this negation of a negation manifest in the Hollywood reconstruction of Hong Kong that makes it possible for Hong Kong to recognize the radicalization of its subject position in relation to the changing, transnational meanings of Chineseness.

Dissemination and Estrangement of Chineseness

The transnationalism of Hong Kong cinema, as discussed in the previous chapter, is evident from a number of signs: an increasing number of coproductions with other countries; the international settings of plots; the ubiquity of foreign stars and stars of half-Chinese, half–other ethnicity in local films; and the visible impact of Hong Kong idiosyncratic film styles on Japanese cinema and on a few mainstream Hollywood movies. But the transnationalism goes beyond these factors. In fact, the Hong Kong film industry displays its transnational sensibility most strongly in its continued attempts to crack open the American market. In the early period of "migration" in the 1970s, Hong Kong films relied for the most part on the "chopsocky" martial arts genres that attracted primarily black and young audiences in America.[5] The phenomenal but brief success of Bruce Lee in the early seventies did not change the picture much either. His untimely death only confirmed the fact that the chopsocky entertainment imported from Hong Kong significantly impeded the crossover of Hong Kong film to the Hollywood mainstream. Throughout the seventies and eighties, Hong Kong movies remained relegated to Chinatown, inner-city theaters, second-run houses, small-town double-bills, and drive-ins. After many failed attempts in the early eighties,[6] in 1996 Jackie Chan was finally able to find a distributor to launch the first U.S. nationwide release of a Hong Kong film, and he managed to make a moderate commercial hit out of his *Rumble in the Bronx*. However, the marketing of Hong Kong films in the United States did not become any easier after that, since Chan's ensuing attempts did not come close to the financial achievement of *Rumble*.[7]

Since the mid-nineties, Hong Kong stars and filmmakers have found a way to become more and more actively involved in Hollywood productions and sometimes have enjoyed miraculous success and widespread popularity among mainstream U.S. audiences. The films in which they are involved are no longer confined to action movies but have become more diversified to include other genres like the horror film and the romantic comedy. John Woo was the pioneering Hong Kong director who was able to secure his position in Hollywood. His *Mission: Impossible II* (2000) further solidified the status he had established with the successes of *Face/Off* (1997) and *Broken Arrow* (1995). Jackie Chan further increased and consolidated his own popularity in Hollywood by pairing with the comedian Chris Tucker in *Rush Hour* (1998), which became one of the year's top ten blockbusters.[8] Michelle Yeoh joined Pierce Brosnan in the James Bond movie *Tomorrow Never Dies* (1997).[9] Sammo Hung appeared on CBS's *Martial Law* every Saturday night for three seasons. After playing an ambivalent lead role in both *The Replacement Killers* (1998) and *The Corruptor* (1999), Chow Yun Fat costarred with Jodie Foster in *Anna and the King* (1999), a remake of the Hollywood classic *The King and I* (1956). Jet Li's spectacular combat in the big-budget hit *Lethal Weapon 4* (1998) impressed a lot of Americans and earned him lead roles in the action movies *Romeo Must Die* (2000), *Kiss of the Dragon* (2001), *The One* (2002), and *Cradle 2 the Grave* (2003). Many Hong Kong directors, such as Tsui Hark, Ringo Lam, Peter Chan, Stanley Tong, Kirk Wong, and Ronny Yu, have already shot their Hollywood debuts.[10] Yuen Wo Ping choreographed Keanu Reeves and designed action sequences for the lucrative sci-fi movies *The Matrix* (1999), *The Matrix Reloaded* (2003), and *The Matrix Revolutions* (2003). Yuen's brother, Corey Yuen, also worked in Hollywood, using his wire work to help Jet Li kick high in all of Li's American films, serving as the action director in *X-Men* (2000), and choreographing Drew Barrymore, Cameron Diaz, and Lucy Liu in *Charlie's Angels* (2000). Donnie Yen, who grew up in Boston's Chinatown, was signed to play the character "Jin" in the fourth installment of the Highlander series, *Highlander: Endgame* (2000), and worked as the martial arts choreographer on the film. Though these works were sheer American productions representing the reassertion of Hollywood hegemony rather than the pride of Hong Kong, they may constitute new kinds of transnational representations within the global cultural exchange, which I will discuss below.

It is not difficult to understand that these Hong Kong film talents are not exported to the global film market as products made in Hong Kong, although it was their work in Hong Kong that first attracted Hollywood's gaze. They are more like expatriates or migrant workers starting a new life in a new host country. Their past reputations in Hong Kong or Asia, upon which their cultural identity was built, become relatively negligible since they are now workers looking for a new career in a different market. It is undeniable that Hong Kong movies have dominated all of Asia.[11] The cinemas in Taiwan, Indonesia, Malaysia, the Philippines, Singapore, and Thailand have long been overwhelmed by Hong Kong films. In South Korea and Japan, films made in Hong Kong are also hugely popular. Though most Hong Kong movies were not officially allowed to enter mainland China in the past, they were commonly pirated. But the Closer Economic Partnership Arrangement (CEPA) signed in 2003 between China and Hong Kong would facilitate the Hong Kong film industry's entry into the mainland market in the future.[12]

Jackie Chan once described himself to a Western interviewer by saying, "In Asia, I am Jurassic Park. I am E.T." (Dannen and Long 1997, 3). But it's a different story in Hollywood. Many Hong Kong stars "could pass by unrecognized on any street in the United States" (1997, 3). When the world media's coverage of Hong Kong dwindled after 1997, the Western masses showed less and less interest in knowing about Hong Kong film personalities' illustrious pasts. The subject position of these personalities is thus, in a sense, out of joint, and they indubitably lack a fixed, established place in the new transnational arena. In a positive sense, these migrating film talents can seek a fluid position among the multiple possibilities offered by the global sphere, and they can reappropriate the discursive formations of race, class, and gender to their own advantage.[13] Indeed the history of Hollywood itself is a history of foreigners and émigrés. Filmmakers from Eastern Europe and Russia in the early twentieth century, those from Germany in the 1920s to the 50s, and also many from Australia in the 1970s and 80s dominated the studio and poststudio eras. The influx of Hong Kong filmmakers and stars could of course be explained as part of the continuous self-rejuvenating process of Hollywood industry.

In the past, foreign filmmakers had a relatively easy time assimilating into the American industry because of their shared white ethnicity. On the other hand, the role of Asians and Asian Americans in the Hollywood industry remains historically ambivalent. The presence of Asian film talents in Hollywood has never been so conspicuous as in the nineties. But the noticeable advent of Hong Kong film people does not mean correspondingly that there is already a definitive position for them there. The cinematic representation of Asians has never been treated as a significant realm for portraying racial tensions within the United States. Instead it appears as a mere digression from the portrayal of the far more intense and immediate racial antagonism between blacks and whites.[14] The interesting result of this is that, because the Asian role is not fixed within the dominant racial discourse, Hong Kong film people can move between one culture and another, thereby increasing their agency by refashioning the transnational code of their identity.

Perhaps the introduction of Asian talents into the white-dominated entertainment industry indicates that today's Hollywood, besides becoming more globalized in the economy of scale, has become more multicultural and politically correct as a result of catering to the increasingly diversified tastes of the world market. But it could also indicate how Hollywood productions of the 1990s increasingly tend to emphasize loose narrative, simple characterization, special effects, and action sequences with spectacular stunts over narrative complexity and deep character development. By and large, Hong Kong cinema displays a similar emphasis.[15] Hong Kong film talent would then be an agency that Hollywood needs in order to implement the new aesthetic.[16] What I am interested in is how the increasingly discernible presence of Hong Kong movie stars and directors in mainstream Hollywood renders cultural identity more complicated, not only in the United States but also in a "global city" like Hong Kong within the Chinese nation-state.[17] In fact, the symptom of one concept of identity can always be kept in check by the use of the conceptual scheme of the other. The transnational crossing of Hong Kong cinema to Hollywood may not only produce something that could generate a possible new and useful reading of cultural globalization; it could also reveal the absurdity of identity formation in general.

Hong Kong stars in Hollywood films are generally portrayed either as foreigners from China or as generic Chinese whose cultural origin has no significance to the plot of the film.[18] In Hong Kong cinema, it is common for Hong Kong artists to play mainland Chinese characters. However, locally, the most popular portrayals of mainland Chinese by Hong Kong stars like Stephen Chiau or Do Do Cheng emerge in comedy films.[19] The farcical depictions of mainland Chinese in the early nineties succeeded at capturing Hong Kong's Chinese imagination and its projection of a backward, premodern but innocent and resourceful China. What is significant for the audience, however, is always the total image of the star rather than the particular character he or she plays in a film. Hong Kong stars who play mainlander characters in comic persona thereby create a strangely familiar effect: the audience can both identify with the characters from (an imposed) distance and ridicule them through a sense of cultural affinity. This is not a simple separation of the self from the other; it is a process of positing otherness and then reappropriating it for the purposes of self-reconstruction. This process became particularly acute in the early nineties, when the people of Hong Kong had to readdress their Chineseness as they prepared for the imminent return of their city to China.

In Hollywood productions, Hong Kong stars playing generic or mainland Chinese characters have a different significance altogether. Like the replicants in *Blade Runner* who challenge the human beings by arguing that they have a greater human sensibility than the humans, Hong Kong actors and actresses in Hollywood productions have to prove themselves to be more Chinese than the mainland Chinese they portray. But they thereby become caught in deviations that could hardly become normative. Sammo Hung is a detective from Shanghai in CBS's *Martial Law*, Michelle Yeoh plays a secret agent for Communist China in the James Bond movie, while Jet Li in *Kiss of the Dragon* is a Zen-like supercop from Beijing who uses an armband of acupuncture needles to take away pain and to inflict it. The Chineseness in these films is converted into a given that can hardly be modified and vigorously reshaped, in comparison to the modifications available in Hong Kong's local productions. Since Chineseness serves as a static ethnicity that American society assigns to the other in order to consolidate its dominant self, the malleability of Hong Kong subjectivity is thereby foreclosed. Mostly fixated on Asian stereotypes and sometimes recreated in a new type—for example, Chow Yun Fat as an F.O.B. (Fresh-Off-the-Boat) hitman in *Replacement Killers,* a corrupted cop associated with Chinese gangs in *The Corruptor,* and an exotic, mysterious, and nameless Tibetan Buddhist monk in *Bulletproof Monk* (2003)—the onscreen images of Hong Kong actors in Hollywood productions are reminiscent of the superficial and stock images of Chinatown-based ethnic portrayals.

It is important to note that the star in a film always has a symbolic function that may differ from the function of the character in the film script. The casting of a particular star is often determined by what symbolic meanings he or she as a star carries, and the star effect can have significant repercussions on the characterization itself. Nevertheless, the characterizations of Hong Kong actors in Hollywood films rely predominantly on American presuppositions of what an Asian should be like as opposed to the specific symbolic values offered by the actors. Their Chineseness appears to both American and Hong Kong audiences as an image of the estranged other. And yet, from a different point of view, these stars may serve as agents of a self-differentiation or self-division that reveals the otherness inherent in Hong Kong subjectivity itself. The formation of Chinese subjectivity within Hong Kong has never been pure and self-sufficient. It has always been an eclectic product of the repeated rearticulations of its difference from Chinese heritage and Western cultural hegemony. If the people of Hong Kong encounter obstacles and adjustments in the process of reconstituting and transforming themselves into a new Chinese subject at the cusp of decolonization and beyond, then in a parallel fashion, the representation of Hong Kong film stars in Hollywood reveals a similarly difficult resubjectivization.[20]

The Chinese characters portrayed by Hong Kong stars in Hollywood films appear estranged and weird to the Hong Kong audience, even as we cheer for their international success. Once again, the negation of negation does not imply a simple rejection of a prior identity but rather implies that there is no difference between the two identities. The "original" identity is no less "artificial" or "unreal" than its copy. The immediate origin proves to be something already foreign, mediated, and secondary. If Chineseness appears in the mode of default in these transnational media productions, we should take into account the fact that the failure to realize the concept also signifies the inadequacy of the concept itself. Why is it difficult for Hong Kong actors who play Chinese characters to allow their local alterity to be universalized in the transnational cinema? The search for a wholly adequate concept goes along with the search for an appropriate form of expression, in the construction of images. Made in Hollywood, these images may have turned into something with which Hong Kong people cannot immediately identify. On the other hand, to a certain extent, nothing actually changes with these representations. The so-called changes just repeatedly "re-mark" what was already there, namely, the re-marking of inherent foreignness within the signifier of the subject.

I should emphasize that the construction of images cannot be read simply in relation to actual, sociohistorical configurations. Even if we presume to grasp images as social and historical markers, we still have to understand that the conditions of production are constitutive of the images through which Hong Kong cultural identities are played out. Crucial to a discussion of Hollywood's orientalizing strategies of labeling, including, and excluding Asians within American culture is an acknowledgment that an inversion may have taken place, which involves the tactics of the marginalized other. The Hong Kong film people who "go Hollywood" have been recoding the colonized subject and appropriating the Asian-Oriental other's position. At first they simulate the traditional clichés of Asians depicted by Hollywood, bringing the image as close as possible to the "original" stereotypes, until at a certain point things reverse. When followed closely, the clichés gradually become so obvious and ridiculous that they make the voyeur aware of his own existence. Such an inversion is comparable to the "affect of exhibitionism" demonstrated by Zhang Yimou's movies, which offer a visually beautiful and exoticized feudalistic China to the craving eyes of the Western audience.[21] But whereas Zhang's works fall into the art-film category and therefore churn up controversies within cross-cultural debate, the Hollywood productions involving Hong Kong film people are all outright mainstream motion pictures, and they can be more easily dismissed for their blatant commercial tricks. And yet, because of their extreme sensitivity to social and cultural shifts, these commercial films bear witness to the delicate mechanism of Hong Kong's Chinese-subject reconstruction within transnational interactions.

To compare the Chineseness constructed in local Hong Kong film production with that of the Hollywood–Hong Kong film, I would characterize the former as an empty concept without a specific ethnic object and the latter as an ethnic object without a proper concept of Chinese national identity. In local Hong Kong movies, the subject emerging as the negativity of Chineseness is an empty concept of Chinese identity without a nationally bound object; it only punches a hole in the symbolic structure of Chinese national identification. On the other hand, in Hollywood films, Hong-Kong-stars-playing-Chinese are like an excessive ethnic object bearing all sorts of superficial icons, one that is displaced from the conceptual structure of Chinese national identity. As I mentioned earlier, Hong Kong's particular identity is negated in these Hollywood productions involving Hong Kong film talent. But negation can be a form of expression for something that cannot be expressed directly and positively. In other words, through negation there may exist in these films a real but empty Hong Kong subjectivity as opposed to an imaginary "full" local identity. The idea that a postcolonial Hong Kong subjectivity can be presented only in a negative mode immediately gives rise to a few questions: What is the thing that cannot be said directly and positively? Is the use of negation conscious or unconscious? Does a negation tell a truth truer than the one told in an ordinary, positive manner? And if an expression by negation is not necessarily truer than a positive expression, what then exactly is the function of negation?

Becoming-Chan and Racial Politics in *Rush Hour*

These questions establish a platform for interrogating the different mode of subjectivity that emerges in Brett Ratner's film *Rush Hour*. Advertisements for the film describe the leading men as the greatest action hero and the most extravagant comedian, a distinction marked by their cultural difference. Jackie Chan has "the fastest hands in the East" while Chris Tucker "has the biggest mouth in the West." The East-meets-West dichotomy is here transfigured from the usual confrontation between a Caucasian and an Asian into a buddy relation between an African American and an Asian, represented as a collaboration between the fastest hands and the biggest mouth.[22] But the merging of the two synecdoches also suggests the image of a young child greedily sucking all of its fingers. And indeed the action comedy plays more on the naiveté, stupidity, and childlikeness of the characters than on the conventional concept of what a hero should be like.

Chan, with his usual likable and unassuming onscreen persona, plays Detective Lee, who is sent for from Los Angeles by a fatherly figure, Consul Han of the People's Republic of China (PRC), to rescue Han's kidnapped daughter. Lee seems to be more responsible and subservient to Han than to the Hong Kong police department for which he works. Such a portrayal of the relation between a Hong Kong detective and a PRC consul may be regarded by Hollywood as normal, since China become Hong Kong's legitimate father again after 1997. This prodigal son who has recently returned home is immediately assigned the huge mission of saving China's future (Consul Han's little daughter) and also of protecting China's past (the antiques that Chan fights to prevent from being smashed by gangsters in the final confrontation). On the other hand, the former British commander of the Royal Police Force, Thomas Griffin (representing the adoptive father), who was very likely Lee's boss before 1997, turns into an evildoer, Juntao, who steals Chinese art treasures, runs a crime organization, and abducts little girls for ransom. Here, the role of the patriarch always serves as the basis of the model and value of masculinity on which the male-dominant action cinema depends. The image of the father runs throughout the movie and becomes obvious when Lee and his black partner, Detective James Carter (Chris

Tucker), at one point suddenly start boasting to each other about their deceased fathers:

> Lee: Your dad was a policeman?
> Carter: Fifteen years LAPD.
> Lee: My father was also a policeman.
> Carter: Your dad was a cop?
> Lee: Not a cop. An officer. A legend all over Hong Kong.
> Carter: My dad a legend too. All over America. My dad once arrested fifteen
>   people in one night by himself.
> Lee: My dad arrested twenty-five people by himself.
> Carter: My dad saved five crackheads from a burning building by himself.
> Lee: My dad once caught a bullet with his bare hands.
> Carter: My dad'll kick your dad's ass all the way from here to China or Japan
>   or wherever you from. All up that Great Wall, too.
> Lee: Don't talk about my father!
> Carter: Don't talk about my dad!

The dead father, it is said, always constitutes the point of ideal identification, while the living father is just the cruel agent of prohibition. In the movie, the living paternal figures are either corrupted (Griffin), untrustworthy (Captain Diel of the LAPD), or impotent (Consul Han). Thus, Lee and Carter have to construct imaginary fathers who bear little resemblance to the living ones. While Jackie Chan keeps questioning his identity in his Hong Kong productions like *Who Am I?* (1998) and *The Accidental Spy* (2001), here he suddenly manages to secure his subject position and create a patrilineality by bragging to a foreigner about his father's ability to catch a bullet with his bare hands. Chan has to reclaim an imaginary father for his new identity in Hollywood, since the available, existing father figures are either too weak (in the case of Consul Han) or too wicked (in the case of Griffin). Neither loyalty to the Chinese patriarch nor attachment to the British ex-colonial master will do any good for Chan's getting a footing in the new global ideological space.

Perhaps a cinematic reinvention of one's paternal origin is precisely what is needed. In fact, unlike many characters in Hong Kong cinema who proclaim themselves outright cynics determined to undermine paternal authority,[23] Chan's usual persona is a nice guy.[24] He believes in and takes seriously symbolic codes, ethical substance, the Name-of-the-Father, and the father of Law.[25] He always acts as if to preserve the fundamental paternal law that forms the order of identity and values, and even to prevent the dissolution of the traditional symbolic father's authority in a world of cynicism. But, the trick is that he believes in the symbolic father without trusting him, because he is also aware that he is dealing with an order of mere semblance. That is to say, the father of Law is treated as if it were still authoritative, respectable, and effective, although in reality it has already become abject and powerless.[26]

Chan's Hong Kong movies may be more radical than many other cynical Hong Kong films that use irony and sarcasm to subvert the ruling ideology represented by the father figures, since Chan "knows" the difference between the ideological veil and the reality but still insists on upholding the veil. He does not renounce the father, because he is too conscious of the particular interest behind the ideological veil. The egotistical interest or brutal lust for power can be satisfied more effectively under the protection of the law or with the legal endorsement of paternal authority. Who then would be the imaginary father or father of semblance anchoring the new subject position for postcolonial Hong Kong within transnational cultural artifice? An answer may be found in an examination of the tradition of American ethnic-based comedy.

Though apparently a Hollywood product with less spectacular stunts than those in Jackie Chan's Hong Kong works, *Rush Hour* is still regarded as a Chan film by some Western critics.[27] But for Hong Kong locals, the film was made primarily to gain U.S. and international acceptance and is regarded simply as an American film made for American taste. Although Jackie Chan, with the success of *Rush Hour,* has shown that he can hang in there in Hollywood,[28] to the people of Hong Kong he has renounced the dimension of his local subjectivity proper in this Western representation. Like many racial discourses implied in Hollywood films, *Rush Hour* presents its minority male leads as some kind of "symbolically castrated men." Carter's motormouth and sexual aggressiveness succeed as flirtation but would never really seduce any women, while Lee is too self-effacing to reveal any interest in the opposite sex. His devotion to rescuing the ten-year-old little girl is conceivably designed to eliminate any possible romantic association. Although Chan's image is by no means effeminized, as many Asian men were in earlier Hollywood films, his ethnicity has already been framed in a passive feminized space.[29] This may partially explain why the small exodus of Hong Kong film talent to Hollywood is largely a male phenomenon, since the muscle men are always already made into "woman."

As some critics have pointed out, the male characters of any racial minority in American cinema always fall into the category of a passive and asexual figure who is not only unthreatening to the white hero but also confirms his sexual domination.[30] However, there is no white hero in *Rush Hour,* let alone one with the sexual appeal. Perhaps it is the mainstream white audience that the film does not want to threaten. Taking up the conventions of the buddy movie, according to which the male duo provide comic relief through witty verbal exchange, *Rush Hour* never hesitates to make good fun of so-called "harmless" Chinese and African American racist jokes in order to entertain mainstream Hollywood spectators. It is almost unimaginable that a local Hong Kong audience would laugh when Lee is misled by Carter to befriend a black bartender by calling him "nigger," or when Carter tells Lee that he has been looking for his "sweet-and-sour-chicken ass." It is not that Hong Kong audiences would be offended by the racist slurs, but rather that they do not understand racial stereotypes in American culture enough to get the gags. In other words, their gazing stance cannot be structured along racial and ethnic lines.

This kind of deployment of ethnic differences and racial stereotypes being played against each other has existed in Hollywood for a long time, the most pertinent example perhaps being the Charlie Chan series, which began in the early 1930s.[31] Based on the character from Earl Derr Biggers's novel, Charlie Chan is one of the most popular American-made screen detectives. Approximately fifty Hollywood feature films have been made about Charlie Chan, from the 1920s to 1981. Although the novelty of the Chan series began to wane in the fifties, the character continued to live on through a television series and countless reruns. Actors of Chinese origin are not strangers to the Chan films. Even Bruce Lee, while involved in the television show *The Green Hornet* (1966–67), was considered for a starring role in *Number One Son,* a spin-off of Charlie Chan movies. Having grudgingly accepted the offer that was never developed into a series, Lee cynically remarked, "Naturally, I was signed to play Charlie Chan's Number One Son. I mean, that's what Chinese actors do for a living in Hollywood, isn't it? Charlie himself is always played by a round-eye wearing six pounds of make-up" (Gaul 1997, 31).[32] This ethnic detective genre is always placed in the comedy format through which the stereotypical image of the Asian male is displaced, inverted, and intermingled with European-American traits that are usually not available to the portrayal of the oriental others. Charlie Chan is depicted as virtuous, mature, rational, and skillful at solving crimes, while his Asian characteristics, such as his speech, dress, and appearance, are still comically maintained.[33]

The embodiment of contradictory images by the protagonist effects a kind of social control over the Asian detective, who could evidently be assimilated to fit into mainstream American culture. "In this move," Norman Denzin observes in his analysis of Charlie Chan films, "the Asian male was simultaneously excluded from, and included inside, a Western-Orientalizing discourse which made him stranger and friend at the same time" (Denzin 1995, 991). Such an "inside-out" or "outside-in" combination of conflicting ideas about the Asian figure is exemplified by the doubled, spectacular structure organizing the film series, wherein Charlie Chan ritually identifies the murderer by restaging the crime in front of all the suspects, thereby becoming a spectacle with his racial distinctions reinscribed. Appearing familiar and different, as subject and object, and with a paradoxically fixed and mutable ethnic identity, the Charlie Chan character offers a certain kind of entertaining exoticism with which the American audience can feel comfortable and through which a white hierarchy continues to assert itself.

Rush Hour certainly accommodates many of the formulaic elements found in the Charlie Chan series, such as playing different racial stereotypes against each other in order to manufacture fun for, rather than present a threat to, the mainstream white audience, and combining contradictory images within the main characters so that they appear both familiar and exotic.[34] The racial hierarchy according to which people of color are subordinated to their Caucasian superiors is institutionalized here in both the police force and the crime organization. After the many attempts made by Asian Americans to fight against the mainstream American grotesque representations of Asians as alien others, and after the declaration of the demise of Charlie Chan, the most famous fake Asian pop icon, by the title of the first anthology of Asian American fiction put out by a commercial publisher in the United States, Charlie Chan Is Dead,[35] the Hollywood–Hong Kong film shamelessly revives his image in a muscular Hong Kong body. The only difference is that in the Hollywood production of the late nineties, the body movement and the stunts performed by Jackie Chan are far more spectacular than those of the Asian Charlie Chan body performed by a Caucasian actor. Does this mean that the reiteration of Charlie Chan in Jackie Chan fails to constitute any new transnational representations within the global cultural exchange?

For Chan's movie fans, the stunts in Rush Hour are less outlandish than those in Chan's Hong Kong films. This may have something to do with the safety-consciousness of the middle-aged star. Or it could represent Hollywood's attempt to contain the image of Asian superheroism being unleashed on the American screen. The outright display of Chan's ferocious athleticism and death-defying stunts has always appeared in repeated shots and even as interruption of the narrative flow in his local productions. In Police Story (1985), Chan slides down a sixty-foot pole covered with sparking electrical wires and lightbulbs. The shot is shown three times in a row and from three different angles. In Project A (1985) he jumps from a clock tower, plummeting through two cloth awnings before he hits the ground. The sequence is done in one take to show that he did not use a safety mat. But the first time he did the stunt, things went wrong. Chan dangled from the clock's minute hand and then let go. As planned, he tore through the first awning. But instead of tearing through the second awning, he accidentally bounced off it and was turned upside down, hitting the ground with his head. He was injured, though not seriously. He tried the stunt again later, and everything went well. When the film was released, both stunts, including the failed attempt, were shown in a row, ignoring the consistency and continuity of the story development. The repetition suspends the linear narrative and its temporal progress, creating an alienating distance from which the stunts are viewed. The audience is suddenly pulled out of the narrative flow and driven into the position of the Master's gaze from which things are seen "objectively" and "totally." But the "objectivity" and "totality" of the stunts that the audience can view outside of the frame is already framed by a part of the narrative. The spectator of Chan's Hong Kong movies is always inscribed inside-out, as if in viewing the outtakes he is posited behind the closing credits.[36] Such an exhibition of Chan's spectacular body-performance in his Hong Kong films is restrained in the Hollywood film.

The two major stunts in *Rush Hour*—one with Lee and Carter falling from a broken bridge, and the other with Lee jumping from the ceiling of a dome—which are modest even by Hollywood standards, are shot in the conventional device of Hollywood action cinema: there is no closeup of the character; there is minimal performance on the actor's part; action is viewed from a distance; and slow motion captures the fall, which is immediately cut to another shot before the action is completed. The convention of using a long shot with closeups displaying every gesture and detail of the movement, which is found in Chan's films, is evident here only in his combats in the bar scene and with the Chinese gangsters in the restaurant scene and in the final showdown.[37] Chan's acrobatic skills and well-choreographed action with cinematographic enlargement are preserved in the Hollywood production, while his death-defying spectacular stunts have been largely toned down. The Hollywood portrayal of Chan is relatively low keyed and unglamorous—he combs back his hair and wears Western suits—and conforms to an ordinary, bourgeois, middle-aged look, in contrast to the boyish Beatles haircut and casual outfits he wears in his Hong Kong films and that emphasize his agility, dynamism, and vitality. Not unlike Charlie Chan, Jackie Chan in Hollywood is tied to a body that has a limited sense of becoming-other and is dressed up like a comedian demonstrating cartoonlike kung fu, which remains legible but bears less of an emotional impact. The tradition of Hong Kong action filmmaking is appropriated to meet Hollywood's realistic style and its racial conventions.

It is no wonder that subject construction is always embedded in a set of conditions of existence that can never be fully controlled or monitored by the subject himself. He can only work on this persistent element of contingent externality in order to transform it into an internal expression of his subjectivity. The local Hong Kong audience cannot identify with the "new" subject assumed by Jackie Chan in his Hollywood endeavors, because they are caught in their own narcissistic, limited frame.[38] Within the cultural logic of the global economy, the "hubris" of asserting one's exclusive particularity perhaps can only lead to an early demise. It is in the realm of the other that the subject is constituted. In the orientalist imagination, Hong Kong film people recreate their own identity under the conditions that are found and imposed on them. The conflation of outsiders from Hong Kong within the American cinematic space has to take place as a smooth integration of the East with the Western psyche and perceptual framework. In order to strive for a new space in the global commercial film market, Hong Kong film talents adopt the position of exploiting the protean multitude—from Fu Manchu through Charlie Chan to all of the material signifiers associated with the Chinatown of the American metropolis—without, however, showing any real engagement in a specifically subjective mode. This is exemplified by the "more-radical-than-cynical" attitude usually found in Chan's films. The humiliated father can be invoked to reclaim one's identity. "Yellow Peril" villains or Charlie Chan stereotypes are appropriated to serve the needs of the new subject formation. Indeed, no father's name cannot be dishonored, although, ironically, in *Rush Hour*, Lee, upon being sent back to Hong Kong for failing to fulfill the rescue mission, accuses Carter of dishonoring his father's name. When combined, the negation of local Hong Kong identity and the confirmation of the negative image of Asians prevailing in Hollywood convey a double sense of negativity. Could this "double negation," however, represent the presence of an absent space connoting a specific type of identity? Could the absence or negation of identity be perceived as a transgressive identity? Can an identity be transgressed and transformed by negating it once, or even twice?

In a radio interview, Jackie Chan told his hosts that although he was more involved in the creative process of *Rush Hour 2* (2001) and was appointed Hong Kong tourism's ambassador to introduce foreigners to the "City of Life"—it was his idea that the sequel's story open in Hong Kong—the stereotypical depictions of the ethnic Chinese in the Hong Kong massage parlor, the karaoke bar, and the chicken market remained far beyond his control. In fact, the successful sequel is not short on negative images of Chinese ethnic groups, including those of the Hong Kong triad of godfather (John Lone), his dragon lady (Zhang Ziyi), and their Chinese gangsters counterfeiting bills and running a money-laundering casino. Though Chan's Asian male sexuality is somewhat foregrounded by his being assigned the prime agency of male voyeurism in watching the white woman undress in front of a window, and by his finally getting to kiss her onscreen,[39] he is nevertheless at the same time reduced to role of sidekick, as if he were playing the Number One Son to Chris Tucker. Perhaps Chan has a lot to learn from Tucker, who, in this second installment of the *Rush Hour* franchise, not only impersonates Michael Jackson and embraces all the old black racial stereotypes, but also becomes something of a racial chameleon by asserting his superior American identity to the Asian girls. On the one hand he victimizes himself as an oppressed black in front of the white people, while on the other hand he boasts about himself as a First World handsome, calling Chan the "Third World ugly" and saying right to his face, "I'll bitch slap you back to Bangkok."

The negation of one's own identity exemplified by the Hong Kong talent's making their way to Hollywood may be interpreted as a conscious and cunning use of negative representation that gesticulates an imaginary transgression of an imaginary subjectivity. It is perhaps just another example of Hong Kong's shameless and shrewd mode of "making it," strikingly manifested by the postcolonial Special Administrative Region government's ventures of a parachuting Disney theme park, a cyberport, and an international hub of Chinese medicine in the city, all of which are part of an attempt to revive the economy after Asia's period of financial turmoil.[40] A new mode of Hong Kong subjectivity emerges only when it is no longer opposed to the other but encompasses it. There is nothing foreign that a local identity cannot incorporate, since the so-called local identity itself is formed by an inherent otherness. The double negation does not provide any miraculous twist guaranteeing the advent of a new transgressive identity; it simply designates the inevitable displacement of the subject after its return to China. Negation here could turn out to be an empty gesture that does not lead to any transgression, imagined or real. A pure negation that fails to transgress anything and lead to a new space is sheer deception.

However, in the history of Hong Kong popular culture, the negation of Chineseness that appears as transgressive has served as the imaginary support for an emergence of a particular local Hong Kong subjectivity. While generally accepted as representative of the city's cultural specificity, the subject manifested in Hong Kong cinema is also the agency of a trans- or pan-Chineseness with which overseas Chinese can relate and identify.[41] Past experience seems to tell Hong Kong locals that negation is constitutive of their identity, even if it constitutes only a semblance of a subject position. If negation has worked for Hong Kong's subjectivization in the past, is it possible that a "negation of negation" would serve as a strategic move for the evolution of a new, postcolonial subject leading up to and following 1997? Can the Hong Kong film people in Hollywood who are undergoing precisely this negation of negation present a new way of constructing a new subject for their home city? And if negation of negation is only a false transgression that cannot create any new space, how can we have any hope that the transnational cinema will beget a new mode of subjectivity?

It would be misguided to argue that false transgression simply reasserts the determining status quo, that is, the racial stereotypes of Asians in American popular culture and the general disbelief on the part of mainland Chinese that Hong Kong people need to maintain their cultural particularity. The reconstruction of Hong Kong identity in Hollywood films, which goes unrecognized by Hong Kong local audiences, remains at a performative level and is by no means a radical act of thoroughly reconfiguring and redefining the very conditions under which a cultural identity is constituted. Suffice it to say that negation of negation provides no magical transformation; it only indicates that Hong Kong people have to come to terms with the wicked situation of being simultaneously integrated into the world of the Chinese nation-state and submitted to the ideological universe of the hegemonic West.

To reclaim a father either in China or in the West becomes a necessary move for Hong Kong. But the rearticulation of Hong Kong subjectivity within a transnational cinema, although it takes place within the dominant ideological field determining what an ethnic identity or racial stereotype should be, still implies a certain subversive displacement. If we conceive Hong Kong's identity reconstruction as a leftover of the mechanisms of Chinese national identity formation and American racial management, the picture can appear quite different. Now it is the dominant system itself that, through its internal contradiction, activates the force of change that ends up challenging its power. This is to say that the return of colonial Hong Kong to China under a nationalist discourse provokes deviations within Chinese-identity portrayal in Hong Kong transnational cinematic production, while the American racial prejudice perpetuated by Hollywood films gives rise to a series of films that blow up the Asian images and may outgrow its conventional confinement. The structure of the power edifice and the dominant ideology, with its inherent inconsistency, is unable to control itself and produces a leftover that subverts its dominion from within. The presence of Hong Kong film people in Hollywood may therefore provide a different perspective from which to reexamine the mechanisms of power and the politics of identity.

6

Racial Passing
and Face Swapping
in the Wild, Wild West

THE ASSIMILATION OF Hong Kong movie stars and directors by
mainstream Hollywood indicates the transnationalization of Hong Kong culture, but it also implies the possibility of a new representation of "Chineseness" within the global media space. Compared with their predecessors in
Hollywood who had to portray the stock array of Chinese domestic servants,
laundrymen, mystics, gangsters, and prostitutes, the Hong Kong stars play
more positive onscreen roles, appear to have more power in the making of
their cinematic images, and enjoy greater popularity among mainstream U.S.
audiences. If Chinese males in American media have long symbolized com-
pliant and passive femininity (Jachinson Chan 2001), the Hong Kong stars
now are mostly associated with the hard-fighting, gun-wielding, and muscular heroes of the action thriller and comedy. However, from one extreme
to the other, the discursive formation of Chineseness within the U.S. media
remains an object of cultural and racial fantasy.

Being stranded in America's Wild West and losing one's memory and identity are the themes of Sammo Hung's Hong Kong work *Once upon a Time
in China and America* (1997), a popular kung fu sequel starring Jet Li. The
series was started in 1991 by Tsui Hark, who creatively revived the legend of
the Cantonese martial arts master Wong Fei-hung/Huang Feihong, who was
the subject of several dozen Cantonese films made after 1949.[1] The 1997 production, in a way, symbolically serves as a pivotal point for our understanding of the phenomenon of Hong Kong film talent's crossing of the Pacific
and landing in Hollywood. After directing the film, Sammo Hung left Hong
Kong and starred in the CBS television action drama *Martial Law*. The movie

was also Jet Li's penultimate Hong Kong production before his Hollywood debut in *Lethal Weapon 4* (1998). The story about the Chinese hero's adventure in the American West seems to foretell the departure of Hung, Li, and other Hong Kong film talents for the Gold Mountain to further develop their careers. As for Tsui Hark, who produced the film, *Once Upon a Time in China and America* was, however, more like an expression of nostalgia for his own homecoming since he had already made the Hollywood film *Double Team* (1997) by that time. Three years later, Jackie Chan, who claimed *Once Upon a Time in China and America* was originally his idea, recycled this kung fu western and proposed it to Disney to make *Shanghai Noon* (2000) after his blockbuster *Rush Hour* (1998).

There are several motifs in *Once Upon a Time in China and America* that may allegorize the experiences of Hong Kong film people working in Hollywood. They are: experiencing amnesia, mixing with or even becoming part of another ethnic group, and selectively deploying Chineseness to advance one's own interest. As the sixth installment of Tsui Hark's series, the film tells the story of Wong Fei-hung, his beloved Aunt Thirteenth, and his disciple Seven, who travel together by stagecoach to visit the Po Chi Lam branch clinic in the late nineteenth-century American West. They have to fight ferocious Indians, white cowboys, and a racist mayor who ruthlessly oppresses Chinese workers, and finally they save the entire community of the overseas Chinese and help to establish the first Chinatown there. Some genre elements of the spaghetti western, such as the bar brawl, the bank robbery, the conventions of the gunfight, and a mass hanging are invoked by this Hong Kong kung fu movie, tailor made for the Chinese New Year. The clashes between Chinese and Western cultures, the final triumph of the Chinese hero, and the match-up between Wong Fei-hung's fast hands and the cowboys' guns all create a comfortably inflated self-image of Chineseness for celebration of the lunar new year. Very much unlike the previous installments in the series, which portray a China in the turmoil of social chaos, revolutions, and Western imperialism, this film gives the kung fu master a vacation by letting him travel overseas and have fun in a foreign wonderland. Trying to leave an agonizing China behind and assert or even redefine one's own Chineseness on new turf resonated with many Hong Kong audiences, who were facing the 1997 handover, which was to happen only a few months after the film's release. Indeed, the film does a good job of integrating the fantasy of amnesia into its story line. Following an Indian raid, Wong Fei-hung hits his head, temporarily loses his memory, and is adopted as a member by a Native American tribe. Only when he regains his

Chinese identity is he able to help the immigrant community fight their white oppressors and engage in the final duel with a Fu-Manchu-look-alike cowboy (which may suggest a symbolic triumph over the stereotypical portrayals of Chinese in the American mainstream media).

The film seems to say that a new beginning (in the New World) is possible only if one can let go of old memories (of China). A real action hero is always required to prove himself in a world where he is deprived of what he once had, and he always needs to fight his way back from a zero degree. This sounds like the myth of the self-made hero, though Wong, the protagonist in the Hong Kong film, and the Hong Kong film stars themselves never begin totally from scratch in the West. When the famous Chinese kung fu master is thrown into a totally foreign environment, the Wild West, his glorious past and records in China are temporarily erased. The traditional image of Wong Fei-hung—in the almost eighty sequences of the series in conventional Cantonese cinema—is of a middle-aged authoritative figure, often played by the Cantonese actor Kwan Tak Hing, who has a horse face and a serious look.[2] He is a patriarch and a local leader who is always surrounded by a group of protégés. The traditional stories of the Wong Fei-hung movies are primarily concerned with how this fatherly hero and his disciples protect the weak and helpless and maintain Confucian values and law and order in Guangdong, beating the local hectors and the villains from northern China. The mood of the early Wong Fei-hung series is basically regional and parochial, paralleling the spirit of Cantonese cinema at that time. And the message of the early films is clear: the local community under Wong, the father figure par excellence, will exhaust every means in order to enable the ethnically homogeneous, the nationally continuous, and the traditionally virtuous to prevail over the heterogeneous, the alien, and the newfangled.[3]

But in Tsui Hark's refreshed nineties version of Wong Fei-hung, the protagonist is played by Jet Li, a young, baby-faced kung fu actor originally from Beijing whose martial arts belong to the school of the North, which puts more emphasis on kicking and the acrobatic pose than does the Southern school. Jet Li is not even fluent in Cantonese (his voice is dubbed in almost all of his Hong Kong movies). The autochthonism and xenophobia are toned down in Tsui's reinvention, which, inversely, is infiltrated with a kind of pluralism that mirrors the reality of contemporary Hong Kong society more than that of Guangdong of the late nineteenth century. Critics generally consider Tsui's *Once Upon a Time in China* series as political allegory for the changes brought to Hong Kong by the 1997 crisis. Mingyu Yang highlights the postmodern characteristics of the film series by seeing it as parody that dismantles and rethinks Chinese history and culture as a collage of real historical events, fictional figures, martial arts legends, popular memory, and the contemporary political situation of Hong Kong. Yang believes "[t]his textual and semiotic hybrid reflects how the [Hong Kong] people make sense of their past experiences and current life in the contingent and fragmented culture of postmodernism" (Mingyu Yang 1995, 169–70).

Tony Williams does not agree that the response offered by Tsui's series to contemporary Hong Kong and China issues is entirely postmodernist in nature: "It is perhaps better to recognize the series as one that takes history seriously" (Williams 2000, 6). Williams asserts that the series, other than dealing with dispersion and China's relationship to the outside world, deserves to be viewed as a whole for its attempt "to construct a new version of an ethnic Chinese identity by moving beyond constricting definitions of nationhood and geographical boundaries and suggesting new ways to define a Chinese hero" (21). Undoubtedly, in the series, Tsui successfully turns the world of martial arts into a symbol for the political tumult of a transitional Chinese society going through modernity. But however hybrid the new appearance of Wong Fei-hung, he still represents the fraternal law, which is only made more appealing and acceptable. And he fundamentally maneuvers within his own sphere of influence, where everyone knows his name, and where he is able to handle the obtrusion of the "foreign elements" that are personified not only by the presumptuous Anglo-American colonial officers, greedy businessmen and missionaries, and villainous martial artists, but also by the westernized Chinese man and woman, including Wong's love interest, Aunt Thirteenth, and his America-educated student.

In *Once Upon a Time in China and America,* however, the situation is entirely reversed. Wong is now the intrusive alien who arrives in a foreign country where very few people are acquainted with his past. The reputed kung fu master is turned into an absolute nobody. He has only his martial arts skills on which to depend for regaining prestige. The accidental amnesia then is an element of the plot and a metaphor for the hero's adverse condition. Such a loss of what represents one's own identity also characterizes the Hong Kong filmmakers and stars trying to launch Hollywood careers. As mentioned earlier, Jackie Chan, years before becoming a household name in the United States, once described himself to a Western interviewer as a major and highly visible star in Asia. But, as he said, in Hollywood, many Hong Kong superstars including him, "could pass by unrecognized on any street in the United States." With the decrease of the world media's coverage of political transition in Hong Kong, the Western masses may no longer be interested in knowing about Hong Kong film people's past glories. Hollywood's reception of the yellow faces is never enthusiastic. Their subject position is out of joint and they do not have their usual places in this new transnational arena. However, from a positive, if not self-congratulating, perspective, the migrating film talent can seek a more flexible position among the multiple possibilities in the global sphere and reappropriate the discursive formations of race and ethnicity for their own advantage. Forgetting is definitely a fundamental act of creation and liberation.

The temporary loss of the hero's past and even cultural identity actually carries a different meaning for diasporic Chinese, whose major concern is adjusting themselves to be able to merge into their adopted lands. The preservation of a stable and inviolable image of being Chinese is not their most urgent consideration. The survival strategy of transmigrating people is to accommodate and assimilate with the host culture. Over different historical periods, many Chinese émigrés and exiles have also been confronted with some host countries' policies of coercive assimilation that foster an oppressive elimination of racial identity and cultural heritage. As one Hong Kong film critic says, alluding implicitly to the painful history of Chinese railroad laborers in the American West, *Once Upon a Time in China and America* "conveys the sense of loss for the diasporic Chinese" (Sek Kei 1999, 86). However, such a "loss" of ethnic identity could be voluntary or involuntary, depending on the situation. It has always been said that ethnic identity is subjected to manipulation and differential presentation. At the threshold of the twenty-first century, Wong Fei-hung's adventure in the American West symbolizes the strategic relocation of the diasporic capital-bearing subjects from affluent Asia, more than the wandering of despised alien Chinese laborers. As a matter of fact, these Hong Kong filmmakers and stars have nothing to lose, even if their Hollywood ventures flop. Their success, however, indicates new possibilities for constituting a more respectable cultural image of the diasporic Chinese modernity. Wong Fei-hung can lose his memory, but he cannot afford to lose his martial arts skills—the cultural capital of Chineseness he owns for investing in his global adventure. That image of a Chinese hero who temporarily becomes oblivious of his Chinese identity implies that a diasporic Chinese does not have to remain a loyal subject to his Chinese origin. Rather, he can rejuvenate himself by symbolically breaking with his past and repositing himself as a subject of fluid identity and as part of a global economy.

A real subject of the global economy should demonstrate the ease with which any color can be appropriated for his own needs and interests. Thus, when Wong Fei-hung is rescued by the peaceful Indians from the river, he has a similar-enough skin color and about the right hairstyle (the long queue worn by Chinese men of the Qing dynasty) to pass as a member of the Native American tribe. His metamorphosis into another race is of course the wishful thinking of Hong Kong filmmakers who generally show almost no sensitivity to racial discourse in local cinema.[4] To emphasize the "racial passing" of Wong and its suggestion of a detachment from specific ethnic roots is not to celebrate the hybridity and flexibility of the so-called postmodern migrant subject. Such a fluid racial imagination is indeed restricted to the elitist protagonist on which Hong Kong filmmakers with Hollywood ambitions project their transnational desires. Belonging to the upper-middle-class, privileged group, Wong is only a sojourner who is notably unlike his fellow countrymen he visits in California. Boundary crossing, whether geographical or racial, has very different meanings for Wong and for the other Chinese men in the film, who have probably been driven by poverty to leave their home country and work in the American West. But, if we take this embarrassingly unreal "racial passing" as an opportunity to examine the very arbitrariness of racial lines within the transnational context, a cultural narrative of passing may emerge here that could shed some light on the contradictions of race and the appropriation of such contradictions for a variety of interests and desires.

For a long time, Hollywood films used white actors to play Asian characters, asking audiences to suspend their awareness that the actors were white people pretending to be Asians. In caricaturing stereotyped Asian features, the Caucasian actors playing Asian roles laid bare the cinematic convention that race has to be performed in order to look "real." At some level, the constructiveness of cinematic representation has encouraged the performativity of racial portrayal. Nevertheless, the unnaturalness of such racial representation may help to debunk the idea of the stability of race, which is not simply a category used to describe visible markers of ethnic difference, but also a kind of authority used to ascribe identity and to quilt the subject to a certain place in the racial hierarchical order. The transnational Chinese subject represented by Wong Fei-hung seeks to defy and rewrite the imposition of racial identities by fantasizing himself as a fluid body that can easily pass from Chineseness to Native American redness for his own needs and interests.

However, such passing cannot easily be read as a form of resistance to the white supremacy that brings inequality and suffering to the Chinese workers in the film. Wong's transformation into a Native American is seen through the white gaze of white hegemony, which is simply unable to distinguish between minority persons of different ethnicities. Hence, Wong's becoming Native

American is actually more like "racial lumping" than racial passing. This often happens to Japanese Americans and Chinese Americans, whom whites describe as looking alike. Perhaps Wong's passing only reinforces the white hegemony's recategorization of marginal, hybrid groups into a monolithic image of a singular race. On the other hand, the film may present new possibilities by deviating from the predominant construction of passing in binary, black-and-white racial terms. As Gayle Wald has pointed out, white passing as black is always elevated to the status of a progressive and heroic act that challenges racial prejudice and promotes cross-racial understanding, whereas black passing as white is depicted as a compromised and self-interested form of racial disloyalty that is complicit with the structures of racial domination (Wald 2000, 16). In *Once Upon a Time in China and America,* Wong's converting to red fits neither the black-and-white binarism of ennobling or compromised representations of racial passing. Perhaps it is only a passing for convenience or a passing by accident, which serves as a means for the Chinese hero to leave his actual and metaphorical home. During his passing as Native American, Wong is not only able to defy his romantic commitment to Aunt Thirteenth and legitimately have an affair with the Indian girl, whose behavior symbolically subverts the Confucian values for which the hero usually stands. He is also temporarily released from the burden of being a Chinese heroic representative, conjuring the fluidity of racial appearance as a transgression of the stable definition of Chinese racial authority. His amnesia and his loss of original identity may reveal the real desire of a Hong Kong subject to control the terms of his racial definition, on the brink of the inevitable return to the Chinese motherland.[5] Not necessarily selling out on his racial origin, the hero capitalizes on the ambiguity of his racial appearance in order to pass as Native American and survive in the Wild West.

Black Connection

In the age of multiculturalism, Hong Kong film people in Hollywood certainly benefit from the blurring of racial boundaries. "Passing for black" is a strategy used by numerous Hollywood productions associated with Hong Kong crews and casts. These works feature team-ups between Hong Kong action stars and African American celebrities, such as Jackie Chan and Chris Tucker in the *Rush Hour* series, Sammo Hung and Arsenio Hall in *Martial Law,* Jet Li and Aaliyah in *Romeo Must Die,* and Jet Li and DMX in *Cradle 2 the Grave.* The Hong Kong "black connection" (Marchetti 2001) is by no

means restricted to the screen. The NBA star Dennis Rodman plays a significant sidekick in *Double Team,* directed by Tsui Hark. The *Replacement Killers,* starring Chow Yun Fat, was directed by the young African American filmmaker Antoine Fuqua. Kirk Wong's first American film, *The Big Hit* (1998),
was produced by the African American actor Wesley Snipes. The relationships
between Hong Kong martial arts movies and African American youth culture began rather early. In the 1973 movie *Enter the Dragon,* the black karate
star Jim Kelly was hired as a supporting character for Bruce Lee. David Desser
has researched the wide popularity of Hong Kong kung fu films in the United States in the seventies, particularly among African American audiences.
The Chinese "chopsocky films" crossed over with blaxploitation, generating
movies like *Cleopatra Jones and the Casino of Gold* (1975), in which a black
female action heroine costarred with a Chinese woman warrior.

For some critics, this cross-cultural mixing and crossover between Chinese and African American affirms the solidarity of people of color in their
struggle against cultural imperialism, political subordination, and the repression of human rights (Gateward 2000). Both martial arts films and hip-hop
culture emphasize the human body as a site of resistance. The collaboration
of Hong Kong kung fu stars and African American celebrities in recent Hollywood productions could be understood as a coalition that empowers and
celebrates the colored body as a positive force and a source of physical ca-
pacities and liberation for fighting against the external, corporeal fixation.
The Hollywood producers, capitalizing on this body appeal of kung fu and
hip-hop to young American audiences, consciously promote *Romeo Must Die*
as a "hip-hop kung fu movie."[6]

Although racial passing has long been considered to have already passed by,
I still want to invoke the term to highlight the representation of Chineseness
through the Hong Kong body on the racially defined American screen. Passing is not out yet, since passing in the age of globalization is never permanent.
The person who has "passed" can always strategically find his way back to his
race. The development of racial equality, racial justice, the growth of racial
pride, and the incorporation of the racial minorities into national discourses
of democratic community, social mobility, and economic opportunity may not
necessarily amount to the end of passing. Alluding to the Shakespearean classic, *Romeo Must Die* tells a story about the children of two rival gang families—
Chinese and African American—falling in love. Of course, the movie is no
Jungle Fever (1991). It does not focus on the interracial romance and tension
between Han, the Chinese ex-cop from Hong Kong, played by Jet Li, and Trish,
the daughter of the black gang boss, played by the late R&B singer Aaliyah in

her feature film debut, in order to open up any dialogue on the border cross-ing of racial sexuality. It is rather an action-packed movie that uses computer-aided special effects in every fight scene. The producer, Joel Silver, apparently appropriates the similarly cutting-edge visual effects from his previous big hit, *The Matrix,* and uses the same high-wire stunts for the knockout action se-quences in *Romeo Must Die.* But in the sci-fi *Matrix,* there is at least a reason for the action heroes to jump high. To film Jet Li's combat sequence via spe-cial effects—to let him leap six feet in the air and rotate 180 degrees while kick-ing several guys—simply misses the point. If special effects can do the job, why does Hollywood bother to hire Hong Kong kung fu masters?

Hollywood's westernization of Hong Kong action stars is always criticized for being like a love relationship in which one partner tries to change the very things in her lover that attracted her in the first place. Ultimately, the charm of Hong Kong martial arts films that originally captured the gaze of the Western audience is lost precisely when Hollywood finally gets what it wants from Hong Kong cinema. In *Romeo Must Die,* however, it is not simply a westernization of the Hong Kong action hero but rather a "negrification," that is, a process of turning Jet Li into "black," that complicates the racial representation of Chineseness in the globalized visual medium. Such a con-version may not have to do with the interracial sexual relationship or with any physical makeup as in the minstrel show. Unlike the way in which he can smoothly transform into a Native American in *Once Upon a Time in China and in America,* Li is so Chinese in *Romeo Must Die* that he could not pass for black by any stretch of imagination. But he is depicted as an Asian im-migrant who can "blend in" easily and successfully with his African Ameri-can love interest and opponents.

In one scene, his African American competitors teach him a lesson on how to play football the hard way. But he finally manages to get on top of his game, hammers a few guys, scores a touchdown, and earns some respect. His ho-mosocial interactions with the black men have been established. Though he can never become a real black, the depiction of his fluidity suggests the flow of identity across the color line. In another scene, he is reminded by Trish to wear his baseball cap backward like a black man before they enter a bar run by another African American gang. Jet Li is continuously portrayed as "act-ing black" throughout the movie. For black audiences, this may constitute a sense of racial alliance and political solidarity among people of color, based on shared experiences of racism in the white-dominant society. For Asian audiences, such an imitation along the line of the racializing narratives of black masculinity could renegotiate and change the stereotypes of Asian male effeminacy. And for the young white audience, the appropriation of black culture is always highly romanticized, as its marginal status makes it an object for the mainstream culture to desire and emulate.

Though set against the antagonistic situation of the two ethnic families, the plot shrewdly reveals that the real enemy lies within the same racial group. Being loyal to one's race is simply unreliable and self-defeating. The henchmen of the Chinese and the African American gang leaders (played, respectively, by Russell Wong and Isaiah Washington) are both eager to outdo each other and even go so far as to assert themselves against their bosses and murder the bosses' sons. The deaths of their brothers unite Han and Trish to look for the real cause of the blood feud between the Chinese and the black organizations, which are involved in a murky plot to buy up the waterfront for a new sports stadium in Oakland, California. After defeating the real foes in each ethnic group, Han has a showdown with his Chinese father and defies his wrongdoing, which leads to the old man's confession and suicide. Meanwhile, Han is warmly accepted by Trish's father, who, however, cannot help making a racialized remark about him: "he a lot shorter than I thought" and "he just a little guy." Han's passing is never complete in the eyes of the blacks. But the death of his brother with the same racial roots could give rise to a new kind of brotherhood across racial lines, while the transgressive act of defying his father may also aid in the formation of an interracial alliance. The implied message of the film is not that if one can transgress one's racial origin, a free zone of multiple identities always awaits. On the contrary, one can cross the racial barriers by attaching to one's ethnic roots on the condition that one is able to avow and discard them at the right moments.[7]

Aihwa Ong has argued that, over the final two decades of the twentieth century, the diasporic movement of Asians to the United States defined an alternative modernity in the Asia Pacific. The Southeast Asian immigrants of the United States developed links with African Americans and constituted a kind of "Black Asian" group that proved to be unassimilable to the stable category of "Asian American" represented by the U.S. racial discourse (A. Ong 1995). Since the black/white division is the typically bipolar construction of race in the United States, Gary Okihiro points out that Asians, along with other minority groups, are rendered invisible in American racial politics. Asians in America are thus perceived as "near-whites" or "just like blacks" (Okihiro 1994, 33). On the other hand, the growing importance of mobile Chinese entrepreneurs on both sides of the Pacific makes them construct themselves as builders of bridges across the Pacific and refuse the model minority image imposed by the U.S. hegemonic understanding (A. Ong 1995).

The "black connection" in Hollywood–Hong Kong films may not simply invalidate the conventional categorization of the minority subject. A simple assertion of hybridity within ethnic subject formation merely goes along with the reproduction of the existing racial power relations. Hybridity, as Lisa Lowe defines it, "does not suggest the assimilation of Asian or immigrant practices to dominant forms but instead marks the history of survival within relationships of unequal power and domination" (Lowe 1996, 67), and she "seeks to challenge the conception of difference as exclusively structured by a binary opposition between two terms, by proposing instead another notion of 'difference' that takes seriously the historically produced conditions of heterogeneity, multiplicity, and nonequivalence" (72). Uneasy racial passing could externalize the problem and compel every subject to recognize that there is always an inherent impossibility at the kernel of its formation. Any claim to refer to the precious internal essence of one's racial being would be rendered ridiculous.

Ubiquitous Whiteness

The combination of Chinese kung fu and hip-hop culture may allow *Romeo Must Die* to claim a multiculturalist edge while fueling the solidarity of a new Chinese nationalism and black nationalism that challenges American racial minority categories. Nevertheless, it also subtly displaces racial politics with the ubiquity and universality of whiteness. The so-called problematization of minority categories and the coalitions between Asians, Asian Americans, and African Americans that undermine the spheres of U.S. global influence is still framed by and emanates from the white field of vision or white gaze. Like *Rush Hour, Romeo Must Die* has no significant white character. But whiteness still occupies the privileged place from which to see and make sense of the world. The portrayals of the people of color are organized along racial order. The minority groups can gain power only through organized crime, and both the sparring Chinese and black gang families have to work for the white boss who is the mastermind of the new stadium plot. The film stereotypes Chinese and African Americans even as it may attempt to recuperate color consciousness. Han remains a taciturn and inscrutable Chinese who can best express himself mainly through his mastery of kung fu. In contrast, the black gang's fat rascal Maurice (played by Anthony Anderson), who repeatedly calls Han "Dim Sum," is always showing off his black talk and lots of propulsive hip-hop with other cast members, Aaliyah and DMX. Hence, a color-blind viewing position is discouraged within the context of whiteness. Instead, the ethnic, culture-clash comic relief in the film is marked and emphasized by its colors while asserting whiteness as natural, nonlocalized, and universal. The invisible but universal whiteness involves a patronizing distance and respect for the ethnic cultures, conceiving the colored as an authentic community toward which it empties its own position of all particular content. The powerful Hollywood film industry can always reassert and renegotiate the centrality of white dominance with the subtlety of not connecting it to the positioning of a white character, in response to social changes and cultural movements.

In the martial arts western comedy *Shanghai Noon,* starring Jackie Chan, the dominance of whiteness is no longer represented by the conventional image of a heroic white cowboy. Rather, it is defined in many different ways as a new nation, as freedom, autonomy, equality, dignity, and so on. *Shanghai Noon* shares many similarities with *Once Upon a Time in China and America.* Both have their Chinese heroes travel the American West in the late nineteenth century and receive a contingent mission during their trip to save the Chinese American laborers. Both films have their protagonists spend time with Indians and become one of them. Both films feature a blond cowboy who is sympathetic to the Chinese, and both films shoot a gallows sequence. Besides all these similarities, there are also major differences between the films, which are constituted by their different relations to whiteness.

Roy O'Bannon (Owen Wilson), the blond cowboy in *Shanghai Noon,* is not like the sharpshooting Billy (Jeff Wolfe) in *Once Upon a Time in China and America.* Roy is an antihero and more humanlike—he is a loquacious lothario and wisecracking but incompetent outlaw-wannabe who is absorbed with his image as a bad guy in order to impress chicks. Although Roy is the whitest guy around, his whiteness is relatively marginalized. The film is a western comedy with an ethnic twist. Ethnic banter is everywhere. Some white settlers think the Chinese are Jews, while other frontiersmen believe the Indians are. On the other hand, the Indians call Chan's character, who is in his Imperial Guard gown, "the man who fights in dress," and when marrying off the daughter of the chief to him, they say, "At least he's not a white guy." It is often said that a racial category is defined only through opposition. Does this imply then that Chineseness is reinforced and empowered vis-à-vis the peripheral white masculinity? However, according to the semiotic assumption, a sign (a racial one in this case) can bear any meaning not only because it signifies in its opposition to another sign but also because it signifies according to its place in a certain context or a determining system. As in *Rush Hour,* the all-action Chan is once again paired with an all-mouth partner. He still plays a man of limited vocabulary and much action and fight. Doing Chris Tucker's job in *Rush Hour,* Wilson in *Shanghai Noon* is the motormouth who covers for Chan's shaky English. His Chineseness is highlighted and exhibited for the consumption of the American audience.

The Chinese Imperial Guard, Chon Wang (Jackie Chan), has traveled a long way to the Wild West to rescue the kidnapped Princess Pei Pei (Lucy Liu), who is being ransomed by a traitorous expatriate in Carson City. Roy keeps telling Chon: "You're not in the East. This is the West. The sun doesn't rise here. It sets here."[8] Unlike Wong Fei-hong, who finally leaves the West after his mission, Chon chooses to stay at the place where the sun sets and to be "naturalized" as an American. But he also chooses to transform his Chinese identity. Though Jackie Chan does not come from Western culture, the story conceived by him pays homage to the western genre he has admired since childhood. He tells reporters that, as a boy, he played with toy pistols in imitation of movie cowboys. Being anachronistic, *Shanghai Noon* is a buddy movie with a cross-cultural spin, turning Butch Cassidy and the Sundance Kid into the Sundance Kid and the Shanghai Kid. The film does not ridicule the old genre at all but makes many references to famous westerns, and it presents a nostalgic fantasy in which the grownup generation can play cowboys and Indians. If Wong Fei-hung becomes a Native American only for a short while and even turns his back on the tribe when he recovers from his amnesia, Chon Wang in *Shanghai Noon* goes so far as to tell his white buddy that the Indian tribe is his family. In the final scene, the Chinese man looks more like the Indian sidekick seen in many westerns who rides with and helps the white sheriff to protect the transcontinental rail from bandits. Chon's Chineseness has been tamed like the Indians conquered by the white man in the untamed Wild West.

Perhaps we should not call it "taming." Minority groups are always required to adopt the norms and values of Anglo Americans in the United States. It is also possibly a strategy employed by the Hong Kong film talent to intervene in the global media controlled by the American entertainment industry. Such a transnational and transracial move may simultaneously invite and deflect control. But it ultimately will subvert the persistent notion of racial categorization constructed by the U.S. white hegemony and give rise to a new Chinese cultural nationalism. As many studies have already indicated, Hong Kong cinema has made use of martial arts within Chinese cultural dimensions to assert a pan-Chinese identity in its overseas exportation. Its impact is not confined to an emergence of Chinese nationalism among the diasporic Chinese. It also creates a kind of pan-Asian cultural nationalism and leads to the formation of U.S. martial arts films and film stars and to the so-called "Asianization" of Hollywood. There is no doubt that Hong Kong–style action thrillers are going to supplant the old styles of action like those of Arnold Schwarzenegger, Bruce Willis, and Sylvester Stallone in Hollywood. However, the Hong Kong stars, such as Chow Yun Fat, whose stature as an action star in the West belies his legitimate acting talent, are not always given an opportunity to show any dramatic range. They always play generic and flat Chinese characters. John Lee in *Replacement Killers* is not very different from Nick Chen in *The Corruptor*. But this is precisely what Hollywood wants: a high-gloss American version of the Hong Kong action picture with the exuberance of a genre where surface is everything. The signs of Chineseness in those Hollywood films starring Hong Kong actors or actresses are merely symbols deprived of actual Chinese people who make them alive. But it is never a straightforward question of racist misrepresentation. The cultural and ethnic differences have never been canceled out in Hong Kong's participation in the global film industry. The Chineseness created by Hong Kong cinema is still in the Hollywood production, though it is not necessarily incarnated by any actual Chinese people.

Peeling Off the Ethnic Face

"If Mr. Cruise peeled off his face and turned out to have been Chow Yun Fat all along, the picture might be saved,"[9] comments one film critic on John Woo's *Mission: Impossible 2*. The sci-fi peel-off latex face in the film may be not only a fabulous device for a spy to switch his identity but also a fantastic trick for a racial minority to sustain its cultural identity behind the white look.[10]

In comparison to the Hong Kong stars who must confront difficulties of representation in their transition to Hollywood, the directors from Hong Kong appear to be in a better position since they only work behind the scenes and their ethnic faces are not required to appear on screen. Their cultural identity is merely mentioned occasionally by film critics or promoters in order to highlight their particular styles or the "ethnic flavor" they add to the mainstream American films they have directed. Without any hustle or hassles in marketing these "Asian" products to different racial groups, Hollywood should always benefit from these nonwhite directors who can adapt their styles to the Hollywood system. Apparently, Hollywood has nothing to lose by having these Hong Kong filmmakers directing movies for the industry and, at the same time, it does not need to worry about playing racial politics in such an employment of foreign labor. The racial ridicule and ste-reotyping usually applied to the ethnic groups in the United States can be easily avoided in their cases.

However, racial politics are always being played by various ideological camps. The global visibility of Hong Kong cinema is considered by scholars of transnational Chinese studies as an invention of a new collective sense of Chineseness among diverse Chinese communities and an unprecedented intrusion of Asian cultural form into the Western-dominated media spaces. The hugely popular action movies by John Woo and other Hong Kong di-rectors are said to embody the spirit of Asian modernity that upholds the myth of fraternal solidarity, valorizes mobile masculinity, and reaffirms a number of traditional Asian values, such as kinship loyalty and a gender di-vision of labor, in the world of capital accumulation. Aihwa Ong suggests a compensatory reading of Woo's films and other Hong Kong action movies by arguing that they provide "a moral counterweight to the heartlessness of capitalism and the upheavals of diaspora."[11] Hence, even before Woo lands in Hollywood, his Hong Kong films already perform the functions of engen-dering emergent global Chinese publics and of subverting the static notion of white supremacy in the mass media.

On the other hand, John Woo's Hollywood position and success have also been immediately recognized by Asian Americanists. They categorize him as one of the significant representations of contemporary Asian American cul-ture, on the assumption that Woo's Hong Kong cultural identity would conflate with the Chinese American one.[12] Lisa Lowe states that the Asian-origin col-lectivity is unstable and changeable, hence the boundaries and definitions of Asian American culture are also continually shifting. "The making of Asian American culture includes practices that are partly inherited, partly modified, as well as partly invented" (Lowe 1996, 65). Some Chinese American filmmak-ers, such as Wayne Wang, who is also originally from Hong Kong, first make independent movies about Chinatown (Wang's reputed debut *Chan Is Miss-ing* [1981] is a low-budget 16 mm black-and-white feature about two Chinese American cabdrivers in San Francisco's Chinatown) and then go beyond the ghetto and deliver for Hollywood. Unlike them, Woo comes to America already as a cult director and a commercial action-genre master through and through. His American productions may add some "Asian flavor" to Hollywood film-making, but, as a critic notes, Woo's films could not be immediately catego-rized as Asian American.[13] However, Woo's being placed as part of Asian Amer-ican culture should be understood within the international frame of global capitalism. Woo's visibility in American culture and his being incorporated into the Asian American discourse could be explained by the fluid concept of trans-national Chinese or Asian cultural identity. Sau-ling Cynthia Wong argues, by looking at a Hong Kong immigrant character named Yuwen in a novel by the popular writer Liang Fengyi, "a Chinese cultural identity for Yuwen is merely one of the many possible alignments to be articulated, even exploited, according to circumstance and need." Wong continues:

> Always relationally defined, "Chineseness" to Yuwen has no a priori ontological status, is neither more nor less intrinsically meaningful than any other identity. When a Canadian women's magazine wants to do a cover story on her, Yuwen is open to presenting herself as a Chinese immigrant entrepreneur, part of the multicultural mosaic of her adopted land. In this case, "Chineseness" (much like education, energy, good looks or linguistic ability) is merely one of many assets, part of the human capital for which Hong Kong emigrants are famed all over the globe. At other times, Yuwen's sense of being Chinese is minimalist, unmobilized: a fact, yes, but hardly something to be exercised about. (S. Wong 1998, 142–43)

Apparently, the alignment or exploitation of and the detachment from a certain cultural identity are always appropriated by various agencies. The "fluidentity" of Chineseness or Asian Americanness could be articulated and manipulated both by the Chinese immigrants themselves and by the Asian scholars advancing an argument. In the case of Woo's Hollywood films, Asian American critics may follow the general conflation of Asian Americans and Asians in mainstream American culture in order to emphasize the ascent of Asian Americans in the motion picture industry and their growing visibility in America's public media. Within the transnational setting, the question of whether Woo should be identified as an Asian American, a Hong Kong film-maker, or a trans-Chinese cultural representative is actually not a significant issue at all, since cultural identity, though it has origins and histories, is always relative, mobile, and subjected to constant changes. On the other hand, the critic always makes his object of study his own, goes forth from himself, and interprets and controls it. The conceptualization or the subjection of the object to the critic's view is the imposition on it of the form of the critic's self. If Woo's Hollywood films that deal only with white Americans can be called Asian American, I don't see any reason why they could not be also labeled as transnational Chinese or Hong Kong cinema. After all, cultural identity is itself a contested terrain of different ideological positions.

Woo may not be the first but he is likely the most popular Hong Kong filmmaker named and acknowledged by the Western world. Considered "the undisputed godfather of Hong Kong cinema and now one of Hollywood's most sought-after directors" (Singer 1998, 321), Woo enjoys well-deserved recognition and a distinct subjectivity across the Asia Pacific. In Western media coverage, Woo's debt to many Western directors in the making of his film style is always mentioned.[14] And he has been portrayed in the American media as a faithful Christian who is never afraid to include a lot of religious imagery in his violent movies.[15] Woo's trans-Pacific subject status is bound by a certain subjection. He is subjected to a designation of multiple cultural identities, which is sometimes rigid, sometimes fluid. As Étienne Balibar has aptly put it, the "subject is basically a responsible, or an accountable, subject, which means that he has to respond, to give an account (rationem reddere) of himself, i.e., of his actions and intentions, before another person, who righteously interpellates him."[16] The other person that interpellates Woo is, of course, in Lacanian terms, the big Other, which is the symbolic order that inscribes him in Western, (trans-)Chinese, or Asian American discourses. But for Woo himself, the attribution to his Chineseness or Asian Americanness could be, at least at the beginning, detrimental to his career in Hollywood film industry.

Besides the phenomenon of numerous Hong Kong directors' beginning to work for Hollywood, Wayne Wang and Ang Lee have already proved that Asian artists could direct prestigious movies with non-Asian casts and handling non-Asian material in *Slam Dance* (1987), *Smoke* (1995), *Blue in the Face* (1995), *Anywhere but Here* (1999), *Maid in Manhattan* (2002), *Sense and Sensibility* (1995), *The Ice Storm* (1997), *Ride with the Devil* (1999), and *The Hulk* (2003).[17] So when Woo's first Hollywood film, *Hard Target* (1993), was described by an American producer as a "Chinese movie in English,"[18] he was devastated and determined to give up his flashy stylistic touches in his following project, *Broken Arrow* (1995), in order to prove that he could make a mainstream American film just like other Asian directors working in Hollywood. The outcome was that *Broken Arrow* fared much better than *Hard Target* in terms of the box office and reviews, but, for Woo's diehard fans, *Broken Arrow* is just another American film and by no means an effective transplant of his Hong Kong action. If style is the man himself, Woo's second Hollywood film is criticized for not bearing his signature style and for thus losing himself in the global entertainment system. But the box-office success of *Broken Arrow* did empower Woo and enabled him to work more freely in his next project, *Face/Off* (1997), which was largely considered a "real John Woo" kind of film.

It seems that the paradox of having to lose one's own style in order to have it holds true to Woo's Hollywood filmmaking experience. The transition from *Hard Target* to *Face/Off* through *Broken Arrow* may explain how Woo could become himself only by renouncing being himself. Such a dialectical self-realization—that is, in order to become himself, he must first lose himself—is what one might call the "symbolic castration" of the ethnic filmmakers' entry into white-dominant Hollywood. Symbolic castration, then, would not be strictly confined to the ethnic actors in Hollywood. But symbolic castration should not be understood as the ultimate barrier that limits the possibilities of subject constructions. On the contrary, it could be the very act that opens up new space for contingent subject formations.

In general discussions of John Woo's movies there is conspicuous consensus as to the concrete existence of a "Woo film-style." This style is presumed to be stable and not vary across time and place. It is cultural capital that supposedly belongs strictly to Woo; even migration and culture shock cannot transform its shareholding and value. When *Hard Target* and *Broken Arrow* were criticized for lacking Woo's stylistic factors, his fans on both sides of the Pacific were disappointed. With the release of *Face/Off*, however, Woo's fans seemed happy again and believed their "auteur director" was back on his recognizable and respectable stylistic track.

What is Woo's style? In what way does the audience conceive of how Woo's films—whether they are made in Hong Kong or produced by Hollywood—work for them? Initially, the first question does not appear difficult. Anyone familiar with Woo's Hong Kong films, such as *A Better Tomorrow* (1986), *The Killer* (1989), and *Hardboiled* (1992), could easily identify recurring images, favored subjects, and characteristic techniques that Woo has always used to achieve the emotional impact of his works. There is, for example, the posture of having both guns outstretched; characters leaping through the air while shooting; guns tossing through the air in slow-motion to be caught by the protagonist; a superhero withstanding the impact of hundreds of bullets; aestheticized violence; well-choreographed action sequences; all kinds of glorifying slow-motion, tracking shots, dramatic dolly-in, freeze-frames, and dissolves; themes of friendship, loyalty, chivalry, and code of honor; and so on. Some of these stylistic features were transplanted to *Hard Target* and *Broken Arrow;* why then did fans and critics still see the two Hollywood films as "non-Woo" works? Are these stylistic particulars just appearances that cannot represent Woo's "real thing"?

To the idea that "style is the man himself," Lacan makes this modification: "style is the man to whom one speaks." While one is defined by his style, he is also defined by his relation to the other. As Judith Miller explains, "Lacan's addition to this definition of style indicates that identity is divided between what style represents and the one before whom it is represented. A subject, says Lacan, by the fact that it is inscribed in the order of language, is represented by a signifier for another signifier" (Miller 1991, 147). Therefore, style does not necessarily suggest the unity of the subject. On the contrary, it designates a constitutive division in the subject that is never guaranteed by an assured identity. In the eyes of his fans, Woo's unique stylistic approach to violence and bloodshed has inspired American "new brutalism" movies,[19] but its authentic being got lost in his own works under the Hollywood system. The "lost object" of Woo's style has nonetheless returned in his third Hollywood production, the highly acclaimed *Face/Off*. The "real" Woo is back and it offers the appearance (in the fantasy of Woo's fans) of being the foundation of the unity of the auteur-subject.

Coincidentally, some obvious questions about subjectivity rarely raised in his previous films are addressed in Woo's *Face/Off*: Is our identity determined by our appearance? Would I become the other person if his face were given to me? How far could I still be myself if my subject is represented by another signifier? In the film, the two main characters swap faces, exchange identities, and are confronted with these very questions. Sean Archer (John Travolta) is a dedicated FBI agent who has been on the force for years and has been obsessively tracking one particular master criminal, Castor Troy (Nicolas Cage), for a long time. Archer knows everything about Troy. The reason Archer is relentlessly pursuing Troy is because, six years ago, he attempted to kill Archer but accidentally killed Archer's son. His desire for revenge and his preoccupation with chasing Troy have alienated Archer from his wife (Joan Allen) and his teenage daughter (Dominique Swain). Troy is finally captured and left in a coma after a violent confrontation. But it seems that Troy has stashed a time bomb somewhere in downtown Los Angeles. Archer's fellow officers believe that the only way to learn the location of the bomb is for Archer to masquerade as Troy and go undercover in prison in order to interact with Troy's brother. Through a highly experimental surgical procedure, Castor Troy's face is removed and transplanted onto Sean Archer. While Archer is disguised as Troy, the faceless Castor wakes up from his coma in the hospital and needs a face. The only one available is, of course, Sean Archer's. Now Troy becomes Archer and Archer is stuck with Troy's face. Troy has found new freedom (and fun) by assuming Archer's identity.

It is not a complicated plot, although it is pretty farfetched.[20] The story is easy to follow because the characters switch faces without their real identities' being changed. As one critic points out, "John Woo seems to suggest that the exterior of the body can be peeled off: faces, voices, body scars can be exchanged, but the inner core of being cannot be changed" (Doraiswamy 1998, 19). Does *Face/Off* simply conform to the idea that appearance is merely an illusion or a false image of reality, implying thereby that appearance is never significant? If so, what is the unchanged inner core of being? Is John Woo implying that he is always the same no matter which system he works for? Can we consider the film an allegorical depiction of transnational identity reconstruction for a Hong Kong filmmaker working in Hollywood?

Perhaps postmodern critics would find *Face/Off* uninteresting precisely because it refuses to enter the age of simulacrum, in which reality or authentic being is no longer distinguishable from its simulated image. The predominance of simulacra in today's world has already dissolved the distinction between reality and appearance. However, *Face/Off* still seems to be obsessed with unchanged being in an outrageously old-fashioned way. In Woo's hands, the original sci-fi plot is turned into a traditional Manichean battle between good and evil. In this plague of simulacra, authentic Being (or the Good), which Woo's films hold on to and do not let go of, is comprised of values usually found in his Hong Kong productions: the old Chinese spirit of chivalry, male bonding, and honor. Woo repeatedly tells interviewers that his movies are never simply about violence. His violence is always based on an ethical stance that has already vanished.[21] However, if what Woo conjures up no longer exists, the so-called Good or authentic Being appearing in his films is then nothing but a mask or a semblance.

Willingly or not, Woo and his characters are condemned to this world of copies and simulacra. Like his fans who anticipate the return of his unique style, Woo is a lack-in-being subject that seeks the lost object to fill out the void. Nevertheless, the old Chinese chivalrous spirit invoked in Woo's films could never be authentic or original since the Hong Kong community was designated, right from the beginning, as a westernized and colonized version of Chinese society. It is a place of lack and inconsistency. Hence, the subject of lack has to seek, in the posited big Other or in tradition, the justification for its being—some ethical mandate with which to identify. In *Face/Off*, however, the exchange of identities between Archer and Troy demonstrates that good/true is the mask of evil/false and vice versa. Ethico-ontological being can never be what it appears to be if it is to give some substance to the divided subject. In *Face/Off* the ethical stance of violence insisted upon by Woo has changed from the code of honor between men to "family values": Archer's battle with Troy and their swapped identities unexpectedly help strengthen Archer's relations with his wife and daughter and save Archer's dysfunctional family. At the end of the film, Archer adopts Troy's illegitimate son to make his family complete again.

The regained unity of Archer's family is constituted through the introduction of certain alien and evil elements by means of the disguised Troy. While Troy plays the role of Archer he succeeds, through his flamboyant approach, in making Archer's listlessly tiresome marriage more exciting and rebuilds trust with his rebellious daughter. Troy's malicious intrusion into Archer's family turns out to be a great help for Archer's final return to the embrace of his wife and daughter. The fine line between good and evil is further blurred as it is Archer, the good guy, who destroys another person's family in order to save his own.

The clamoring of family values, though a bit unusual in Woo's previous movies, actually reinforces the mainstream American perception of Asian (Americans) as a "model minority" cherishing the significance of family and kinship. If the film is viewed from the perspective of family values in a scenario of the other's desire, however, it may take on a different meaning. The film could be looked at through Archer's gaze as one who presumes he knows that he is meant for the other's desire. Then Archer would no longer be an innocent hero whose identity is bereft, whose wife is stolen by his enemy, and who is thus left with no choice but to fight back to retrieve what he has lost. On the contrary, Archer would be the great conspirator who designs the whole plot. While he is free to choose to become Troy, it is Troy who wakes up from his coma without a face and is forced to take the only available face. He has to settle for Archer's identity. At first it appears that Archer makes an "ethical" decision by giving himself up and negating his identity in order to save the innocent people of Los Angeles from Troy's time bomb. Apparently his rescue attempt fails because it is Troy, after taking over Archer's face, not Archer, who unplugs the bomb. On the other hand, Archer succeeds in saving the innocent lives of Los Angeles at the expense of lending his face to Troy, although he gets credit under his own name. The mission is completed while the hero is displaced and misidentified.

If, however, we consider that this rescue plan is in fact Archer's desperate attempt to save his crumbling family and to pursue the ideal image of being a father, then actually nothing runs aground in the hero's mission. His self-negation turns out to be a means for Archer to become what he ultimately wants to achieve being. Such a decision involves the dimension of the death drive, suggesting a negative gesture of suspending the symbolic order. By inviting another man to take his place in the family, Archer lets Troy have sex with his wife and exposes his daughter to possible paternal sexual harassment.

The strategy of "nothing ventured, nothing gained" is of course a convention in action movies. But, Archer's move also bears witness to the fact that, in cop movies, the only true transgression is always the adventure of the defender of the law, whereas the criminals, in comparison, appear like indolent petit-bourgeois, careful conservators (Žižek 1990, 93).

Archer's transgression is even subtler. His attempt to venture expresses a death drive that throws the symbolic order out of joint. Still, it is not Archer but the proxy, who literally wears his face, who has really made the transgression. Perhaps the unruliness and destructiveness of Troy are only the external reflections realizing Archer's innermost whims—such as killing without any justifiable cause, having an extramarital affair, and sexually harassing his own daughter. His self-negation is merely an encounter with himself in the form of his opposite, a self-differentiation through a negative self-relation, or a self-referential movement of negativity. What appears as the threat of an intruding alien that can undermine and steal our identity is actually the inherent antagonism of identity itself. Archer's obsession with hunting Troy has already gone so far that a mere arrest would not satisfy him. Only by changing identities and positions with Troy can Archer make himself appear as the object that attracts his gaze. In a way, he gets caught up in the picture he is looking at and he loses all distance from it. His hunt for the enemy turns into his "getting himself hunted."

When Archer falls into his own plot or picture, the gaze under which he makes himself seen reveals in him also his shadowy double, that is to say, that which is in him more than him. The scene that most clearly stages this "making oneself seen" has Troy and Archer standing on opposite sides of a wall with a double-sided mirror between them. As they point their guns, preparing to shoot each other, they see their reflections in the mirror. Since their identities have already been switched, the mirror images are not reflections of who they are but who they are trying to kill. So the real aim of the bullet is not to hit the target opposite but to return in a loop to make oneself hit. The evil Troy thus embodies the good guy Archer in the form of his opposite. And Archer then is the form of the appearance of evil (when Archer acts and appears as himself, he is far more monstrous and disgusting to his family and coworkers than after Troy takes up his face).

Thus the hidden message in *Face/Off*, if there is any, is not that there is some authentic Being or reality, such as ethnicity, value, or the Good, that could remain unchanged no matter how far it is concealed by appearance. Identity and value do change when they migrate to different cultural and social spaces, and they always adapt themselves to the new environment. What is revealed, however—if we read *Face/Off* as an allegorical description of Woo's own situation in the transnational crossing—is that appearance or the body can be separated successfully from the inner being or the soul. What Woo finally proves is that he can make a mainstream American blockbuster, thus affirming that the merging of Hong Kong filmmakers with Hollywood's global system is a deterritorializing body capable of overcoming various boundaries and crushing all barriers and resistances, such as those of the nation, race, and value. The fantasy of a man who would not be entrapped in his body and could move freely is somewhat realized.

From vampire movies to alien body-snatcher sci-fi, Hollywood cinema has always been populated by characters whose bodies are invaded by external forces. This is probably an expression of Hollywood's anxiety about outside ideological impact—one is always exposed to the alien spectral other. In the 1990s, Hollywood films continued to portray people whose bodies have been switched. However, now only the external body is drastically changed, with the internal self remaining the same. Although the white male body that defines the qualities of American masculinity as violence, autonomy, possession of women, and lack of emotion has been repudiated, these bodily transformations never challenge the privileges associated with white U.S. masculinity.[22] Now, in the twenty-first century, a Chinese director, accompanied by the deterritorializing forces of the cinematic mode of production under the global media syndicate, subverts traditional codes that restrict and control social relations: for example, racial limits, kinship systems, class structures, religious beliefs, folk customs, and so on. The multinational capital that makes Woo's Hollywood success possible is precisely the fluid and hybrid body that can always change faces and, in its deterritorializing guise, set adrift fluxes of things, people, words, customs, and beliefs in the global circuit. The force of deterritorialization is precisely the gist of "Pacific Rim discourse."

However, if Woo's success in *Face/Off* and *Mission: Impossible 2* may satisfy the passion for the semblance (of a cult director's personal style and of an ethnic minority's so-called inner being), the box-office and critical failures of his *Windtalkers* (2002) probably tell us about a violent return to the strong desire for reality. This movie is based on the true story of Navajo soldiers' using their unwritten language during World War II to create an unbreakable code that helped win the combat against the Japanese in the Pacific. In it, Woo obviously attempts to meld into the cliché of the war film genre his own intimate style, such as the visually hyperbolic and weightily emotional approach and the dramatic themes of male bonding, honor, and loyalty, accompanied with his trademarks of the slow-motion birds in flight and the standoff with firearms held on one another, in order to prove that he is more than a choreographer of violent mayhem. But there is always a limit for the deterritorializing drive since reterritorialization is also an intrinsic moment of the fluid global flows. Even though Woo can break the racial and religious boundaries, he is by no means considered the right man to handle the overly familiar nationalist materials of the World War II for the American audience. Indeed, after the spectacular attack on the World Trade Center, and when America was consequently engaged in wars on terrorism with Afghanistan and Iraq, reality has already become the best appearance of itself. No catastrophe movies and no large-scale war films could create similar effects, let alone the one by an Asian director who is only good at staging shootouts in enclosed spaces.

The Rim-like Structure of the Global Capital Drive

Pacific Rim discourse is nothing but the rim-like structure of the global capital drive. It is said that the Asia Pacific is the last frontier of the spatial imagination of Euro-American capitalism.[23] It is the "last thing" because this object of drive can no longer be infinitely substituted for by any other objects of desire. This is *it*. There is no possibility of any further postponement of the encounter. It can no longer shift from one object to another through metonymical displacement. But the final border could also be a return to its supposed origin, since America's Pacific is only a loop of the American West. The circular movement of boundless expansion may eliminate as well as reinforce the frontier that separates "us" from "them." Asia Pacific is less a geographical concept than a conceptual construct. Fantasies of immense wealth projected by Euro-American capitalism onto the Pacific Rim have lured many Westerners to the mapping and domination of the region. Many Asians, at the same time, have also been attracted to America to pursue their "Gold Mountain" dreams. The Gold Mountain soon turned into a place of disillusionment for early Asian immigrants. Racial segregation, denial of citizenship, restrictions on land-ownership, physical abuse, and even internment paved the ways for the immigrants from Asia Pacific to traverse their fantasy of America. Over the last four decades, however, Asia Pacific has produced new successful models of transnational capitalism that go beyond even the visions and fantasies of the Euro-American capitalist system that triggers it. The economic growth of Asia Pacific and the potential rise of China in the region are considered a threat to U.S. hegemonic power, which no longer hesitates to allow the language of "the Yellow Peril" to emerge again in its politics of culture. It does not, however, necessarily bring about a resurgence of anti-Asian sentiment. Rather, it leads to "a single mouth kissing itself"—using Asians to "smooch" the Asians on the other shore.[24] The circuit of self-affected drive becomes a solution for curbing the excessive expansion of global capitalism and rendering possible the nation-state's rescaling and restructuring.

The absorption of Hong Kong film talent by Hollywood (from the 1990s on) is perhaps a good illustration of the circular movement of global capital drive. As John Woo himself has observed, Hollywood is copying Hollywood insofar as Hong Kong films are an imitation of Hollywood. In a sense, Hollywood can get back its own message from the otherness of Hong Kong cinema. In the early 1990s, Hong Kong cinema was "discovered" by Hollywood for its refreshing differences, especially for its physical vitality and political mirror-effect. By looking at Hong Kong films, the American audience could once again experience the bizarre articulations of energy that had long since disappeared from Hollywood cinema.

Because of the 1997 political handover, Hong Kong films are commonly received in the United States as allegories of the city's sociohistorical situation. The political relevance and function of cinematic production as the collective mode of social expression that had vanished in Hollywood now pops up again in Hong Kong filmmaking. Not only can the style of Hong Kong action cinema be found in quite a few Hollywood productions, but also a number of Hong Kong directors have already thrived in American mainstream productions. A handful of Hong Kong actors and actresses have already starred in several major features and blockbusters. As I have argued in the previous chapter, the infiltration of Asian film talent into the white-dominant entertainment industry may imply that the new Hollywood has followed the direction of multiculturalism in order to adjust itself to American cultural policy and to meet the growing diversified tastes of the domestic and the world markets. Nevertheless, the transnational crossing of Asian film people to Hollywood may only offer an alibi for the continued hegemony of the Anglo-American global entertainment industry. The small-scale "Asianization" of Hollywood is simply a new face of the old hegemony, as white America dresses itself up in a new representation of its own self and of the world. Far from being the other of the United States, Hong Kong cinema is rather the United States itself in its otherness. Presumably through such a relation, the United States is able to externalize and transfer onto the other the dimension of internal difference that dwells in itself, thereby avoiding any confrontation with it. Such an avoidance of or a defense against one's own otherness still belongs, however, to the logic of desire. The inscription of Hong Kong film styles in Hollywood production is, instead, actually defined by the order of drive. The economy of drive can never act like a lizard that jettisons its own tail when it is in distress, for it is hooked too closely to it.

The assimilation of Hong Kong film styles into the Hollywood system and the hiring of Asian film talent do not necessarily construct a new identification with a totality that conjoins with multiracial and multicultural America in a harmonious fashion. Right from the beginning, there is never a striving for any form of unity. There is no necessary correspondence between the thrust and the object, since the aim of Hollywood's outreach to the Asia Pacific is not the consumption of any external object. It is merely a montage, in the sense that it links together two heterogeneous things.

Some critics might want to believe that Hollywood is no longer the puppeteer of the global economy of images but only a nodal point of a complex transnational construction of cinematic landscapes, and therefore that a radical heterogeneity of the object as gaze is produced in Hollywood. The film industry in California, however, does not play the role of a unique mastering subject that oversees the entire field of vision. Now, it is also "in the picture." Despite the success of Jackie Chan, Jet Li, and John Woo, Asian American moviemakers are still finding it tough to break into Hollywood. Many Asian American directors have expressed their discontent at having their works rejected by distributors and festivals, including Sundance (Hodgson 2000).

Since the Hong Kong artists mostly play alien characters from Asia on-screen, they only further confirm the prevailing prejudice that Asian Americans are forever seen as "strangers" in their own country. While many Americans enjoy the Hollywood productions starring or directed by Hong Kong actors and filmmakers, the Asian American community remains under a humiliating cloud of suspicion. A number of Chinese Americans were the target of the furor that broke out over the illegal donations by Asians to President Clinton's 1996 reelection campaign. Finally they all pleaded guilty to the charge of improper political fund-raising.[25] About the same time, the Chinese American scientist Wen Ho Lee was suspected of spying for China. He was fired from the nuclear weapons laboratory he worked for, on charges that he violated security policies by downloading confidential data to an unsecured computer. He was detained for nine months and finally prosecuted for crimes unrelated to espionage. His case has been widely covered and debated in the national media.[26] It is believed that, in order to save face, the U.S. government had to prosecute Lee even without having strong evidence. The Cox Report further spread fear among the American public about China's theft of nuclear secrets from U.S. institutions.[27] The Republicans, apparently, exploited the racist fears for political gain, whereas the Democrats did very little to openly defend the integrity of Chinese Americans. At the same time as the controversies over human rights, nuclear espionage, Taiwan–U.S. military ties, the bombing of China's embassy in Belgrade, and the clash of an American spy plane with a Chinese fighter jet over the South China Sea, the U.S. government sought support from the Chinese government on the war against terrorism and continued to act on trade agreements with Beijing, which helped clear the way for China to join the World Trade Organization in 2001. In a way, while American spectators are excited by the aesthetic violence produced by the ethnic directors from the Asian Pacific, a different form of violence is raging in American society.

The montage of global capital drive links heterogeneous partial objects together and brings a little bit of the Real inside the symbolic order. The Real is the impossible, in the sense that it is the impossibility of any relationship that could bring different things to the formation of a whole. The circuit of global capitalism in the Pacific turns around this failed relationship and marks it in its very impossibility. The globalization process does not generate a multicultural and multiracial total order that can quilt all nations and peoples to the synchronic chain of economic operation. California is a window state that shows us how people of different racial and cultural origins can learn to live with one another. And Hollywood is the self-appointed progenitor of this multiculturalist idea by hiring diverse races and representing people of color in its globally distributed entertainment products. However, the "progress" of this multiculturalism in Hollywood productions is never a revolt against or a subversion of the dominant system representing whiteness. Instead, it is founded upon the very excessive strength of the worldwide image-producing syndicate. The larger the share Hollywood can get of the Asian Pacific market, the more yellow and brown faces will probably be seen in the mainstream American cinema and television.

Under the global economy and the capital drive to the Pacific, Hollywood is renouncing its usual dimension of subjectivity by chasing multiple modes of representation, without fidelity to any specific subjective engagement. Hollywood's drive to Asia Pacific is only a closed circular pulsation that finds satisfaction in endlessly repeating the same. There may be no new opening to the outside or no real introduction of otherness into the system. Only the eternal return of the same is fully endorsed. But simply to condemn the multiculturalism practiced in America as nothing but Eurocentrism at heart could easily miss the point.

In the eyes of the newly immigrant Asian film people, America is still seen as a land of good health, easy living, and open fairness to people of different ethnic heritages. Now living with his family in Los Angeles, John Woo tells his interviewer that the American lifestyle allows him a rebalancing of film career and family:

> Hong Kong is a place that will drive you crazy. It's very competitive, lots of pressure, people don't respect your privacy. You always have to work faster and smarter than the other guy, or else you'll get beaten down. Hong Kong people train for that. You work seven days a week, and it's really unhealthy. I spent all, or most of my time, in the office and the studio. I was never able to give enough time to my children, and my family was being torn apart. . . . There's pressure here, of course, but it's normal pressure. People have to work hard and do a good job, but everyone is more respectful of each other's lives. I can have my own privacy, and not work on weekends to spend more time with my wife and children. . . . Even if I fail in the United States, I still don't want to go back. . . . I couldn't stand that kind of lifestyle anymore. (Singer 1998, 322)

Living in the United States seems to stabilize his life of madness in Hong Kong. Woo's favorite leading man in his Hong Kong films, Chow Yun Fat, apparently also shares Woo's view of the American lifestyle. Chow is said to reside "in a lovely hillside home, designed by Frank Lloyd Wright, in Los Angeles and by all indications, he is here to stay. He loves California." In Chow's own words: "I have a lot of freedom here. I enjoy the food and the atmosphere. I enjoy the air here, it's better than Hong Kong. Mostly I enjoy hiking, it's kind of my hobby. Every Sunday I go for a two-hour hike; I prefer to go on the open side of the hills so I can have a view of the city and the ocean" (Heard 2000, 228). In the restructuring of global capitalism the American West is turned into a safe haven or a breathing zone from the competitive and stressful Asia Pacific for the celebrities and the new rich. The general assumption that Asian migrants are displaced in Western worlds and that their families are broken up by emigration is now reversed. It is only the displacement that can save their marriage and can reposition and offer comfort to these Asian immigrants caught up in the chaotic world on the other shore. Like Sean Archer in *Face/Off,* who needs an alien element to hold his family together, the concept of Chineseness also requires a transnational setting to reaffirm its cohesiveness and legitimacy. The American West acts like a symbolic order that pulls them out of the experience of abyss and chaos.

The influx of Hong Kong film people to the United States may be instigated by the return of the city's sovereignty to China. Their underlying motivation could be to escape from the totalitarian rule of the Communist regime. But this drive to the United States from Asia is unlike previous Asian immigrations, because the host country is never really their final destination. The "new" Asian immigrants are more interested in the Pacific shuttle, finding enjoyment in the very circular movement along the Pacific Rim. It is still more profitable to work and do business in Asia, while North America is a better place for these new Asian immigrants to settle their families. To live in California helps in resolving the unbearable tension in their Asian homeland. Although Woo and other Hong Kong directors complain about rigid American filmmaking schemes, the Hollywood system is for them a medium of differentiation that creates order out of chaos and transforms a Hong Kong subject who has already plunged into an abyss of craziness into a free subject—a subject that can migrate not just from one place to another, but from one face to the next. But are they avoiding the abyss of life in Asia or the abyss of their pure subjectivity in the transnational world? Perhaps denying one's place of origin and clinging to one's particular cultural heritage no longer make any difference. Both only enable one to implement the process of globalization.

The fantasy of California is a misrecognition of the global capital drive. The drive of Asian film talent to Hollywood has nothing to do with the flawed model of multiculturalism that essentializes particular ethnic cultures by attributing to them unity or stability. It is not about the desire for recognition of the marginal identity or tolerance of racial and cultural differences. Nor does it have to do with any "unhomely" quality of dispossession that is haunted by otherness. Rather, according to Lacan, it is more the color of an emptiness that is suspended in the light of a gap. The identification of the Asian element in Hollywood is only a self-reflexive turn of unrestrained global capitalism. Žižek argues that the mark of particular cultural or ethnic roots is nothing but an imaginary veil that covers up the fact that the subject is already thoroughly ungrounded, and that its real position is the void of universality (Žižek 1999). The open mouth of the Pacific Rim does not signal a want-to-be but rather the black hole of drive and its blissful enclosure of sucking everything in.

The rearticulation of Chineseness in the age of globalization is not only a displacement of the ideology of nation-state domination; it also is a form of narrative that endeavors to organize all the contingent experiences of Chinese diaspora. It is more a form than any content or substance, serving as the a priori condition of possibility for the synthesis and coordination of the Chinese contingent experiences into a coherent narrative. However, a form that comes before any positive content is always an unfailing indication of some traumatic, repressed antagonism. Thus, even as a form, Chineseness is never exactly—as some poststructuralist critics would say—a contingent discursive construction, although it is not necessarily a biological and trans-historical essence either. Perhaps it is an uncanny dimension that emerges with the advent of global capitalization and haunts the global economy from within. Apparently, its traditionally sanctioned proper place is lost in the new millennium, and yet, it is precisely its unplaceability in this world that enables it to flourish and take a strong hold in the popular discourses of the global entertainment industry.

7

Tigers Crouch and Dragons Hide in the New Trans-Chinese Cinema

IN WHAT WAY DOES Ang Lee's *Crouching Tiger, Hidden Dragon* (2000) give us a new view of the confrontation of Chineseness with the cinematic images circulated in the world? Can the resistance to U.S. imperialism or the struggle against globalization still be fought on a national or nationalist terrain, when cultural and ethnic particularity can be successfully fabricated and reproduced by such a Hollywood-distributed, multinational-funded Chinese film?[1] Does the film suggest that there is no longer any place for Hong Kong now that the global film industry is making way for a pan-Chinese or trans-Chinese culture and wiping out those who are occupying a place to which they have no title? The discussion of *Crouching Tiger, Hidden Dragon* in a book on Hong Kong transnational popular culture is necessary not simply because the use of kung fu conspicuously marks the film as part of the tradition of Hong Kong martial arts cinema. The transnational backdrop of the film also provides a precious chance, as many cultural products from Hong Kong might do, to reflect upon the manufacture and representation of Chineseness or any kind of ethnicity in the context of global capitalism.

At the threshold of the twenty-first century, when many Hong Kong films were beginning to deliver dialogue in English in order to compete with Hollywood and go international,[2] some in Hollywood went in the opposite direction and produced a Chinese-language movie, *Crouching Tiger, Hidden Dragon*. Although this swordplay-and-kung-fu movie in Mandarin did not become a blockbuster in Hong Kong, where it was premiered for public release,[3] it surprisingly turned out to be the most popular Chinese language film ever in the West. It is the highest-grossing foreign-language film to open in Britain. In the United States it has surpassed the unprecedented American box-office success of Roberto Benigni's Oscar-winning Italian film, *Life Is Beautiful* (*Crouching Tiger* has grossed about US$127 million in the United States alone).[4] The response of American critics to the film was generally positive, helping it to reap many film awards and finally four Oscars.[5] What is more significant is that *Crouching Tiger, Hidden Dragon* may have changed the Western impression of the martial arts movie. To most Western moviegoers, swordplay-and-kung-fu films mean badly dubbed Asian flicks with actors gruntingly performing chopsocky violence, and such films get little respect outside of the downmarket fanbase. For a long time it has been a marginalized genre received only by followers of camp and by admirers of trash movies and relegated to fan-boy cult status. However, *Crouching Tiger, Hidden Dragon* could be the one martial arts film that legitimizes the genre as bona fide cinema in the mainstream market.[6] Hong Kong media treat the film as the pride of Hong Kong by focusing on its Hong Kong cast, Chow Yun Fat and Michelle Yeoh, and its action choreographer, Yuen Wo Ping, though its director, Ang Lee, originally comes from Taiwan and its actual protagonist, Zhang Ziyi, is a Beijing Film Academy student who had her feature debut in Zhang Yimou's *The Road Home* (1999).

I would like to situate the film within the framework of Hong Kong cultural transnationalization, because it is not the first time that a transnational Chinese production that gains international success has been considered a "Hong Kong film." The Palme d'Or winner and Oscar-nominated *Farewell My Concubine* (1993) is a typical case. The Mandarin-language film, directed by Chen Kaige, a well-known fifth-generation director from mainland China, is based on the best-selling novel of the same title by the popular Hong Kong writer Lillian Lee. The company that produced *Farewell My Concubine* is a Hong Kong–based Taiwan firm headed by the Taiwan ex–kung fu movie actress Hsu Feng. The major cast includes the internationally famous mainland Chinese actress Gong Li and the Hong Kong movie star and pop singer Leslie Cheung. Because of this pan-Chinese production background, *Farewell My Concubine* was registered as a "Hong Kong movie" when it was nominated for the Oscar for Best Foreign-Language Film. The background of *Crouching Tiger, Hidden Dragon* is even more complicated in terms of its transnational Chinese formation. This is not only because it is fundamentally a Hollywood-funded and -distributed Chinese film with the collaboration of some Hong Kong, Taiwan, and mainland Chinese companies,[7] but also because it designates a stronger sense of Chinese cultural diaspora and a more fluid spatial identity of Chineseness.[8] Ang Lee's filmography is already remarkably hybrid, combining the Taiwan of his Chinese trilogy with the diversified milieus of his Hollywood features: Jane Austen's nineteenth-century British society (*Sense and Sensibility*), 1970s American white suburbia (*Ice Storm*), and the Civil War period (*Ride with the Devil*). The martial arts epic set during the Qing dynasty also offers the balletic actions choreographed by the Hong Kong kung fu master Yuen Wo Ping; the Oscar-caliber photography of Peter Pau, who is also originally from Hong Kong; and the spectacular mise-en-scène and costumes by the Hong Kong artistic designer Tim Yip. The soundtrack composed by the mainland exile Tan Dun, the cello interludes of the Chinese American Yo-Yo Ma, and the English theme song by Hong Kong–born Coco Lee also create an exemplified Chinese heteroglossia. The cast members come from different Chinese communities, including Hong Kong (Chow Yun Fat), mainland China (Zhang Ziyi), Taiwan (Cheng Chen), and Southeast Asia (Michelle Yeoh).

Representing a combined effort of many reputed diasporic Chinese, *Crouching Tiger, Hidden Dragon* is a "flexible production" made possible by Hollywood capital and constitutes a new kind of pan-Chinese identity that commands new cultural allegiances. The movie title already presents a high-sounding message to the Chinese audience. *Crouching Tiger, Hidden Dragon* may symbolize that the economic tiger states (Taiwan, Hong Kong, and other Chinese-populated Southeast Asian countries) and the rising dragon (the emerging power of mainland China) are seeking their chance to triumph in the West in order to reassert Chinese national or ethnic glory. The dream of a powerful China is somewhat realized through the transnational Chinese cinematic imagination. However, the Chinese joint force does not necessarily suggest a single cultural unity. A Chinese imagining of success and modernity is not necessarily driven by the desire for any form of consistency and unification.

In the film, even the names of the characters appear in competing romanization systems in the English subtitles. For example, "Li Mu Bai" is in pinyin romanization, while "Yu Shu Lien" and "Jen" are in Wade-Giles. The juxtaposition of the two systems of romanization in the film may reveal more about the cultural difference and tension between mainland China and Taiwan than their perfect harmony. According to the Jewish screenwriter of the film, James Schamus, who has worked closely with Ang Lee on many of Lee's Chinese films since *Pushing Hands* in 1992, *Crouching Tiger, Hidden Dragon* was first written by him in English, then translated into Chinese, and finally retranslated back into English subtitles again by himself. This may explain why the romanizations of the characters names are inconsistent. But it also reveals that the modern meaning of Chineseness is always constructed and seen through the eyes of the Western other. Perhaps we can claim that the immediate sense of Chineseness manifested in the film is always already mediated, that is to say, it is its own self-negation. A foreign perspective through the Jewish scriptwriter may perceive the disavowed part of the Chineseness itself, forcing it to become aware of its own "repressed" truth. The transnational cultural background of the film proves that the decentering of Chineseness is original and constitutive. From the outset, it is a "bricolage" of different components that requires an external, foreign gaze to perceive it as an apparently cultural and ethnic unity.[9]

To Be Westernized in Order to Be More Chinese

As many studies of contemporary globalism have already pointed out, ethnic cultural diversity and difference are no longer seen as obstacles to the development of multinational capitalism. Rather, they are the marketable features for the expansion of the commodification that is aesthetically consumed. Commodity nowadays is primarily marketed for its image rather than for its immediate use, and a product with an ethnic cultural image is definitely a magnified form and all the better for aesthetic consumption. The ethnic difference itself exists only as a commodified spectacle to be consumed in a global capitalist world where exterior boundaries are no longer as thinkable as in the past. This is precisely why the world entertainment syndicate needs to finance and produce an ethnic Chinese swordplay period film to reconstitute an exteriority from within,[10] in order to stage the phantasm of cultural and national distinction in a spatial economy that is irreducible to geographical dichotomies.

Unlike the other previous Chinese-language movies of Zhang Yimou, Chen Kaige, or Wong Kar-wai, which are aesthetically consumed and applauded by Western audiences as ethnic exhibits shown in art-house theaters, *Crouching Tiger, Hidden Dragon,* though having a similar thematic sophistication and spectacular cinematography, is a different kind of Chinese-language film and is more transnational in its nature and marketing. For the Chinese audience of *Crouching Tiger, Hidden Dragon,* the rendering of a fictional and superficial China is no longer seen as a betrayal or a selling out to the West. Indeed, the film is precisely about a fabricated China that not only fascinates the Chinese themselves but also lures the craving eyes of Western spectators. On the other hand, the movie also differs from the "Hongkongified" Hollywood

English action films, like those starring Jackie Chan or Jet Li, or the few directed by John Woo, because it is far more high-brow or serious than those martial arts movies. This Mandarin-language action and fantasy film highlights its cultural otherness and particularity more than its easy assimilation into the American mainstream, posing a gesture of resistance to the American standardization of world culture. It shares some of the characteristics of the internationally known Chinese films but also deviates from them. Situating itself in between the localization of cultural production and the transnationalization of capital, the film succeeds at invoking a timeless and dreamlike China that poses no threat to anyone but arouses some nostalgic feelings in its Chinese audience.

The swordplay fiction on which the film relies already carries such characteristics, and Bordwell has explained that the martial arts tales (*wuxia*) "represent a China made for exiles. Roger Garcia has called martial arts films a form of 'mythic remembrance' for the diaspora, a legitimating fantasy. However unhappy Chinese history has really been, one can imagine belonging to a country of stable traditions—not of law or government, but of honorable personal conduct. The wuxia tales make honor a matter of family, school, and ultimately the individual" (Bordwell 2000b, 194). This statement indicates that the martial arts film is never simply an imaginary expression of Chinese culture, as Western critics tend to presume. In fact, Chinese culture itself needs the phantasmic support of the martial arts film to make everyday life more bearable. The wuxia novels become a "portable China" that sustains the nostalgic feelings of the diasporic Chinese.[11] The discursively invented China in martial arts films is no longer bound by any historically geographic reality; but in the transient process of transnational deterritorialization, it could reterritorialize the national and cultural cravings to a certain locality. It is true that Chinese film under the immanent logic of global capitalism can be produced anywhere at any time, liberated from fixed spatial referents. But still an imagined spatial reconfiguration is necessary for such transnational production, especially when the martial arts genre is generally seen as the signifier of traditional Chinese spiritualities, including Confucianism, Buddhism, and Taoism. Indeed, the immanent transnational nature of capitalist development always relies on a nationally girded place to manifest its full potential. The ahistorical China reinvented in the swordplay film could serve precisely such a purpose. Like the glamorous and magnificent ancient Rome recreated in *The Gladiator* (2000), a similar cyber Beijing with long-lost glory reappears in *Crouching Tiger, Hidden Dragon*, aided by advanced Hollywood visual effects.

Numerous Chinese film critics have categorized Ang Lee's *Crouching Tiger, Hidden Dragon* within the tradition of King Hu's intellectual swordplay films, which bear a Zen-like philosophical overtone. In a sense, *Crouching Tiger, Hidden Dragon* is even seen as a new film that pays homage to King Hu's classics. Not only is Hu's favorite actress, Cheng Pei Pei, cast in the film, but the confrontation and flying in the bamboo forest especially make critics recall a similar scene in Hu's *A Touch of Zen* (1971).[12] Ang Lee is not shy about acknowledging Hu's influence on him:

> The first time I met Hu was in 1984. That was a long time ago, when I graduated from film school and I wanted to go back to Taiwan to look for opportunities to make films. . . . I drove 17 hours up there [in New York] to see him. I really worshipped him, because he was the first Chinese director to be known internationally, because of the "swordsman" movies, a real special theme with unique visual effects. For this reason, I thought that maybe I could work for him, get to know him, hear him speak. People like me who grew up in Taiwan, receiving Chinese education, have lost touch with the mainland, because I was brought up as a Chinese, but I haven't really been to mainland China. That's why I sometimes feel strange about my Chinese identity. *This identity was obtained from Mr. Hu's movies and Li Hanxiang's movies, from TV and textbooks. It was very abstract, not because of blood relationship or land but rather an ambiguous cultural concept. It was like a dream.* You couldn't make sense of everything, but it was a holistic Chinese influence and it is in my blood. I think his martial arts films are different from modern kung fu action pictures. It was swordsman, not action and fighting. In his time, his style was relevant to Chinese history. He used the world of the swordsman to present the abstract part of Chinese culture. He guides you into Chinese landscape paintings, a legendary atmosphere which was very special. His cinema skills were very modern. He used quick editing techniques to all action, all visual effects . . . *very Chinese, yet very modern.* He was an amazing and unique director. (Raymond Chow et al. 1998, 107; my emphases)

As a fresh graduate of film school, Lee saw Hu somewhat as his ideal model although in fact Lee has had a much better career and perhaps enjoyed more fame than Hu in the West.[13] But, to be Chinese and to be modern seem to be Lee's criteria of achievement in filmmaking and something he learned from Hu's swordsman movies. Being "very Chinese, yet very modern" for Lee is not a synthesis of two different or even conflicting things because, as he has said in an interview, contemporary Chinese are westernized and modernized, allowing no space for the existence of the old system. Nostalgia for the old China then becomes the common mood of contemporary Chinese.[14] Does he mean that Chineseness for a Chinese like him is only an appearance while the real content is always already westernized? When asked if he can make a "purely Asian mainstream movie," Lee responds: "With *Crouching Tiger,* for example, the subtext is very purely Chinese. But you have to use Freudian or Western techniques to dissect what I think is hidden in a repressed society—the sexual tension, the prohibited feelings. Otherwise you don't get that deep. Some people appreciate it; others don't because it twists the genre. It's not 'Chinese.' *But to be more Chinese you have to be Westernized,* in a sense. You've got to use that tool to dig in there and get at it" (Hajari 2001, 79; my emphasis).

In other words, the appearance cannot be easily dismissed as a mere illusion because it possesses a power of its own and conceals a different reality. In Lee's own description, his Chinese identity (in his words, "it is an abstract cultural concept, very illusive but also very real" [qtd. in C. Wong 2000, 35]) is completely mediated by martial arts and period films mostly produced by exiled Chinese directors like King Hu and Li Hanxiang in Hong Kong. In other words, the power of pseudo-concrete images manufactured in the British colony has structured the subject position of a diasporic Chinese like him. Being an image maker himself, Lee is well aware that disclosing the illusiveness and superficiality of the image production would not dissolve its magical effects. Rather, it strengthens the fetishist status of the image. Hence, a highly fictional Chinese film like *Crouching Tiger, Hidden Dragon* should not alienate Chinese audiences from culturally identifying with the Chinese images portrayed in the film. The dematerialization of the very image on which transnational Chinese identity is based does not weaken its power, but rather further endows it with a stronger spectral spirit that dominates the subject who thinks he can maintain a distance from it. The mechanism of ideology, like that of nationalist identification, is already outside, on the surface, or belongs to the realm of appearance in the age of postmodernity. Its normal functioning no longer depends on its state of being hidden in some unfathomable depth. In other words, the unveiling of ideology could never be a critique of it.

Ma Sheng-mei has pointed out that there is always a duality in Ang Lee's earlier Chinese films (including the trilogy *Pushing Hands* [1992], *Wedding Banquet* [1993], and *Eat Drink Man Woman* [1994]) that contributes to their global box-office success and winning international awards. Such a duality is able, by rendering the same thing, to both evoke nostalgic feelings in some

Chinese audiences and provide an exotic tour for Westerners (Ma Sheng-mei 1998). Obviously, Lee is more skillful than Zhang Yimou in selling Oriental exoticism to Western audiences without offending the Chinese viewers. While lingering with a sense of immigrant nostalgia for the lost Chinese tradition, Lee's trilogy succeeds in exoticizing Chinese culture within a new package of gender, race, and age representation. In her brilliant critique of Ang Lee, Shu-mei Shih argues that Lee is very good at integrating the Chinese national subject and the Asian American minority subject in his Chinese-language films by making a nationalist appeal to the Taiwan audience and employing exotic orientalist structures for the approval of the U.S. moviegoers. Operating on the two nodal points of nationalist patriarchy and gendered minoritization, Lee has always been able to maneuver in the global film market with his well-planned ethnic trajectories, such as the traditional banquet customs, the fetishized Chinese food, the taichi meditation, and the erotic and exotic Oriental women (Shih 2000).

While agreeing with the critiques of Lee mentioned above, I believe that it is not exactly the perfect match between the nostalgic and patriarchal space for Chinese moviegoers and the self-orientalizing discourse catering to the craving eyes of the U.S. audience that renders the success of Ang Lee in Chinese and American communities. On the contrary, it is the inconsistency or incompatibility between the two cultural allegiances that makes Ang Lee's films well acclaimed in both societies. The Chineseness depicted in his films is basically deprived of the immanent localism of Chinese communities anywhere. For the Chinese audience to identify culturally with Lee's works, an ambiguous pan-Chinese subject position has to be conjured. Such a position can liberate the Chinese viewer precisely from the subjection to the sovereignty of any local or national regime, offering an illusive sense of emancipation from national politics and a racially interpellated secured place. On the other hand, for the American audience, the stress on the Chinese ethnic difference in Lee's films is less a domestication of Chinese culture in multiculturalist America than an estrangement of the minority group from within, which reconstitutes the distinct racial and cultural lines separating the white majority and the ethnic minority under the immense deterritorializing forces of the U.S.-led globalism. The welcoming reception of ethnic cultural products in the United States could affirm the consistency of the American symbolic structure in which the myth of the melting pot and its ideology of racial hierarchy are proved to be still valid.

To return to *Crouching Tiger, Hidden Dragon,* we find that the picture has been well received by Western liberal critics and viewers because, according to the reviews, it frees the martial arts genre from a world exclusive to men by giving women a commanding presence within the narrative. In fact, the woman warrior is not at all foreign to conventions of the wuxia genre. For a long time, in its fiction, folktales, Peking opera, and films, Chinese popular culture has been known for its tradition of celebrating female action heroines to a degree without parallel in Western adventure stories.

The real action begins when the Green Destiny Sword is stolen by the beautiful daughter of a provincial governor. She fantasizes about the exciting life of a swordsman from reading martial arts stories and desperately longs for her own personal freedom in the face of an impending arranged marriage. The two major marathon combats are fought between the two female characters. The two women engage in a pulse-pounding hand-to-hand combat in the first fight scene, running across rooftops, silently high-flying through the air, and executing gymnastic flips and kicks. And in the second long combat scene, which displays unparalleled wit, grace, and energy, the two women fight intensely, with one of them using any and every weapon she can get her hands on. The fact that the most daring and successful fighters in the film are the so-called weaker sex definitely empowers and enlivens Ang Lee's female audience.[15] The emphasis on the awesome power of women fighters in *Crouching Tiger, Hidden Dragon* particularly impresses the American audience since it relates itself to the current Hollywood trend of feminizing kung fu in popular movies like *Charlie's Angels* (2000). The feminization of martial arts within the U.S. context may inspire its female viewers, who constitute a significant portion of moviegoers nowadays,[16] but it could also lessen the masculine nationalist dimension of the Hong Kong genre, thereby containing its threat to American masculinity. The fantasy of all-powerful women could therefore be merely a construction of the patriarchal discourse reasserting the male subjectivity.

Based on a 1920s serialized fiction by the Manchurian Chinese writer Wang Dulu,[17] *Crouching Tiger, Hidden Dragon* tells the conventionally complex and convoluted storyline of serialized swordsman fiction in a rather concise way. The renowned Wudan swordsman, Li Mu Bai (Chow Yun Fat), has decided to resign from a legendarily heroic life of the *jiang hu* (which literally means rivers and lakes and metaphorically refers to the world of martial arts) and asks his unattainable love, Yu Shu Lien (Michelle Yeoh), a kung fu fighter herself who makes her living by providing security for transported goods, to carry his symbolic blade, the Green Destiny Sword, cross-country to his elderly mentor, an aristocrat of the Qing dynasty, Sir Te (Lung Sihung), for safekeeping in Beijing. But almost immediately after Yu has finished her mission and given Sir Te the sword, the prop that triggers the whole story is stolen by a masked intruder in the aristocrat's compound. Yu feels obligated to assist in its recovery and investigate the case. The veiled thief is found out to be Jen Yu (Yu Jiaolong, in pinyin, literally meaning Jade Dragon), who is played by Zhang Ziyi. Jen is a Manchurian governor's daughter who is going to marry a high official to help her father's political career. But she has been involved in a secret, passionate affair with a member of the non-Han ethnic minority, a desert bandit named Lo (Luo Xiaohu, equivalent to Little Tiger), played by Cheng Chen. Jen steals the sword merely to relieve her boredom and, by doing so, to imagine herself as a swordsman who can enjoy the freedom that she desires.

In the process of investigating the theft, there resurfaces a woman warrior at large, Jade Fox (Cheng Pei Pei), who teaches Jen martial arts and who had poisoned Southern Crane, Li's master, years ago. Li's failure to avenge Southern Crane's death drags him back into the struggle and violence of the jiang hu. Jade Fox uses the scroll she stole from Southern Crane to teach Jen kung fu. Hence, Jen is also learning Li's Wudan school of martial arts. While Li is pursuing Jade Fox for revenge, he discovers Jen's talent but finds that she has learned the kung fu incorrectly. He wants to recruit her as his own disciple by taking her back from the evil Jade Fox to what he calls the "right path." But the rebellious Jen does not accept the offer. She runs away from her arranged marriage, takes out her anger by beating up many swordsmen, and causes trouble for the jiang hu. Finally, she is caught by Li, who keeps trying to convert her. In order to save Jen, Li falls into a trap set up by Jade Fox in an abandoned kiln. Though he kills Jade Fox, like his master, Southern Crane, he is poisoned by the needle in her booby trap; he passes away in the arms of his beloved Yu Shu Lien. Li's death seems to be a blow to Jen. She leaves for Wudan mountain, the home of Li, to meet her lover, Lo. In the finale, Jen mysteriously jumps from the high mountain apparently to fulfill a legend she heard from Lo. The legend is that a young man who wants to make a wish that his parents recover from illness jumps from a high cliff. The belief is that a faithful heart will make wishes come true. According to what Lo tells Jen, the man does not die or get hurt from the jump; his wish is granted and he floats far away to some remote place where no one sees him again. Does Jen wish to resurrect Li and so make the plunge? Or is the jump her redemption for all the wrongs her overwhelming passion has caused? The film ends with such an enigma.

What attracts the audience of the film is, of course, not only the action sequences and the plot twists. The film also tells the tales of two pairs of lovers, one of them (Li and Yu) too mature and repressed, and the other (Jen and Lo) unformed and wildly reckless. At first glance, the two couples seem to represent the opposition between sense and sensibility, old and new, the dominant Han and the non-Han minority cultures, collective interest and individual desire, and, all in all, between tradition and modernity—a rather hackneyed topic of many non-Western cultural works. But the film is not so naive as to celebrate the triumph of one and lament the defeat of the other. In a way, both relationships end in physical separation, suggesting a certain failure in accomplishing the romantic unity of body and soul.

The two relationships do not simply parallel and mirror each other. They intersect and provoke the "hidden dragon" in the other's hearts. Li and Yu at first behave very traditionally by repressing their desires for each other. The appearance of Jen causes some changes, especially in Li, who finally expresses his passion by calling Yu "my love" in such a straightforward way that many Chinese critics have deemed it too westernized and contrived. On the other hand, the youthful and energetic go-getter, Jen, who acts far more like a contemporary American teenage girl than a Chinese woman in the martial arts genre, is suddenly, by the end of the movie, so immersed in the mysterious atmosphere of Zen metaphysics as to renounce her love as well as her life, probably because of the profound influence of Li.

If the system of global capitalism is constitutive of the imbalance of social and economic exchange, the film attempts, at least at the cultural level, to reinstall a certain state of equilibrium. While one side gives the Chineseness over to westernization, the other, whose cultural entry is already westernized, remodels itself on the traditional ethnic form. The depiction of love is like a clichéd blending of Western and Eastern senses and sensibilities, just as the film itself is a martial arts story filled with romance, or a love story filled with martial arts adventure. But the blending of different cultures does not mean that one can have it all. On the contrary, in the transnational context of cultural exchange, one can have what one possesses only on the basis of a certain renunciation.

The filmmaker keeps reminding the audience that the movie itself is *Sense and Sensibility* with martial arts: "at the core they're a lot alike. It just cinematically looks very different. There's 'sensibility,' a passionate, romantic force; if you go overboard it can be destructive. On the other hand there is 'sense,' restraint, social code, obedience, repression. My films always seem to be about how these conflicts resolve themselves" ("Conversation with Ang Lee," 2000).[18] Does Lee imply that the passionate, destructive force, far from effectively threatening the system of social code and repression, is only its inherent transgression? Are sense and sensibility just two sides of the same coin? To put it differently, it is probably the system of social code and restraint, that is, the "sense," that creates the passionate destructive force, that is, the "sensibility," as the inherent threat to be conquered and subdued. The embodiment of conflicts and contradictions could become a new transnational commodity that prevails across different national boundaries, as have many of Ang Lee's previous movies. Is the film *Crouching Tiger, Hidden Dragon* then a perfect example of "global culture," wherein East-meets-West leads to a consummation of love (though not without conflict and difference) as its unity or homogeneous formation? Isn't it true that the contradictions between East and West no longer need to be suppressed in a transnational cultural product but can be displayed as a new spectacle for consumption in the global capitalist system?

Perhaps we could never come close to a thing called global culture in film. However, under the immense expansion of global communications and trade markets, the circulation of cinematic images is carried out in the balance of cultural exchange. What I mean by this balance of exchange is not a simple combination of having it all or an equivalent transfer in return for something with identical value. Cultural exchange has never been a fair trade. Rather, the very balance of this exchange is grounded precisely on a lack that opens up the space of exchange. It is always the fleeting and elusive appearance, not the hard and inert reality, that spellbinds the other in the course of exchange. Cinematic production is built upon the dematerialization of the commodity form, which characterizes the mode of production in global capitalism. Such eviction of the materiality or substance enables the easy accessibility and transmissibility of the cross-cultural exchange, while simultaneously flattening cultural hierarchies and dismantling the foundations on which different cultural histories are built. The balance of this exchange could be maintained because appearance is not the opposite of the underlying reality. Ang Lee's self-explication that "to be more Chinese you have to be Westernized" makes sense only when appearance and reality are no longer opposed. Believing in appearances, we see the cultural other the way he or she effectively is, and we like that person just for those very appearances, not in spite of them. What is at first appearance in the end becomes almost the essence in the cultural exchange operating under the global economy.[19]

If the word "exchange" is substituted for "translation" in the following quote from Rey Chow, the coevality of cultures in the global context would become more revealing: "Genuine cultural translation is possible only when we move beyond the seemingly infinite but actually reductive permutations of the two terms—East and West, original and translation—and instead see both as full, materialist, and most likely equally corrupt, equally decadent participants in contemporary world culture" (Rey Chow 1995a, 195). What has been corrupted or decayed is precisely the substance itself. And through the cultural exchange, at least appearance could be reinvented for the gaze of the cultural other and recognized as real in effect. Perhaps, it is already enough to create new verisimilitudes in order to create new essences in the long run. Whenever there is appearance that the essence shines through in the cultural exchange, there is no longer any removal or leveling of cultural distinction in the process of globalization.

Noir Martial Arts, Noir Chineseness

The construction of feminine subjectivity and the gaze in the patriarchal order in *Crouching Tiger, Hidden Dragon* may remind us somewhat of the characteristics of film noir. First, as an adaptation of pulp fiction, the movie reenacts the close connection between film noir and the hard-boiled novel. Second, many of its fight scenes take place in darkness, which is a significant style of noir lighting. Third, its plot is modeled on the structure of the noir detective story: the narrative begins with the discovery of the lost sword, continues with the pursuit of the wanted murderer, and entails the discovery of the darkness of the human soul. Yu is a self-appointed private detective and there is also a minor character, an undercover agent, who has been pursuing Jade Fox for years in order to avenge his wife. These characteristics may reveal to us the film's Hollywood origins rather than its self-acclaimed Chinese one. But projecting the concept of film noir onto Ang Lee's film not only allows us to see clearly how the narrative of transgression can never be severed from the paternal law. Any submission to transgressive passion is only the obscene inversion of a fallible phallic regime. In addition, film noir is a loose term that can be easier to perceive than to define, since it resists any stable identity and clear boundaries. The closer one tries to approach the noir as a definitive object, the more ambiguous and elusive it will become. In a similar fashion, the wuxia movie is a cultural object that can be easily recognized. It is an outstanding signifier of Chineseness: "you know right away what it is, the object being only the synecdoche of a continent, a history and a civilization, or more precisely of their representation for non-natives" (Vernet 1993, 1). But like noir, wuxia film only appears to be Chinese in origin but it is not necessarily a specifically national and ethnic form representing the essential characteristics of Chineseness. Perhaps, it is not only the genre of *Crouching Tiger, Hidden Dragon* but also its Chinese content that is noir per se. That is to say, its Chineseness is nothing but a fuzzy image that lures the eyes rather than a substance with any foundation.

By no means is *Crouching Tiger, Hidden Dragon* the first "martial arts noir" or "action noir" in Chinese or Hong Kong cinema (I would name Wong Karwai's *Ashes of Time* [1994], Tsui Hark's *Black Mask* [1996], and John Woo's *The Killer* [1989] as examples of this category).[20] However, it transforms the very standard notion of noir itself and displays its dynamics. The character of Jen is a contradictory combination of femme fatale and the exemplary youth of adventure genre. On the one hand, she represents the myth of a strong and aggressive woman who expresses her dangerous power and causes frightening results, presenting a female threat to the male patriarchal dominance. On the other hand, she is the restless adolescent protagonist who topples apprenticeship and dismantles the continuity of traditions and rules, symbolizing the new and destabilizing forces of modernity. In contrast to Li, who is the enforcer of the old rules with Yu as his faithful supporter, Jen defies all regulations. She embodies a new kind of ideology that subverts the conventional moral laws that prevail in the world of the martial arts genre. Apparently, Jen is not interested in the totalizing narrative of good versus evil that governs the minds of Li, Yu, and many other swordsmen in the jiang hu. Rather, she stands for a new liberation from moral servitude. Jen is very much identified with mobility, even to the point of transgression. She travels from the desert to the capital city, from the aristocracy to the class of knight errant, and even from one sexual identity to another. She is a "trans-subject" capable of smoothly crossing the gender boundary (she is a transvestite who sometimes dresses as a boy), ethnic borders (she as a Manchurian is romantically involved with a Muslim ethnic and arouses the desire of the Han hero Li), and ethical barriers, denoting the mobility and fluidity of the new transnational force maneuvering across heterogeneous spaces.

The common narrative of the martial arts genre or adventure story is that of the journey and the mobility that accompanies it, which is always seen as the ideal opportunity for the hero or the heroine to create and try out his or her new identities. But in *Crouching Tiger, Hidden Dragon*, the protagonist's journey does not necessarily help her to find and affirm what she is as an individual or to verify and establish her identity. Even at the end of the journey, the most crucial aspect of romance and of the adventure genre of ordeal—the protagonist's fidelity to her lover—has not yet been affirmed. Indeed, unlike the self-made identity of the conventional adventure hero, Jen's identity is more inherited than produced anew, as it carries an explicit sense of aristocracy. She has all the attributes of the upper aristocratic class. This may explain why she is not interested in acquiring the new and supposedly better martial arts skills persuasively offered by Li to reshape herself. She already owns the best and has it all. Belonging to the privileged class, she treats her kung fu master, Jade Fox, like a maidservant and asks her to leave when Fox gets into trouble. Her aristocratic inheritance inevitably weakens the revolutionary spirit she could have brought to the old and conservative martial arts world. Portrayed more like a spoiled child than a highly motivated young adult, she has no ambitious goals or any inner devotion to fight for values not yet socially accepted, such as the individual right to autonomy.

Appearing to have a strong and even disturbing personality, Jen remains nontransparent to us. Sometimes she embodies the power of corruption more than the spirit of revolution. Her character is too mutable to allow for any easy identification with her. Ang Lee even says that Jen "is in some ways the villain in the movie, but a most likable one" ("Conversation with Ang Lee"). Unlike many adventure movies that invite the audience to identify with their young hero or heroine, the film presents Jen as a woman of rebellion and even of some evil when projected through a certain external paternal viewpoint, though she cannot be totally contained by it.

Although Li Mu Bai is the most powerful and skillful swordsman in the movie, he dies in the hands of the weaker woman, implying the triumph of the new power represented by the female character over the traditional patriarchal authority. Jen does not literally kill Li, but she is primarily responsible for Li's death—Li is poisoned in his attempt to save her, and Jen fails to come back on time to provide the antidote that the dying Li desperately needs. In the last battle, Jen symbolically eliminates both her actual master (Jade Fox) and her virtual master (Li)—her presence simply offers a chance for them to destroy each other. A direct reading of the film might conclude that a new trans-Chinese form of modernity represented by woman has successfully replaced the old conservative paternal power of China. It would be an allegory of generational conflict, resulting with the dominance of the new liberal and more flexible and multiple Chinese cultural identity in the age of global capitalism. In fact, the picture of oppressed young women rebelling against the tyrannous fatherly figure is always perceived through the frame of the Western media reporting Chinese affairs, and it is commonly constituted in Chinese American literature, modern Chinese fictions translated into English, and in some contemporary Chinese films that reaffirm the Western assumption.

However, a more cautious reading of the film suggests that it is the aseptic and drab paternal figure Li who asks for his own demise with his insistence on passing on his skills to the young and rebellious Jen. His pursuit of Jen is perhaps never simply motivated by his so-called goodwill to convert her to become a morally decent person. His encounter with Jen is his fatal attraction. In the eyes of the suspicious Jen, Li's desire is illicit. Jen simply refuses to believe that Li would unconditionally pass the kung fu skills to her. She has probably heard from her master, Jade Fox, that the leader of the Wudan school, Southern Crane, sexually exploited Fox and refused to teach her martial arts skills, forcing her to poison him to steal the scroll. But in a way, Jen is puzzled by Li's intentions and by the question of what the other wants from her. In a love relationship, the loved one does not know what she has in herself that makes her worthy of the other's love. Thus, in order to solve her puzzle and escape from the pressure, she returns her love.

Being drugged (or is this an excuse?) in the kiln hole, Jen directly challenges (or offers herself to) Li by wearing a soaked robe through which her half-naked body is easily visible and seductively asks him whether he really wants the sword or her. (It is already obvious in the previous scene that Li is not interested in getting back the sword at all. He simply throws it in the rapids when Jen refuses to go with him to Wudan mountain.) Jen's seductive challenge to Li is supposed to be a misperception or a drama of false appearance because Jen is out of her mind under the drug. But what is revealing is that, through the false appearance, a forbidden wish is permitted to be articulated. The misperception is able to express the disavowed desire of the hero and the heroine, while allowing them to insist on their innocence.

Though Li never answers Jen's question and does nothing when Jen collapses in his arms, the audience has already been able to enjoy the pleasurably aberrant viewing (Maltby 1996, 455). That Li intimately touches Jen's body in order to restore her to consciousness with his *qi gong* (breath exercise) is erotic enough to make Yu frown. The narrative line of the film has already implied that it is Li's few brief encounters with Jen that help release his repressed passion for his long-beloved Yu. He becomes more and more expressive of his feelings to Yu every time after he runs into Jen. Is the lively and youthful Jen a love catalyst that the dreary and repressed Li desperately needs to motivate him to act out his innermost passions for Yu? Or is Li actually displacing his real burning desire for Jen onto a more morally acceptable love object, Yu, in the jiang hu on which his fame depends? The very defense against the prohibited sexual transgression may actually generate a stronger wave of sexual passion.

The phrase "Crouching Tiger, Hidden Dragon" in Chinese metaphorically refers to something hidden deep behind appearances, undoubtedly reiterating the noir theme of the darkness in human hearts, which are far from being innocent. The serious, poised, and restrained fatherly figure Li could always have another face deep down. It is said that the regulations of the jiang hu and the moral principles of ancient Chinese society always deter people from becoming themselves. Li and Yu are the apparent victims of these dehumanizing forces. Jen seems to be the bravest character who can be true to her self. But what exactly is a true self? Jen's evil master, Jade Fox, accuses Jen of hiding the martial arts skills from her. (The skills are contained in the scroll Jade Fox has stolen from Wudan school. Since Jade Fox is illiterate, she has to depend on Jen to learn the craft from the scroll. Obviously, Jen not only can read but is far more talented than her master at understanding the skills.) Jade Fox feels betrayed and wants to kill Jen. So beneath the mask of every human face there is always a secret underside that may surface at any time to horrify others. Thus, Li's continued "stalking" and "harassment" of Jen in the name of correcting her and recruiting her to be his disciple is driven by his desire for her. But what exactly does he want from her? Being disturbed by this enigma, Jen angrily warns Li that if she learned his kung fu secret, she would use it to kill him. But Li is surprisingly indifferent to the possibly terrible outcome—he doesn't care whether he would be killed by her.

His attitude could be interpreted as his unconditional demand and the absolute intensity of his love.[21] Therefore, Jen's mysterious dive from the mountain in the final scene is not a means of compensating for her guilt over causing Li's death. Rather, it is an act of returning her love for Li's irresistible sacrifice. By sacrificing his life, Li wins the hearts of two women and gains their eternal love. The radical renunciation (even of one's life) could result in the most intense and satisfactory fulfillment. In a way, Li is probably the one, like the hero in the noir world, who can be true to his own self by surrendering to dangerous and disturbing passions. The skills and values Li desperately tries to pass on to the new generation could only be continued and achieved in his own death. Is this precisely the ideology of diasporic Chinese—that the loss and renunciation of the real China could lead to the full realization of a China at heart? There is probably a vague idea in the minds of overseas Chinese that the authentic Chinese culture actually continues in the diasporic Chinese community.

On the other hand, the phrase "Crouching Tiger, Hidden Dragon" also reveals a fable of the other space—the other cultural space imagined and constructed by the diasporic Chinese. Besides the official totems of tiger and dragon in Chinese culture, there are other tigers and dragons crouching and hiding somewhere else than in China and that represent the reinvented Chineseness of the diasporic group. Perhaps the film does not go so far as to suggest that the true Chinese self is not what it appears to be but is actually that of the other Chinese, or of the Chinese diaspora. But it never hesitates to announce that there is always another Chinese space that coexists with and is nothing less than the so-called authentic one. Isn't the goal of the modernization or capitalization of China precisely to attain what the successful overseas Chinese already have—transnational wealth and the respect and recognition of the West?

It is crucial for us to avoid the trap of perceiving the two spaces of Chineseness along the axis of appearance versus reality. The reiteration of the binary opposition between false appearance and deep-down reality is replete with its artificial character. The film always suggests that there is no distinct and simple opposition between right and wrong in the fairy-tale-juridical world of martial arts. The thing one sees is always not exactly what it is. As Li Mu Bai says in the film, "Jiang hu is a world full of crouching tigers and hidden dragons, and so with human hearts. Our weapons carry danger, and so does our emotion." Apparently, there is some deep and innermost kernel of our subjectivity that is always inaccessible to us. If we delve too far beneath the surfaces, we will come face to face with a horror and the price we pay will be much higher than we think.

However, there is something fake in the film about such an assumption of concealed depth and such an act of rendering visible the hidden reality. Perhaps, the so-called secret behind the mask is itself a phantasmic construction. The theme of discovering the inner depth or truth is probably the mask of its exact opposite, of the growing loss of the hidden dimension of authentic self. What if there is no crouching tiger or hidden dragon within the human being? Are we actually robots or automatons pretending to be unique individuals with depth and inner authenticity? What if there is no unspoken rule prescribing everything in the jiang hu? Isn't it true that the jiang hu exists only when people believe in it or act in their social exchange as if they believe in it? What if the symbolic Chineseness that gives the movie a distinct cultural identity is not endowed with any substance?

Practicing Taoist philosophy and Wudan martial arts, Li never passes up any chance to show off his Zen-like wisdom. In one scene, while obviously playing an upper hand in the fight with Jen and being challenged by her with respect to being good enough to be her master, he humbles himself by saying that his fame is nothing but an illusion. And so are the Wudan school, the martial arts skills, and even the Green Destiny Sword he is holding at that moment. They are all human projections. (In the English subtitles, his words become, "Like most things, I am nothing. It is same for this sword. All of it is simply a state of mind.") If the kung fu skill is just an illusion, how could Li justify his insistence on passing on the skill to Jen? Undoubtedly, the answer would be that contradiction is part of the Zen practice and that the contradiction is not as it appears to be. In another scene, grabbing her hand to touch his face, he again preaches his Taoist ideas to Yu: "The things we touch have no permanence. My master would say there is nothing we can hold on to in this world. Only by letting go can we truly possess what is real." On both occasions, however, his theories are either ridiculed or disputed by the women whom he tries to convince. In the first scene, Jen lashes out bluntly to Li, "Stop talking like a monk just because you're in a temple! Just fight!" In the second one, Yu Shu Lien simply disagrees with Li that everything is an illusion. She tells Li tenderly that her hand he just held is real—it is rough and callused from kung fu practice.

What does the film try to convey to us here, other than invoking the Zen words as cultural markers to assert its Chineseness? Is it a cruel mockery of the old Chinese wisdom spoken through the mouth of a drab and boring patriarch? Is the truth on the side of the women who somewhat represent the viewpoint of pragmatic modernity? Is the film suggesting that external, phenomenal manifestation is all that the Chinese of today's transnational world have? Does it imply that any pursuit of inner depth and unique identity is futile because at the core everything is just the same? Or, does the film actually abstain from taking sides, by juxtaposing the two different views that correlate to Ang Lee's understanding of what it means to be modern Chinese, that is to say, to a Chinese identity that is only an appearance and the real content of which has already been emptied out by the process of westernization or modernization? Is the Chinese appearance merely used to cover up the void of the Chineseness, because beneath the manifest phenomena there is actually nothing? In this sense, Li Mu Bai's words would have some truth for our understanding of the modern sense of Chineseness: when we close our hands tightly into fists, there is nothing inside; but if we release our fists, then what we can possess is everything.

Does the most globally successful Chinese-language movie ever reveal to us, through the ancient wisdom of Zen, that holding on to the inner truth or essence, no matter whether it is a psychological, cultural, or ethnic one, is only an illusion? When there is no valid difference between essence and appearance, what matters in the transnational world is the power of representing and fabricating. This power that produces images and appearances no longer holds itself behind the images. Rather, it circulates and comes to light in the images. In short, images give themselves as reality fully. If the world is merely an appearance and there is nothing true outside of it, then why is it necessary to maintain the word "appearance," which inevitably carries a traditionally negative connotation and brings back the opposition between the thing-in-itself and the phenomenon? Within the global nature of the capitalist system, however, the appearance of Chineseness is a significant force of fiction making. It keeps sustaining the fictional difference between the originary and the derived, the hidden truth and the manifest phenomenon, being and becoming, in order to assign us with stable positions and offer us fictitious identities. The rearticulation of goal, truth, and essence by means of representation and appearance falls under the concept of the phantasm. For the blind machine of global capitalism there is no question of the ideal and final goal. It only wills but does not know why or even what. Appearance is essential in the sense that it prevents the disintegration of the symbolic order of our world, which is still divided into races and nation-states. The appearances and images of Chineseness circulated through the Chinese-language films are signs that indicate the beyond or the beneath of the phenomena, covering up the fact that there is nothing inside.

PART 3

A Show Boat
to China

8

Giant Panda, Mickey Mouse, and Other Transnational Objects of Fantasy in Theme Park Hong Kong

I WOULD LIKE to begin this chapter with a fantasy I wrote some time ago:

Since the giant panda pair, An An and Jia Jia, have become widely popular in the Hong Kong Special Administrative Region, the Chinese central government has decided to continuously export an excessive number of giant pandas to the ex-colony. In the next five years, one million six hundred seventy thousand giant pandas from Sichuan will be given to Hong Kong for the historic commemoration and early celebration of the city's complete integration with the mainland in 2046.

Although giant pandas are lovely, cutesy ambassadors, one million six hundred seventy thousand is not an insignificant figure for the tiny SAR to handle easily. Under such extraordinary circumstances, the SAR government has no choice but to establish an emergency unit to deal with the crisis. With the goodwill of the central government and the enthusiastic reactions of the SAR citizens, in addition to the fact that the giant panda has been upheld as a national treasure, the Hong Kong government did not have the guts to openly categorize the imminent arrival of one million six hundred seventy thousand giant pandas as a "crisis." Hence, the work of the emergency unit has been disguised as fervent preparations for the upcoming festive event.

The SAR Chief Executive who is also the chairman of the emergency unit told the press that "it is a very extraordinary, very complicated situation. We have to deal with it quickly. There is no time to spare. Just think about the figure! Think about the panda shits left by one million six hundred seventy thousand giant pandas!"

The report composed by the emergency unit stated that the most difficult problem brought on by the advent of over a million pandas was not necessarily the problem of limited space for their accommodation. Indeed, the SAR government had already planned many grand projects to build numerous theme parks in order to settle the pandas. Those theme parks that have agreed to provide homes for the pandas include Disneyland, Cyberport, Chinese Medicine Hub, Oriental Hollywood Film City, and others. Unexpectedly, the report pointed out, the area that would be most affected by the million pandas was actually the health of Hong Kong residents. Scientific research has shown that watching pandas too much could cause people to develop "panda eye-patches" and could damage normal vision. The food supply for the million pandas would also put a lot of pressure on the limited number of bamboo trees in the SAR. In the long run, the pandas would empty out all the greens in the city and create severe environmental problems. The report also called our attention to an issue that has rarely been discussed: the naming of the million pandas. Giant pandas have been traditionally called double names, such as "Gui Gui," "Yan Yan," etc. It was very likely that one million six hundred seventy thousand giant pandas could exhaust all the double names, constituting the legitimate crisis of proper naming. If we were forced to follow the tradition of double names by calling the pandas "Ba Ba" (father), "Ma Ma" (mother), or "Ye Ye" (grandfather), this would clearly subvert our family hierarchy and values, blur the boundary between human and animal, and topple the Confucian ruling order of the postcolonial Hong Kong regime.

According to a reliable source that refused to disclose its identity, there was a classified item in the report that had never been released to the public. It said that the leaders of the central government revealed to the SAR that giving out the million pandas was not simply a handover present but also a warning to any hostile powers in the West. If they ever tried to disturb the peace of China and to intervene into Chinese internal affairs, millions of giant pandas would be released to all over the world. At that time, swarms of pandas would cross all national borders, trample the sovereignty of every country, and cause severe ecological problems to the world. The SAR government did not want to get involved in this foreign affair issue that was outside the limits of its autonomy. Therefore, the issue of a million pandas was only casually categorized as the general issue of new immigrants from mainland China. (K. Lo 1999)

Facts

In 1999, Beijing gave a pair of giant pandas to Hong Kong to commemorate the former British colony's return to Chinese rule. An An, a fourteen-year-old male panda, and Jia Jia, a twenty-one-year-old female, made their public debut in May 1999 at Hong Kong Ocean Park, a private amusement theme park established by the Hong Kong Jockey Club and the designated spot for visitors from mainland China.[1]

By the end of 1999, a HK$21 billion theme park deal was signed by the Hong Kong SAR government to pay the Walt Disney Company to build the world's first "Chinese Disneyland," which is due to open in 2005 at Penny's Bay on Hong Kong's Lantau Island. With its economy having been in the doldrums for years since the 1997 Asian financial crisis, the Hong Kong Disneyland project is expected to spark the city's recovery and induce more investments. It is predicted that Hong Kong Disneyland will primarily attract visitors from mainland China.[2]

The negative feelings of Hong Kong locals toward the new mainland arrivals have been on the rise since 1997. In January 1999, the Hong Kong Court of Final Appeal ruled that mainland residents with at least one parent who was a legal resident of Hong Kong had a constitutional right to join their parents in Hong Kong. The ruling intensified the Hong Kong people's anti-immigrant sentiments. The SAR government further provoked hostility with its announcement that there could be 1,670,000 mainlanders moving to Hong Kong if their rights of abode were granted. Later on, the Hong Kong government asked the standing committee of China's National People's Congress to review the ruling and overthrow it. On the other hand, mainland visitors make up the largest portion of the city's tourist industry. Twelve million tourists are expected to visit Hong Kong per year and about one-third will come from China. Hong Kong's fear of a huge influx of mainlanders results in the SAR authorities' erecting hurdles to restrict the flow of tourists and immigrants to the city. But when the city's economy is in straits and it becomes desperate for tourist money, the SAR government pleads with Beijing to relax visa restrictions on mainland visitors and business people who want to visit. However, mainlanders are not duped by Hong Kong's welcoming gestures. Surveys show that mainland tourists feel they have been looked down upon and find prices too high in Hong Kong (Chow and Chan 2001).

Fantasy

Pandas, the Disney theme-park project, and the continuous influx of people from China are interwoven into a phantasmic scenario of the post-1997 Hong Kong Chinese community. The message of this fantasized picture is rather enigmatic. When many people expect the postcolonial Hong Kong to become more Chinese, the city turns its back on Chinese cultural productions and opens its arms to the growing American influence. The presence of "aliens" from China is perceived by Hong Kong Chinese as a threat to their unique identity and a major cause of conflicts that divide the community, though many local residents also recognize that their economic fortunes are increasingly and inextricably tied to the mainland. Indeed, post-1997 Hong Kong's recourse to Chinese national identity or Chinese nationalism could emerge at any moment, and not only pragmatically when the city needs to compete with other global opponents and to protect itself from the disorientation caused by the forces of globalization. When the decolonized Hong Kong people feel unable to bear the internal traumatic contradictions of their modernity and capitalist development, and when they unconsciously attempt to repress the very contradictions of that development, a unified sense of national belonging could cover up the tension. Hence, what I mean by fantasy in this context is never simply an illusion that cannot be sustained when confronted with a correct apprehension of reality. Rather, fantasy here is a construction or an imaginary scene in which the subject becomes the object of fantasy to support the reality of Hong Kong after 1997. The formula of a fantasy essentially consists of four elements. They are a subject, an object, a signifier, and images (Nasio 1998). These elements are organized according to a scenario that is always expressed through a certain narrative. In short, fantasy operates as a narrative that resolves fundamental contradictions and antagonisms by rearranging their terms into sequential, cause-and-effect orders (Žižek 1997).

In this way, the contingent occurrences before and after 1997 are incorporated into a diachronically fantasized historical narrative that functions to evoke, erase, and thereby resolve the traumatic antagonism. The sequential relationship and the continuously progressive story in the fantasy scenario replace the radical historical ruptures that usually defy the logic of narration and paradoxically generate the synchronicity of losses and gains. If "1997" is the signifier of the phantasmic scene, it both separates and reunifies the subject and the object of fantasy. Having lost the object, the subject always becomes the object itself. We should recognize that the loss of the object occurs at the same moment as the identification of the subject with the object of desire. There will not be any loss without the subject's identification with what it loses. In the fantasy picture of post-1997 Hong Kong, is the postcolonial city itself necessarily the fantasizing subject? Would it be possible that Hong Kong is only acting as a proxy to assume the fantasy of the other as its own? And what is the object that has been lost and for which the subject of fantasy mourns? Most likely we are not only unable to measure what has been lost and what has been gained for Hong Kong after the 1997 historical break, we are also unable to determine the definite positions of the subject and the object in the scenario. However, if fantasy is at issue, it could also provide an answer for the changed city that is puzzled by its constitutive position in relation to the desires of others. What does mainland China want from a decolonized Hong Kong? What does the West see in a Hong Kong that has been integrated into the territory of China? What is the significance of post-1997 Hong Kong to others?

In the phantasmic formation, a certain object is needed to offer some degree of consistency to the subject's being. Through such an object of fantasy, the subject is able to fill out the place of a response that is not given, to identify with the object that is seen as the extension of the subject, and, through such an identification, to perceive itself as worthy of the desire of others. While post-1997 Hong Kong fantasizes itself as unique and alluring to China by offering the mainland visions of an alternative "Chinese" modernity, China also views the repossessed city as a phantasmic picture in order to conceal the antagonistic situation of its own capitalist development and to showcase a kind of enjoyment to which only Hong Kong is allowed to have access. In a way, the fantasy is mutual. But a Hong Kong that hangs on to a fantasy is actually becoming fantasy itself—becoming a fantasyland filled with cutesy, fluffy cartoon figures and cartoonlike living beings. When post-1997 Hong Kong attempts to conceal the void of its new subjectivity and to erase the antagonism in its past experience of modernity with the fascinating effects of the new fantasy objects, it also unwittingly exposes the internal contradictions of the modernity of the Chinese nation-state. In a strange circularity, the fantasy of post-1997 Hong Kong fills the lack it itself opens up by creating and bearing witness to what it means to cover up.

Panda Watching

The giant panda is one of the world's most endangered species. Like all other endangered species, giant pandas confront the problems of human encroachment into their habitat and the deforestation of their natural range. The small population of the bearlike animals is also due to their very selective eating habits and extremely short mating seasons. But unlike any other endangered animals, giant pandas exert a tremendous, fascinating hold on the human psyche. Probably no other animals, except the costumed figures of human-ized ones like Mickey Mouse or Donald Duck, are so appealing to and favored by different people and age groups. The panda's worldwide popularity could be attributed to its large but cuddly and soft body, clumsy and clownish move-ments, childlike and innocent look, and seemingly harmless and friendly char-acter. Critics also point out that the animal with distinctive black and white markings and large eye-patches would not have won a significant place in human hearts were it not that the teddy bear was already a popular toy when pandas first began to arrive in the West. Rarity surely accounts for the pan-da's appeal. Found only in Sichuan, the black-and-white animals are consid-ered national treasures in China. Only about a thousand giant pandas are believed to survive in the wilds of southwestern China. The Chinese govern-ment is never shy about using the popularity of giant pandas to advance its diplomatic and political interests. Giving out pandas has become an honor-able gesture of China for befriending other nations. Living pandas were first given to the United States by the Nationalist government in the 1930s. When the Communist government wanted to rebuild international relations with the world in the 1970s, pandas were presented to the heads of different nation-states, including the U.S. president Richard Nixon. Besides ping-pong, the giant panda has become a symbol of friendship between China and other nations. Europe, Japan, and Mexico also benefited from China's panda diplomacy. But, beginning in the 1980s, China was no longer giving out giant pandas for free. The panda loan program started because the Chinese desperately needed money to help the animals survive. The beasts could be leased on short-term loans by various zoos primarily in the West for about US$200,000 a month.

The arrival of the pandas in postcolonial Hong Kong was definitely seen as a generous act from the Chinese central government. But it was at first op-posed by animal rights and environmental groups, because the humidity and subtropical climate of the port city was regarded as unsuitable for the giant animals. So a US$10.2 million 2,000-square-meter temperature-controlled facility, one of the biggest giant panda habitats in the world, was built at Ocean Park as the new home for the special guests from China. The enclosed giant panda habitat is kept at 68 degrees Fahrenheit all day long, with humidity at 50 to 60 percent, and fresh, cool air circulates freely in the winter. Hence, vis-itors of Hong Kong's giant pandas may need to wear jackets even in the heat of summer. The panda habitat extends behind the back wall, where there are four large sleeping dens for the VIP animals. In addition, in back of the hab-itat, there are advanced medical and husbandry facilities to ensure the big bears' health. Bushes are planted throughout the constructed habitat to play the role of barriers in case the pandas need some privacy. The giant pandas in the concrete-and-glass house constitute a certain representational sign that not only demonstrates the simulated wild life of a precious species in order to educate visitors as to how they can help ensure the survival of the threatened animals. The pandas also project a kind of heterogeneous quality that is not necessarily compatible with and even is foreign to the local environment of the Hong Kong community.

The mission of the giant pandas is revealing in terms of the China–Hong Kong relationship after 1997. Hong Kong did not ask for this national treasure, because, obviously, Hong Kong does not know what it can want from China (other than the economic benefits). But with the generosity of the Chinese central government, Hong Kong had to accept the gift and view it as grace from the north. Despite their impressively cute and friendly look, the giant pandas connote a meaning that might not be too different from that of the garrison of the People's Liberation Army in Hong Kong. As national symbols, they convey the presence of a well-designed Chineseness both overseeing and being seen in the postcolonial city. However, it is not necessarily true that the public authority of China maintains a gentle appearance behind which is the brutal exercise of power. Rather, pandas and the Liberation Army execute the double operation of the concept of the panopticon. In order to control and monitor people's behaviors, power in modern society is imposed through putting the people under surveillance without itself being seen. On the other hand, power also makes itself as transparent as possible to serve as a fetish that fascinates with its conspicuous presence. The more the Liberation Army becomes invisible, the stronger is its spectral effective control over the city. Whereas the more the giant pandas from China can turn themselves into an attractive spectacle, the more they function as a powerful ideological call addressing the viewing subject. Hong Kong people are thus reminded of the two faces of the Chinese sovereign: one is appeasing and seemingly harmless; another, strict and potentially relentless.

However, the giant pandas are never simply an ideological interpellation targeted only at the wavering Hong Kong people who may have doubts about their new Chinese Communist master. Since the home of the giant pandas in Hong Kong is at Ocean Park, visited by many people from the mainland, the Chineseness represented by the big bears also functions as a self-seeing or self-mirroring spectacle. It is the mainland visitors, not necessarily the Hong Kong locals, who are assured the visibility of the national symbol when traveling to this city that once was a British colony and has lately returned to the Chinese motherland.[3] Hence, the gaze of China is always already included in the picture of panda watching. Unlike other giant pandas sent to overseas zoos, the pair at Hong Kong is not simply staged for external eyes but is also posed as a fantasized setting in order to attract the mainland Chinese gaze itself. Self-reflection in the making of Chinese national identity is clearly involved here. It is a narcissistic act of beholding and recognizing oneself in a mirror image. The significant meaning for mainland tourists who visit Hong Kong after 1997 is never simply to travel to just another Chinese city; rather it is to reclaim a long-lost territory where the truly essential dimension of national characteristics should be visible. The giant panda is precisely the living master signifier (the "dead" but far more mythic and powerful one is of course the dragon, which the Hong Kong SAR government has recently appropriated as its "new" logo) that stands for such an essential dimension about which the Chinese visitors need not make any other claim in order to feel like they are "home." What Hong Kong means for China is that, against the withering-away of the traditional nation-state, the inner truth of Chineseness can seemingly reappear through a form of animal-externalization in the regained tiny postcolonial space.

The return of Hong Kong constitutes precisely the reemergence of Chinese nationalism that is needed to fill out the ideological void left by dying Communist doctrines. By giving the giant pandas to Hong Kong, China places the bears in a fantasized setting in which China appears caught up as a participant in order to see itself in a likable image as worthy of love. The subject of the fantasy hence becomes the signifier that marks the place of the object of desire. In other words, the presence of Chineseness relies on the assurance of self-seeing and the phantasmic scene of turning itself into a desirable object for the other. In the fantasy scenario of panda watching, any alienation, contradictory elements, and divisiveness between the recovered territory and the motherland would be minimized, masked, and rearranged into a coherent narrative of identification that melds all differences into one totality.

As an object of fantasy that fills the lack in the Chinese subject constituted in the early twentieth-first century, the giant panda is also elevated to the status of the Thing that could promise an imaginary fullness among all Chinese, from the mainland, Hong Kong, Taiwan, or elsewhere. It has been reported that the mainland Chinese government is willing to offer Taiwan giant pandas as a gift, since the panda is a symbol of peace, and according to the Chinese officials, what the mainland has been relentlessly pursuing is a peaceful unification with Taiwan. The offer of giant pandas to Taiwan is thus a well-intended act on the part of the mainland. However, Taiwan is afraid to let pandas come to Taiwan lest it imply that the Taiwanese government has to accept the one-China premise in the political negotiations for unification. Even though Shanghai is willing to give Taipei the giant pandas for free and the mayor of Taipei is eager to have them, the deal is still pending ("Dalu yuanzengtai daxiongmao" 2001).

Insofar as the giant pandas designate the agency of the symbolic authority of China in Hong Kong, they also remind us of their fragile and endangered state. In fact, the presence of the powerful Thing could paradoxically be the signifier of weakness. The imposed Chinese "reality" with which the recovered Hong Kong is pledged to merge, since it is regulated by a symbolic fiction, conceals or forecloses something that may return in an alien form. If the giant pandas denote the symbolic presence of Chineseness planned and planted by China, it is not necessarily a dominant one that can be seen as the answer to any possible disintegration of imaginary unity. Rather, it is an endangered kind of Chineseness that might have difficulties reproducing itself and could probably not survive by itself without tremendous care and protection. The Chineseness manifested by the pandas is only something that has to be isolated and encircled (in the glass house of a foreign zoo, in the conservation area at Sichuan, or in the Hong Kong theme park) in order to make sure it can last. The national Thing of the panda is a negative idea of a particular vanishing being, a being that represents its own gradual disappearance.

The fantasy scenario staged by the giant pandas is not exactly used to cover over the uneasy tension between Hong Kong and China in order to indulge the people of the two places in the dream of a unified and harmonious Chinese nation held together by solidarity and cultural cohesiveness. On the contrary, the fantasy of panda watching in Hong Kong articulates a kind of ironic distance for the Hong Kong subject not to identify too much with the displayed Chineseness. However, far from suggesting the failure of the ideological edifice, it is such a distance that functions as the positive condition of its performance. Although the resubjectivizing process of Hong Kong people into a unified Chinese identity may not be very smooth, the ideological interpellation always involves a certain "forced choice." That is to say, when the subject recognizes himself as a member of the united China, he would freely choose the fact that he has always already been a member of the organic Chinese whole. An interpellated subject emerges out of the act of freely assuming the inevitable. For the majority of Hong Kong people, an inner distance is still firmly maintained in their consciousness to differentiate themselves from the mainlanders and to assert their superiority complex. Even after 1997, Hong Kong locals continually subject mainlanders to slurs and discriminate against them as unsophisticated country bumpkins or corrupted entrepreneurs from across the border.

New immigrants from China are generally seen as uneducated, uncivilized, violent, and lazy. There is a looming prejudice against new mainland arrivals, especially after the Asian financial turmoil. Hong Kong people believe that mainlanders will take away their jobs, worsen Hong Kong society, and destroy the city's prosperity and stability.

However, paradoxically, Hong Kong people also depend on the new immigrants from China to act as a "proxy" to make them believe that the city is still an ideal place to live—that it is still a great city to which many aliens desperately want to come. The Hong Kong fantasy about the new immigrants' fantasy of Hong Kong, in a way, can partially take care of Hong Kong's confidence crisis. Hong Kong people believe that there are immigrants who are naïve enough to believe in the future of Hong Kong. This delegated belief can thus sustain the subjectivity of Hong Kong. Hence, the kernel of the fantasy is that China can be duped and China is kept at bay, so Hong Kong people can love the pandas and at the same time express their discontent about the new immigrants from the mainland, though both of them are the external existence of Chineseness. Such distancing of the Hong Kong self from the mainland Chinese does not pose any threat to China. On the contrary, it is constitutive of the power of the nationalist ideology. Ideology can exert its hold over the subject precisely because of the very insistence that there is a gap between the innermost subjectivity and the ideological legitimization. Hong Kong's belief that it is able to dupe and sometimes manipulate China is actually tolerated by China and is precisely what guarantees Hong Kong's subservience to the nation.

Hong Kong's anti-immigrant attitude, indeed, does not conflict with the interest of China and the ideological grip of national subjectivization. As a matter of fact, discrimination against the poor and the lazy has become the common value judgment of China and Hong Kong nowadays. In the process of extensive capitalization and economic reforms, China also projects the disavowed part of itself onto the figure of the "immigrants" (who are identified as "rural migrants" or "migrant workers" on the mainland). In the dispute of the ruling of the Hong Kong Court of Final Appeal over the 1,670,000 mainlanders' constitutional right of abode in Hong Kong, it is the Chinese government, not just the SAR authority, that restricts the immigration of mainland Chinese to the postcolonial city. The hostility toward the "aliens" (the poor, the migrant, and other kinds of minorities) bears witness to the fact that the experience of belonging to a well-defined social body that gives meaning to the individual is rapidly losing ground. The phantasmic production of perceiving the presence of "aliens" as a threat to social identity only reveals that the subject is disoriented by the inherent antagonism within the meaning and logic of capitalist development. In addition, it is even easier to assume that not only the social but also the national identity or cohesiveness is in jeopardy because it is menaced by the growing presence of other aliens coming from the outside. In post-1997 Hong Kong, the aliens that are able to compete with the popularity of the giant pandas and their symbolic national presence are of course the Western humanized animal-figures, such as Mickey Mouse or Goofy, from the American-owned multinational corporation Disney.[4]

Go to the Chinese Disneyland

The presumed opposition between the real, natural panda that symbolizes inherent Chineseness and the artificial, fabricated American imperialist token of Mickey Mouse is, in fact, false and misleading. The giant pandas in Hong Kong are no less fictional and imperialistic than Mickey Mouse, whereas the Disney cartoon figures could also be regarded as a "natural" part of the growth of capitalism in the Chinese community. It is not only Hong Kong but China as well that embraces the advent of "Disneyfication" on the regained Chinese soil, because what Disney the corporation stands for is no longer simply American cultural imperialism or the omnipresence of American mass culture. The Disney theme park is always related to many other projects in urban planning, ecological development, product merchandising, technological innovation, and construction of national character (Smoodin 1994). In addition, it manifests the utopian vision made possible by capitalism and technology (Prager and Richardson 1997) or even carries the promise of social progress for the masses without revolution. Perhaps the Chinese leaders long for Disney to convey its emblem of family values and hypercleanliness, that is, a kind of "Singaporization," in the sense that economic integration with the global system is at full speed with the depoliticization of social life. Despite some local intellectuals' expressing doubts about and critiques of the future opening of Disneyland in Hong Kong (Sze and Ip 1999), the general public in the port city as well as in mainland China strongly supports the project and anticipates enjoying the cultural and economic benefits the theme park will bring.[5] The Hong Kong government and the local media are frank in admitting that the Disneyland venture is expected to serve as a leading project to induce other investments and to resolve the confidence crisis after the Asian financial crash. So, right from the beginning, Hong Kong Disneyland is considered as a pure business generator or a money machine. Simultaneously, it is also perceived as a phantasmic springboard for the ex-colony to project itself as the most cosmopolitan city in Asia and to imagine itself, in the words of the SAR chief executive Tung Chee-hwa, "enjoying status similar to that of New York in America and London in Europe" (though neither New York nor London has a Disneyland).

Unlike the French elite who dismissed Euro Disneyland by calling it a "Cultural Chernobyl" or a "Tragic Kingdom" that infringes upon their community, Hong Kong people never conceive their city as a place of innocence that would be contaminated by the invading U.S. culture. If there is any discussion of the cultural impact of the Disney theme park on Hong Kong, it merely functions as an ideological screen or a phantasmic scene for rescuing the domain of appearance. Appearance has to be maintained because it functions as a symbolic order that prevents a world divided into racial and cultural differences from falling apart. It is tempting to pursue Baudrillard's idea that Disneyland as a simulacrum is used to cover up the loss of non-simulated reality in Los Angeles and the America surrounding it, by arguing that the host city of the Chinese Disneyland is itself turning into a gigantic imaginary theme park. Mitsuhiro Yoshimoto has already made similar claims about Tokyo Disneyland: it is a Disneyland in Tokyo and Tokyo as a Disneyland, since Tokyo has already become a large theme park visited by people from all over Japan who want to have fun (Yoshimoto 1994, 190). A Hong Kong–based journalist writes,

> Perhaps this is to be Hong Kong's future: to peddle a fake Chinese style to the West, a user-friendly model China, complete with avuncular mandarins and miniature Great Walls—while simultaneously peddling a fake version of the West to China, replete with smiling Mickeys and Minnies. . . . [T]he new Hong Kong will be a "virtual" city. . . . Theme park Hong Kong is far too "virtual" to consider its actual location on the south China coast. It likes to project itself as everywhere and anywhere, a cyber-city, more notional than physical. (Colvert 2000)

Notwithstanding its insight, the above comment mistakenly presumes that playing the middleman between China and the West and selling "fake" things to both parties is simply the future of Hong Kong, when in fact it is an old business that the ex-colony has been doing for a long time. Any easy historicization of a city that distinguishes between the past/old as something authentic/real and the future/new as something virtual/imaginary only casts a veil over the hard kernel that always returns as the same through different kinds of historical narratives. The so-called "fake" cultural styles that Hong Kong has been marketing to its clients are nothing but the mise-en-scène of the fantasy that supports the cultural reality itself. Hong Kong's customers know that what they consume is not the real thing, but still they enjoy it. Indeed, many tourists come to Hong Kong precisely for the counterfeited brand names.[6]

One of the earliest amusement parks built in Hong Kong and one that attracted the attention of tourists around the world was the Tiger Balm Garden, which opened in 1935. The Burma-born overseas Chinese entrepreneur Aw Boon Haw (Hu Wenhu in pinyin), who ran a successful medical-ointment business with the brand-name of Tiger in Southeast Asia, designed and constructed from scratch a bizarre and outrageous "Chinese theme park" for promotional and moral purposes. The concept of the theme park probably didn't exist in the 1930s. The Tiger Balm Garden, however, could be categorized as an amusement park that pretends to be a theme park about Chinese culture. There are many tiger sculptures that not only allude to a significant totem in Chinese tradition but also remind visitors of the commercial logos of Aws Tiger Brand products. Described in many guidebooks as having "grotesque statuary in appallingly bad taste," "a landscape nightmare," and "garish staircases, animals, and grottoes," the Tiger Balm Garden appropriates stories and legends of immortal figures from Chinese folklore and history in order, in the mind of the nationalist merchant, to teach traditional Chinese values to overseas Chinese mingling with Westerners (Brandel and Turbeville 1998). But the special kind of Chineseness (reflected through its excessiveness, hyperbolism, hybridity, and stylistic inconsistency) evoked in the park, for many Chinese visitors, arouses alienation and repulsion more than it summons nostalgia for a rich cultural heritage. What embarrasses visitors is not necessarily that the Chineseness invoked in the garden is purely forged or simply a semblance without any substance. Rather, such a flamboyant Chinese theme park shamelessly reveals too much of the intimate fantasy domain of Chineseness in the mind of a frantic overseas Chinese. The problem of Chineseness in the Tiger Balm Garden is not that it is just a sham to be easily dismissed, but that it is too much and too close to a publicly confessed fantasy. With commercialism running rampant in the rapidly developing Hong Kong, Aw's descendants gradually sold more and more portions of the garden terrain to property development firms. The garden has found itself overwhelmed by the surrounding westernized high-rise apartments. Its extravagant Chineseness, symbolized by the remaining pagoda and the honeycombed cave, has become more eccentric and unreal, serving as a footnote not to the way in which the enclave of the fabricated Chineseness in Hong Kong could be easily swallowed by the raising tide of the economy,[7] but rather to how a comfortable feeling of Chineseness could emerge only under the shadow of commanding commercialization.[8]

To maintain a distance from an intimate phantasmic domain or to virtualize the ideal cultural essence is indeed a way to avoid intruding into the fantasy that forms the disavowed kernel of our subjectivity. Perhaps, the belief in the virtuality of Hong Kong city is precisely a shield that protects us from exposing the secret fantasies of Chineseness.[9] But when everything becomes fake or virtual and when cities become cyber theme parks no longer located in particular places, then appearance remains the only magic that sustains the very fundamental structure of our world. The magic the city attempts to conjure is to make invisible the fact that already many Chinese cities have built their own theme parks and that the market economy has been changing the nation-space into a huge commodified virtual reality. The Disneyland project in Hong Kong is, in fact, a sleight of hand for glossing over the naked truth that virtual reality is already everywhere, although the appearance is maintained by having Hong Kong singled out as the one and only "theme park city" in China.[10]

Unlike many theme parks built in post-Mao China that simulate and display the cultural history, national landscape, and ethnic diversity of the Chinese nation as an eternal unity, Hong Kong Disneyland appears to introduce some foreign American monuments and landscapes to threaten the totality and integrity of the Chinese nationscape. Almost an exact copy of the Disneyland in Anaheim, California, Hong Kong Disneyland is easily associated in the minds of its predominantly Chinese visitors with the overwhelming presence of the United States as a hegemonic power in Asia, especially during some occasional hard times between China and the States.[11] There is some cultural sensitivity, certain tactical adjustments (such as emphasizing the Chinese heroine Mulan, offering some other Chinese elements of attraction, and serving dim sum and Chinese cuisine other than hamburgers and hotdogs), and cautious removal of any apparent icons that may remind people of strong American nationalism. Nonetheless, Hong Kong Disneyland still carries the mission of giving its Chinese guests a true sense of Americanness. The complex will clearly be a celebration of Americana as seen through the eyes of Hollywood. According to surveys conducted by the SAR, Hong Kong locals and mainland tourists want an American-style Disneyland with its classic characters and themes, rather than one with Chinese characteristics. The Chinese will find the Hong Kong Disneyland more appealing if it is an

English-speaking venue that presents programs and music in English and is served by English-speaking staff. For the Chinese visitors, "only this would be the real thing," remarked the chairwoman of the Hong Kong Tourist Board. "If people want a Chinese theme park, they will go to China. People come here for a Disney theme park," the Hong Kong commissioner for tourism has also commented (Y. Chung 1999, 53).

As mentioned earlier, many Chinese amusement parks, cultural villages, historical museums, and *fangujie* (reconstructed old towns), such as Splendid China in Shenzhen and the Chinese Ethnic Culture Park in Beijing, have been built since the early 1990s.[12] These national parks are often jointly owned by the local Chinese government and overseas investors from Taiwan and Hong Kong. For a decade Chinese people have been used to consuming the commodified forms of the cultural past that their theme parks can provide in the rapid expansion of a market economy.[13] And the Chinese government obviously grasps the trick of manipulating the amusement park to demarcate "the space of representation, within which the nation can be rendered as a total concept, a timeless essence," and to narrativize "the nation as an eternal unity, made of an essence that does not change, that allows it to cohere together" (Anagnost 1997, 162, 165). Hence, the Hong Kong Disneyland project cannot be innocently assumed by the Chinese to be a sheer tourist attraction or a pure symbol of the age of global capitalism and advanced technology. The proper questions to be asked then are: Why does the Chinese authority, with a keen awareness of the fact that Disneyland is an apparatus of U.S. nationalism, reproducing America as an imagined community of the nation-state, still welcome the project in its special administrative zone? Is it possible that by permitting Hong Kong's attempt to bring a gigantic token of possibly hostile foreign nationalism onto Chinese soil, the Chinese authority can thereby reconstruct its own cultural, particular roots in order to shroud its social reality of the reign of abstract capital?

The Hong Kong Disneyland project could help China to maintain a balance between the pervasive commodification of everyday life by the mechanism of global capitalist economy and the continuous narrativization of Chinese nationalism in opposition to the looming Americanization. As the various "lands" (for instance, Main Street USA, Fantasyland, or Adventureland) in Disney's theme park are all displacements, the Hong Kong Disneyland is itself a "displaced fantasy." That is to say, it is never simply a phantasmic scenario of Hong Kong by which it perpetuates its cosmopolitan dream of becoming one of the world's top cities while duping the Chinese central government that the city is sufficiently patriotic enough to be left alone. Hong Kong's misidentification of itself as the subject in this displaced fantasy turns out to be merely a substitute that enables the Chinese subject to sustain its desire for a strong hold on the national imaginary through its encounter with the conspicuous manifestation of American hegemony. The fantasy is displaced also in the sense that the Disneyland tailor-made for Chinese consumers is located in the Hong Kong SAR, a place both inside and outside the Chinese nation-space. In other words, the Hong Kong Disneyland is a place on the move. It is close enough to be effectively contained within the political territorial boundaries, and yet it is far enough to be seen as a fetish and conceal the lack around which the symbolic logo of contemporary China is articulated—and by means of which the Chinese subject can sustain itself at the level of its vanishing desire.

Just as Bush's America needs an evil enemy to shore up the resurgence of its conservatism, China also relies on a Disneyland as one of the ways to cover up the inconsistency of its own ideological system. Being no longer a rival to capitalism,[14] "Communist" China can at least recreate itself as a rival to hegemonic Americanness and mask the fact that it is launching a tougher, harder, and more inherently exploitative capitalist campaign within its own country. With the worldwide triumph of capitalism without communism, China has to look for a scene in which its position could be redefined. Hence, what the handover symbolizes is not capitalism versus communism, freedom versus authoritarianism, Western democratic ideas versus Oriental despotism, or Western interference in the name of human rights versus Chinese national integrity and sovereignty. If there is any confrontation, it is an illusory one. All of these forces find accord in a fundamental discord: the renaturalization of capitalism through reference to Chinese nationalization. The Chinese invention of "one country, two systems" and Chinese-style socialism are nothing but a veil for the wholesale acceptance of capitalism. The return of Hong Kong to China, which would ostensibly pose a threat to the Communist regime (by inviting the spread of corrupt, capitalist ideas and political intervention on the part of Western human rights watchers), actually facilitates China's increasing involvement in the global capitalist system.

The gigantic theme park Hong Kong is thus well designed for China to reposition itself in the new global scenario. The "fun" that theme park Hong Kong can offer ranges from cutesy kiddy animals to terrifying thrill rides, from which the city is never able to stand aside. The retired chief secretary for administration, Anson Chan Fang On-sang, has said, "We have forged a partnership between two of the world's best-known brand names—Hong Kong and Disney" (Y. Chung 1999, 54). Perhaps it is not merely wishful thinking on the part of the Hong Kong official to see the city as just another transnational company and to try to benefit from associating itself with the other big name. I am not simply suggesting that, to an extent, both brand names are in decline and desperately seeking some help to revitalize themselves in the twenty-first century. What I am trying to say is that post-1997 Hong Kong is endeavoring to undergo the evolutionary transformation that Disney's symbol, Mickey Mouse, has been through. When Mickey Mouse hit the theaters in the late 1920s, his behavior and appearance were not like what we are familiar with today. Instead of the cute, inoffensive, and well-behaved cartoon character we now see, Mickey was mischievous and slightly sadistic in his early appearance. Soon Mickey's personality was softened, with his look becoming more and more like that of a child. As the natural scientist Stephen Jay Gould points out, Mickey Mouse has been evolving over the last several decades toward the characteristics of a young child: his head size, eyes, and cranium have been gradually and persistently growing larger to appeal to people as cute and friendly (Gould 1980). These babyish features manage to elicit strong human affection and maintain a hold over us.[15] Wild animals with features mimicking those of human babies can also draw powerful emotional responses from us. Isn't it true that the appealing power of the giant panda rests precisely on our reaction to the same set of features in our own babies? Could we then say that the evolution of Mickey Mouse is indeed a process of "pandarization"? In this particular sense, the myth of East–meets/merges with–West could continue in the ex-colony that always worries about losing its cosmopolitan flavor after the handover. These two cutesy animals sharing some human baby features give body to the failure of the signifying representation of the post-1997 Hong Kong subject. They serve as fantasy objects that fill out the lack in the signifying order of the decolonized Hong Kong.

Instead of being programmed by a purposeful higher-order force such as globalization, Hong Kong as a well-designed screen for the emergence of any fantasy is only a side effect of its own struggle for individual reproduction. To use the Heideggerian language, an ex-colonial community like Hong Kong is determined as "being thrown" into a contingent situation within which it has to assume its destiny. Instead of finding itself disoriented and lost during the fifteen years of the transitional period to the handover, post-1997 Hong Kong is more and more "freely assuming" its imposed historic destiny. Trying to be young or returning to childishness is a target the city chooses to hit and a selected means for avoiding becoming too Chinese and becoming too dangerously politicized. The child image embodied by the real and unreal babyish-looking animals from afar forms a point of identification through which post-1997 Hong Kong attempts to reconstitute itself. The reverse route of juvenilization is accompanied by cleaning up one's act and behaving properly at all times. To retrieve a juvenile image and features implies not only a recovery of a bygone childhood but also a return to the state of subordination. Post-1997 Hong Kong thus understood is not a city at its end but one in the nascent, newborn childlike state, and this state is going to be constant and will be carefully monitored. But a (youthful) "city of life," a slogan used by the tourism board to promote the city to foreigners, is a representation that betrays the Hong Kong subject because it deforms what it is supposed to reveal. There is always a certain remnant in the childlike image that Hong Kong strives to fit in. The city that takes out its anger and frustration on the new immigrants from mainland China and Southeast Asia may have difficulty matching a happy, angelic, and submissive child-image. The remnant that resists the subjectivization in the fantasy scenario, however, is the positive condition of the Hong Kong subject. Fantasy, indeed, could create multiple subject positions among which the fantasizing subject is free to choose its identification.

Post-1997 Hong Kong is always thinking of playing the game of miniaturization or minorization to China while dreaming of itself being big or major in the construction of the new meanings of Chineseness. Thinking big and simultaneously expanding the childlike image do not come together to form a clear picture of a post-1997 Hong Kong that is regressing from an adult city with growing demands for political reforms to a happy kiddyland that any totalitarian regime would love to govern. The propensity for the infantile may not necessarily suggest that the postcolonial city is nostalgic for its colonial good old days. Hong Kong does need Disney to get out the child in it. Mickey Mouse is never a cultural intrusion but somewhat of a solution to the China–Hong Kong relation. It is a solution that alleviates Hong Kong's anxiety about directly confronting the desire of China. Constantly renewing links with childhood could be more a mode of becoming than a sort of remembering. A becoming-child, or even a becoming-baby, is an intense rupture for Hong Kong's reconception of itself for China. Deleuze states: "With a baby, one has nothing but an affective, athletic, impersonal, vital relationship. The will to power certainly appears in an infinitely more exact manner in a baby than in a man of war. For the baby is combat, and the *small* is an irreducible locus of forces, the most revealing test of forces" (Deleuze 1997, 133). The fantasy of Hong Kong is always to use its "smallness" to take hold of any larger force in order to make it its own.

Hong Kong's becoming-child does show its revolutionary potential. On

July 1, 2003, during the sixth-anniversary celebrations of the Hong Kong handover to Chinese rule, a half million citizens, with good order and without causing any problems, peacefully vented their anger and marched in protest at antisubversion legislation, the possible implementation of mainland Chinese–style security laws by the SAR government, that many in the former British colony fear could erode freedom. The rallying point was the demand for the stepping down of Chief Executive Tung Chee-hwa, more openness of the government, and, eventually, universal suffrage. Not unlike a big festive parade on a carnivalesque holiday, it was the largest pro-democracy demonstration anywhere in China since the Chinese government's bloody crackdown against the student campaign in Beijing's Tiananmen Square in 1989. China's leadership could not have expected a democracy movement to flower suddenly in the showcase city's soil, which had long been barren. Media on the mainland had a blackout on the mass demonstration in Hong Kong. A senior mainland official later warned that Hong Kong, which promotes itself as a "city of life" (dong*gan* zhidu), might become a "city of turmoil" (dong*luan* zhidu) if it could not maintain its political stability—that is, be pacified and obedient, like a mannerly child. However, not simply showing that Hong Kong is more than just another Chinese city following the politically imposed "Chineseness" from the central government, this effective statement of popular will may manifest for China a possible example of progressive democratization in parallel to the historical role played by Hong Kong in creating as well as transforming the modern meanings of Chineseness.

Whether exhibiting East-meets-West images and selling fabricated Chinese cultural flavors to the world in the colonial period or displaying the success of Chinese unification to the mainland's gaze and the model of "one country, two systems" to the suspicious eyes of Taiwan and the international community in the postcolonial age, "Theme Park Hong Kong"—the so-called mega-Chinatown on earth—strives continuously to define its own positions in relation to the notion of Chineseness within a transnational setting. Hong Kong's Chinese cultural identity is never built upon the identification with the image representing what it likes to be. It is rather identification with the very point from which Hong Kong is being seen through the perspectives of the other. What it means to be Chinese today in Hong Kong culture always depends on an external gaze to perceive it as a symbolic unity. But the unified image could never be coherent without at the same time producing a certain excess or leftover that disrupts the system from within. No matter how faked, contrived, and artificial is the Chineseness constructed in Hong Kong culture, it functions as a fantasy screen to conceal the inherent inconsistency of today's Chinese identity in the era of globalization. This fantasy, however, could not be discarded as something false. If Hong Kong holds on to this fantasy object status all the way, it may realize the emancipatory potential of the fantasy not only by changing all those involved but also by leading them to a new scenario of life.

Notes

Introduction

1. For instance, the avowed globalist and internationally acclaimed management guru Kenichi Ohmae said that Hong Kong should benefit from the "Commonwealth of Chunghwa (or Chinese)," that is, greater China's economy, by enforcing a "Closer Economic Partnership Arrangement" with mainland China, treating upper-middle-class Chinese as customers, and positioning itself as a hub for professional services in China (J. Lo 2003).

2. The scholarly works I refer to here are mainly those by scholars and critics in Hong Kong and published in Chinese. See, for instance, Lui (1983, 1997); P. Leung (1993, 1995); Ng and Sze (1993); F. Lok (1995); S. Chan (1997); Chan, Li, and Wong (1997); C. Ng (1996b, 1997); Ma Kwok-ming (1998); Ng and Cheung (2001); and Chu (2002).

3. For Western writers like Jan Morris, Chinese culture is ubiquitous in and fundamental to Hong Kong. She writes, "Hong Kong is in China, if not entirely of it, and after nearly 150 years of British rule the background to all its wonders remains its Chineseness. . . . The very smells are Chinese smells—oily, laced with duck-mess and gasoline," and "the British Empire at its most tremendous failed to make much impression upon this down-to-earth genius, and the mass in Hong Kong today are not a jot less Chinese because they live beneath the Union Jack. A surprising number, after 150 years of British rule, still speak no English." Furthermore, Morris underscores "the reluctance of the vast majority of Chinese in Hong Kong to become in the least Anglicized" (Morris 1990, 38, 130).

4. The Chineseness constructed in Hong Kong is not confined to the realm of popular culture. There were a number of Chinese scholars and philosophers, such as Qian Mu, Luo Xianglin, Mou Zongsan, Tang Junyi, and Xu Fuguan, who were

associated with the prominent "new Confucianism" and who took refuge in Hong Kong after 1949. They published their major works in the intellectual oasis that colonial Hong Kong provided, training a generation of scholars and philosophers in the local universities.

5. Indeed, it is never an easy task to map out even a "local" position for Hong Kong, since the construction of Hong Kong identity always involves class differentiation (Wong and Lui 1993; Siu 1996), gender division, sexual orientation, Chinese and non-Chinese ethnicities, and tensions between natives and new immigrants and urban and rural cultures (Hung 2001). If there is a "unique Hong Kong identity," it is by no means a product of multiple subjectivities or an entity of negotiation. A discussion of Hong Kong identity cannot perpetuate a postmodern identity politics of multiple, particular lifestyles. Rather, it has to acknowledge a particular identity that claims to articulate impossible universal demands and to bear the dimensions of political struggle and confrontation.

6. In an interview, Chow said that instead of multiplying or pluralizing Chineseness, she prefers not to be a "full-time" Chinese (Yuen 1998, 30); in this sense, reducing or negating half of one's Chineseness may appear to be an effective strategy for addressing a nationalist discourse about Chinese identity.

7. For more on the concept of inherent transgression, see Slavoj Žižek (2000a, 2000b).

8. Denis Bray, a former senior Hong Kong civil servant, suggested in 1971 that the stability of the Hong Kong colony's way of life rested on a tripod of consents of China, Britain, and Hong Kong (Miners 1991, 251). During his visit to the colony in 1982, the British minister of state, Lord Belstead, used the term "three-legged stool" to describe how things can go smoothly only when China, Britain, and Hong Kong are in agreement (Tang and Ching 1996, 42).

9. Yu was so enthusiastic about Hong Kong's role in Chinese culture that he even urged leading Hong Kong academics to consolidate their efforts and form schools like the Frankfurt school (A. Leung 2001). See also "Xunzhao duhui he tadewenhua" [In Search of the Metropolis and Its Culture], *Hong Kong Economic Journal,* August 1, 2001, 32.

10. For surveys of the cultural changes within post-Mao China, see, for instance, Zha (1995a), J. Wang (1996), X. Zhang (1997), Huot (2000), X. Tang (2000), and S. Lu (2001).

11. The phrase literally means punk, hoodlum, or hooligan literature. The Chinese authorities have deemed Wang Shuo a source of "spiritual pollution," since his characters, which indulge in drinking, gambling, and promiscuity, are bad role models for his readers. His works occasionally have been banned in China. At the same time, he is a best-selling author there, with over twenty novels and ten million copies in print, and his work appeals to audiences across multiple social strata. For more on the Wang Shuo phenomenon in China, the reader can consult J. Wang (1996, 261–86).

12. Compared with advanced capitalist countries, China still has a long way to go.

However, Chinese-made products have penetrated every corner of the world. In 2001, China's export commodities reached US$266 billion, of which 90 percent were industrial manufactured products. At the same time, 80 percent of the world's top 500 transnational enterprises have entered China, and 390,000 foreign-funded enterprises have been operating in China. China has rocketed to second place in the absorption of foreign direct investment. Because of its cheap labor, China has been depicted as the "world factory" by Western media and as a major factor contributing to the worldwide deflation of the prices of some consumer goods.

13. Chan is the founder of Hong Kong's "Yuppies" magazine *City Magazine,* which advocates the use of hybrid language, a combination of Cantonese and English, in written texts. Its style of writing has been characterized as a major feature of Hong Kong culture. On Chan and his cultural enterprise, see J. Zha (1995b).

14. The challenge to China figures in the subtitle of Michael Yahuda's book, *Hong Kong: China's Challenge* (Yahuda 1996).

15. For instance, the influx of Hong Kong Chinese immigrants and capitalism into North America was not particularly welcomed. See K. Mitchell (1995, 1996).

16. The flood of Chinese immigrants in the United States and Canada has radically changed the cultural landscape of the North American suburb. The downtowns are full of signs in Chinese and Chinese stores in which Hong Kong videos and publications are widely available. Monterey Park in California became America's first majority-Chinese town in the 1980s. At least seven nearby towns also attained majority or near-majority Chinese populations in the 1990s (Piore 2001).

Chapter 1: Much Ado about the Ordinary in Newspaper-Column and Book Culture

1. The Official Languages Ordinance was passed in 1974 to promote the parity of Chinese and English, but the civil service has been slow to use Chinese in administrative practice. The majority of secondary schools continued to use English as the primary language of instruction even after 1997, because general opinion still held that the English language was of greater value than the Chinese language in terms of career success. On the other hand, in the Official Languages Ordinance, what the term "Chinese" means—whether it is standard Chinese (Putonghua) or Cantonese—was never specified, leaving some kind of fuzziness surrounding the term "Chinese language" in Hong Kong.

2. Rey Chow has lucidly described her experience of high school education in colonial Hong Kong: "What needs to be emphasized is that Chinese culture was never eradicated tout court but always accorded a special status—and that this was actually the more effective way to govern. During the era when I was in secondary school (1970s), for instance, English was the mandatory medium of instruction in Hong Kong's Anglo-Chinese schools (there were also Chinese schools where Cantonese was the medium of instruction), but Chinese language and literature and Chinese his-

tory were also possible subjects (for public examinations). The native culture, in other words, continued to be taught (all the way to university and postgraduate levels) and allowed a certain role in the colonized citizens' education. Rather than being erased, its value became specialized and ghettoized over time precisely through the very opportunities to learn it that were made available. Albeit not a popular one, the study of Chinese remained an option. It was in this manner that British colonialism avoided the drastic or extremist path of cultural genocide (which would have been far too costly) and created a social stable situation based on the pragmatist hierarchization of cultures, with the British on top and the Chinese beneath them. . . . Racism was, indeed, very much in operation, but it was a racism that had turned race and culture into *class* distinctions so that, in order to head toward the upper echelons of society, one would, even (and especially) if one was a member of the colonized race, have no choice but to collaborate with the racist strategies that were already built into the stratification informing the distribution and consumption of knowledge as well as its compensation" (Rey Chow 2002, 11–12).

3. There are occasionally idiosyncratic, stylish supplements in Hong Kong Chinese-language dailies, such as the "Magpaper," which ran in the *Hong Kong Daily News* from June 3, 1996, to September 30, 1997. But stylistic experiments in the supplements generally have not been well received by readers.

4. Clement Y. K. So has done a comparative survey on the supplement sections of Hong Kong's *Mingpao Daily,* Taiwan's *China Times Daily,* China's *People's Daily,* and the *New York Times.* He finds that although all papers have supplement sections, columns make up 29.5 percent of the content of Hong Kong dailies, the highest of all. See So (1999).

5. For a more detailed look at the *Apple Daily,* see So (1997a). The tabloid's preoccupation with the downfall of celebrities may reflect not only the traditional content of tragedy (as one critic points out [Simon 1999]), but also upon the psyche of its readership, which, in the context of a transitional Hong Kong, is obsessed with the potential reversal of prosperity.

6. As Michael Hardt and Antonio Negri would say, this new globalism, which they call "Empire," makes conquests beyond imperialism and the nation-state, in the guise of peacemaking and local incorporation (Hardt and Negri 2000).

7. For more on this rumor, see Evans (1997).

8. Studies of Hong Kong newspaper columns are numerous, but academic treatments of the subject still are rare. For the general comments on columns, see, for instance, "Zhuanlan yu wenxue zuotanhui" [Forum on Column and Literature], *Kung Kao Po,* September 5, 1986; "Special Issue on the Column," *Boyi* 9 (1988); Lian Xihua, "Zhuanlan yi" [Column 1], *Lianhe wenxue* [Unitas] 94 (1992): 29–30; Chen Huiyang, "Zhuanlan er" [Column 2], *Lianhe wenxue* [Unitas] 94 (1992): 31–32; Karen Chan, "Tuojie zhuanlan" [Columns Not in Sync with Times], *Hong Kong Cultural Studies Bulletin* 2 (April 1995): 48–49; Xie Xiwei, "Shuxie yu jilu zhijian: lun baozhi fukannei de zhuanlan" [Between Writing and Recording: On Columns in Newspaper Supple-

ment], *Hong Kong Cultural Studies Bulletin* 2 (April 1995): 50–51; Feng Weicai, "Xianggang de zhuanlan wenhua" [Hong Kong's Column Culture], *Dushu ren* [Readers] 6 (1995): 97–102; Li Zhanpeng, "Fukan, wenxue, xie" [Column, Literature, Writing], *Mingpao,* November 19, 1997; Huang Canran, "Baozhi fukan de zhuanji" [A Favorable Turn for the Newspaper Supplement], *Mingpao,* December 30, 1997; Ma Ka-fai, "Zhuanlan shuxie yu quanli caozuo" [Column Writing and Power Manipulation], paper presented at Hong Kong Culture Conference, Hong Kong Polytechnic University, October 8–9, 1999.

9. See, for instance, Karen Chan (1994, 39), He Liangmao (1997, 48–52).

10. For such a sociological perspective, see So (1997b, 1999).

11. For a discussion of the role of the column in Hong Kong literature, see, for example, Yip (2000); Wong Yan Wan (1997); "Wenxue fukan sheng yu si" [The Life and Death of the Literary Supplement], *Mingpao,* August 26–27, 1997; Huang Canran, "Baozhi yu wenxue" [Newspapers and Literature], *Mingpao,* February 22, 2000; Ye Si, "Zhuanlan yu xinganxing" [Columns and the New Sensibility], *Boyi* 9 (1988): 154–157; "Zhuanlan yu wenxue zuotanhui" [Forum on Column and Literature] (1986); Ye Si, "Zai Xianggang xie zhuanlan" [Writing Columns in Hong Kong], *Literary Quarterly* 5 (March 1983): 51–53.

12. For English translations of the works of these Hong Kong writers, see M. Cheung (1998), Tam, Yip, and Dissanayake (1999).

13. The Sino-British Declaration states that "Hong Kong's previous capitalist system and life-style shall remain unchanged for 50 years." For a discussion on the political implications of the Hong Kong lifestyle, see Turner (1995).

14. There is a Chinese phrase, *luoye guigen,* that metaphorically characterizes Chinese emigrants as "fallen leaves that will return to their roots" in the soil of China.

15. What I mean by "book" here is different from Derrida's concept of the book as a metaphor of God's writing, the book of Nature, the divine inscription in the heart and the soul, or the determination of absolute presence. Although my concept of "book" is strictly that of an artificial human product, I agree with Derrida that the idea of the book is the idea of totality. See Derrida (1976, 18).

Chapter 2: Leftovers of Film and Television Subtitles in a Transnational Context

Portions of this chapter appeared, in a different form, as "Look Who's Talking: The Politics of Orality in Transnational Hong Kong Mass Culture" in "Modern Chinese Literary and Cultural Studies in the Age of Theory: Reimagining a Field," ed. Rey Chow, special issue, *Boundary 2* 25.3 (1998): 151–68.

1. Some viewers prefer subtitled films because they find the out-of-sync dialogue in dubbed movies irritating, while others like dubbed versions since they feel subtitles disrupt the visual experience of a film. American audiences see subtitled foreign

films in "art-house theaters," whereas Hong Kong audiences usually enjoy subtitled Hollywood blockbusters in mainstream theaters. Recently Hong Kong film distributors have begun to release both dubbed and subtitled versions of foreign movies— mainly animated Disney features, Japanese anime, and children's films like *Harry Potter*—to accommodate the different needs of local audiences.

2. More than three hundred Chaozhouese-speaking and two hundred Amoy-dialect films were made in Hong Kong over those two decades (*Fifty Years of the Hong Kong Film Production* 1997).

3. I thank Law Kar, renowned Hong Kong film critic and programmer of the Hong Kong Film Archive, for providing this information.

4. For more comprehensive and detailed historical accounts of the developments of Hong Kong's Cantonese and Mandarin cinemas and their interconnection, see Fu (2000), Stokes and Hoover (1999a), Teo (1997, 2000), Fonoroff (1997), Armes (1987, 158–61), and Jarvie (1977).

5. Shohat and Stam write, "For those familiar with both source and target language, subtitles offer the pretext for a linguistic game of 'spot the error'" (Shohat and Stam 1985, 46).

6. See Shohat and Stam (1985, 48), Nornes (1999, 30, 34 n. 39), and Bordwell (2000b, 87). Such practice could also be considered as a situationist exercise of "détournement" that reuses the preexisting elements in a new ensemble.

7. Shu Kei, the director of *Sunless Day* (1990) and *Hu-Du-Men* (1996), observes that the post-synch shooting of most Hong Kong films encourages extraordinarily quick editing: "Editing with sound you would realize film can be slowed down a little, and you can play more with the rhythm of not only sound but also visuals. Actually, the sound slows up the rhythm of the visuals. But without it you tend to do everything in a very fast way, and I think this is something that is very subconscious that the [Hong Kong] filmmakers do not realize" (qtd. in Wood 1998, 114).

8. Michel Chion argues that an audiovisual analysis aims to understand the interplay of sound and images in film. But in audiovisual media, such a combination is always a forced marriage (Chion 1994). For other comprehensive studies on the topic, see Weis and Belton (1985).

9. By the end of 2003, English subtitles had become mandatory on news, weather, and current affairs shows and emergency announcements on Hong Kong English language channels in order to help local audiences to improve their English. As a member of the Subsidized Secondary Schools Council said, "Many students are turned off because the dialogue in some English programs is spoken too fast or they don't understand the accent, even though they know the words. If students can read and hear the words, it would definitely help in learning" (A. Lo 2002).

10. The Broadcasting Authority regularly receives complaints from local TV viewers about Chinese words that have been misused or mistyped in the subtitles. The complaints reveal that TV viewers do read the subtitles, and that they enjoy picking out mistakes in them.

11. The advent of VCD and DVD technology could allow a viewer either to tune into a Mandarin or Cantonese soundtrack or to select subtitles in different languages.

12. On the other hand, American film critics are also able to appreciate the spectacle of Hong Kong film's reinvention of an "apocalyptic crisis cinema" with political, historical, and cultural density. See, for instance, Williams (1997). Because of the 1997 handover, Hong Kong films have largely been received in the West as an allegory of the city's sociohistorical situation. The political relevance and the function of cinematic production as a collective mode of social expression, which has vanished in Hollywood, suddenly is relevant to Hong Kong filmmaking. The growing popularity of Hong Kong movies in the West may say more about current conditions in the West than of those in Hong Kong. Perhaps, far from being the other of the West, Hong Kong cinema embodies the West in its otherness.

13. For a detailed description of the subtitling routine, see Bordwell (2000b, 126–27). In order to improve the quality of the subtitles, the Chinese University of Hong Kong has announced recently that its translation department will teach courses on film subtitling.

14. Obviously, not all Western viewers like the dubbed versions of Hong Kong action cinema. Some would prefer to see the original with the subtitles. An American critic, while reviewing the DVD version of *Contract Killer* (1998), starring Jet Li, laments that "*Contract Killer* is a completely different film at the same time, simply because the DVD is dubbed. And although your stereotypical Ugly American may not like to read and watch films at the same time, the fact that the subtitles option isn't even offered by Columbia Tristar is an immense disservice to the genre, the actors, and their skills. Contrary to what the market may dictate when it comes to action cinema—especially anything originating somewhere else besides the States—film is not exclusively a visual medium. And although Jet Li may not be Hong Kong's finest actor (even within the action genre, which he more or less owns), the fact that you can't *listen* to him do his job devalues what the guy has to offer" (Thill 2002).

15. Bordwell explains that "there are subtitles straight out of Raymond Roussel, passed happily around the world through e-mail: 'I am damn unsatisfied to be killed in this way.' 'Same old rules: no eyes, no groin.' 'I have been scared shitless too much lately.' 'How can you use my intestines as a gift?' 'You always use violence. I should've ordered glutinous rice chicken.'" (Bordwell 2000b, 91). Indeed, quotations of fractured English subtitles in Hong Kong film saturate the Internet.

16. As Bordwell points out, Western admirers of Hong Kong cinema "tend to offer rhapsody rather than analysis" of their favorite flicks. They dismiss the question of the appealing power of Hong Kong film as "academic" (Bordwell 2000b, 96).

17. Quoted from the back cover of David Bordwell's *Planet Hong Kong*.

18. This is a term I borrow from Roland Barthes, who defines it as something manifest, stubborn, and beyond the meaning of the words. See Barthes (1977).

19. Bordwell observes that, like "Japanese anime, Indian melodramas, Italian horror, Mexican masked-wrestler films, Indonesian fantasies, and other off-center me-

dia materials from various countries," Hong Kong cinema is a form of ethnic culture and "a local cinema [that] has achieved international reach by becoming a subcultural cinema" in the United States, having become "so powerful that it can seize Hollywood's attention" (Bordwell 2000b, 96).

20. There are always exceptions. The protagonist of Ng Hui Bun's epistolary story, "Xin" (Letters), works for a Hong Kong television station translating American programs such as *Quincy* and *The A-Team*. He is so sensitive to language that he can't help changing his translations in order to resist the ideology spread by those programs. For instance, when a U.S. documentary says "the benightedness and ignorance of the Third World deter it from receiving advanced technology," he creatively renders it, "those Anglo-American technologies may not be appropriate to resolve the poverty and disasters of the Third World" (Ng Hui Bun 1987, 143).

21. Canto-pop refers to the Hong Kong popular music in Cantonese dialect. The Canto-pop boom began in the early 1970s. The music industry continued to expand throughout the 1980s by producing stars and products cheaply and quickly, until it was hit hard by piracy. In the 1990s, Canto-pop stars began to record Mandarin-language versions of their hits and even entire Mando-pop albums. The mainland market offers an unprecedented new world for Canto-pop (which could easily evolve into Mando-pop) to conquer.

22. By "modern concepts of the sign," I mean those proposed by Ferdinand de Saussure, Roman Jakobson, Jacques Lacan, Roland Barthes, and Emile Benveniste. See, for example, de Saussure (1966), Jakobson (1956), Lacan (1977), Barthes (1973), and Benveniste (1971).

23. In order to attain "reconciliation," we do not have to "overcome" the scission between the two parties. We only need to construct a new frame of reference and place the conflicting parties in a new symbolic order.

24. According to Matthew Turner, the so-called Hong Kong identity was carefully designed by the British colonial government to alienate the Chinese population from Communist China after the 1967 anticolonial riot. Because of social and political changes that have taken place in the last two decades, the Hong Kong lifestyle has been displacing traditional cultural attachments to China. In the mid-1980s a majority of the local population identified themselves as "Hong Kong people," not "Chinese people." The return of sovereignty to China has forced Hong Kong people to rethink their identity and their relation to China. See Turner (1995).

25. See, for example, Anderson (1983, 41–49).

26. When the documentary was released on video compact disc (VCD) in 1997 by the Guangdong Haiyan Audio-Visual Company, it was retitled *Xianggang Bainian*.

27. This notion of subject formation, according to Judith Butler, is full of religious implications. The interpellating call comes from God and is a command to align oneself with the law through the appropriation of guilt. The submission to the law is necessary to prove one's innocence in the face of accusation. Butler points out: "To

become a 'subject' is thus to have been presumed guilty, then tried and declared innocent" (Butler 1997, 118).

28. It is a written language that combines Cantonese, classical Chinese, and standard Chinese. Standard Chinese usually dominates in such a text while classical Chinese and Cantonese are used only at certain points for emphasis. The origin of the term *saam kap dai* has been explained differently. Some believe it is derived from the Chinese classical examination system. The top three places of the classical examination, in Cantonese, are known as *saam yun kap dai,* or *saam kap dai,* for short. Others point out there is a kind of porridge in Canton that is made with three different kinds of pig innards. The porridge is called *saam kap dai juk.* Parents bring their children to eat such porridge in the hope that the kids will score well in the examination as the top three of the classical examination system (Snow 1991; Huang 2002).

29. *Her Fatal Ways IV* (Biaojie, Ni Haoye! 4 zhi Qingbuzijin) was directed by Alfred Cheung Kin-Ting and released in 1994. The Chinese title means "Cousin Sister, You're Great Stuff! 4: Uncontrollable Love." For a detailed analysis of the series in terms of China–Hong Kong relations, see Shih (1999).

30. The mainland Chinese policewoman is called "Miss Cheng" while the name of the Scottish character is "John" in the movie. In the following table, the right-hand column shows the English and Chinese subtitles seen onscreen (the English errors are printed as such). The left-hand column tells the language(s) the characters choose to speak in the scene. The Cantonese phrases are transliterated in Yale romanization while the standard Chinese is in pinyin:

John (speaks in English)	hai [Cantonese] Hi.
Cheng (speaks in English)	hai [Cantonese] Hi.
John (in English)	hai [Cantonese] Hi.
	néih yiu ngh yiu joh hah? [Cantonese] Do you want to sit down?
Cheng (in English)	ngh gòi [Cantonese] Oh, thank you.
	néih jùng yi sihk taat? [Cantonese] You like tarts?
John (in English)	haih a, ngóh jùng yi sihk taat, daahn haih jihng haih jùng yi hèung góng gei taat. [Cantonese] Yes, I like tarts, but I only like Hong Kong tarts.

	ngóh làm go go dòu jùng yi sihk, haih mài a? [Cantonese] I think everybody does, right?
Cheng (in English)	haih a [Cantonese] Yes.
John (in English)	ngóh juhng yáuh léuhng go, néih juhng sihk ngh sihk? [Cantonese] I still have two left; would you like one?
	nàh, béi yāt go néih. [Cantonese] Here we go, one for you,
	nèih go ngóh gei. [Cantonese] And one for me.
	ngóh móuh làm gwo néih gàm jùng yi sihk taat gà [Cantonese] I didn't think you like tarts so much.
	néih yìu jí gàn màh? [Cantonese] You want a tissue?
Cheng (in English)	ngh gòi [Cantonese] Thank you.
	néih jùng yi cheung gō gà? [Cantonese] You like sing song?
John (in English)	haih [Cantonese] Yes.
Cheng (in English)	néih cheung di mé gō gà? [Cantonese] What song you sing?
John (speaks in English except for the term "Cantonese song" in Cantonese)	dò sok yìng màhn gō [Cantonese] I sing mostly English. ngóh dòu hó yíh cheung yāt di gwóng dùng gō [Cantonese] But I can also sing a little bit of Cantonese song.
Cheng (in English)	jàn gà? me gō a? [Cantonese] Oh, really? What song?
John (in English)	ngóh sīk cheung yāt sáu sìhm yún jùng sing [Cantonese] I can sing one called "Sim Yuen Chung Sing."
Cheng (in English)	chìng néih cheung béi ngóh ting ngò? [Cantonese] Please sing.

John (sings in English)	hou ngò [Cantonese] Ok.
	"ngóh heui gàai síh máaih sung" [Cantonese] I went shopping in the market.
	"seung máaih di mihn bāau sihk hah" [Cantonese] Wanted to buy some bread and food to eat.
	"ngóh dāk yāt hòuh jí" [Cantonese] I had 10 cents
	"daahn di sihk maht maaih léuhng hòuh jí" [Cantonese] But the food was 20 cents.
	"ngóh mé dòu máaih ngh dou, wái yáuh fáan ngūk kéih" [Cantonese] There was nothing for me to do but to return home.
	dou néih là, dāk meih? [Cantonese] Your turn; are you ready?
Cheng (sings in English)	hóu. [Cantonese] Ok.
	"chàhm yaht, gàm yaht, ting yaht, ting máahn, sìng kèih luhk" [Cantonese] Yesterday, today, tomorrow, tonight, Saturday
	"sìng kèih yāt, sìng kèih yih" [Cantonese] Monday, Tuesday
	"sìng kèih yaht wúih Ok" [Cantonese] Sunday it will be . . . Ok.
	"múih yaht dòu haih hóu yaht jí" [Cantonese] Everyday is good day, good day.
John (speaks in English)	cheung dāk hóu hóu a. [Cantonese] Very good.
Cheng (in English)	duō xiè [Cantonese] Thank you.
	nǐ kě yī wéi wǒ chàng shǒu gē ma? [Cantonese] Can you sing song for me?
John (in English)	wǒ yǒu yī shǒu gē shì sòng gěi nǐ dì [Cantonese] Yes, I have one for you.
Cheng (speaks in Cantonese)	hóu a [Cantonese] Great.
John (sings in English)	wǒ yī zhí yǐ wéi wǒ dì shēng mìng yǐ jīng wú quē [standard Chinese]

I always thought my life complete.

wǒ bù yǐ wéi huán yǒu shèn mó xū yào
[standard Chinese]
Never thought I'd need anything more.

gōng zuò hé péng yǒu wǒ chuí shǒu kē dé
[standard Chinese]
Work and friends were always there for me.

méi xiǎng dào wǒ huán quē shǎo liǎo shèn mó
[standard Chinese]
Never thought that I might be needing
something more.

zhí zhì wǒ kān jiàn nǐ nà zhāng qiào liǎn
[standard Chinese]
Until the first time I saw your lovely face.

wǒ kān jiàn nǐ zuò zhuó, chōng mǎn āi yuàn dì yǎn
jīng [standard Chinese]
I saw you sitting there with despair in your eyes.

wǒ cái zhī dào wǒ men liǎ yǒng bù néng tuǒ xié
[standard Chinese]
I know then that you and I could never compromise.

Cheng
(speaks to herself
in Cantonese)
kéuih gàm yeuhng jouh, haih ngh jīk haih deui ngóh
yáuh yi sì nèih? [Cantonese]
Isn't it a sign of love?

John
(sings in English)
wǒ dì shū nǔ ā, qǐng dá yīng wǒ, zuò wǒ dì nǔ rén
[standard Chinese]
My lady, please say yes, please be mine, please
be mine.

ràng wǒ lìng nǐ dì shēng mìng dé yǐ biàn dé
chóng gāo [standard Chinese]
Let me make your life sublime.

nǐ xǐ huān ma? [standard Chinese]
Do you like it?

Cheng
(speaks in English)
héi fùn [Cantonese]
Oh, yes.

John
(in English)
je sáu gō ngóh dahk yi waih néih
sé dik [Cantonese]
I write this song specially for you.

néih gok dāk láahng a? [Cantonese]
You feeling cold?

hóu yāt dím a? [Cantonese]
Is it better?

Cheng
(speaks the first
line in English,
then the rest in
Cantonese)

ngóh di yìng màhn ngh haih géi hou
  [Cantonese]
My English is not so . . . so good.

só yíh [Cantonese]
So . . .

júng jì nèih jauh . . . [Cantonese]
Anyway . . .

néih haih daih yāt go waih ngóh jok yāt sáu gō
  gei yàhn là [Cantonese]
You are the first one who has composed a
  song for me.

sèui yìhn ngóh ngh haih hou jì douh di noih yùhng
  góng mé yéh [Cantonese]
Although I don't quite understand the content.

bāt gwo ngóh dòu hou . . . [Cantonese]
I . . . I am very . . .

(speaks the word
"Touch" in English)

hou gám duhng [Cantonese]
Touch.
ngóh háng dihng nèih néih jauh haih géi héi fùn
  ngóh gà là [Cantonese]
I am sure you like me.

daahn haih ngóh yauh meih hàng dihng jih géi haih
  me ngoi seuhng néih [Cantonese]
But I am not sure whether I have fallen for you
  or not.
bāt gwo nèih, ngóh jauh deui néih yáuh hóu
  gám [Cantonese]
But, I like you.

ngóh juhng haih yuhk nǔ laih gà, wah béi néih ting
  dòu ngh pa là [Cantonese]
I am still virgin, I am not afraid of telling you.

bāt gwo néih dòu ngh mìhng ngóh góng mé yéh
  [Cantonese]
But, you won't understand what I am talking.

júng jì nèih, ngóh jauh ngh haih go di hóu chèuih
  bihn gei néuih yàhn là [Cantonese]
Anyway, I am not an easy-going woman.

ngóh góng gàm dò yéh néih dòu haih ngh mìhng
gà là [Cantonese]
You won't understand.

(speaks the last two lines in English again)

dím dòu hou, baai baai [Cantonese]
Anyway, bye bye.

dò jeh néih sáu gō [Cantonese]
Thank you for your song.

John
(speaks in Cantonese)

mài jyuh [Cantonese]
Wait.

Cheng
(speaks in Cantonese)

hàh? mài jyuh? [Cantonese]
What? Wait?

John
(in Cantonese)

kèih saht néih tàuh sìn góng gei yéh nèih
[Cantonese]
In fact, all you have just talked

ngóh chyùhn bouh dòu mìhng baahk [Cantonese]
I understand all.

Cheng
(in Cantonese)

hóu cháu a [Cantonese]
How shameful!

John
(in Cantonese)

síu sàm di a [Cantonese]
Be careful.

ngóh yáuh móuh mouh faahn néih a? [Cantonese]
Did I offend you?

Cheng
(in Cantonese)

néih jouh mé ngh wah béi ngóh ting néih sīk jung
màhn gà? [Cantonese]
Why don't you tell me you know Chinese?

John
(in Cantonese)

néih yauh móuh mahn dou [Cantonese]
You didn't ask me.

yāt hòi chí dòu haih néih góng yìng màhn sìn gei
[Cantonese]
You speak English first.

31. Cantonese subtitling did draw criticism from Chinese audiences abroad. For example, a Taiwanese reviewer complains that his DVD copy of *Days of Thunder* (1990), starring Tom Cruise, carries only Cantonese subtitles. As his English-language proficiency does not allow him to understand the original dialogue, he has no choice but to read the Cantonese subtitles. However, he could not comprehend some of the Hong Kong car racing idioms; thus, he prefers to turn off the subtitling (see <http://www.dng.idv.tw/dvdreviews/tom_dvd/day_of_t.htm>, accessed January 12, 2003).

Chapter 3: Hong Kong Muscles and Sublime Chinese Subjectivity

An earlier version of this chapter appeared as "Muscles and Subjectivity: A Short History of the Masculine Body in Hong Kong Popular Culture," *Camera Obscura* 39 (1996): 105–25.

1. But for the pro-China nationalists, the Hong Kong Olympic victory was simply interpreted as a token gift and part of the celebration of the city's return to its Chinese motherland.

2. Probably because of lingering colonial influence, Hong Kong sports fans are also used to following English soccer and have displayed a strong passion for the national soccer team of England even after 1997.

3. The sublime has been an important topic in Western aesthetics and philosophy. The earliest conceptualization of the sublime is ascribed to Longinus (first century A.D.). In modern times, the sublime was given prominent consideration by Burke in his "Essay on the Sublime and Beautiful" (1756), in which the sublime, caused by a mode of terror or pain, is contrasted with the beautiful. In Kant's *Critique of Judgment,* the sublime applies to the mind but not to the object. It is a feeling brought about by objects that are infinitely large or overwhelmingly powerful. Kant distinguishes between a mathematical sublime of extension in space or time and a dynamical sublime of power. There is a great deal of contemporary scholarship on this issue. The "postmodern sublime" has become a basis for contemplation of art, literature, and philosophy. While beauty is associated with a form that can be apprehended, the sublime is connected with the formless and unpresentable. The sublime is also given a political meaning, understood as a resistance to rule and as that which marks the limits of representational thinking, while beauty is associated with a conservative acceptance of existing social structures. *Of the Sublime: Presence in Question* (Courtine 1993), an anthology of essays by Lacoue-Labarthe, Lyotard, Nancy, Rogozinski, and others, is one recent outstanding example of this scholarship. While grounded in this intellectual history, my invocation of the notion of the sublime primarily stems from a colloquial understanding of the term in order to develop a specific concept that helps us to better understand the cultural identity of Hong Kong.

4. The impossible representation of Hong Kong identity has been keenly discussed by a number of critics. See, for instance, Rey Chow (1992, 1995), Abbas (1997), and P. Leung (1995, 1996a, 1996b, 1996c).

5. For a critique of such an ahistorical Western reception of Hong Kong cinema, see Stringer (1997).

6. See, for instance, Eizykman (1976). See also Kaminsky (1984, 73–80), Polan (1986, 167–69), and Sandell (1997, 23–34). However, Yvonne Tasker argues that the juxtaposition of Chinese martial arts and dance in Western culture carries the kind of feminized association that the Western imaginary has long ascribed to the East, since "dance

offers the possibility of occupying a feminine position that involves, as with the martial arts film, an explicit location of the male body on display" (Tasker 1997, 320).

7. The Western scholarship on Hong Kong cinema, and on John Woo's movies in particular, in the 1990s tends to see the cinematic body of work as responsive to the political crisis of 1997. Hence, the cinema is regarded as a means for expressing the Hong Kong people's anxiety, uncertainty, and vulnerability in the face of the Chinese government's takeover. See Stringer (1997) and Williams (1997). Like Matthew Turner, these critics, though offering interesting readings of Woo's films, tend to overemphasize the direct historical reflexivity of Hong Kong cinema.

8. Although Hong Kong people are Cantonese speaking, a lot of Mandarin films were produced in Hong Kong following the 1950s, nearly extinguishing Cantonese cinema in the early 1970s (only one Cantonese film was made in 1971–72). At the time, Mandarin films were more cosmopolitan, technically sophisticated, and related to the modern urban world. Cantonese films, with their lower budgets, were considered to be too parochial and of poor quality.

9. Lee was able to complete only four features in the three years before his untimely death in 1973. They are *The Big Boss, Fist of Fury* (also titled as *The Chinese Connection*), *The Way of the Dragon,* and *Enter the Dragon.*

10. When Cantonese cinema revived and swept away the entire Mandarin film industry, Golden Harvest redubbed Bruce Lee's movies in Cantonese. As a child, Bruce Lee had starred in several Cantonese films, such as *My Son Ah Cheung* (1950), *Thunder Storm* (1957), and *The Orphan* (1961). For biographical studies of Bruce Lee, consult Thomas (1994), J. Wen (1992), Linda Lee (1989), and Clouse (1988).

11. One critic even argues that the popularity of Bruce Lee is intimately associated with the Chinese "Boxer Rebellion idea" and anti-Western and anti-imperialist attitudes of that time. See Cheng Yu (1984).

12. Many studies on the meaning or the ideological content of Bruce Lee's films decode him as either a nationalist or a narcissist. See, for instance, Rayns (1980, 110–12) and Teo (1991, 70–80).

13. This American connection of Lee is played up in the Hollywood film *Dragon: The Bruce Lee Story* (1993), starring Jason Scott Lee, which obviously attempts to reclaim Bruce Lee's body as an incarnation of the myth of the American dream. In the film, Lee is portrayed as a struggling immigrant who is able to overcome racial discrimination, smoothly developing a harmonious relationship with other racial minorities, fighting against the conservative Chinese, and making his dream of success come true at the end. He is also described as a faithful husband and a responsible father, upholding American family values.

14. While this phenomenon is probably an effect of the technical problems of the post-synched soundtrack, I believe its significance extends well beyond the technical dimension.

15. It is locally called "fighting manhua." For a brief history and colorful graphics of the Hong Kong violent action comics, see W. Wong (2002, 100–131).

16. Anti-Japanese sentiment has been a dominant theme in Hong Kong kung fu cinema and comics, even though, ironically, they are heavily influenced by Japanese popular culture.

17. The techniques indebted to cinema used in the comics include closeups, special angles, various depths of field focus, and other frame-size changes.

18. For descriptions of the Hong Kong comics market in the 1970s and 80s, see Lau Ting-kin (1993).

19. Ma's two major comics have already been adapted into big-budget Hong Kong movies. They are *The Stormriders* (1998) and *A Man Called Hero* (1999).

20. See Wong Yuk Long's own memoirs, *Longzhonghu* (The Tiger in Jail) (Wong Yuk Long 1994a) and *Shiyi fuhuameng* (The Dream of a Billion Dollars) (Wong Yuk Long 1994b). Note that Wong refers to himself here as "Tiger."

21. Jackie Chan came from a poor family. His parents once offered to sell him for twenty-six dollars to a British doctor, and they later left him in a Beijing Opera training school for ten years when they migrated to Australia. He never received any formal education and only learned English in Los Angeles when he was sent by Golden Harvest to crack the American market in 1979. For the early history of Jackie Chan, see *Cheng Long* (Taipei: Linba chubanshe, 1981) and his autobiography (1998).

22. It has already been widely adopted by Hollywood movies to merge with the blooper-show tradition.

23. The term "MacGuffin" figured in a joke told by Alfred Hitchcock in an interview with François Truffaut. The joke goes as follows: MacGuffin is a Scottish name that relates to a story about two men on a train. One man says, "What's that package up there in the baggage rack?" The other man answers, "Oh, that is a MacGuffin." The first one asks, "What's a MacGuffin?" "Well," the other man says, "it's an apparatus for trapping lions in the Scottish Highlands." The first man says, "But there are no lions in the Scottish Highland." The other one answers, "Well, then that is no MacGuffin!" (Truffaut 1985, 138).

24. When he refers to Hong Kong culture as "a culture of disappearance," Abbas does not merely mean that its cultural specificity is going to be extinct after the handover to China in 1997. "Dis-appearance" is understood as a kind of pathology of cultural presence that no familiar modes of representation can contain. Abbas believes that filmmakers such as Stanley Kwan and Wong Kar-wai are able to work with disappearance and invent a form of visuality that problematizes the visual itself. See Abbas (1997).

25. This costume martial arts movie is about a man who, in order to learn a powerful fighting skill, pays the price of emasculating himself and being transformed into a woman. Although the film implies that the foundation of phallic power is paradoxically based on the loss of the penis, and the fluid sexual identity displayed by the film also reveals the gender confusion of today, I still think a feminist critique of the film is valid. For a direct criticism of the film, see T. Cheung (1993, 182–88). Cheung fails to offer a sophisticated reading of the film, but she has surveyed more than one hundred Hong Kong films made between 1989 and early 1993, and she comes to the

conclusion that, despite the increasing physical strength of the female roles on screen, women continue to be subordinate to men and are portrayed as those who are better at using their fists than their brains.

26. For further discussion of Tsui Hark's movies, see my "Once Upon a Time: Technology Comes to Presence in China" (K. Lo 1993).

27. Ironically, Jackie Chan collaborated with Spielberg's production company DreamWorks on *Tuxedo* (2002), an action movie full of special effects.

28. Another popular, heavily digitized Hong Kong movie is Stephen Chiau's *Shaolin Soccer* (2001), a comedy in which Shaolin monks play soccer as if performing supernatural kung fu.

29. For more detailed discussion on Hong Kong action heroines, see Logan (1995), Ciecko and Lu (1999), Giukin (2001).

30. Referring to Kazuo Ishiguro's "more English than the English" novel, *The Remains of the Day,* Ma Sheng-mei states that "postethnicity seems to be an excess indulged in only by those who have already made it, partly by virtue of their ethnicity" (Ma Sheng-mei 2000, 150).

Chapter 4: Transnationalization of the Local in a Circular Structure

This chapter has been greatly modified from an essay published as "Transnationalization of the Local in Hong Kong Cinema" in *At Full Speed: Hong Kong Cinema in a Borderless World,* ed. Esther C. M. Yau (Minneapolis: University of Minnesota Press, 2001), 261–76.

1. See Hu (1997).

2. Hong Kong films are considered by the Taiwan government as "domestic products" that could be exempted from the quota restriction on foreign-made movies. See Liang (1997, 163).

3. For the history of Taiwan's investment in Hong Kong cinema, see Liang (1997, 158–63) and Shen (1995, 4–12).

4. Other Hong Kong directors make similar claims. For example, Gordon Chan says: "To survive in the market place, Hong Kong cinema must cast off its local, inward-looking tendency. I very much want to make Asian films" (Li Cheuk-to 2000, 65). Teddy Chen, in explaining his *Purple Storm* (1999), explains: "We just didn't want to make an action film that's too localized. We wanted a more international Hong Kong film and we looked for terrorists with interesting backgrounds. . . . After some work, we decided on Pol Pot's Khmer Rouge" (Ho 2000, 60). And Johnnie To, in referring to his *Fulltime Killer,* presented in a mixture of Japanese, English, and Putonghua, says: "We are hoping it will be viewed as an Asian movie. When we were making it, there was a strong reminiscence of old European movies where the action takes place from Rome, to Paris and Switzerland. *Fulltime Killer* takes place in Hong Kong, Macau and Japan. This is like a half-way point; maybe later we might make a movie that's fully in English. The market is in a moulding stage and everyone can try anything with it. Co-operating with

Thailand, Singapore, Korea or Japan is inevitable. In many aspects it's for our mutual interest. If my actors and your actors work together, we win markets on both sides. There's nothing new about the concept" (Chung 2001).

5. As history has proved, the European model with multiple languages and multi-national crews could hardly compete with the one-dominant-language Hollywood model that absorbs talents from different places. Indeed, the European model in the 1950s was primarily Franco-Italian coproductions. The French then came to copro-duce with Americans, forming a new genre of film called Euro-American art cine-ma. In order to remain internationally competitive, the French were willing to make English-language films, imitating Hollywood formulae and even financing films like *Terminator 2* and *J.F.K.*, evincing the failure of the European model in filmmaking (Nowell-Smith and Ricci 1998; Kuisel 2000).

6. Such "Asianization" is not a Lee Kuan Yew (the founding father of the Singapore republic) kind of reactionary search for shared Asian values such as Confucianism, discipline, and collectivism, all of which are opposed to Western individualism, he-donism, and democratic spirit. Rather, the Asianization referred to here is more of a "forward-thinking" entity than something nostalgic. It is "primarily articulated through a shared pursuit of urban consumption, of Americanized (westernized) popular culture" (Iwabuchi 1999, 192). See also Iwabuchi (2002).

7. Surveys show that there is a rise of (racial) discrimination cases in the post-1997 Hong Kong, especially against the new immigrants from mainland China, and in-creasingly there have been assaults against maidservants from the Philippines and Indonesia. The SAR government has been strongly urged to legislate against discrim-ination on the grounds of race.

8. For studies on the transnational and transcultural dimensions of Hong Kong cinema, see, for instance, S. Lu (1997, 2001), Teo (1997), Stokes and Hoover (1999a), Bordwell (2000b), Fu and Desser (2000), Law (2000), Yau (2001), and Y. Zhang (2002).

9. For a detailed study of the New Wave auteurs in Hong Kong cinema, see Teo (1997), especially "Part Three: Path Breakers."

10. For a discussion of diasporic Chinese culture, see the special issue entitled "The Living Tree: The Changing Meaning of Being Chinese Today," *Daedalus* 120.2 (Spring 1991). For a pointed and rigorous critique of Chinese centrism, see Rey Chow (1993).

11. For the discussion on the new American global cinema, see Polan (1996).

12. It was a production of Media Asia, a Hong Kong company founded in the 1990s.

13. *First Option* was another production by Media Asia and was a box-office hit.

14. After a long lapse, the deceased Teresa Teng was recently appropriated by the Hong Kong Tourism Board as one of the major "local" icons to attract tourists.

Chapter 5: Charlie Chan Reborn as Jackie Chan in Hollywood–Hong Kong Representations

Portions of this chapter appeared as "Double Negations: Hong Kong Cultural Iden-tity in Hollywood's Transnational Representations" in "Becoming Hong Kong in

Postcolonial Times," ed. John Nguyet Erni, special issue, *Cultural Studies* 15.3/4 (2001): 464–85.

1. Ironically, in *Blade Runner* the company that produces the replicants promotes its product as "more human than human." In his analysis of the film, Slavoj Žižek argues that only when the replicant assumes his replicant-status does he become a truly human subject. "I am a replicant," according to Žižek, is the statement of the subject in its purest—the same as in Althusser's theory of ideology, where the statement "I am in ideology" is the only way for me to truly avoid the vicious circle of ideology (Žižek 1993, 41). The question, however, is whether the negation of the negation can really result in a positive way out.

2. When asked how he feels about the fact that American stunt coordinators copy a lot from his movies, Jackie Chan responds humbly that for a long time he has also learned from American stuntmen: "When I looked at Spielberg's *Indiana Jones and the Temple of Doom,* I see that he totally copied my bicycle sequence from *Project A;* I used a bicycle, he used a motorcycle. But I'm so happy that even the biggest director has learned something from me! . . . But I have also learned from other movies. . . . *I think that in the world of movies everybody copies everybody*" (Little and Wong 1999, 135; my emphasis).

3. Perhaps one of the reasons that Hong Kong film talents are courted by Hollywood studios is precisely because Hong Kong movies imitate Hollywood. In Hong Kong cinema, Hollywood rediscovers its own lost energy and seeks its own lost original experience of what a film should be.

4. This negation of Chineseness is not a denial of Chinese origin but rather an articulation of the difference within Chinese identity. As one critic has argued, Hong Kong identity is never constituted by a stable narrative, but instead emerges out of a clash of discourses. "It was precisely the inability to articulate identity . . . along any stable narrative that marked out Hong Kong people from Chinese on the mainland or Taiwan" (Turner 1995, 20).

5. In 1973, American audiences were entranced by a number of Hong Kong action films besides those starring Bruce Lee. In May of that year, three Hong Kong kung fu movies, *Fist of Fury, Deep Thrust—the Hand of Death,* and *Five Fingers of Death,* were listed, respectively, at positions 1, 2, and 3 on *Variety*'s list of the weekly top box-office draws. In the following month, no less than five Hong Kong kung fu movies appeared in the American top fifty list. See Desser (2000).

6. Chan made several U.S. films between 1980 and 1985. He starred in *The Big Brawl* (1980) and in *The Protector* (1985) and had a minor role in *Cannonball Run* (1981) and its sequel (1983). All these American productions only led him back to making his own action films in Hong Kong, where he could have full control.

7. Some critics have suggested that the success of *Rumble in the Bronx* represents an attempt to redefine global cinema as something other than the U.S.-produced and English-speaking Hollywood entertainment film. But this interpretation is too eagerly optimistic. See for instance Fore (1997) on Jackie Chan's impact on global en-

tertainment. *Rumble in the Bronx* opened nationwide in the United States in February 1996 and quickly become the top box-office draw of the month. It grossed US$32 million total. But the box-office performance of Chan's subsequent Hong Kong films declined consistently. *Supercop* grossed less than *Rumble,* at US$16 million, and *First Strike* grossed less than *Supercop,* at US$14 million.

8. Unlike many action films that do great business in the first week but quickly exhaust their young-male audience base, *Rush Hour* was able to continuously find new fans. In its first seventeen days it amassed US$84 million, and overall it grossed US$244 million (including $141.2 million in the United States and $102.8 million overseas). Its sequel, *Rush Hour 2,* grossed US$67.4 million in its first three days, which is a record for a comedy in the United States.

9. For a detailed study on Yeoh, see Williams (2001).

10. The Hollywood filmography of these Hong Kong directors includes: *Maximum Risk* (Columbia Pictures, 1996), directed by Ringo Lam; *Double Team* (Columbia Pictures, 1997), directed by Tsui Hark; *Mr. Magoo* (Walt Disney Pictures, 1997), directed by Stanley Tong; *Warriors of Virtue* (MGM, 1997), directed by Ronny Yu; *The Big Hit* (Tristar Pictures, 1998), directed by Chek-Kirk Wong; *Bride of Chucky* (Universal, 1998), directed by Ronny Yu; *Knock-Off* (Tristar Pictures, 1998), directed by Tsui Hark; *The Love Letter* (DreamWorks, 1999), directed by Peter Chan; and *Freddy vs. Jason* (Warner, 2003), directed by Ronny Yu.

11. Compared to Hollywood, Hong Kong cinema is more capable of blending into Asian countries, taking into account the local characteristics of Asian markets and yielding to its other. For this reason Hong Kong movies are able to compete with Hollywood in Asia. See Lii (1998). However, Lii's binary model of Hollywood films on the one hand and Hong Kong films on the other hand is too rigid for understanding the Hollywood tactics of absorbing overseas talent in their productions.

12. Under CEPA, Hong Kong–produced films can be exempt from the annual twenty-film foreign production quota. Hong Kong investors can hold a majority stake/management control in mainland cinemas, and there is no restriction on China-wide distribution of Hong Kong Chinese coproductions. The agreement also provides opportunities for overseas companies to collaborate with Hong Kong film companies to explore the mainland market.

13. For a positive view of the Chinese diaspora, see for instance A. Ong (1993) and Ong and Nonini (1997).

14. There have been some studies of Asian representations in Hollywood films, for instance E. Wong (1978), Law (1992), and Marchetti (1993). But an Asian-white dichotomy could hardly occupy the center stage of American racial conflict.

15. "The two movie capitals [Hong Kong and Hollywood] have a great deal in common," writes Fredric Dannen, "in fact, Hong Kong is often called *Dongfang Haolaiwu,* the Hollywood of the East. . . . Perhaps the best way to describe the Hong Kong genre is to speak of its comic-book aesthetic: it is a cinema of incessant action, eye-popping effects, and cartoon-like violence" (Dannen and Long 1997, 5).

16. Peter Chan admits in an interview that Hollywood hires him and other Hong Kong directors because they are skilled craftsmen. Peter Chan, interview with Stella Sze, *Dream Factory,* RTHK, ATV Home Channel, Hong Kong, July 3, 1999.

17. The arrival of Hong Kong stars within the American mainstream media may stir up the debate, among Asian Americanists, about whether the focus of research should shift from a claiming of America (which would assert the American identity and root of Asian minorities) to a denationalization or globalization of Asian American studies. Undeniably, Asian Americans can to some extent identify with the success of Hong Kong film people in Hollywood. As MTV's Chinese American video jockey, Allan Wu, comments, "Growing up in the U.S., I only saw Asian actors in stereotype roles. . . . People like Jackie Chan and Chow Yun-Fat busted their asses getting to where they are today and Hollywood is beginning to see Asian actors on a wider scope and not just as a token." Wu admits that the representation of Asians in the United States is moving in the right direction, although it is still difficult for Asian American actors to get mainstream roles that are not stereotypical. For this reason Asian Americans try to use the images of Hong Kong stars to transform their own subject positions in the States. See "VJ Hunk Allan Eyes Film Career," *South China Morning Post,* September 24, 1999, 20.

18. Although the story of *Rush Hour 2* begins in Hong Kong, a number of scenes, such as the one in the massage parlor, were actually shot in Thailand. In this way, Hong Kong as a place is reduced to a mere name or sign with which Hong Kong locals find it hard to relate.

19. I am referring to those popular films such as *All for the Winner* (1990), *God of Gamblers II* (1990), *God of Gamblers III: Back to Shanghai* (1991), *From Beijing with Love* (1994), all starring Stephen Chiau Sing-Chi, and *Her Fatal Ways* and its three sequels (1990–94), starring Do Do Cheng.

20. To use the Althusserian term, this can be understood as the way in which an individual relates to the conditions of his existence, understands his specifically designated place in a sociopolitical formation as natural, and is thereby interpellated as a subject.

21. For an innovative and provocative interpretation of Zhang's exhibitionism, see Rey Chow (1995a).

22. Historically, Hollywood's portrayal of the East-West encounter has taken the form of an interaction between a white protagonist and an Asian sidekick or opponent, from *The World of Suzie Wong* (1960) to *Year of the Dragon* (1985).

23. Typical of these ultra-cynical characters is the persona played by Stephen Chiau Sing-Chi in his *mou lei-tau* (nonsense slapstick) comedies of the early 1990s.

24. Chan has starred in a movie called *Mr. Nice Guy* (1997), directed by Sammo Hung.

25. As Jacques Lacan writes, "It is in the name of the father that we must recognize the support of the symbolic function which, from the dawn of history, has identified his person with the figure of the law" (Lacan 1977, 67). A father figure is never

missing from Chan's films. Bill Tung, playing Chan's boss, uncle, or his senior, has a small part in virtually every Chan movie in order to represent the father's law, to which the action hero can resort in the final moment.

26. Chan's "semblance play" with the father of Law is further evidenced by his scandalous extramarital affair with the ex–beauty queen Ellen Ng, who gave birth to his daughter in late 1999. Chan described the affair, after it was long over, as a "playful act" with "shameful" consequences.

27. This is probably due to the outtakes seen at the end of the film, since the closing credits in all of Jackie Chan's Hong Kong productions feature multiple outtakes that show him missing on stunts and hurting himself.

28. There is a scene in which Lee, escaping from Carter, jumps from a double-decker bus and hangs on to a Hollywood Boulevard sign. Chan told a reporter that "[t]he director had me hanging off a Sunset Boulevard sign . . . and I asked him if I could change it to a Hollywood sign. That sign has meaning to the Chinese. It's like I grab Hollywood." See Richard Corliss, "King of America," *Time* (Asian edition), October 19, 1998, 54–55.

29. The cultural prejudice according to which an Asian man is assumed as a submissive Oriental woman by the white man is exemplified in David Henry Hwang's play *M. Butterfly* (1988). Rey Chow argues, in a different context (1991), that Hollywood's reception of ethnic culture reproduces it as a feminized spectacle.

30. See for instance Tasker (1993), Bogle (1994), and Yearwood (1982). There is also the stereotype that constructs the black hero as abnormally libidinous and hypersexual. Carter obviously does not belong to this type but is designated as a "castrated" comic figure.

31. For a chronological study of the Charlie Chan series, see Hanke (1989) and C. Mitchell (1999).

32. Ironically, those Asian American actors who had played Charlie Chan's sons, such as Keye Luke, Victor Sen Yung, Benon Fong, Philip Ahn, and James Hong, all ended up appearing in the pilot of *Kung Fu* (1972–75), a television series first conceived and developed by Bruce Lee, who wanted to play the lead role.

33. The comic aspect is apparent because the Charlie Chan character is always played by a Caucasian actor. Among the white men who played the Chinese detective, Warner Oland was the most popular Charlie Chan. Born in Sweden to Swedish and Russian parents, he was considered to have an exotic look, and with the addition of an Oriental-style mustache and goatee, the transformation was complete. Oland said that "I owe my Chinese appearance to the Mongol invasion" (Hanke 1989, 1).

34. Both Chan and Tucker's characters are smart, brave, and cerebral when it comes to solving crimes. These traits present the audience with the familiar image of a Western hero. At the same time, Tucker's outrageously fast talk and super-sassy derisiveness, along with Chan's reticence and fascinating acrobatic skills, together are reminiscent of an old-fashioned, exotic minstrel show. One British reviewer, for instance, writes that "Tucker's Eddie Murphy-ish schtick, all jive-ass mockery

and shrill falsetto disbelief, plays off divertingly against Chan's self-deprecating humor, and their scenes together convey a genuine sense of mutual enjoyment" (Kemp 1998, 61).

35. The complete title of the book is *Charlie Chan Is Dead: An Anthology of Contemporary Asian American Fiction*, edited by Jessica Hagedorn, preface by Elaine Kim (Harmondsworth, Middlesex, Eng.: Penguin, 1993).

36. For a discussion of the effects of the outtakes in Jackie Chan's films, see chapter 3.

37. For a thought-provoking analysis of the difference between Hollywood and Hong Kong action cinemas, see Bordwell (1997).

38. The Hong Kong box-office earnings of the two U.S. blockbusters *Rush Hour* and *Rush Hour 2*, though not bad at all in a time when the city has been struggling to recover from recession, could hardly compete with those of any of Jackie Chan's local productions.

39. Neither Chow Yun Fat in *Anna and the King* nor Jet Li in *Kiss of the Dragon* got to kiss their white female leads, Jodie Foster and Bridget Fonda, respectively. Chan's romantic act with Roselyn Sanchez in *Rush Hour 2*, by contrast, is a notable exception that implies the breaking of the cultural taboo forbidding a white woman's sexual attraction to an Asian man, although Sanchez is Argentine and not exactly Anglo-Saxon.

40. Following Singapore's example, the Hong Kong Special Administrative Region government under Chinese rule is attempting to further integrate its culture and economy with global capitalism while paradoxically enhancing an appreciation of traditional Chinese values. This contradictory combination of globalized economic logic and traditional Asian ethics is what Žižek means by globalization without universalism—a system that aims at precluding any political dimension of social life. See Žižek (1998).

41. Gina Marchetti remarks in a footnote that, traditionally, Hong Kong cinema appropriated this "pan-Chineseness" in order to make its way in the lucrative overseas Chinese markets. But I disagree with her claim that the past success of Hong Kong cinema in the overseas Chinese market took place at the expense of a uniquely Hong Kong voice. See Marchetti (1998, 72).

Chapter 6: Racial Passing and Face Swapping in the Wild, Wild West

A short version of this chapter was published as "Pacific Asia's Drive to Hollywood and Back: The *Jouissance* of California Hong Kong Movies," *(a)—a Journal of Culture and the Unconscious* 1.1 (2002): 47–58.

1. The first Wong Fei-hung film series was directed by Hu Peng. Since then, films and television shows about the kung fu master continued to be made in Hong Kong.

Even Jackie Chan has played the young Wong Fei-hung in the kung fu comedy *Drunken Master* (1979), which immediately turned him into a star.

2. More than one hundred films featuring Wong Fei-hung have been produced since 1949 by the Hong Kong film industry. Seventy-seven of them starred Kwan Tak Hing, who became identified with the role. For a complete filmography of the series that were released from 1949 to 1995, see *Wong Fei Hung: The Invincible Master* (1996). For more detailed discussion on this film series, see Yu (1980), Rodriguez (1997), and Williams (1998).

3. Although the original film series may sound traditional, moral, and parochial, Hector Rodriguez points out that the movies have "even incorporated narrative norms and situations from popular Hollywood films, especially the Saloon fight characteristic of countless Westerns, transplanted in various [Wong Fei-hung] installments to the more indigenous setting of a dim sum restaurant" (Rodriguez 1997, 3).

4. Lisa Odham Stokes and Michael Hoover argue that in the film "Wong Fei-hung is twice marginalized, first for his Chineseness and second for identifying with Native Americans. Unfortunately, the film fails to draw out the implications of the two peoples' marginalized histories. . . . [T]he genocidal treatment of Native Americans is reduced to the comment that 'we were forced off our land' and a Mel Brooks–type scene in which three are forced to 'dance' when bigoted whites fire bullets at their feet" (Stokes and Hoover 1999a, 97).

5. The overwhelming majority of Hong Kong business people and middle-class professionals have foreign passports and have established rights to foreign domicile, especially in Canada, the United States, and Australia.

6. For the discussion on the cross-identification between African American and Asian American in terms of hip-hop or kung fu, see Ongiri (2002) and Sunaina (2000).

7. In a parallel fashion, many members of Hong Kong society choose to stay and to migrate at the same time in order to cope with the return of Hong Kong sovereignty to China. While maintaining their livelihoods in Hong Kong, they spread assets and family members around the world. For instance, they buy houses in Canada, invest in the mainland and Southeast Asia, send their children to British boarding schools, and hold Australian passports.

8. The lines of course remind audiences of Rudyard Kipling's famous verses, "Oh, East is East, and West is West, and never the twain shall meet, / Till Earth and Sky stand presently at God's great Judgment Seat."

9. A. O. Scott, "Mission? Improbable, but the Pigeons Are Nifty," *New York Times on the Web,* May 24, 2000 <http://www.rottentomatoes.com/movies/titles/mission_impossible 2/ click.php?review=77>

10. In *The Tuxedo* (2002), Jackie Chan wears not a mask but a special high-tech tuxedo owned by a secret agent to convert himself into a Bond-like superhero. The film is not simply about a man wearing a costume that gives him extraordinary power, but also about a Chinese minority putting on the Caucasian master's suit, assuming his identity, and finally gaining the recognition from the white folks.

11. See Ong's chapter "'A Better Tomorrow'? The Struggle for Global Visibility" (A. Ong 1999, 164). There, Ong primarily uses Woo's *A Better Tomorrow* and its sequels as examples for illustrating how these Hong Kong action films hold on to Chinese values in the chaotic world of Asian capitalism. But she also adds that "[i]t is no secret that John Woo, like film directors the world over, honed his skills by studying American movies and in the process picked up techniques as well as modernist themes. . . . Western themes include the importance of male bonding for surviving in a lawless world, men fighting for a space in which domesticity is safe, and making a last stand against outsiders and authorities. These good, old-fashioned American frontier values are transposed or rather merged with representations of ethnic-Chinese fraternal culture" (165–66).

12. See, for instance, Timothy P. Fong's "Charlie Chan No More: Asian Americans and the Media" (Fong 1998, 180). The trend of "Asian filmmakers and actors such as John Woo and Jackie Chan, who are literally marching or hurtling into Hollywood . . . [may] represent future directions for the booming Asian American cinema" (Jun Xing 1998, 28).

13. Peter Feng writes, "Hong Kong directors have also helmed diverse mainstream productions, including Stanley Tong's *Mr. Magoo* (1997), Ronnie Yu's *Bride of Chucky* (1998), and Peter Chan's *The Love Letter* (1999). . . . While these films represent a marriage of Hong Kong and Hollywood production styles, none of them tells a story about Asian Americans, any more than Fritz Lang's *Fury* (1936) was a German American film." But like other Asian Americanists, Feng also identifies Woo as an Asian American filmmaker. See P. Feng (1999, 20–21).

14. Major figures such as Sam Peckinpah, Martin Scorsese, Stanley Kubrick, Jean-Pierre Melville, and John Ford are said to have inspired Woo to build his own style.

15. According to many Western depictions, Woo grew up on the streets and in the shacks of Hong Kong, where he was exposed to crime and drugs. Just before he almost joined a street gang, the Christian church helped him and his family. An American family sent money through the church to support his education. At one point, Woo even considered becoming a minister. A Christian magazine comments, "Many Christians have problems with the very genre of the violent action picture, but Mr. Woo insists that his movies bolster his own strong family values. His heroes are 'always reaching out a helping hand,' he points out, 'even sometimes sacrific[ing] himself for the others.' Though Mr. Woo's vocation lies in making movies that are primarily exciting, rather than theological, he demonstrates the value of saving pennies to send overseas." See Pamela Johnson, "John Woo: Training up a Director," *World Magazine* 12.13 (1997), <http://www.worldmag.com/world/issue/07–26–97/cultural_3.asp>, accessed August 2, 1997. Woo also emphasizes his close American connection to his Western interviewers. For instance, he says, "My wife is an American citizen and two of my kids were born here. . . . I also received so much support from the film community in the United States. A producer once told me that nobody in the film industry was jealous of me. Every-

one seemed very excited about me to come here. Everybody wanted me to be successful, and no one wanted to see me fail" (Singer 1998, 322, 323).

16. Balibar also tells us that the word "subject" is a translation of the Latin word *subjectus*—"a political and juridical term, which refers to subjection or submission." See Balibar (1994, 8–9).

17. Another Asian director who has excelled in Hollywood recently is M. Night Shyamalan, whose features *The Sixth Sense* (1999), starring Bruce Willis and Haley Joel Osment, and *Signs* (2002), starring Mel Gibson, became the blockbusters of those years. But unlike Wayne Wang, Ang Lee, and Joan Chen (whose Hollywood directorial debut was *Autumn in New York* [2000], starring Richard Gere and Winona Ryder), who are immigrants from Hong Kong, Taiwan, and mainland China respectively, Shyamalan is an American-born Indian. On the other hand, Shekhar Kapur, the Indian director from Asia, also managed to make the leap from Bollywood to Hollywood with his Oscar-nominated feature *Elizabeth* (1998) and with *The Four Feathers* (2002).

18. See, for instance, Havis (1998, 16). Woo's business partner and producer, Terence Chang, also commented that "a lot of people said [*Hard Target*] is a Hong Kong movie in English" (Dannen and Long 1997, 152). It apparently makes no difference to American audiences whether Woo's first American film is a "Hong Kong" movie or a "Chinese" movie in English, although it is Terence Chang who qualifies it with the Hong Kong identity.

19. "New brutalism" is a term used by Annette Hill to refer to *Reservoir Dogs* (1992), *Pulp Fiction* (1994), and the like, which—according to the audience—provide "realistic" representations of violence, in contrast to Hollywood action movies, such as the *Die Hard* series (1988, 1990, 1995) or *Terminator 2* (1991), which are just "fun, playful and unrealistic." See Hill (1999).

20. *Face/Off* was at first a sci-fi film. But Woo told the producers that he wasn't any good at making sci-fi movies. So the producers had a rewrite done to lessen the sci-fi aspect and to enhance the characters and the drama according to Woo's wishes. See Stokes and Hoover (1999b, 37).

21. In Woo's own words, "My movies have a lot of heart, passion, and emotion. They aren't only about violence. I try to show something good and pure about the human spirit in them. Qualities like loyalty, honor, dignity, and a spirit of chivalry that has disappeared" (Havis 1998, 12–13); see also Server (1999, 32).

22. This is an argument made by Susan Jeffords when she talks about *Kindergarten Cop* (1990), *Robocop 2* (1990), *Terminator 2* (1991), *Beauty and the Beast* (1991), and *Switch* (1991). See Jeffords (1993).

23. For the idea of "Pacific Rim Discourse," and "Asia-Pacific Idea," see Connery (1995, 1996), Cumings (1998), Dirlik (1998).

24. For the discussion on the Asian American subject's symbolizing the shifting identities of Asian transnational diasporas, see Palumbo-Liu (1999).

25. John Huang, a Democratic Party employee, was accused of bringing in some illegal donations from Asian Americans and some Asian companies. The fund-raising event Huang organized in a Buddhist temple near Los Angeles was charged by the Republicans as a Clinton-Gore campaign money laundry. For more detailed coverage of the incident, see Brooks Jackson, "Democrats Have to Give Back More Money," *All Politics*, <http://www.cnn.com/ALLPOLITICS/1996/news/9610/18/soft.money/index.shtml>, accessed February 4, 2003.

26. Elaine Shannon, a *Time* correspondent, found that the American media had played a major role in Wen Ho Lee case. The reason the FBI confronted Lee in 1999 was because the *New York Times* was on the story and said that the Chinese espionage did very severe damage to the American interest. See "Wen Ho Lee: A Discussion with *Time* Correspondent Elaine Shannon Hosted by Court TV (Transcript from September 13, 2000)," <http://www.time.com/time/community/transcripts/2000/091400wenho.html>, accessed February 4, 2003.

27. Christopher Cox, a six-term Republican congressman from California, headed the committee to investigate allegations that China stole U.S. nuclear secrets. He released his report, which was full of factual errors, in 1999. See James Oberg, "Errors Mar Cox Report," *ABC News,* <http://abcnews.go.com/sections/science/DailyNews/oberg990602.html>, accessed February 4, 2003.

Chapter 7: Tigers Crouch and Dragons Hide in the New Trans-Chinese Cinema

1. It is difficult to categorize Lee's *Crouching Tiger, Hidden Dragon* as Chinese or Hollywood, since the financing scheme that funded the movie was based on the advance sale of the international distribution rights to a horde of American, Japanese, and European companies. The major money came from different divisions of Tokyo-based Sony. Sony Pictures Classics in New York bought the U.S. distribution rights. Columbia Pictures in Hollywood owned the rights for Latin America and several Asian markets. Columbia Pictures Asia, a Hong Kong–based production company, also contributed funds, and Sony Classical Music financed the soundtrack. The actual cash for the film was provided by a bank in Paris, while a bond company in Los Angeles insured the production. For more details, see Klein (2002). However, I won't celebrate the film as a typical representative of global cinema. Rather, I would use it to rethink the function of national-cultural terms in the global world.

2. In the past, Hong Kong films have been divided into Cantonese and Mandarin ones. It was the Mandarin-language films of Hong Kong that first succeeded in creating a global audience. But beginning in the 1980s, the reemergence of Cantonese language and culture dominated the screen of Hong Kong cinema. Cantonese is spoken by all the characters, including the Westerners, in Hong Kong films, much the same way that Hollywood cinema has every screen character speak English. But when Hong Kong Cantonese cinema began losing its market in the 1990s, many compa-

nies started producing Hollywood-styled movies with a lot of characters speaking English. For instance, Stanley Tong believes that the mastery of the English language in future Hong Kong productions has become the requisite initial step toward globalization (S. Cheung 2000, 125). See chapter 4.

3. *Crouching Tiger, Hidden Dragon* barely made US$2 million in Hong Kong and US$1.3 million in mainland China in 2001, though it performed strongly in Taiwan, Thailand, Singapore, and other Asian countries. For Hong Kong audiences, there is not enough action in the film—audiences complain that fighting doesn't begin until after the first fifteen or so minutes—and many scenes are too familiar.

4. Its global box-office revenue was US$208 million in 2001, while the film was made for only about US$15 million.

5. The list of the awards won by the film is long. To name a few: Best Foreign Language Film, Best Cinematography, Best Score, and Best Art Direction, 73rd Annual Academy Awards; Best Feature, Best Director, and Best Supporting Actress (Zhang), 2001 Independent Spirit Awards; Best Director, 2001 Directors Guild Awards; Best Cinematography, Best Foreign Film, Best Original Score, and Most Promising Actress (Zhang), 2001 Chicago Film Critics Awards; Best Director, Best Foreign Language Film, Best Music, and Best Costume, 2001 British Academy of Film and Television Arts (BAFTA); Best Director and Best Foreign Language Film, 2001 Golden Globes; People's Choice Award, 25th Annual Toronto International Film Festival; Best Foreign Film, 2000 National Board of Review; Best Cinematography, 2000 New York Film Critics Circle; Best Picture, Best Cinematography, Best Production Design, and Best Music, 2000 Los Angeles Film Critics Association; Best Cinematography and Best Foreign Film, 2000 Boston Society of Film Critics; Best Foreign Film, 2000 Broadcast Film Critics Association; Best Foreign Film and Best Cinematography, 2000 Online Film Critics Society. In Taiwan and Hong Kong the film's awards include: Best Picture, Best Sound Effects, Best Action Choreography, Best Original Film Score, Best Film Editing, and Best Visual Effects, 2000 Golden Horse Awards (Taiwan's version of the Oscars); Best Film, Best Director, Best Actress in a Supporting Role, Best Cinematography, Best Action Director, Best Original Film Score, Best Sound Effects, and Best Original Song, 20th Annual Hong Kong Film Awards.

6. The victory of *Crouching Tiger, Hidden Dragon* in the Oscars and in the U.S. box-office race led Zhang Yimou to try to duplicate Ang Lee's magic formula in making his first martial arts epic, *Hero* (2002), with similar multinational funding (from mainland China, the United States, and Hong Kong) and a transnational (Chinese) cast and crew (four Hong Kong stars—Jet Li, Tony Leung, Maggie Cheung, and Donnie Yen; the Hong Kong choreographer Ching Siu-tung; the Chinese-speaking Australian cinematographer Christopher Doyle, who has shot many of Wong Kar-wai's films; the Japanese designer Emi Wada; and the composer Tan Dun and the "princess" Zhang Ziyi from *Crouching Tiger*). It was the most expensive film ever made in mainland China and did well in China's box office. But it didn't win any Oscar and was not released in the United States until August 2004. Miramax sat on

the film for almost two years. Another Zhang Yimou crowd-pleasing martial arts movie, *House of Flying Daggers* (2004), starring Takeshi Kaneshiro, Andy Lau, and Zhang Ziyi, was also made with international funding. Its release to the Western market is very likely, due to the box-office success of *Hero* in the United States.

7. The production companies involved in the film include Columbia Pictures Film Production Asia, Sony Pictures Classics, Good Machine International, Edko Films, Zoom Hunt International, China Film Co-production Corporation, and Asian Union Audio Visual and Cultural Company.

8. Probably only the name "Hong Kong" could accommodate the complicated background of the film. David Bordwell even confines all of the film's references to the traditions of Hong Kong martial arts cinema: "From a historical perspective, *Crouching Tiger, Hidden Dragon* becomes a millennial synthesis of the great wuxia tradition. . . . The serene self-possession of Li Mu Bai is reminiscent of King Hu's fighters. . . . Yu Shu Lien's rooftop pursuit of the mysterious thief echoes 1960s adventures, and her unfussy prowess puts her in the line of women warriors played by Wu Lizhen, Josephine Siao Fong-fong, and Cheng Pei Pei. . . . The young couple, Jen and Lo, recall the combative couples of *Shaolin vs. Ninja;* by the end, however, their love affair, told through sumptuous desert flashbacks, acquires a sweeping poetic anguish akin to that of *Ashes of Time.* . . . Blending everything is Ang Lee, fully aware of the landmarks of the genre he's working in, and like his predecessors he at once pays homage to them and reworks them to new effect" (Bordwell 2000a, 20–21).

9. For American audiences, it is a subtitled Chinese-language film. But for Chinese audiences, especially the Mandarin-speaking ones, the film is not "really" Chinese enough because Chow is a Cantonese who fails to deliver proper Mandarin and Yeoh can't even read Chinese and had to learn her part line by line in pinyin.

10. The acquisition of Columbia Pictures by Sony a few years ago does not necessarily represent the penetration of Japanese culture or otherness in Hollywood, which would designate a clear line between the foreign outsider and the internal American self. On the contrary, it only shows that Hollywood has been incorporated into the transnational media conglomerate and has become the major producer of global images, gradually losing the sense of an outside.

11. Joseph S. M. Lau argues that the wuxia novels of Jin Yong/Louis Cha could become a means of Chinese education for the overseas Chinese. See J. Lau (1998).

12. The difference is that in Hu's film, the fight takes place on the ground under bamboo trees, while in Lee's work the characters float high and dance on the tops of the trees, with cranes and wires digitally removed from the frames. The spatial opposition may allegorize the rather different receptions of the two Chinese filmmakers in the United States. In the last few years of his life, Hu tried hard to find investors for his film on Chinese American railway workers to no avail.

13. The so-called "fame in the West" is of course only relative. King Hu's *Touch of Zen* was presented at the 1975 Cannes Film Festival and won the Technical Award.

His *Touch of Zen* and *The Fate of Lee Khan* (1973) have been released in France. Hu's films received considerable attention in France and other parts of Europe.

14. See C. Wong (2000, 35). In an interview given to the Taiwan media in 1993, Lee had already made similar statements about the westernization of Chineseness and went so far as to say that, "in the process of Westernization, Taiwanese people have already done many of the kinds of work that [Chinese immigrants in the United States] do. Although their bodies are not in the United States, they are immigrants psychologically. . . . What is the difference between living in Flushing, New York and Taipei? Except that one knows America better and sees more Americans, there is not much difference." See *China Times Weekly* 65, March–April 1993, 75; qtd. from Shih (2000).

15. Lee has acknowledged that his films are more popular among female audiences. He chose to adapt Wang Dulu's martial arts novel precisely because it focuses on the role of female warriors. Furthermore, he cast Chow Yun Fat instead of Jet Li as the male lead because Chow looks more feminine.

16. Hollywood recognizes its female market because the top-grossing record of *Titanic* (1997) was largely made by young girls seeing the film over and over again. According to the Motion Picture Association of America, half of teenage movie-going audiences are girls. Hollywood pictures aimed at girls and younger women have produced good box-office successes since the late 1990s. The track record led some in Hollywood to speculate that young females are on their way to becoming one of the film industry's most reliable audience blocs. See Cieply and Eller (2003) and Elias (2003).

17. As Ni Kuang, who has written the scripts of some three hundred martial arts films, says, "There have been two periods when wu xia novels reached new peaks. The first was during the 20s and 30s with the sudden appearance of such excellent writers as Huanzhu Louzhu, Chu Zhenmu, Wang Dulu, Zheng Zhengyin and Pai Yu. The second wave began simultaneously in Hong Kong and Taiwan around 1955 when the works of Jin Yung launched the so-called 'new style' martial arts novels." Qtd. from Koo Siu-fung (1981, 25).

18. For an elaborate comparison between *Crouching Tiger, Hidden Dragon* and *Sense and Sensibility*, see W. Leung (2001). Leung sees *Crouching Tiger, Hidden Dragon* as a continuity of *Sense and Sensibility* and calls the martial arts film "a Jane Austen plot with a Taoist twist" (49).

19. Žižek has argued that there are four senses of appearance: (1) illusion; (2) symbolic order; (3) a sign indicating that there is something beyond; and (4) something that fills the void in the midst of reality (Žižek 1999, 197–98).

20. John Woo's *The Killer* has been widely considered by Western critics as "noir-based libretto." See Naremore (1998, 228–29) and Hirsch (1999, 104–6).

21. Of course, there is another way to understand Li's persistence with Jen. Jen could serve as the object of exchange between Li and his enemy Jade Fox. To a certain extent, they fight their battle through her. The cruelest way for Li to take out his re-

venge on Jade Fox is not simply to kill her but to take away her disciple, to whom she is emotionally attached. Taking this interpretation further, we could say that the fact that Li goes so far as to break the rule of the Wudan school by recruiting a female disciple is a symbolic gesture of fulfilling what his late master, Southern Crane, failed to do. Southern Crane has been murdered by Jade Fox because he only sleeps with her but rejects her as his disciple. It also connotes Li's sexual desire for Jen. Such a reading takes into account the male bonding and the patriarchal conspiracy against the weaker and wicked women.

Chapter 8: Giant Panda, Mickey Mouse, and Other Transnational Objects of Fantasy in Theme Park Hong Kong

1. The unprofitable amusement park is running an accumulative deficit of HK$142 million following the effects of the Asian economic turmoil in 1997. It extended its hours to 11 P.M. on Saturdays in July and August starting in the summer of 2001. Between July 1999 and June 2000, about three million people visited the venue, and Ocean Park is the city's third-most popular spot for tourists. But the continuing deficit has urged the park's board to seek government permission to rejuvenate the park by allowing it to form a partnership with an internationally known theme park. Choices for partners include Sea World on the Gold Coast, Queensland, or in Florida, or Universal Studios in Los Angeles.

2. Surveys indicate that millions of tourists are expected to come to Hong Kong in 2005 purely for the opening of Disneyland. About 75 percent of these are expected to be mainlanders. The expected figures of mainland visitors to Hong Kong would skyrocket to 10 million annually. Beginning in 2004, mainland residents could come to Hong Kong on an individual basis. Previously they were allowed to visit only as part of tour groups. In light of Hong Kong's round-the-clock opening of the border and further relaxation of mainland tourism policies, the Walt Disney group raised its projection for visitors to the $22 billion Hong Kong Disneyland to 5.6 million, up from the initial forecast of 5.4 million per year, starting in 2005–6.

3. The statues at Bauhinia Plaza, where mainland tourists mostly visit, also serve the function of marking the reconquered space with the hegemonic meaning of Chineseness.

4. Another popular humanized animal figure, Hello Kitty, which Hong Kong people have loved for almost two decades, comes from Japan. The most popular locally made cartoon figures are two piglets named McMug and McDull, which were incorporated by the transnational fast food chain McDonald's to be toys for sale in their restaurants. Some union activists accused McDonald's of exploiting the Hong Kong cartoon pigs, since McMug and McDull were created in the late 1980s to symbolize the spirit of a simple life, friendship, and environmental protection, which runs counter to the transnational corporation's tradition of exploiting cheap labor and

causing environmental damage. Indeed, the popularity of the two piglets has already spawned a tie-in industry that includes the production of toys, educational material, and accessories. The two little pigs even have their own credit cards for a local bank. The comics of McDull has been developed into an animated feature film, *My Life as McDull* (2001), which immediately became a hit film in Hong Kong and won many awards in Asia and the Grand Prix Annecy Award in Cannes. A French-dubbed version was released in France during the summer of 2003.

5. At that time, top Chinese leaders from Prime Minister Zhu Rongji down had been pushing Disney to cut a deal with the local government to build a theme park on Chinese soil, and the Chinese government did endorse the building of Disneyland in Hong Kong. Early in 1996, the Chinese government held a number of discussions about a possible Disneyland, but the two sides could not get as far as choosing an appropriate Chinese city for the site. Since then, discussions have reached a stalemate. As China's thriving metropolis and one of the most densely populated cities, Shanghai was first considered a good choice for a Disney amusement park. But a project like this has to convince international investors, who have lost money before in similar operations in China. There are already more than thirty theme parks operating in Shanghai, and most of them are in a deficit. Finally, Disneyland chose Hong Kong instead of Shanghai, and the mayor of Shanghai congratulated Hong Kong for winning the bid. However, mainland China wants a Disneyland so much that mainland media report that a Beijing Disneyland will be opened in time for the 2008 Olympic Games. The Disney company's chief, Michael Eisner, has denied the report but admitted that the company is engaged in ongoing talks with authorities in Beijing and Shanghai, and he has said that a mainland Disney theme park is feasible because of the size of the Chinese market.

6. After the Hong Kong government showed a strong commitment to combating piracy, the center of counterfeited goods moved to Shenzhen, the show place of China's economic reform. To put it differently, the usual copying trick of Hong Kong has now been appropriated by its motherland, and China is becoming more and more Hongkongized.

7. The Tiger Balm Garden was sold in 1998 to the Hong Kong tycoon Li Ka-shing's Cheung Kong Property Limited and will be demolished for an upscale housing development. Only the mansion inside the garden will be preserved and is designated as a historical monument. But there is another Tiger Balm Garden that was built by Aw Boon Haw in Singapore. It has been renovated by the Singapore government as the "Dragon World" theme park to "support the state's claims to an alternative modernity . . . trumpeting the triumphant Asian appropriation of Western modernity" (Oakes 1998, 43–44). On the other hand, there is another Chinese ancient-culture theme park named Tang Dynasty Village, which recreates the seventh-century Chinese village of Xian in Singapore.

8. The commercialization of traditional Chinese culture in Hong Kong theme

parks is not unusual. For example, the Sung Dynasty Village, a recreation of an old Chinese community in Sung Dynasty (960–1279) with costumed reenactors portraying courtesans, soldiers, and workers, was a popular tourist spot before it was closed in March 1997. The Middle Kingdom, right next to Hong Kong Ocean Park, is another recreation site that sells to visitors the ancient Chinese cultural heritage of thirteen dynasties with full-size replicas of temples, shrines, street scenes, pavilions, pagodas, and palaces.

9. Another way to understand the thesis of the theme park Hong Kong is to associate it with the new type of amusement park, such as Virtual World in San Diego, California, Acuarinto of Nagasaki, or the Circus Theater of Zandvoort in Holland (Cerver 1997), where adventures do not take place in real space but only behind the screen. The virtuality of Hong Kong lies precisely in its function of serving as a displayed image of Chineseness.

10. Shenzhen, the special economic zone, has been China's undisputed theme park capital since it built the first theme park, owns over twenty large-scale attractions and its tourist industry is worth several billion yuans. But it can hardly compete with Hong Kong in terms of international status.

11. U.S.-China relations became tense over incidents such as those mentioned in chapter 6, including the U.S. bombing of the Chinese embassy in Belgrade in 1999 and the collision of a U.S. spy plane with a Chinese fighter jet over the South China Sea in 2001. China is now considered as the strategic military competitor of the United States in Asia Pacific under the presidency of George W. Bush, even though the United States needs China's cooperation occasionally in its war on terrorism.

12. China experienced "theme park fever" in the 1990s. Within three years after the opening of Splendid China, there were about sixteen large-scale theme parks and hundreds of small-scale parks in mainland China (Oakes 1998). By 1998, there were an estimated two thousand amusement or theme park attractions in China. But many of them have not been successful from a financial and operational perspective (Ap 2003).

13. A Western anthropologist has described the reactions to these Shenzhen theme parks: "For most of the people in Hong Kong with whom I discussed the parks, they were an expression of economic achievement and cooperation in the period leading up to the handover, although one cynical Danish journalist noted that Window of the World might protect the 'real world' from an invasion of Chinese tourism" (Hendry 2000, 110).

14. In a speech commemorating the eightieth anniversary of the Chinese Communist Party on July 1, 2001, President Jiang Zemin announced that Beijing now wants to draw private entrepreneurs into the Party, probably as his strategy of jointly promoting economic reform and the Communists' political monopoly. But private business people have traditionally been seen by the Chinese Communists as "exploiters." For many die-hard and veteran Communists, such a move is simply a betrayal of the workers and farmers whom the Party was supposed to represent. At the Six-

teenth Congress, in 2002, the Chinese Communist Party officially reshaped its ideology in its constitution and embraced as members the capitalists that it once loathed.

15. However, other critics also point out that the big heads of Mickey and his crew have the power of the grotesque that can scare young children. Many kids run away from the cartoon characters in Disneyland theme parks, tearful and screaming (Project on Disney 1995).

References

Abbas, Ackbar. 1994. "The New Hong Kong Cinema and the Déjà Disparu." *Discourse* 16.3:65–77.

———. 1997. *Hong Kong: Culture and the Politics of Disappearance.* Hong Kong: Hong Kong University Press.

———. 1996. "Cultural Studies in a Postculture." In *Disciplinarity and Dissent in Cultural Studies.* Ed. Cary Nelson and Dilip Parameshwar Gaonkar. 289–312. New York: Routledge.

Adorno, Theodor W. 1991. "Culture Industry Reconsidered." In *The Culture Industry: Selected Essays on Mass Culture.* Ed. J. M. Bernstein. 85–92. London: Routledge.

Agamben, Giorgio. 1991. *Language and Death: The Place of Negativity.* Trans. Karen E. Pinkus and Michael Hardt. Minneapolis: University of Minnesota Press.

Ah Cheng. 1994. *Xianhua xianshuo—zhongguo shisu yu zhongguo xiaoshuo* [Leisure Talks: Chinese Secular Culture and Chinese Fiction]. Taipei: Times Cultural Press.

Althusser, Louis. 1971. "Ideology and Ideological State Apparatuses (Notes towards an Investigation)." *Lenin and Philosophy and Other Essays.* Trans. Ben Brewster. 127–88. New York: Monthly Review Press.

Anagnost, Ann. 1997. *National Past-Times: Narrative, Representation, and Power in Modern China.* Durham, N.C.: Duke University Press.

Anderson, Benedict. 1983. *Imagined Communities: Reflections on the Origin and Spread of Nationalism.* New York: Verso.

Ang, Ien. 1993. "To Be or Not to Be Chinese: Diaspora, Culture, and Postmodern Ethnicity." *Southeast Asian Journal of Social Science* 21.1:1–17.

———. 1994. "On Not Speaking Chinese: Postmodern Ethnicity and the Politics of Diaspora." *New Formations* 24:1–18.

———. 1998. "Can One Say No to Chineseness? Pushing the Limits of the Diasporic Paradigm." *Boundary 2* 25.3:223–42.

Ang, Ien, and Jon Stratton. 1996. "Asianing Australia: Notes toward a Critical Transnationalism in Cultural Studies." *Cultural Studies* 10.1:16–36.

Ap, John. 2003. "An Assessment of Theme Park Development in China." In *Tourism in China*. Ed. Alan A. Lew et al. 195–214. New York: Haworth Hospitality Press.

Armes, Roy. 1987. *Third World Film Making and the West*. Berkeley: University of California Press.

Ascheid, Antje. 1997. "Speaking Tongues: Voice Dubbing in the Cinema as Cultural Ventriloquism." *Velvet Light Trap* 40 (Fall): 33–41.

Bacon-Stone, John, and Kingsley Bolton. 1998. "Charting Multilingualism: Language Censuses and Language Surveys in Hong Kong." In *Language in Hong Kong at Century's End*. Ed. Martha C. Pennington. 43–90. Hong Kong: Hong Kong University Press.

Balibar, Étienne. 1994. "Subjection and Subjectivation." In *Supposing the Subject*. Ed. Joan Copjec. 1–15. New York: Verso.

Barthes, Roland. 1973. *Elements of Semiology*. Trans. Annette Lavers and Colin Smith. New York: Hill and Wang.

———. 1977. "The Grain of the Voice." In *Image-Music-Text*. Trans. Stephen Heath. 179–89. Glasgow: Fontana.

Baudrillard, Jean. 1983. *Simulations*. Trans. Paul Foss, Paul Patton, and Philip Beitchman. New York: Semiotext(e).

Benjamin, Walter. 1973. "The Work of Art in the Age of Mechanical Reproduction." In *Illuminations*. Trans. Harry Zohn. 219–53. New York: Fontana.

———. 1985. *One Way Street and Other Writings*. Trans. Edmund Jephcott and Kingsley Shorter. London: Verso.

Benveniste, Emile. 1971. *Problems in General Linguistics*. Trans. Mary Elizabeth Meek. Coral Gables, Fla.: University of Miami Press.

Bogle, Donald. 1994. *Toms, Coons, Mulattoes, Mammies, and Bucks: An Interpretive History of Blacks in American Films*. 3rd ed. New York: Continuum.

Bordwell, David. 1997. "Aesthetics in Action: Kung Fu, Gunplay, and Cinematic Expressivity." In *Fifty Years of Electric Shadows*. Ed. Law Kar. 81–89. Hong Kong: Urban Council.

———. 2000a. "Hong Kong Martial Arts Cinema." In *Crouching Tiger, Hidden Dragon: A Portrait of the Ang Lee Film*. Ed. Linda Sunshine. 14–21. New York: Newmarket Press.

———. 2000b. *Planet Hong Kong: Popular Cinema and the Art of Entertainment*. Cambridge, Mass.: Harvard University Press.

Brandel, Judith, and Tina Turbeville. 1998. *Tiger Balm Gardens: A Chinese Billionaire's Fantasy Environments*. Hong Kong: Aw Boon Haw Foundation.

Brownell, Susan. 1999. "Strong Women and Impotent Men: Sports, Gender, and Nationalism in Chinese Public Culture." In *Spaces of Their Own: Women's Public Sphere in Transnational China*. Ed. Mayfair Mei-Hui Yang. 207–31. Minneapolis: University of Minnesota Press.

Bruche-Schulz, Gisela. 1997. "'Fuzzy' Chinese: The Status of Cantonese in Hong Kong." *Journal of Pragmatics* 27:295–314.

Buck-Morss, Susan. 1977. *The Origin of Negative Dialectics: Theodor W. Adorno, Walter Benjamin, and the Frankfurt Institute.* Sussex, Eng.: Harvester Press.

Butler, Judith. 1997. *The Psychic Life of Power: Theories in Subjection.* Stanford, Calif.: Stanford University Press.

Cerver, Francisco Asensio. 1997. *Theme and Amusement Parks.* New York: Hearst Books International.

Chan, Jachinson. 2001. *Chinese American Masculinities: From Fu Manchu to Bruce Lee.* New York: Routledge

Chan, Jackie. 1998. *I Am Jackie Chan: My Life in Action.* New York: Ballantine Books.

Chan, Karen. 1994. "Columns on Columns." *Hong Kong Cultural Studies Bulletin* 1 (December): 39.

Chan Koon-Chung. 1997. "Bantangfan—meixue biji" [Half-Chinese and Half-Western—Aesthetic Notes]. *Mingbao Daily.* October 10, D4.

———. 2001. "Fangwen Huang Yulang" [Interview: Wong Yuk Long]. In *Xianggang wei wancheng de shiyan* [The Incomplete Experiment of Hong Kong]. 183–86. Hong Kong: Compass Ltd.

Chan, Stephen Ching-kiu, ed. 1997. *Wenhua xiangxiang yu yishixingtai: dangdai xianggang wenhua zhengzhi lunping* [Cultural Imaginary and Ideology: On Cultural Identity Politics in Contemporary Hong Kong]. Hong Kong: Oxford University Press.

Chan, Stephen Ching-kiu, Siu-leung Li, and Wang-chi Wong. 1997. *Fouxiang Xianggang: lishi, wenhua, weilai* [Hong Kong Un-Imagined: History, Culture and the Future]. Taipei: Rye Field.

Cheng, Manli. 2001. *Haiwai huawen zhuanmei yanjiu* [A Study of Overseas Chinese Language Media]. Beijing: Xinhua chubanshe.

Cheng Yu. 1984. "Anatomy of a Legend." In *A Study of Hong Kong Cinema in the Seventies.* Ed. Li Cheuk-to. 18–25. Hong Kong: Urban Council.

Cheung, Martha P. Y., ed. 1998. *Hong Kong Collage: Contemporary Stories and Writing.* New York: Oxford University Press.

Cheung, Suk-yee. 2000. "Hong Kong Filmmakers in Hollywood: Stanley Tong, Terence Chang, Peter Chan Ho-sun." In *Border Crossings in Hong Kong Cinema.* Ed. Law Kar. 124–35. Hong Kong: Leisure and Cultural Services Department.

Cheung, Tammy. 1993. "Who Are the Women in Hongkong Cinema?" *Cinemas* 3.2–3:182–88.

Chion, Michel. 1994. *Audio-Vision: Sound on Screen.* Ed. and trans. Claudia Gorbman. New York: Columbia University Press.

Chow, Chung-yan, and Carrie Chan. 2001. "Unfriendly, Unhelpful, Exorbitant Prices . . . Welcome to the SAR." *South China Morning Post,* August 22, 3.

Chow, Raymond, et al. 1998. "Remembering King Hu." In *Transcending the Times: King Hu and Eileen Chang.* Ed. Law Kar. 79–112. Hong Kong: Provisional Urban Council.

Chow, Rey. 1991. *Woman and Chinese Modernity: The Politics of Reading between West and East.* Minneapolis: University of Minnesota Press.

———. 1992. "Between Colonizers: Hong Kong's Postcolonial Self-Writing." *Diaspora* 2.2:151–70.

———. 1993. *Writing Diaspora: Tactics of Intervention in Contemporary Cultural Studies.* Bloomington: Indiana University Press.

———. 1995a. *Primitive Passions: Visuality, Sexuality, Ethnography, and Contemporary Chinese Cinema.* New York: Columbia University Press.

———. 1995b. *Xiezai jiaguo yiwai* [Alternative Perspectives on Hong Kong Culture]. Hong Kong: Oxford University Press.

———. 1997. "Larry Feign, Ethnographer of a 'Lifestyle': Political Cartoons from Hong Kong." *Boundary 2* 24.2:21–45.

———. 1998a. *Ethics after Idealism: Theory-Culture-Ethnicity-Reading.* Bloomington: Indiana University Press.

———. 1998b. "Introduction: On Chineseness as a Theoretical Problem." *Boundary 2* 25.3:1–24.

———. 2000. "Introduction: On Chineseness as a Theoretical Problem." In *Modern Chinese Literary and Cultural Studies in the Age of Theory: Reimagining a Field.* Ed. Rey Chow. 1–25. Durham, N.C.: Duke University Press.

———. 2002. *The Protestant Ethnic and the Spirit of Capitalism.* New York: Columbia University Press.

Chu, Stephen. 2002. *Bentu shenhua: quanqiuhua niandai de lunshu shengchan* [Local Myths: The Production of Discourse in the Age of Globalization]. Taipei: Student Book.

Chun, Allen. 1996. "Fuck Chineseness: On the Ambiguity of Ethnicity as Culture as Identity." *Boundary 2* 23.2:111–38.

Chung, Winnie. 2001. "To's Numbers Game." *South China Morning Post.* July 30, Features, 1.

Chung, Yulanda. 1999. "Making a Magic Kingdom." *Asiaweek.* November 12. 52–55.

Ciecko, Anne T., and Sheldon H. Lu. 1999. "The Heroic Trio: Anita Mui, Maggie Cheung, Michelle Yeoh—Self-Reflexivity and the Globalization of the Hong Kong Action Heroine." *Post Script* 19.1:70–86.

Cieply, Michael, and Claudia Eller. 2003. "'Girl Power' Flexing Muscle in Hollywood." *Los Angeles Times.* April 11. Reprint, Honolulu Advertiser.com. <http://the.honoluluadvertiser.com/article/2003/Apr/11/il/il06a.html>, accessed July 18, 2003.

———. 2003. "Girls Just Wanna Have Films." *Harvard Independent: Harvard's Weekly Newsmagazine.* May 2. <http://www.harvardindependent.com/main.cfm/include/smdetail/synid/84480.html>, accessed July 18, 2003.

Clouse, Robert. 1988. *Bruce Lee: The Biography.* Burbank, Calif.: Unique Publications.

Colvert, Kieran. 2000. "Welcome to Our Mickey Mouse City." *South China Morning Post.* June 15, Analysis, 18.

Connery, Christopher L. 1995. "Pacific Rim Discourse: The U.S. Global Imaginary in the Late Cold War Years." In *Asia/Pacific as Space of Cultural Production*. Ed. Rob Wilson and Arif Dirlik. 30–56. Durham, N.C.: Duke University Press.

———. 1996. "The Oceanic Feeling and the Regional Imaginary." In *Global/Local: Cultural Production and the Transnational Imaginary*. Ed. Rob Wilson and Wimal Dissanayake. 284–311. Durham, N.C.: Duke University Press.

"A Conversation with Ang Lee and James Schamus." 2000. *Crouching Tiger, Hidden Dragon*. DVD. Columbia Pictures.

Courtine, Jean-François, et al. 1993. *Of the Sublime: Presence in Question*. Trans. Jeffrey S. Librett. Albany: State University of New York Press.

Cumings, Bruce. 1998. "Rimspeak; or, The Discourse of the 'Pacific Rim.'" In *What Is in a Rim? Critical Perspectives on the Pacific Region Idea*. 2nd ed. Ed. Arif Dirlik. 53–72. Boulder, Colo.: Rowman and Littlefield.

"Dalu yuanzengtai daxiongmao" [Mainland Willing to Give Taiwan Giant Panda]. 2001. *Mingpao*. March 2, B15.

Dannen, Fredric. 1995. "Hong Kong Babylon." *New Yorker*. August 7, 30–38.

Dannen, Fredric, and Barry Long. 1997. *Hong Kong Babylon: An Insider's Guide to the Hollywood of the East*. New York: Miramax Books.

Deleuze, Gilles. 1997. *Essays Critical and Clinical*. Trans. Daniel W. Smith and Michael A. Greco. Minneapolis: University of Minnesota Press.

Deleuze, Gilles, and Felix Guattari. 1988. *A Thousand Plateaus: Capitalism and Schizophrenia*. Trans. Brian Massumi. London: Athlone.

Denzin, Norman K. 1995. *The Cinematic Society: The Voyeur's Gaze*. London: SAGE.

Derrida, Jacques. 1976. *Of Grammatology*. Trans. Gayatri Chakravorty Spivak. Baltimore: Johns Hopkins University Press.

Desser, David. 2000. "The Kung Fu Craze: Hong Kong Cinema's First American Reception." In *The Cinema of Hong Kong: History, Arts, Identity*. Ed. Poshek Fu and David Desser. 19–43. New York: Cambridge University Press.

Dirlik, Arif. 1997. *The Postcolonial Aura: Third World Criticism in the Age of Global Capitalism*. Boulder, Colo.: Westview Press.

———. 1998. "The Asia-Pacific in Asian-American Perspective." In *What Is in a Rim? Critical Perspectives on the Pacific Region Idea*. 2nd ed. Ed. Arif Dirlik. 283–308. Boulder, Colo.: Rowman and Littlefield.

———. 1999. "Globalism and the Politics of Place." In *Globalization and the Asia-Pacific: Contested Territories*. Ed. Kris Olds, Peter Dicken, Philip F. Kelly, Lily Kong, and Henry Wai-chung Yeung. 39–56. New York: Routledge.

Dolar, Mladen. 1996. "The Object Voice." In *Gaze and Voice as Love Objects*. Ed. Renata Salecl and Slavoj Žižek. 7–31. Durham, N.C.: Duke University Press.

Doraiswamy, Rashmi. 1998. "The Spectacle of Action: John Woo's Face/Off." *Cinemaya* 39–40:17–19.

Eizykman, Claudine. 1976. *La jouissance-cinéma*. Paris: Union generale d'editions.

Elias, Justine. 2003. "What Women Want." *New York Daily News*. April 25. <http://

www.nydailynews.com/entertainment/story/78392p-72229c.html>, accessed July 18, 2003.

Evans, Grant. 1997. "Ghosts and the New Governor: The Anthropology of a Hong Kong Rumour." In *Hong Kong: The Anthropology of a Chinese Metropolis.* Ed. Grant Evans and Maria Tam. 267–96. Honolulu: University of Hawaii Press.

Feng Bing. 2001. *Zhongguo wenyi fukanshi* [History of Chinese Literary Supplement]. Beijing: Hauwen chubanshe.

Feng, Peter. 1999. "The State of Asian American Cinema: In Search of Community." *Cineaste* 24.4:20–24.

Fifty Years of the Hong Kong Film Production and Distribution Industries: An Exhibition (1947–1997). 1997. Hong Kong: Hong Kong Film Archive.

Fong, Timothy P. 1998. *The Contemporary Asian American Experience: Beyond the Model Minority.* Upper Saddle River, N.J.: Prentice Hall.

Fonoroff, Paul. 1997. *Silver Light: A Pictorial History of Hong Kong Cinema, 1920–1970.* Hong Kong: Joint Publishing Co.

Fore, Steve. 1994. "Golden Harvest Films and the Hong Kong Movie Industry in the Realm of Globalization." *Velvet Light Trap* 34 (Fall): 40–58.

———. 1997. "Jackie Chan and the Cultural Dynamics of Global Entertainment." In *Transnational Chinese Cinemas: Identity, Nationhood, Gender.* Ed. Sheldon H. Lu. 239–62. Honolulu: University of Hawaii Press.

Friedman, Lester D., ed. 1991. *Unspeakable Images: Ethnicity and the American Cinema.* Urbana: University of Illinois Press.

Fu, Poshek. 2000a. "Between Nationalism and Colonialism: Mainland Émigrés, Marginal Culture, and Hong Kong Cinema 1937–1941." In *The Cinema of Hong Kong: History, Arts, Identity.* Ed. Poshek Fu and David Desser. 199–226. New York: Cambridge University Press.

———. 2000b. "Going Global: A Cultural History of the Shaw Brothers Studio, 1960–1970." In *Border Crossing in Hong Kong Cinema.* Ed. Law Kar. 43–51. Hong Kong: Leisure and Cultural Services Department.

Fu, Poshek, and David Desser, eds. 2000. *The Cinema of Hong Kong: History, Arts, Identity.* New York: Cambridge University Press.

Gateward, Frances. 2000. "Wong Fei Hung in Da House: Hong Kong Martial Arts Film and Hip Hop Culture." Paper presented at "Year 2000 and Beyond: History, Technology, and Future of Transnational Chinese Film and Television: The Second International Conference on Chinese Cinema." Hong Kong Baptist University.

Gaul, Lou. 1997. *The Fist That Shook the World: The Cinema of Bruce Lee.* Baltimore, Md.: Midnight Marquee Press.

Giddens, Anthony. 1991. *Modernity and Self-Identity: Self and Society in a Late Modern Age.* Oxford: Polity.

Giukin, Lenuta. 2001. "Boy-Girls: Gender, Body, and Popular Culture in Hong Kong Action Movies." In *Ladies and Gentlemen, Boys and Girls: Gender in Film at the*

End of the Twentieth Century. Ed. Murray Pomerance. 55–69. Albany: State University of New York Press.

Gould, Stephen Jay. 1980. "A Biological Homage to Mickey Mouse." In *The Panda's Thumb: More Reflections in Natural History.* 95–107. New York: Norton.

Hajari, Nisid. 2001. "Erasing the Boundaries." *Newsweek.* Special edition, "Issue Asia." July–September, 79.

Halbertsma, Tjalling. 2001. "Crosses in the Dust." *South China Morning Post.* September 20, Features, 2.

Hall, Stuart. 1997. "Old and New Identities, Old and New Ethnicities." In *Culture, Globalization and the World-System: Contemporary Conditions for the Representation of Identity.* Ed. Anthony King. 41–68. Minneapolis: University of Minnesota.

Hamamoto, Darrell Y. 1994. *Monitored Peril: Asian Americans and the Politics of TV Representation.* Minneapolis: University of Minnesota Press.

Hammond, Stefan, and Mike Wilkins. 1996. *Sex and Zen and a Bullet in the Head: The Essential Guide to Hong Kong's Mind-Bending Films.* New York: Simon and Schuster.

Hanke, Ken. 1989. *Charlie Chan at the Movies: History, Filmography, and Criticism,* Jefferson, N.C.: McFarland.

Hardt, Michael, and Antonio Negri. 2000. *Empire.* Cambridge, Mass.: Harvard University Press.

Havis, James. 1998. "A Better Today: Hong Kong's John Woo Finally Does It His Way in Hollywood." *Cinemaya* 39–40:10–16.

He Liangmao. 1997. *Dianfu Zhuanmei* [Subverting Media]. Hong Kong: Subculture.

He Wenlong. 1994. "Chen Kexin yaozhuahui yiliushi de guanzhong" [Peter Chan Wants to Regain the Confidence of the Audience]. *City Entertainment.* February, 50–51.

Heard, Christopher. 2000. *Ten Thousand Bullets: The Cinematic Journey of John Woo.* Los Angeles: Lone Eagle.

Heidegger, Martin. 1962. *Being and Time.* Trans. John Macquarrie and Edward Robinson. New York: Harper and Row.

Hendry, Joy. 2000. *The Orient Strikes Back: A Global View of Cultural Display.* Oxford: Berg.

Herskovitz, Jon. 2001. "'The Great Wall' Towers over NBA." *South China Morning Post.* March 31, Sport, 21.

Hill, Annette. 1999. "Risky Business: Film Violence as an Interactive Phenomenon." In *Identifying Hollywood's Audiences: Cultural Identity and the Movies.* Ed. Melvyn Stokes and Richard Maltby. 175–86. London: British Film Institute.

Hirsch, Foster. 1999. *Detours and Lost Highways: A Map of Neo-Noir.* New York: Limelight Editions.

Ho, Sam. 1999. "Merchandising as Filmmaking: Andrew Lau on the Miracle of *The Stormriders.*" *Hong Kong Panorama 98–99.* 43–44. Hong Kong: Provisional Urban Council.

———. 2000. "Everybody's a Terrorist: Teddy Chen's *Purple Storm.*" In *Hong Kong*

Panorama 1999–2000. 60–61. Hong Kong: Leisure and Cultural Services Department.

Hodge, Bob, and Kam Louie. 1998. *The Politics of Chinese Language and Culture: The Art of Reading Dragons.* New York: Routledge.

Hodgson, Liz. 2000. "Frozen Out in Hollywood." *South China Morning Post.* May 4, 27.

Hong Kong Film Critics Society. 1997. Review of *Lost and Found.* <http://filmcritics.org.hk/lost&found/review.html>, accessed July 15, 2001.

Huang Zhongming. 2002. *Xianggang sanjidi wenti liubianshi* [The Changing Histories of Hong Kong Saam Kap Dai Literary Genre]. Hong Kong: Hong Kong Writers' Association.

Hu Ke. 1997. "The Influence of Hong Kong Cinema on Mainland China." In *Fifty Years of Electric Shadows.* Ed. Law Kar. 171–78. Hong Kong: Urban Council.

Hung Ho-fung. 2001. "Identity Contested: Rural Ethnicities in the Making of Urban Hong Kong." In *Hong Kong Reintegrating with China: Political, Cultural and Social Dimensions.* Ed. Lee Pui-tak. 181–201. Hong Kong: Hong Kong University Press.

Huntington, Samuel P. 1996. *The Clash of Civilizations and the Remaking of World Order.* New York: Simon and Schuster.

Huot, Marie Claire. 2000. *China's New Cultural Scene: A Handbook of Changes.* Durham, N.C.: Duke University Press.

Iwabuchi, Koichi. 1999. "Return to Asia? Japan in Asian Audiovisual Markets." In *Consuming Ethnicity and Nationalism: Asian Experiences.* Ed. Kosaku Yoshino. 177–99. Honolulu: University of Hawaii Press.

———. 2002. *Recentering Globalization: Popular Culture and Japanese Transnationalism.* Durham, N.C.: Duke University Press.

Jakobson, Roman. 1956. "Two Aspects of Language and Two Types of Aphasic Disturbances." In *Fundamentals of Language.* 69–96. The Hague: Mouton.

Jarvie, I. C. 1977. *Window on Hong Kong: A Sociological Study of the Hong Kong Film Industry and Its Audience.* Hong Kong: Centre of Asian Studies, University of Hong Kong.

Jeffords, Susan. 1993. "The Big Switch: Hollywood Masculinity in the Nineties." In *Film Theories Goes to the Movies.* Ed. Jim Collins, Hilary Radner, and Ava Preacher Collins. 196–208. New York: Routledge.

Kaminsky, Stuart M. 1984. "Comparative Forms: The Kung Fu Film and the Dance Musical." In *American Film Genre.* 2nd ed. 73–80. Chicago: Nelson-Hall.

Kemp, Philip. 1998. "Rush Hour." *Sight and Sound* 8.12:60–1.

Klein, Christina. 2002. "When Chinese Martial Arts Flies through the Global Box Office." *YaleGlobal Online.* December 9. <http://yaleglobal.yale.edu/display.article?id=535>, accessed August 2003.

Koo, Siu-fung. 1981. "Philosophy and Tradition in the Swordplay Film." In *A Study of the Hong Kong Swordplay Film (1945–1980).* Ed. Lau Shing-hon. 25–46. Hong Kong: Urban Council.

Kozloff, Sarah. 2000. *Overhearing Film Dialogue*. Berkeley: University of California Press.

Kuisel, Richard F. 2000. "The French Cinema and Hollywood: A Case Study of Americanization." In *Transactions, Transgressions, Transformations: American Culture in Western Europe and Japan*. Ed. Heide Fehrenbach and Uta G. Poiger. 208–23. New York: Berghahn Books.

Lacan, Jacques. 1977. *Ecrits: A Selection*. Trans. Alan Sheridan. New York: Norton.

———. 1992. *The Ethics of Psychoanalysis, 1959–1960*. Trans. Dennis Porter. New York: Norton.

Lau, Joseph S. M. 1998. "Jin Yong xiaoshuo yu qiaojiao" [Louis Cha's Novels and the Education of Overseas Chinese]. In *Wuxia Xiaoshuo Lunjuan* [On the Martial Arts Novel]. Vol. 2. Ed. Chan Wing-ming and Joseph S. M. Lau. 434–65. Hong Kong: Mingheshe.

Lau Ting-kin. 1993. *Lianhuantu dajuezhan* [The War of Comics]. Hong Kong: Free Person.

Law, Kar, ed. 1992. *Overseas Chinese Figures in Cinema*. Hong Kong: Urban Council.

———, ed. 2000. *Border Crossing in Hong Kong Cinema*. Hong Kong: Leisure and Cultural Services Department.

Lee, Leo. 1995. "Piping kongjian: lun xiandai zhongguo de wenhua piping lingyu" [Critical Space: The Field of Cultural Criticism in Modern China]. In *Huigu xiandai wenhua xiangxiang* [In Remembrance of Modern Cultural Imagination]. 4–25. Taipei: Shibao.

Lee, Leo, and Andrew J. Nathan. 1985. "The Beginnings of Mass Culture: Journalism and Fiction in the Late Ch'ing and Beyond." In *Popular Culture in Late Imperial China*. Ed. David Johnson, Andrew J. Nathan, and Evelyn S. Rawski. 360–95. Berkeley: University of California Press.

Lee, Linda. 1989. *The Bruce Lee Story*. Santa Clarita, Calif.: Ohara Publications.

Lee Pik Wah. 2001. "Shui gei Ladeng kankanxiang?" [Who Will Give bin Laden a Face Reading?] *Apple Daily*. September 16, E12.

Lee, Quentin. 1994. "Delineating Asian (Hong Kong) Intellectuals: Speculations on Intellectual Problematics and Post/Coloniality." *Third Text* 26:11–23.

Lee, Rachel. 1999. "Asian American Cultural Production in Asian-Pacific Perspective." *Boundary 2* 26.2:231–54.

Leung, Ambrose. 2001. "SAR Culture Impresses Shanghai Writer." *South China Morning Post*. August 1, 4.

Leung, Grace, and Joseph Chan. 1997. "The Hong Kong Cinema and Its Overseas Market: A Historical Review, 1950–1995." In *Fifty Years of Electric Shadows*. Ed. Law Kar. 136–51. Hong Kong: Urban Council.

Leung Ping-kwan, ed. 1993. *Xianggang liuxing wenhua* [Hong Kong Popular Culture]. Hong Kong: Joint Publishing Co.

———. 1995. *Xianggang wenhua* [Hong Kong Culture]. Hong Kong: Hong Kong Arts Center.

———. 1996a. "Liuchang de shujian: zenyang keyi tongguo bieren de kuanjia qu shuoziji" [The Fluent Letters: How to Look at Oneself through the Frame of the Other]. In *Evans Chan's To Liv(e): Screenplay and Essays*. Ed. Wong Tak-wai. 151–55. Hong Kong: Hong Kong University.

———. 1996b. *Xianggang wenhua kongjian yu wenxue* [Hong Kong Cultural Space and Literature]. Hong Kong: Youth Literary Press.

———. 1996c. *Yuejie shujian* [Letter across Borders]. Hong Kong: Youth Literary Press.

Leung, William. 2001. "Crouching Sensibility, Hidden Sense." *Film Criticism* 26.1:42–55.

Li Cheuk-to. 2000. "Gordan Chan Goes Global in *2000 AD*." *Hong Kong Panorama 1999–2000*. Trans. Au Jing-wong. 65–66. Hong Kong: Leisure and Cultural Services Department.

Li, David Leiwei. 1998. *Imagining the Nation: Asian American Literature and Cultural Consent*. Stanford, Calif.: Stanford University Press.

Liang Hai-chiang 1997. "Hong Kong Cinema's 'Taiwan Factor.'" In *Fifty Years of Electric Shadows*. Ed. Law Kar. 158–63. Hong Kong: Urban Council.

Lii, Ding-Tzann. 1998. "A Colonized Empire: Reflections on the Expansion of Hong Kong Films in Asian Countries." In *Trajectories: Inter-Asia Cultural Studies*. Ed. Kuan-Hsing Chen. 122–41. New York: Routledge.

Ling, Jinqi. 1998. *Narrating Nationalisms: Ideology and Form in Asian American Literature*. Oxford: Oxford University Press.

Little, John R., and Curtis F. Wong, eds. 1999. *Jackie Chan: The Best of Inside Kung-Fu*. Lincolnwood, Ill.: Contemporary Books.

Liu, Melinda. 2001. "A Chinese Century?" *Newsweek*. Special edition, "Issue Asia." July–September, 10–14.

Lo, Alex. 2002. "English Subtitles for ATV and TVB." *South China Morning Post*. November 13, 1.

Lo, Joseph. 2003. "HK Can 'Be Everything It Wants': A Leading Management Guru Says We Should Be More Upbeat on the Future." *South China Morning Post*. August 30, A1–2.

Lo, Kwai-Cheung. 1993. "Once Upon a Time: Technology Comes to Presence in China." *Modern Chinese Literature* 7.2:79–96.

———. 1999. "Xiongmao de gushi" [The Story of Giant Pandas]. *Mingpao Daily*. May 22.

Logan, Bey. 1995. *Hong Kong Action Cinema*. London: Titan Books.

Lok Fung. 1995. *Shijimo chengshi: Xianggang de liuxing wenhua* [The Decadent City: Hong Kong Popular Culture]. Hong Kong: Oxford University Press.

Louie, Kam. 2002. *Theorizing Chinese Masculinity: Society and Gender in China*. New York: Cambridge University Press.

Lowe, Lisa. 1996. *Immigrant Acts: On Asian American Cultural Politics*. Durham, N.C.: Duke University Press.

Lu Jinrong and Lu Feiyun. 2002. "Wang Zhan jiaoshou tan Xianggang fazhan ding-wei" [Professor Wang Zhan on Hong Kong's Positioning]. *Warring States: Strategic Business World Monthly* 1. August, 46–52.

Lu, Sheldon H., ed. 1997. *Transnational Chinese Cinemas: Identity, Nationhood, Gender.* Honolulu: University of Hawaii Press.

———. 2001. *China, Transnational Visuality, Global Postmodernity.* Stanford, Calif.: Stanford University Press.

Lui Tai-lok, ed. 1983. *Puji wenhua zai xianggang* [Popular Culture in Hong Kong]. Hong Kong: Twilight Books.

———. 1997. *Wugai, maidan! yige shehuixuejia de xianggang biji* ["Check, Please!": A Sociologist's Notes on Hong Kong]. Hong Kong: Xian Ren Hang.

Ma, Eric Kit-wai. 1999. *Culture, Politics, and Television in Hong Kong.* London: Routledge.

Ma Kwok-ming. 1998. *Lubian zhengzhi jingjixue* [A Political Economy of the Street]. Hong Kong: Twilight Books.

Ma Sheng-mei. 1998. *Immigrant Subjectivities in Asian American and Asian Diaspora Literatures.* Albany: State University of New York.

———. 2000. *The Deathly Embrace: Orientalism and Asian American Identity.* Minneapolis: University of Minnesota Press.

MacDougall, David. 1998. *Transcultural Cinema.* Ed. and intro. Lucien Taylor. Princeton: Princeton University Press.

Major, Wade. 1997. "Third Team: Tsui Hark Joins Van Damme's Hong Kong Club with *Double Team*." <http://www.boxoff.com/feb97story5.html>, accessed July 2000.

Maltby, Richard. 1996. "'A Brief Romantic Interlude': Dick and Jane Go to 3 ½ Seconds of the Classic Hollywood Cinema." In *Post-Theory: Reconstructing Film Studies.* Ed. David Bordwell and Noel Carroll. 434–59. Madison: University of Wisconsin Press.

Marchetti, Gina. 1993. *Romance and the "Yellow Peril": Race, Sex, and Discursive Strategies in Hollywood Fiction.* Berkeley: University of California Press.

———. 1998. "Chinese and Chinese Diaspora Cinema—Plural and Transnational: Introduction." *Jump Cut* 42:68–72.

———. 2000. "Buying American, Consuming Hong Kong: Cultural Commerce, Fantasies of Identity, and the Cinema." In *The Cinema of Hong Kong: History, Art, Identity.* Ed. Poshek Fu and David Desser. 289–313. Cambridge: Cambridge University Press.

———. 2001. "Jackie Chan and the Black Connection." In *Keyframes: Popular Cinema and Cultural Studies.* Ed. Matthew Tinkcom and Amy Villarejo. 137–58. New York: Routledge.

mat x. 2002. "Beast Cops Bad-ass at the Film Festival." *The e.peak* 100.5 (October 1998). <http://www.peak.sfu.ca/the-peak/98-3/issue5/badass.html>, accessed December 26, 2002.

Miller, Judith. 1991. "Style Is the Man Himself." In *Lacan and the Subject of Language.* Ed. Ellie Ragland-Sullivan and Mark Bracher. 143–51. New York: Routledge.

Miners, Norman. 1991. *The Government and Politics of Hong Kong.* 5th ed. New York: Oxford University Press.

Mitchell, Charles P. 1999. *A Guide to Charlie Chan Films.* Westport, Conn.: Greenwood Press.

Mitchell, Katharyne. 1995. "The Hong Kong Immigrant and the Urban Landscape: Shaping the Transnational Cosmopolitan in the Era of Pacific Rim Capital." In *Asia/Pacific as Space of Cultural Production.* Ed. Rob Wilson and Arif Dirlik. 284–310. Durham, N.C.: Duke University Press.

———. 1996. "In Whose Interest? Transnational Capital and the Production of Multiculturalism in Canada." In *Global/Local: Cultural Production and the Transnational Imaginary.* Ed. Rob Wilson and Wimal Dissananyake. 219–51. Durham, N.C.: Duke University Press.

Morris, Gary. 2002. "Recent Hong Kong Films." *Bright Lights Film Journal* 20 (November 1997). <http://www.brightlightsfilm.com/20/20_hk_recent.html>, accessed December 26, 2002.

Morris, Jan. 1990. *Hong Kong: Epilogue to an Empire.* London: Penguin.

Nakayam, Thomas K., and Judith N. Martin, eds. 1999. *Whiteness: The Communication of Social Identity.* Thousand Oaks, Calif.: Sage Publications.

Naremore, James. 1998. *More Than Night: Film Noir in Its Contexts.* Berkeley: University of California Press.

Nasio, Juan-David. 1998. *Five Lessons on the Psychoanalytic Theory of Jacques Lacan.* Trans. David Pettigrew and François Raffoul. Albany: State University of New York Press.

Ng Chun-hung. 1996a. "Social Indicators and the Hong Kong Way of Life." In *New Frontiers of Social Indicators Research in Chinese Societies.* Ed. Lau Siu-kai et al. 121–36. Hong Kong: Chinese University Press.

———. 1996b. *Wenhua lache* [Cultural Chat]. Hong Kong: Xianggang renmin kexue chubanshe.

———. 1997. *Wenhua zai lache* [Cultural Chat Again]. Hong Kong: Xianggang renmin kexue chubanshe.

———. 1998. "Xunzhao xianggang bentu yishi" [In Search of the Hong Kong Local Consciousness]. *Mingpao Monthly* 3:23–29.

Ng Chun-hung, and Charles Cheung, eds. 2001. *Yuedu Xianggang puji wenhua 1970–2000* [Reading Hong Kong Popular Cultures, 1970–2000]. Hong Kong: Oxford University Press.

Ng Chun-hung, and Stephen Sze, eds. 1993. *Xianggang puji wenhua yanjiu* [Studies on Hong Kong Popular Culture]. Hong Kong: Joint Publishing Co.

Ng Hui Bun. 1987. *Wu Xubin xiaoshuoji: yige yundao zai shuichi pangbian de yindianren* [The Collected Stories of Ng Hui Bun: An Indian Who Collapsed beside a Pool]. Taipei: Grand East Book Enterprise.

Nornes, Abé Mark. 1999. "For an Abusive Subtitling." *Film Quarterly* 52.3:17–34.

Nowell-Smith, Geoffrey, and Steven Ricci, eds. 1998. *Hollywood and Europe: Economies, Culture, National Identity 1945–95.* London: British Film Institute.

Oakes, Tim. 1998. *Tourism and Modernity in China.* New York: Routledge.

Okihiro, Gary Y. 1994. *Margins and Mainstreams: Asians in American History and Culture.* Seattle: University of Washington Press.

Ong, Aihwa. 1993. "On the Edge of Empires: Flexible Citizenship among Chinese in Diaspora." *Positions: East Asia Culture Critique* 1.3:745–78.

———. 1995. "Southeast Asian Refugees and Investors in Our Midst." *Positions: East Asia Cultures Critique* 3.3:806–13.

———. 1999. *Flexible Citizenship: The Cultural Logics of Transnationality.* Durham, N.C.: Duke University Press.

Ong, Aihwa, and Donald Nonini, eds. 1997. *Ungrounded Empires: The Cultural Politics of Modern Chinese Transnationalism.* New York: Routledge.

Ong, Walter. 1993. *Orality and Literacy: The Technologizing of the Word.* New York: Routledge.

Ongiri, Amy Abugo. 2002. "'He Wanted to Be Just Like Bruce Lee': African Americans, Kung Fu Theater and Cultural Exchange at the Margins." *Journal of Asian American Studies* 5.1:31–40.

Palumbo-Liu, David. 1999. *Asian/American: Historical Crossings of a Racial Frontier.* Stanford, Calif.: Stanford University Press.

Piore, Adam. 2001. "Colonizing California." *Newsweek.* Special edition, "Issue Asia." July–September, 62–67.

Polan, Dana. 1986. "Brief Encounters: Mass Culture and the Evacuation of Sense." In *Studies in Entertainment: Critical Approaches to Mass Culture.* Ed. Tania Modleski. 167–87. Bloomington: Indiana University Press.

———. 1996. "Globalism's Localisms." In *Global/Local: Cultural Production and the Transnational Imaginary.* Ed. Rob Wilson and Wimal Dissanayake. 255–83. Durham, N.C.: Duke University Press.

Prager, Brad, and Michael Richardson. 1997. "A Sort of Homecoming: An Archeology of Disneyland." In *Streams of Cultural Capital: Transnational Cultural Studies.* Ed. Hans Ulrich Gumbrecht and David Palumbo-Liu. 199–219. Stanford, Calif.: Stanford University Press.

Prashad, Vijay. 2001. *Everybody Was Kung Fu Fighting: Afro-Asian Connections and the Myth of Cultural Purity.* Boston: Beacon Press.

———. 2003. "Bruce Lee and the Anti-imperialism of Kung Fu: A Polycultural Adventure." *Position: East Asia Cultures Critique* 11.1:51–90.

Project on Disney. 1995. *Inside the Mouse: Work and Play at Disney World.* Durham, N.C.: Duke University Press.

Rayns, Tony. 1980. "Bruce Lee: Narcissism and Nationalism." In *A Study of Hong Kong Martial Arts Film.* Ed. Lau Shing-hon. 110–12. Hong Kong: Urban Council.

Rickitt, Richard. 2000. *Special Effects: The History and Technique.* New York: Billboard/Watson-Guptill.

Robertson, Roland. 1995. "Glocalization: Time-Space and Homogeneity-Heterogeneity." In *Global Modernities*. Ed. Mike Featherstone, Scott Lash, and Roland Robertson. 25–44. London: Sage.

Rodriguez, Hector. 1997. "Hong Kong Popular Culture as an Interpretive Arena: The Huang Feihong Film Series." *Screen* 38.1:1–24.

Sandell, Jillian. 1997. "Reinventing Masculinity: The Spectacle of Male Intimacy in the Films of John Woo." *Film Quarterly* 49.4:23–34.

Sarkar, Bhaskar. 2001. "Hong Kong Hysteria: Martial Arts Tales from a Mutating World." In *At Full Speed: Hong Kong Cinema in a Borderless World*. Ed. Esther C. M. Yau. 159–76. Minneapolis: University of Minnesota Press.

Saussure, Ferdinand de. 1966. *Course in General Linguistics*. Trans. Wade Baskin. New York: McGraw-Hill.

Schwartz, Hillel. 1996. *The Culture of the Copy: Striking Likeness, Unreasonable Facsimiles*. New York: Zone Books.

Sek Kei. 2002. "Yueyu 'gangwen' zimu" [Cantonese "Hong Kong Style" Subtitles]. *Mingpao*. August 21, D7.

———. 1999. *Shiqi yinghuaji* [Selected Film Criticisms of Sek Kei]. Vol. 8. Hong Kong: Subculture.

Server, Lee. 1999. "John Woo Interview." *Asian Pop Cinema: Bombay to Tokyo.* 28–36. San Francisco: Chronicle Books.

Shen, Shiao-ying. 1995. "Where Has All the Capital Gone: The State of Taiwan's Film Investment." *Cinemaya* 30:4–12.

Shih, Shu-mei. 1999. "Gender and a Geopolitics of Desire: The Seduction of Mainland Women in Taiwan and Hong Kong Media." In *Spaces of Their Own: Women's Public Sphere in Transnational China*. Ed. Mayfair Mei-hui Yang. 278–307. Minneapolis: University of Minnesota Press.

———. 2000. "Globalization and Minoritisation: Ang Lee and the Politics of Flexibility." *New Formations* 40:86–101.

Shohat, Ella, and Robert Stam. 1985. "The Cinema after Babel: Language, Difference, Power." *Screen* 26.3–4:35–58.

Simon, Richard Keller. 1999. *Trash Culture: Popular Culture and the Great Tradition*. Berkeley: University of California Press.

Singer, Michael. 1998. "John Woo." In *A Cut Above: 50 Film Directors Talk about Their Craft.* 321–27. Los Angeles: Lone Eagle.

Sinn, Elizabeth, ed. 1995. *Culture and Society in Hong Kong*. Hong Kong: Center of Asian Studies, University of Hong Kong.

Siu, Helen F. 1996. "Remade in Hong Kong: Weaving into the Chinese Cultural Tapestry." In *Unity and Diversity: Local Cultures and Identities in China*. Ed. Tao Tao Liu and David Faure. 177–96. Hong Kong: Hong Kong University Press.

———. 1999. "Hong Kong: Cultural Kaleidoscope on a World Landscape." In *Cosmopolitan Capitalists: Hong Kong and the Chinese Diaspora at the End of the Twentieth Century*. Ed. Gary G. Hamilton. 100–117. Seattle: University of Washington Press.

Smoodin, Eric. 1994. "Introduction: How to Read Walt Disney." In *Disney Discourse: Producing the Magic Kingdom*. Ed. Eric Smoodin. 1–20. New York: Routledge.

Snow, Donald Bruce. 1991. *Written Cantonese and the Culture of Hong Kong: The Growth of a Dialect Literature*. Ph.D. diss. Indiana University. Ann Arbor, Mich.: UMI.

So, Clement Y. K. 1997a. "Pre-1997 Hong Kong Press: Cut-throat Competition and the Changing Journalistic Paradigm." In *The Other Hong Kong Report 1996*. Ed. Nyaw Mee-kau and Li Si-ming. 485–505. Hong Kong: Chinese University Press.

———. 1997b. "Wanquan shichang daoxiang xinwenxue: pingguo ribao gean yanjiu" [The Completely Market-Driven Journalism: The Case Study of Apple Daily]. In *Dazhongzhuanbo yu shichang jingji* [Mass Communication and Market Economy]. Ed. Joseph Man Chan, Leonard L. Chu, and Zhongdang Pan. 215–33. Hong Kong: Lo Fung Learned Society.

———. 1999. "Xianggang baozhi fukan suo fanying de xiaofei wenhua" [The Consumer Culture Reflected in Hong Kong Newspaper Supplement]. Paper presented at Hong Kong Culture Conference. Hong Kong Polytechnic University. October 8–9.

Spivak, Gayatri Chakravorty. 1990. "Postcoloniality and Value." In *Literary Theory Today*. Ed. Peter Collier and Helga Geyer-Ryan. 219–44. Ithaca, N.Y.: Cornell University Press.

Stokes, Lisa Odham, and Michael Hoover. 1999a. *City on Fire: Hong Kong Cinema*. New York: Verso.

———. 1999b. "Hong Kong to Hollywood." *Cinemaya* 46:30–39.

Stringer, Julian. 1997. "Your Tender Smiles Give Me Strength: Paradigms of Masculinity in John Woo's *A Better Tomorrow* and *The Killer*." *Screen* 38.1:37, n. 20.

Sun, Wanning. 2000. "Internet, Memory, and the Chinese Diaspora—The Case of the Nanjing Massacre Website." *New Formations* 40 (Spring): 30–48.

Sunaina, Maira. 2000. "Henna and Hip Hop: The Politics of Cultural Production and the Work of Cultural Studies." *Journal of Asian American Studies* 3.3:329–69.

Sunshine, Linda, ed. 2000. *Crouching Tiger, Hidden Dragon: A Portrait of the Ang Lee Film*. Foreword by Ang Lee and James Schamus. Intro. David Bordwell and Richard Corliss. New York: Newmarket Press.

Sze Pang-cheung and Ip Iam-chong, eds. 1999. *Dishini bushi leyuan* [Disney Is No Paradise]. Hong Kong: Step Forward Press.

Tam, Kwok-kan, Terry Yip, and Wimal Dissanayake, eds. 1999. *A Place of One's Own: Stories of Self in China, Taiwan, Hong Kong, and Singapore*. New York: Oxford University Press.

Tan, See Kam. 2001. "Chinese Diasporic Imaginations in Hong Kong Films: Sinicist Belligerence and Melancholia." *Screen* 42.1:1–20.

Tang, James T. H., and Frank Ching. 1996. "Balancing the Beijing-London-Hong Kong 'Three-Legged Stool,' 1971–1986." In *The Hong Kong Reader: Passage to Chinese Sovereignty*. Ed. Ming K. Chan and Gerard A. Postiglione. 41–64. London: M. E. Sharpe.

Tang, Xiaobin. 2000. *Chinese Modern: The Heroic and the Quotidian.* Durham, N.C.: Duke University Press.

Tasker, Yvonne. 1993. *Spectacular Bodies: Gender, Genre and the Action Cinema.* New York: Routledge.

———. 1997. "Fists of Fury: Discourses of Race and Masculinity in the Martial Arts Cinema." In *Race and the Subject of Masculinities.* Ed. Harry Stecopoulos and Michael Uebel. 315–36. Durham, N.C.: Duke University Press.

Tay, William. 1994. "Xianggang wenxue, zhimindi wenxue, xianggang jiuqi yihou" [Hong Kong Literature, Colonial Literature, Post-1997 Hong Kong]. *Youshi wenyi,* June, 33–37.

———. 1998. "Yiwang de lishi, lishi de yiwang" [The Forgotten Histories, the Forgetting of History]. *Zhuiji xianggang wenxue* [In Search of Hong Kong Literature]. 1–9. Hong Kong: Oxford University Press.

Teo, Stephen. 1991. "The True Way of the Dragon: The Films of Bruce Lee." In *Overseas Chinese Figures in Cinema.* Ed. Law Kar. 70–80. Hong Kong: Urban Council.

———. 1997. *Hong Kong Cinema: The Extra Dimensions.* London: British Film Institute.

———. 2000. "The 1970s: Movement and Transition." In *The Cinema of Hong Kong: History, Arts, Identity.* Ed. Poshek Fu and David Desser. 90–110. New York: Cambridge University Press.

Theroux, Paul. 1997. *Kowloon Tong.* London: Penguin.

Thill, Scott. 2002. "Contract Killer (Sat Sau Ji Wong)." *Pop Matters.* <http://www.popmatters.com/film/reviews/c/contract-killer.shtml>, accessed December 26, 2002.

Thomas, Bruce. 1994. *Bruce Lee: Fighting Spirit.* Berkeley, Calif.: Frog Ltd.

Truffaut, François. 1985. *Hitchcock.* New York: Simon and Schuster.

Trinh T. Minh-ha. 1992. *Framer Framed.* New York: Routledge.

Tsao Chip. 2001. "Disanci shijiedazhan qianxi?" [The Eve of World War Three?] *Oriental Daily.* September 12, B20.

Tsui, Athena. 1997. "Interview with Peter Chan." *Hong Kong Panorama 96–97.* 26–27. Hong Kong: Urban Council.

Tu Wei-ming. 1994. "Cultural China: The Periphery as the Center." In *The Living Tree: The Changing Meaning of Being Chinese Today.* Ed. Tu Wei-ming. 1–34. Stanford, Calif.: Stanford University Press.

Turner, Matthew. 1995. "Hong Kong Sixties/Nineties: Dissolving the People." In *Hong Kong Sixties: Designing Identity.* Ed. Matthew Turner and Irene Ngan. 13–34. Hong Kong: Hong Kong Arts Center.

Vernet, Marc. 1993. "Film Noir on the Edge of Doom." In *Shades of Noir: A Reader.* Ed. Joan Copjec. 1–31. New York: Verso.

Wald, Gayle. 2000. *Crossing the Line: Racial Passing in Twentieth-Century U.S. Literature and Culture.* Durham, N.C.: Duke University Press.

Wang Gungwu. 1991a. "The Chineseness of China." In *The Cambridge Encyclopedia of China*. Ed. Brian Hook. 31–34. Cambridge: Cambridge University Press.

——. 1991b. *The Chineseness of China: Selected Essays*. New York: Oxford University Press.

——. 1999. "Chineseness: The Dilemmas of Place and Practice." In *Cosmopolitan Capitalists: Hong Kong and the Chinese Diaspora at the End of the Twentieth Century*. Ed. Gary G. Hamilton. 118–34. Seattle: University of Washington Press.

Wang Gungwu and Wang Ling-chi, eds. 1998. *The Chinese Diaspora: Selected Essays*. Singapore: Times Academic Press.

Wang, Jing. 1996. *High Culture Fever: Politics, Aesthetics, and Ideology in Deng's China*. Berkeley: University of California Press.

Wang Shigu. 1998. *Haiwai huawen xinwenshi yanjiu* [A Study of the History of Overseas Chinese Language News]. Beijing: Xinhua chubanshe.

Wang Shuo. 2000. "Wokan dazhongwenhua gangtaiwenhua jiqita" [My Views on Mass Culture, Hong Kong and Taiwan Cultures, and Others]. *Wuzhizhewuwei* [The Ignorant Has No Fear]. 2–46. Shenyang: Chunfeng wenyi chubanshe.

Weis, Elisabeth, and John Belton, eds. 1985. *Film Sound: Theory and Practice*. New York: Columbia University Press.

Wen, Juan, ed. 1992. *Li Xiaolong yanjiu* [Studies on Bruce Lee]. Hong Kong: Just for Fun Book.

Williams, Tony. 1997. "Space, Place, and Spectacle: The Crisis Cinema of John Woo." *Cinema Journal* 36.2:67–84.

——. 1998. "Kwan Tak-Hing and the New Generation." *Asian Cinema* 10.1:71–77.

——. 2000. "Under 'Western Eyes': The Personal Odyssey of Huang Fei-Hong in Once Upon a Time in China." *Cinema Journal* 40.1:3–24.

——. 2001. "Michelle Yeoh: Under Eastern Eyes." *Asian Cinema* 12.2:119–31.

"Women meitian de jingshen shiliang—xianggang baozhi fukanwenhua de tantao" [Our Daily Spiritual Food: An Investigation on the Supplement Culture of Hong Kong Newspapers]. 1989. *Wenhua jiaodian* [Cultural Focus] 4 (March): 7–11.

Wong, Cecilia. 2000. "Ang Lee: Nostalgic Dreamer." *City Entertainment*. July 6, 34–36.

Wong, Eugene Franklin. 1978. *On Visual Media Racism: Asians in the American Motion Pictures*. New York: Arno.

Wong, Sau-ling Cynthia. 1992. "Ethnicizing Gender: An Exploration of Sexuality as Sign in Chinese Immigrant Literature." In *Reading the Literatures of Asian American*. Ed. Shirley Geok-lin Lim and Amy Ling. 111–29. Philadelphia: Temple University Press.

——. 1995. "Denationalization Reconsidered: Asian American Cultural Criticism at a Theoretical Crossroads." *Amerasia Journal* 21.1&2:1–27.

——. 1998. "'Astronaut Wives' and 'Little Dragons': Identity Negotiations by Diasporic Chinese Women in Two Popular Novels of the 1980s." In *The Chinese Diaspora: Selected Essays Volume I*. Ed. Wang Ling-chi and Wang Gunwu. 133–51. Singapore: Times Academic Press.

Wong Fei Hung: The Invincible Master. 1996. Hong Kong: Urban Council.

Wong, Thomas W. P., and Lui Tai-lok. 1993. *Morality, Class and the Hong Kong Way of Life.* Hong Kong: Occasional Paper, Hong Kong Institute of Asia-Pacific Studies, Chinese University of Hong Kong.

Wong, Wendy Siuyi. 2002. *Hong Kong Comics: A History of Manhua.* New York: Princeton Architectural Press.

Wong Yan Wan. 1997. "Guanyu zhuanlan de yixie wenti" [Some Questions about Column]. *Ruci* [Bygones]. 139–42. Hong Kong: Youth Literary Bookstore.

Wong Yuk Long. 1994a. *Longzhonghu* [The Tiger in Jail]. Hong Kong: Jade Dynasty.

———. 1994b. *Shiyi fuhuameng* [The Dream of a Billion Dollars]. Hong Kong: Jade Dynasty.

Wood, Miles. 1998. "Shu Kei." *Cine East: Hong Kong Cinema through the Looking Glass.* 104–15. Guildford, Surrey, Eng.: FAB Press.

Xiang Yang. 1995. "Fukanxue de lilun jiangou jichu—yi Taiwan baozhi fukan zhi fazhan guocheng jiqi shidai beijing wei changyu" [The Theoretical Basis for the Study of Supplement]. In *Wenxue yu zhuanbo de guanxi* [The Relationships between Literature and Communication]. 193–226. Taipei: Xuesheng Bookstore.

Xing, Jun. 1998. *Asian America through the Lens: History, Representations, and Identity.* Walnut Creek, Calif.: AltaMira Press.

Yahuda, Michael. 1996. *Hong Kong: China's Challenge.* London: Routledge.

Yang, Mayfair Mei-Hui, ed. 1999. *Spaces of Their Own: Women's Public Sphere in Transnational China.* Minneapolis: University of Minnesota Press.

Yang, Mingyu. 1995. *China: Once Upon a Time/Hong Kong: 1997: A Critical Study of Contemporary Hong Kong Martial Arts Films.* Ph.D. diss., University of Maryland. Ann Arbor, Mich.: UMI.

Yau, Esther C. M., ed. 1997. "Ecology and Late Colonial Hong Kong Cinema: Imaginations in Time." In *Fifty Years of Electric Shadows.* Ed. Law Kar. 107–13. Hong Kong: Urban Council.

———. 2001. *At Full Speed: Hong Kong Cinema in a Borderless World.* Minneapolis: University of Minnesota Press.

Yearwood, G. L. 1982. "The Hero in Black Film." *Wide Angle* 5.2:42–50.

Yeung, Yin Lin. 2000. "Understanding the Japanese Market of the 1980s: Interviewing Peter Lam and Lau Fong." In *Border Crossing in Hong Kong Cinema.* Ed. Law Kar. 150–53. Hong Kong: Leisure and Cultural Services Department.

Yip Fai. 2000. "Qishiniandai de zhuanlan he zhuanlan wenxue" [Columns of the Seventies and Column Literature]. *Su Yeh Literature* 68 (December): 136–40.

Yoshimoto, Mitsuhiro. 1994. "Images of Empire: Tokyo Disneyland and Japanese Cultural Imperialism." In *Disney Discourse: Producing the Magic Kingdom.* Ed. Eric Smoodin. 181–99. New York: Routledge.

Yuen, Jeanie. 1998. "Zhou Lei: Buzuo 'quanzhi' zhongguoren" [Rey Chow: Not to Be a "Fulltime" Chinese]. In *Guanjingchuang* [Viewfinder]. Ed. Kwai-Cheung Lo. 25–30. Hong Kong: Youth Literary Bookstore.

Yu Mo-wan. 1980. "The Prodigious Cinema of Huang Fei-Hong: An Introduction." In *A Study of the Hong Kong Martial Arts Film.* Ed. Lau Shing-hon. 79–86. Hong Kong: Urban Council.

Zha, Jianying. 1995a. *China Pop: How Soap Operas, Tabloids, and Bestsellers Are Transforming a Culture.* New York: New Press.

———. 1995b. "Citizen Chan: Is Hong Kong Poised to Take Over Mainland China?" *Transition* 65:69–94.

Zhang Che. 1999. "Creating the Martial Arts Film and the Hong Kong Cinema Style." In *The Making of Martial Arts Film—As Told by Filmmakers and Stars.* Trans. Stephen Teo. 16–24. Hong Kong: Provisional Urban Council.

Zhang, Xudong. 1997. *Chinese Modernism in the Era of Reforms: Cultural Fever, Avant-garde Fiction, and the New Chinese Cinema.* Durham, N.C.: Duke University Press.

Zhang, Yingjin. 2002. *Screening China: Critical Interventions, Cinematic Reconfigurations, and the Transnational Imaginary in Contemporary Chinese Cinema.* Ann Arbor: Center for Chinese Studies, University of Michigan.

"Zhuanlan yu wenxue zuotanhui" [Forum on Column and Literature]. 1986. *Kung Kao Po.* September 6, 12–13.

Žižek, Slavoj. 1990. "The Limits of the Semiotic Approach to Psychoanalysis." In *Psychoanalysis and . . .* Ed. Richard Feldstein and Henry Sussman. 89–110. New York: Routledge.

———. 1993. *Tarrying with the Negative: Kant, Hegel, and the Critique of Ideology.* Durham, N.C.: Duke University Press.

———. 1996. "I Hear You with My Eyes; or, The Invisible Master." In *Gaze and Voice as Love Objects.* Ed. Renata Salecl and Slavoj Žižek. 90–126. Durham, N.C.: Duke University Press.

———. 1997. *The Plague of Fantasies.* New York: Verso.

———. 1998. "A Leftist Plea for 'Eurocentrism.'" *Critical Inquiry* 24:988–1009.

———. 1999. *The Ticklish Subject: The Absent Center of Political Ontology.* London: Verso.

———. 2000a. *The Art of the Ridiculous Sublime: On David Lynch's Lost Highway.* Seattle: Walter Chapin Simpson Center for the Humanities, University of Washington.

———. 2000b. "Da Capo senza Fine." In *Contingency, Hegemony, Universality: Contemporary Dialogues on the Left.* 213–62. London: Verso.

Index

KWAI-CHEUNG LO teaches in the Department
of English Language and Literature at Hong Kong
Baptist University. He is the author of numerous
fiction pieces and critical essays in collections and
in journals such as *Cultural Studies*, *Boundary 2*,
and *Camera Obscura*. He is also the author of the
first book-length study of Gilles Deleuze in the
Chinese language.

The University of Illinois Press
is a founding member of the
Association of American University Presses.

———————————————

Composed in 10.5/13 Adobe Minion
by Celia Shapland
for the University of Illinois Press
Manufactured by Maple-Vail Book
Manufacturing Group

University of Illinois Press
1325 South Oak Street
Champaign, IL 61820-6903
www.press.uillinois.edu